W9-AQN-077

THE NEW TESTAMENT
in Its
FIRST CENTURY SETTING

Essays on Context and Background

in Honour of

B. W. WINTER

on His 65th Birthday

THE NEW TESTAMENT
in Its
FIRST CENTURY SETTING

Essays on Context and Background

in Honour of

B. W. WINTER

on His 65th Birthday

• •

Edited by

P. J. Williams,
Andrew D. Clarke,
Peter M. Head,
David Instone-Brewer

WILLIAM B. EERDMANS PUBLISHING COMPANY
GRAND RAPIDS, MICHIGAN / CAMBRIDGE, U.K.

Wm. B. Eerdmans Publishing Co.

255 Jefferson Ave. S.E., Grand Rapids, Michigan 49503 /

P.O. Box 163, Cambridge CB3 9PU U.K.

www.eerdmans.com

Printed in the United States of America

09 08 07 06 05 04   7 6 5 4 3 2 1

Library of Congress Cataloging-in-Publication Data

ISBN 0-8028-2834-5

Contents

Gospels

Apocalypse

Preface

With this volume the editors and contributors join together in honouring Bruce Winter. We hope it will be a pleasant surprise on his sixty-fifth birthday, but, if the element of surprise is lacking (secrets are hard to keep and Bruce has always had a knack for finding things out), we hope it will nevertheless be pleasant.

We, the editors, have all worked as researchers under Bruce in various capacities and for various lengths of time at Tyndale House in Cambridge. In discussing how we should mark Bruce's sixty-fifth birthday we all felt that in view of his contributions to Christian scholarship — as an encourager of many young scholars, as a creative New Testament scholar, as (longest ever serving) Warden of Tyndale House, and as editor of the important series of studies on The Book of Acts in Its First Century Setting — it would be very appropriate to organise a celebratory volume in his honour. Our judgement was swiftly confirmed by the publishers and by the responses of those asked to contribute. Indeed, Bruce has various networks of scholarly friends, made through his writings and his attendance at many conferences, especially the annual SNTS and SBL congresses. We could have easily doubled the number of essays if we had wished. However, we felt that the appropriate focus for the volume should be Tyndale House and the network of grateful alumni which encircles the globe. Of course we also included some old friends from 'down under', but all the antipodean contributors have also benefited from and contributed to the atmosphere of learning and encouragement that characterises Tyndale House (on the good days).

In terms of subject and approach, our appreciation of Bruce's own contributions to the study of the New Testament in its context, made it inevitable that this would also be a controlling feature of this volume. No text can be understood in a vacuum, and this is abundantly true of the New Testament. Serious study of the New Testament has therefore always sought to understand its context or setting and has been prepared to explore the many avenues of enquiry which shed light on the context in which the New Testament arose. These naturally include consideration of the Old Testament as providing a significant proportion of the literary and theological context for the New, but also include varied disciplines such as epigraphy, sociology, history and linguistics. This volume brings together a range of approaches to understanding the setting and background of the New Testament, consciously presenting them as illustrative of the fruitful methods that may be adopted. An effort has also been made to ensure that the essays cover all the main sections of material in the New Testament. Not a few bring forth new documentary evidence to support particular interpretations, three deal explicitly with the social issue of interpersonal relationships, and all engage with the question of the context in which the New Testament text should be understood. Despite the contributors' interest in questions of history and background for their own sake each essay engages substantially with the questions of the meaning of the New Testament text in the light of their enquiry. The end product, we hope, is therefore a sounder understanding of the text. It is this link between background and text that has always been of interest to Bruce Winter and it is in recognition of his achievements in this area that the title contains the words 'in Its First-Century Setting'.

The Editors

Foreword

The Rt. Revd John B. Taylor

This volume of essays has been compiled as surreptitiously as possible by friends and colleagues of Bruce Winter, the Warden of Tyndale House, Cambridge, to celebrate his sixty-fifth birthday in 2004. That is a time when most right-thinking people announce their retirement from hard work, unless they have been fortunate enough to extricate themselves earlier still, but such conventions seem not to apply either to scholars or ministers of the gospel. Bruce of course is both, so no one who knows him is expecting him to withdraw from his busy lifestyle of research, writing and preaching. Nevertheless, it is the hope of these essayists that he will find time to peruse these contributions to scholarship from the pens of many of his friends, and think back with gratitude over a full and productive life spent both in his native Australia as well as in Singapore and Cambridge. The hope is that he will be encouraged by those who have been his former pupils and admirers to believe that his work will be continued in them for many a long year to come.

Bruce William Winter was born on July 2nd 1939 just as Great Britain and the Commonwealth were about to be embroiled in the Second World War, but that became a distant memory as he enjoyed his schooling and subsequent university career at the University of Queensland, where he took a B.A. in History, Political Science and Biblical Studies. He worked for the Australian Civil Service, achieving a Diploma in Public Administration, before changing direction and training for ordination at Moore Theological College in Sydney. After a curacy in Brisbane, he was instituted to the parish of St George's Singapore in 1973, and three years later became Warden of St Peter's Hall within Trinity Theological College, Singapore, where he lectured in New Testament studies. Over the next ten years, partly in Singapore and partly in Sydney, he built on his studies in biblical theology which had brought him an M.Th. from the South East Asia Graduate School of Theology and went on to develop an interest in papyrology and epigraphy as they touched on the New Testament. This ultimately led to a Ph.D. from Macquarie University which was later published under the title of 'Philo and Paul among the Sophists'.

It was as a result of his visits to Cambridge to study at Tyndale House for his doctorate that he came to apply for the Wardenship and to follow in the distinguished footsteps of his fellow-Australian, Leon Morris, later to be Principal of Ridley College, Melbourne, Derek Kidner, former Senior Tutor of Oak Hill College, London, Dick France, later to be Principal of Wycliffe Hall, Oxford, and the New Zealander Murray Harris. He was duly appointed in August 1987 and has served generations of scholars at Tyndale House ever since.

The hallmark of his Wardenship has undoubtedly been his concern for each one of those who have studied at Tyndale House. He has welcomed them, often with their family too, he has helped them to settle into their studies in a strange university and city, he has in many cases supervised them or offered informal direction or encouragement. Whatever he is doing he invariably tries to break off at the time of morning coffee or afternoon tea to be available for the readers in the library as they leave their desks to gather in the lounge for a refreshing drink. Then is the time when ideas can be bandied around, new theories tested and problems brought out into the open. Research is stressful at the best of times, and the pastoral care of a more experienced scholar as Warden and the fellowship of like-minded colleagues can be a great strength to those who are going through testing times.

At the heart of the life of Tyndale House is the corporate meeting together in the Upper Hexagon on Tuesday morning for half an hour of 'chapel'. A hymn or two, some prayers about current concerns and a brief biblical address from the Warden are the standard fare.

Bruce's contributions are invariably prepared and delivered with care and attention to detail. They variously encourage, challenge and exhort from the scriptures. If there is an enduring message, it is that all biblical scholarship is to be for the building up of the Church, not for the massaging of the scholarly ego, and certainly not for the sake of an additional line in the individual's academic c.v. The scholar is a servant, as every minister of Christ is, and this must never be forgotten.

Bruce's vision has also led to significant expansion of the residential facilities available for scholars, students and their families at Tyndale House. He masterminded the building of five new family houses, and the conversion of a further five flats on the upper floors of the original 36 Selwyn Gardens. His energies have more recently turned towards the significant expansion of the library itself, incorporating much more shelving, office, study and seminar space, all in further fulfilment of the founding aims of Tyndale House as a residential, biblical studies centre.

Another task of the Warden is to foster good relations with the University and particularly with the two faculties most closely associated with the work of Tyndale House, namely the Divinity Faculty and the Oriental Studies Faculty. It was through Bruce Winter's vision and initiative that he was able to persuade a generous benefactor to fund two research fellowships, one for each of these departments, so that an up and coming scholar could be appointed jointly by Tyndale House and the Faculty concerned to lecture in the University part-time and to continue their post-doctoral research at Tyndale House to the benefit of both bodies. Bruce has also helped to establish a link between Tyndale House and St Edmund's College, of which he is a Fellow, which has enabled several visiting scholars to be accorded the privileges of the college and in some cases a visiting fellowship.

At the same time the Warden is expected to spend the major part of his time doing original research. A cursory glance at the bibliography later in this volume will give some idea of how fully Bruce has used his time. He has drawn upon his New Testament studies, his early fascination with archaeology and his classical studies to concentrate on the Pauline epistles, particularly 1 Corinthians, and although attracted by linguistics he has also wanted to see the texts against the social and cultural background of life in the Eastern Mediterranean in the first century AD. Some of his discoveries are already being reflected in new commentaries, as well as broadcast in the pulpits of those who take their biblical preaching seriously. Worthwhile scholarship must, in his own words, always benefit the Church.

In addition to his own research, Bruce has also been the driving energy behind a number of edited publications. He increased the size and frequency of the *Tyndale Bulletin*, and has witnessed a significant growth in its number of subscribers. One further and far-reaching project has been his masterminding of 'The Book of Acts in Its First-Century Setting' series. This timely collection of volumes has made an international mark among Acts commentators and scholars.

So I have no doubt that, though Bruce will welcome and be grateful for these offerings made to wish him well as he comes to an important milestone in his life (he might say a midway point!), he will also be concerned that, beyond their role as part of a Festschrift, they will have a usefulness for Christians in the pews who may know little of Tyndale House, the *Tyndale Bulletin* or the Tyndale Fellowship, but who value the Bible and long to understand better the riches it contains.

List of Publications by Bruce W. Winter[1]

1978

"The Lord's Supper at Corinth: An Alternative Reconstruction," *RTR* 37: 73-82.

1986

Coauthor: *The Gospel of Luke: New International Version* (Singapore: SU).

1988

"Philo and Paul among the Sophists: A Hellenistic Jewish and a Christian Response," doctoral thesis (Sydney: Macquarie University).

1996: Published as *Philo and Paul among the Sophists* (SNTSMS 96; CUP).

2002: Second edition including new material, published as *Philo and Paul among the Sophists: Alexandrian and Corinthian Responses to a Julio-Claudian Movement* (Grand Rapids: Eerdmans).

"Providentia for the Widows of 1 Timothy 5:3-16," *TynB* 39: 83-99.

"The Public Honouring of Christian Benefactors: Romans 13.3-4 and 1 Peter 2.14-15," *JSNT* 34: 87-103.

"'Seek the Welfare of the City': Social Ethics according to 1 Peter," *Themelios* 13: 91-94.

Editor: *Tyndale Bulletin* (1988 to the present).

1989

"Secular and Christian Responses to Corinthian Famines," *TynB* 40: 86-106.

---

[1] Prepared by David L. Baker.

"'If a Man Does Not Wish to Work ...' A Cultural and Historical Setting for 2 Thessalonians 3:6-16," *TynB* 40: 303-15.

1990

"Theological and Ethical Responses to Religious Pluralism — 1 Corinthians 8–10," *TynB* 41: 209-26.

1991

"Civil Litigation in Secular Corinth and the Church: The Forensic Background to 1 Corinthians 6.1-8," *NTS* 37: 559-72. Reprinted 1995 in *Understanding Paul's Ethics: Twentieth Century Approaches* (ed. Brian S. Rosner; Grand Rapids/Carlisle: Eerdmans/Paternoster), 85-103.

"The Importance of the *Captatio Benevolentiae* in the Speeches of Tertullus and Paul in Acts 24:1-21," *JTS* 42: 505-31.

"The Messiah As the Tutor: The Meaning of καθηγητής in Matthew 23:10," *TynB* 42: 152-57.

"In Public and in Private: Early Christian Interactions with Religious Pluralism," in *One God, One Lord in a World of Religious Pluralism* (Cambridge: Tyndale House), 112-34.

Coeditor with Andrew D. Clarke: *One God, One Lord in a World of Religious Pluralism* (Cambridge: Tyndale House). Revised and enlarged edition 1992 with title *One God, One Lord: Christianity in a World of Religious Pluralism* (Carlisle/Grand Rapids: Paternoster/Baker). Indonesian translation *Satu Allah, Satu Tuhan: Tinjauan Alkitabiah tentang Pluralisme Agama* (Jakarta: BPK Gunung Mulia, 1995).

1992

"The Problem with 'Church' for the Early Church," in *In the Fullness of Time: Biblical Studies in Honour of Archbishop Donald Robinson* (ed. David Peterson and John Pryor; Homebush West, New South Wales: Lancer), 203-17.

1993

"The Entries and Ethics of Orators and Paul (1 Thessalonians 2:1-12)," *TynB* 44: 55-74.

"Imitate Paul — He Imitated Jesus (1 Corinthians 8:1–11:1)," in *Mercy, Community and Ministry: Essays in Commemoration of the Twenty-fifth Anniversary of Eagles Communications 1968-1993* (ed. M. L. Y. Chan; Singapore: Eagles), 151-60.

"Official Proceedings and the Forensic Speeches in Acts 24–26," in *The Book of Acts in Its Ancient Literary Setting* (ed. Bruce W. Winter and Andrew D. Clarke; The Book of Acts in Its First Century Setting, vol. 1; Grand Rapids/Carlisle: Eerdmans/□Paternoster), 305-36.

Coauthor with T. Hillard and A. Nobbs: "Acts and the Pauline Corpus I: Ancient Literary Parallels," in *The Book of Acts in Its Ancient Literary Setting* (ed. Bruce W. Winter and Andrew D. Clarke; The Book of Acts in Its First Century Setting, vol. 1; Grand Rapids/Carlisle: Eerdmans/Paternoster), 183-213.

"Rhetoric," in *Dictionary of Paul and His Letters* (Leicester: Inter-Varsity), 820-22.

Series editor: *The Book of Acts in Its First Century Setting* in 5 volumes (Grand Rapids/Carlisle: Eerdmans/Paternoster, 1993-1996).

1994

Seek the Welfare of the City: Christians As Benefactors and Citizens (First-Century Christians in the Graeco-Roman World; Grand Rapids/Carlisle: Eerdmans/Paternoster).

"Acts and Food Shortages," in *The Book of Acts in Its Graeco-Roman Setting* (ed. David W. J. Gill and Conrad Gempf; The Book of Acts in Its First Century Setting, vol. 2; Grand Rapids/Carlisle: Eerdmans/Paternoster), 59-78.

"Acts and Roman Religion: B. The Imperial Cult," in *The Book of Acts in Its Graeco-Roman Setting* (ed. David W. J. Gill and Conrad Gempf; The Book of Acts in Its First Century Setting, vol. 2; Grand Rapids/Carlisle: Eerdmans/Paternoster), 93-103.

"1 Corinthians" in *New Bible Commentary: 21st Century Edition* (ed. D. A. Carson et al.; Leicester: Inter-Varsity), 61-1187.

"Is Paul among the Sophists?" *RTR* 53: 28-38.

1995

"The Achaean Federal Imperial Cult II: The Corinthian Church," *TynB* 46: 169-78.

"The Public Place for the People of God," *Vox Evangelica* 25: 7-16.

1996

"On Introducing Gods to Athens: An Alternative Reading of Acts 17:18-20," *TynB* 47: 71-90.

1997

"1 Corinthians 7:6-7: A Caveat and a Framework for 'The Sayings' in 7:8-24," *TynB* 48: 57-65.

"Gluttony and Immorality at Élitist Banquets: The Background to 1 Corinthians 6:12-20," *Jian Dao* 7: 77-90.

"Homosexual Terminology in 1 Corinthians 6.9: The Roman Context and the Greek Loan-word," in *Interpreting the Bible: Historical and Theological Studies in Honour of David F. Wright* (ed. A. N. S. Lane; Leicester: Apollos), 275-90.

"Pilgrim's Progress and Contemporary Evangelical Piety," St. Antholin's Lectureship Charity Lecture.

"St Paul As a Critic of Roman Slavery in 1 Corinthians 7:21-23," in *St Paul and the European Civilization: Proceedings of the International Congress* (ed. I. Karavidopoulos et al.; Pauleia

3; Veria, Greece: Diocese of Veria, Naousa and Kabania), 337-54.

"'The Seasons' of This Life and Eschatology in 1 Corinthians 7:29-31," in *'The Reader Must Understand'*: *Eschatology in Bible and Theology* (ed. K. E. Brower and M. W. Elliot; Leicester: Apollos), 323-34. US edition with title *Eschatology in Bible and Theology: Evangelical Essays at the Dawn of a New Millennium* (Downers Grove: InterVarsity).

1998

"*Christentum und Antike*: Acts and Paul's *Corpus* As Ancient History," in *Ancient History in a Modern University*, vol. 2 (ed. T. W. Hillard et al.; Grand Rapids: Eerdmans), 121-30.

"Puberty or Passion? The Referent of ὑπέρακμος in 1 Corinthians 7:36," *TynB* 49: 71-89.

1999

"Gallio's Ruling on the Legal Status of Early Christianity (Acts 18:14-15)," *TynB* 50: 213-24.

2000

"Dangers and Difficulties for the Pauline Missions," in *The Gospel to the Nations: Perspectives on Paul's Mission: In Honour of Peter T. O'Brien* (ed. Peter Bolt and Mark Thompson; Leicester: Apollos), 285-95.

"The 'New' Roman Wife and 1 Timothy 2:9-15: The Search for a *Sitz im Leben*," *TynB* 51: 285-94.

2001

After Paul Left Corinth: The Influence of Secular Ethics and Social Change (Grand Rapids: Eerdmans).

"Punishment As Remedy," *Relational Justice Bulletin* 12: 6-7.

Member of translation oversight committee: *The Holy Bible: English Standard Version* (Wheaton: Good News).

2002

"The Imperial Cult and Early Christians in Roman Galatia (Acts XIII 13-50 and Galatians VI 11-18)," in *Actes du Ier Congrès International sur Antioche de Pisidie* (ed. Thomas Drew-Bear et al.; Collection Archéologie et Histoire de l'Antiquité, vol. 5; Lyon: Université Lumière-Lion), 67-75.

"Roman Law and Society in Romans 12–15," in *Rome in the Bible and the Early Church* (ed. Peter Oakes; Carlisle/Grand Rapids: Paternoster/Baker), 67-102.

2003

Roman Wives, Roman Widows: The Appearance of New Women and the Pauline Communities (Grand Rapids: Eerdmans).

"Introducing the Athenians to God: Paul's Failed Apologetic in Acts 17?" in *A Graced Horizon: Essays in Gospel, Culture and Church in Honour of Choong Chee Pang* (ed. M. Chan and R. Chia; Singapore: Armour).

"The Toppling of Favorinus and Paul by the Corinthians," in *Early Christianity and Classical Culture: Comparative Studies in Honor of Abraham J. Malherbe* (ed. John T. Fitzgerald et al.; NovTSup 110; Leiden: Brill), 291-306.

"The 'Underlays' of Conflict and Compromise in 1 Corinthians," in *Paul and the Corinthians: Studies on a Community in Conflict: Essays in Honour of Margaret Thrall* (ed. Trevor J. Burke and J. Keith Elliot; NovTSup 109; Leiden: Brill), 139-55.

"You Were What You Wore in Roman Law: Developing the Dress Codes of 1 Timothy 2:9-15," *Whitefield Briefing* 8.4.

2003

"Philodemus and Paul on Rhetorical Delivery (ὑπόκρισις)," in *Philodemus and the New Testament World* (ed. John T. Fitzgerald et al.; NovTSup 111; Leiden: Brill), 323-342.

Abbreviations

Modern works and Editions

AB	Anchor Bible Commentary
Aeg	*Aegyptus*
ANTC	Abingdon New Testament Commentary
BAGD	*W. Bauer, W. F. Arndt, F. W. Gingrich, Frederick W. Danker, eds.,* A Greek-English Lexicon of the New Testament and Other Early Christian Literature *(2nd ed.; Chicago/London: University of Chicago Press, 1979).*
BCH	*Bulletin de correspondance hellenique*
BDAG	Frederick W. Danker et al., eds., *A Greek-English Lexicon of the New Testament and Other Early Christian Literature* (3rd ed.; Chicago/London: University of Chicago Press, 2000).
BECNT	Baker Exegetical Commentary on the New Testament
BGU	*Berliner Griechische Urkunden (Ägyptische Urkunden aus den königlichen Museen zu Berlin)*
BibSac	*Bibliotheca Sacra*
BJRL	*Bulletin of the John Rylands University Library of Manchester*
BNTC	Black's New Testament Commentary
BTB	*Biblical Theology Bulletin*
CBQ	*Catholic Biblical Quarterly*
CIL	*Corpus Inscriptionum Latinarum*
CNT	Commentaire du Nouveau Testament
CP	*Classical Philology*
CPJ	*Corpus Papyrorum Judaicorum*

CPR	*Corpus Papyrorum Raineri*
CSEL	Corpus Scriptorum Ecclesiasticorum Latinorum
DGE	*Diccionario Griego-Español*
EC	Epworth Commentaries
EDNT	*Exegetical Dictionary of the New Testament*
EKK	Evangelisch-Katholischer Kommentar zum Neuen Testament
EvQ	*Evangelical Quarterly*
ExpT	*Expository Times*
FTS	Frankfurter theologische Studien
HGV	*Heidelberger Gesamtverzeichnis der Griechischen Papyruskunden Ägyptens*
HTK	Herders theologischer Kommentar zum Neuen Testament
IBS	*Irish Biblical Studies*
IC	M. Guarducci, ed., *Inscriptiones Creticae* (1935-50)
ICC	International Critical Commentary
IG	*Inscriptiones Graecae*
IGR	*Inscriptiones Graecae ad res Romanas pertinentes*
ILS	H. Dessau, *Inscriptiones Latinae Selectae* (1892-1916)
IVPNTC	IVP New Testament Commentary
JbAC	*Jahrbuch für Antike und Christentum*
JBL	*Journal of Biblical Literature*
JBLMS	Journal of Biblical Literature Monograph Series
JEA	*Journal of Egyptian Archaeology*
JETS	*Journal of the Evangelical Theological Society*
JJP	*Journal of Juristic Papyrology*
JRS	*Journal of Roman Studies*
JSHJ	*Journal for the Study of the Historical Jesus*
JSNT	*Journal for the Study of the New Testament*

JSS	*Journal of Semitic Studies*
JTS	*Journal of Theological Studies*
KEK	Kritisch-exegetischer Kommentar über das Neue Testament
KNT	Kommentar zum Neuen Testament
LCL	Loeb Classical Library
Louw and Nida	J. P. Louw and E. A. Nida, *Greek-English Lexicon of the New Testament Based on Semantic Domains* (New York: United Bible Societies, 1988).
LSCG	F. Sokolowski, *Lois sacrées des cites grecques* (1969)
LSJ	Liddell, H.G., Scott, R. & Jones, H.S., *A Greek-English Lexicon* (Oxford: Clarendon Press, 1985 reprint incorporating 1940 & 1968 Supplement)
LTQ	*Lexington Theological Quarterly*
LumVie	*Lumière et vie*
MeyerK	Meyer Kommentar
MM	J. H. Moulton and G. Milligan, *The Vocabulary of the Greek Testament Illustrated from the Papyri and Other Non-literary Sources* (London: Hodder & Stoughton, 1914-29).
MT	Masoretic Text
NAC	New American Commentary
NCBC	New Century Bible Commentary
NIBC	New International Biblical Commentary
NICNT	New International Commentary on the New Testament
NICOT	New International Commentary on the Old Testament
NIDNTT	New International Dictionary of New Testament Theology
NIGTC	New International Greek Testament Commentary

NovT	*Novum Testamentum*
NTD	Das Neue Testament Deutsch
NTS	*New Testament Studies*
P. Abinn.	*The Abinnaeus Archive:* (Oxford 1962)
P. Alex.	*Papyrus grecs du Musée Gréce-Romain d'Alexandrie* (Warwaw, 1964)
P. Fam. Tebt.	B. A. van Groningen, *A Family-archive from Tebtunis* (Papyrologica Lugduno-Batava 6; Leiden: E. J. Brill, 1950)
P. Gur.	*Greek Papyri from Gurob* (Dublin 1921)
P. Haun.	*Papyri Graecae Haunienses* (Copenhagen 1942; Bonn 1981-1985)
P. Heid.	*Veröffentlichungen aus der Heidelberger Papyrussammlung* (Heidelberg, 1956-2001)
P. Herm.	*Papyri from Hermopolis and Other Documents of the Byzantine Period* (London, 1964)
P. Lille	*Papyrus grecs* (Institut Papyrologique de l'Université de Lille, 1907-1929)
P. Kell.	*Papyri from Kellis* (Oxford, 1995-1999)
P. Münch.	*Die Papyri der Bayerischen Staatsbibliothek München* (Stuttgart, 1986)
P. Oxy.	*The Oxyrhynchus Papyri* (London: Egypt Exploration Society in Graeco-Roman Memoirs, 1898-)
P. Paris	*Notices et textes des papyrus du Musée du Louvre et de la Bibliothèque Impériale* (Paris, 1865)
P. Petrie	*The Flinders Petrie Papyri* (Dublin, 1891-1905)
P. Ryl.	*Catalogue of the Greek and Latin Papyri in the John Rylands Library* (Manchester, 1911-1952)
P. Tebt.	*The Tebtunis Papyri* (London 1902-1976)
P. Hamb.	*Griechische Papyrusurkunden der Hamburger Staats- und Universitätsbibliothek* (Leipzig-

	Berlin, 1911-1924, Hamburg 1954, Bonn 1984, Stuttgart and Leipzig 1998)
PG	*Patrologia Graeca* (ed. J.P. Migne; 162 vols; Paris, 1857-1866)
PIR²	E. Groag et al., eds., *Prosopographia Imperii Romani Saeculi I, II, III* (2nd ed., 1933-)
PSI	*Papiri Greci e Latini*, Pubblicazioni della Società italiana per la ricerca dei papiri greci e latini in Egitto (1912-)
RAC	*Reallexikon für Antike und Christentum*
RE	*Real-Encyclopädie der klassischen Altertumswissenschaft*
RevBib	*Revue Biblique*
SB	F. Preisigke et al., eds., *Sammelbuch griechischen Urkunden aus Ägypten* (1915-)
SBS	Stuttgarter Bibelstudien
SC	Sources Chrétiennes
SEG	*Supplementum epigraphicum Graecum* (1923-)
SIG³	W. Dittenberger and F. Hiller von Gaertringen, eds., *Sylloge Inscriptionum Graecarum* (3rd ed.; Leipzig: S. Hirzel, 1915).
SJT	*Scottish Journal of Theology*
SNTSMS	Studiorum Novi Testamenti Societas Monograph Series
SP	Sacra Pagina
TAPA	*Transactions of the American Philological Association*
TDNT	*Theological Dictionary of the New Testament*
TLNT	*Theological Lexicon of the New Testament*
TNTC	Tyndale New Testament Commentary
TynB	*Tyndale Bulletin*
WBC	Word Biblical Commentary

WUNT	Wissenschaftliche Untersuchungen zum Neuen Testament
ZPE	*Zeitschrift für Papyrologie und Epigraphik*
ZWT	*Zeitschrift für wissenschaftliche Theologie*

Biblical Books and Versions

AV	Authorised Version
RV	Revised Version
RSV	Revised Standard Version
ESV	English Standard Version
NEB	New English Bible
TEV	Today's English Version
NRSV	New Revised Standard Version
JB	Jerusalem Bible
NIV	New International Version
TNIV	Today's New International Version
GNB	Good News Bible
REB	Revised English Bible
NLT	New Living Translation

Gen	2 Kgs	Isa	Nah	Rom	Titus
Exod	1 Chr	Jer	Hab	1 Cor	Phlm
Lev	2 Chr	Lam	Zeph	2 Cor	Heb
Num	Ezra	Ezek	Hag	Gal	Jas
Deut	Neh	Dan	Zech	Eph	1 Pet
Josh	Esth	Hos	Mal	Phil	2 Pet
Judg	Job	Joel	Matt	Col	1 John
Ruth	Ps (Pss)	Amos	Mark	1 Thess	2 John
1 Sam	Prov	Obad	Luke	2 Thess	3 John
2 Sam	Eccl	Jonah	John	1 Tim	Jude
1 Kgs	Song	Mic	Acts	2 Tim	Rev

Apocrypha, Pseudepigrapha and Qumran

Tob	Tobit
Jdt	Judith
Sir	Sirach
Macc	1, 2, 3, 4 Maccabees
Esd	1, 2 Esdras
En.	*1, 2, 3 Enoch*
Bar.	*2, 3, 4 Baruch*
apGen	*Genesis Apocryphon*
CD	*Damascus Document*
11Q19	fragment 19 from Qumran cave 11
1QH	*Hodayot*
Jub.	*Jubilees*
Let. Aris.	*Letter of Aristeas*
Pss. Sol.	*Psalms of Solomon*
T. Ab.	*Testament of Abraham*
T. Naph.	*Testament of Naphtali*
T. Sim.	*Testament of Simeon*
T. Jud.	*Testament of Judah*
T. Zeb.	*Testament of Zebulun*
T. Ben.	*Testament of Benjamin*
T. 12 Patr.	*Testament of the 12 Patriarchs*

Rabbinic Literature

m. Ab.	Mishnah, *Abot*
m. Bik.	Mishnah, *Bikkurim*
m. Ket.	Mishnah, *Ketubot*
m. Nid.	Mishnah, *Niddah*
m. Zeb.	Mishnah, *Zebahim*
b. San.	Babylonian Talmud, *Sanhedrin*
b. Shab.	Babylonian Talmud, *Shabbat*
Gen. R.	*Genesis Rabbah*

Exod. R.	*Exodus Rabbah*
Num. R.	*Numbers Rabbah*
Pirqe R. El.	*Pirqe de Rabbi Eliezer*

Graeco-Roman Literature

Aeschylus
Eum.	*Eumenides*

Alexander of Aphrodisias
Comm. Metaph.	*In Aristotelis Metaphysica commentaria*
Comm. Sens.	*In librum De sensu commentarium*

Aristophanes
Av.	*Aves*
Pax	*Pax*

Aristotle
Frag.	*Fragmenta varia*
Sens.	*De sensuet sensibilibus*
Pol.	*Politica*
Rhet.	*Rhetorica*

Augustine
Epist.	*In Epistolam*

Caesar
Bell. civ.	*Bellum civile*

Cicero
Att.	*Epistulae ad Atticum*

Crantor
Frag.	*Fragmenta*

Demosthenes
Philippum	*In Philippum*
Orat.	*Orationes*

Dinarchus
Aristog.	*In Aristogitonem*
Phil.	*In Philoclem*

Dio Cassius
Hist. Rom.   *Historia Romana*
Diodorus Siculus
Bibliotheca   *Bibliotheca Historica*
Diogenes Laertius
Vit. Phil.   *Vitae Philosophorum*
Sib. Or.   *Sibyline Oracles*
Dionysius of Halicarnassus
Is.   *De Isaeo*
Hist.   *Notitia historica*
Ant. rom.   *Antiquitates romanae*
Epictetus
Diatr.   *Diatribai (Dissertationes ab Arriano digestae)*
Eusebius
Hist. eccl.   *Historia ecclesiastica*
Praep. ev.   *Praeparatio evangelica*
Homer
Il.   *Ilias*
Od.   *Odyssea*
Irenaeus
Haer.   *Adversus haereses*
Isocrates
Frag.   *Fragmenta*
Isidorus (Aegyptius)
Hymn   *Hymni in Isim*
Josephus
A.J.   *Antiquitates judaicae*
C. Ap.   *Contra Apionem*
B.J.   *Bellum judaicum*
Vita   *Vita*
Livy
Epon.   *Ab urbe condita libri (Eponymous)*

Lucian

Luct.	*De luctu*
Ver. hist.	*Vera historia*

Macrobius

Sat.	*Saturnalia*

Mantheo

Frag.	*Fragmenta*

Marcus Aurelius

Med.	*Meditationes*

Origen

Comm. Jo.	*Commentarii in evangelium Joannis*
Or.	*De oratione*
Hom. Luc.	*Homiliae in Lucam*

Paulinus of Nola

Epist.	*Epistolae*

Pausanias

Descr.	*Graeciae descriptio*

Philo

Opif.	*De opificio mundi*
Somn.	*De somniis*
Mos.	*De vita Mosis*
Flacc.	*In Flaccum*
Leg.	*Legum allegoriae*
Legat.	*Legatio ad Gaium*
Migr.	*De migratione Abrahami*
Abr.	*De Abrahamo*
Cher.	*De Cherubim*
Sacr.	*De sacrificiis Abelis et Caini*
Post.	*De posteritate Caini*
Her.	*Quis rerum divinarum heres sit*
QG	*Quaestiones et solutiones in Genesin*
Conf.	*De confusione linguarum*

Philostratus

Vit. Apoll.	*Vita Apollonii*

Plato

Crat.	*Cratylus*
Leg.	*Leges*

Pliny the Elder

Nat.	*Naturalis historia*

Pliny the Younger

Ep.	*Epistulae*

Plotinus

Enn.	*Enneades*

Plutarch

Conj. praec.	*Conjugalia Praecepta*
Alex.	*Alexander*
An seni	*An seni respublica gerenda sit*
Cleom.	*Cleomenes*
Cons. Apoll.	*Consolatio ad Apollonium*
Sept. sap. conv.	*Septem sapientium convivium*
Ages.	*Agesilaus*
An. procr.	*De animae procreatione in Timaeo*
Comm. not.	*De communibus notitiis contra stoicos*
Def. orac.	*De defectu oraculorum*
E Delph.	*De E apud Delphos*
Exil.	*De exilio*
Fac.	*De facie in orbe lunae*
Is. Os.	*De Iside et Osiride*
Lat. viv.	*De latenter vivendo*
Her. mal.	*De Herodoti malignitate*
Mulier. virt.	*Mulierum virtutes*
Prim. frig.	*De primo frigido*
Rect. rat. aud.	*De recta ratione audiendi*
Sera	*De sera numinis vindicta*
Soll. an.	*De sollertia animalium*

Lys.	*Lysander*
Mor.	*Moralia*
Praec. ger. rei publ.	*Praecepta gerendae rei publicae*
Adol. poet. aud.	*Quomodo adolescens poetas audire debeat*
Rom.	*Romulus*
Sert.	*Sertorius*

Polybius

Hist.	*Historiae*

Pomponius Mela

Chror.	*De chorographia*

Pseudo-Philo

L.A.B.	*Liber Antiquitatum Biblicarum*

Seneca

Ep.	*Epistolae morales*

Statius

Silv.	*Silvae*

Suetonius

Dom.	*Domitianus*
Tib.	*Tiberius*

Tacitus

Ann.	*Annales ab Excessu Divi Augusti*
Hist.	*Historicae*

Tertullian

Virg.	*De virginibus velandis*
Bapt.	*De baptismo*

Theophilus

Autol.	*Ad Autolycum*

Thucydides

Hist.	*Historiae*

Velleius Paterculus

Gest.	*Res gestae divi Augusti*

Xenophon

Hell.	*Hellenica*

Mem.   *Memorabilia Socratis*
Zeno
Stoic.   *Stoicorum veterum fragmenta*
Unknown
Mir. ausc.   *On Marvellous Things Heard*
Various
Sc. Hist. Aug.Mar. *Scriptores Historiae Augustae, vita Marci Antonini philosophi*

The Linguistic Background to Jesus' Dereliction Cry (Matthew 27:46; Mark 15:34)

P. J. Williams

Jesus' Aramaic in Greek Manuscripts

If we wanted to divide up people who copied early manuscripts of the Greek New Testament we could do it in several ways. We could categorize them by their theological profile, their location, their handwriting or their skill. Less conventionally, however, we could distinguish scribes by whether they understood Hebrew and/or Aramaic. This is a less usual means of classification because knowledge of Hebrew or Aramaic, or a lack thereof, does not often become apparent in a Greek text. However, in a few places in the Gospels it clearly does.

When Jesus told the girl in Mark 5:41 to get up, did he say 'Talitha cum'[1] (ταλιθα κουμ) as in the NRSV or 'Talitha cumi' (ταλιθα κουμι) as in the ESV?[2] The variant in the Greek manuscripts about whether there is an *iota* at the end of the second word agrees exactly with a dialectal difference in the Aramaic pronunciation of the feminine singular imperative. In some dialects it was *qumi* and in some it was *qum*. *Qumi* was the earlier form and the one preferred in

---

[1] The precision of transcription used in this article varies according to the needs of the point being made.

[2] The NRSV is supported by ℵ B C L ƒ[13] et al., and the ESV by A Δ ƒ[1] 𝔐 et al., though there are numerous spelling variations (ταλειθα κουμει, etc.), and the variants with 'Tabitha': Θαβιτα (D), Ταβιθα (W) and Ταβηθα (157). The authorities reading 'Tabitha' show sufficient spelling variation amongst themselves as to raise the possibility that they have arrived at this corrupt reading independently.

most dialects, while the elision of the *i* is only found in the eastern dialects of Aramaic, such as Babylonian Jewish Aramaic and Syriac (the oral but not the written form). Some scribe clearly knew enough Aramaic to know what the form ought to be in his dialect and 'corrected' the text to that form. We do not know for certain which was the form in Galilean Aramaic (the presumed dialect of Jesus), though it is likely on linguistic grounds that the ESV is right and the NRSV wrong, and the external textual evidence does not seem strong enough to overturn this decision.[3]

But whichever form Jesus used he certainly did not say the nonsensical *tabea acultha cumhi* as recorded in the Latin manuscript *e*. This is clearly not the work of someone who knew Aramaic.

Similarly, in transmitting Jesus' cry of dereliction on the cross, recorded in Matt 27:46 and Mark 15:34, scribes show different levels of knowledge. At the nonsense end of the spectrum there is manuscript 118, the thirteenth century Oxford manuscript, which is part of the textual family f^{13}. In Mark it records *Eloi, Eloi, limas abachthane* (ελωι ελωι λιμας αβαχθανη)[4] — the *sigma* gently gliding from the

---

[3] See the comments on New Testament Aramaic words in Rudolf Macuch's learned yet ignored *Grammatik des samaritanischen Aramäisch* (Berlin: de Gruyter, 1982), 61-64. There are two serious problems with the form *qum* rather than *qumi*. First, that the disappearance of the final vowel is only attested in East Aramaic dialects, whereas all those which most probably relate to Jesus' speech preserve it: Biblical Aramaic, Palestinian Jewish Aramaic, Samaritan Aramaic, Christian Palestinian Aramaic. Even East Aramaic dialects like Syriac may have pronounced the vowel during the New Testament period. Secondly, *sabachthani* (Matt 27:46 and Mark 15:34) preserves a final *i* in a similar phonetic position on the lips of Jesus. The final vowels in *qumi* and *sabachthani* are of the same length and immediately after a stressed syllable. It is therefore likely that if the final vowel in *qumi* were elided the final vowel in *sabachthani* would be too, though one could produce *ad hoc* explanations for why it might not be.

[4] The spellings of manuscripts in this study are based largely on Reuben Swanson, *New Testament Greek Manuscripts, Variant Readings Arranged in Horizontal Lines against Codex Vaticanus: Matthew, Mark, Luke, John* (4 vols.; Sheffield: Sheffield Academic Press, 1995).

beginning of the last word to the end of the penultimate one takes away any chance of intelligibility. In Mark, manuscript F manages *sabachthachthani* (σαβαχθαχθανι), likewise incomprehensible.

On the other hand, it is not surprising, given the prominent position of this cry in accounts of the Passion, that the majority of Greek authorities have transmitted it correctly, even though, at least in the Middle Ages, they certainly did not understand its Aramaic morphology. The first thing they establish is that Matthew has the beginning of the cry, 'My God, my God' as *Eli, Eli* (ηλι ηλι), but Mark has *Eloi, Eloi* (ελωι ελωι).[5] The third word, 'why', according to the Nestle-Aland *Novum Testamentum Graece* is *lema* (λεμα) in both Matthew and Mark.

There is some variation in manuscripts with the forms *lama* (λαμα), *lema* (λεμα) and *lima* (λιμα or λειμα) occurring, but in Aramaic the first vowel would be unstressed and possibly indistinct, and this adequately explains the variations introduced by scribes. The final word, 'you have forsaken me', was certainly *sabachthani* (σαβαχθανι or σαβαχθανει) in both Matthew and Mark.

The readings of select witnesses are shown in the table:

Matt 27:46

ℵ	ελωι ελωι	λεμα	σαβαχθανει
A	ηλι ηλι	λιμα	σαβαχθανει
B	ελωει ελωει	λεμα	σαβακτανει
C	—	—	—
D*	ηλει ηλει	λαμα	ζαφθανει (corrector, σαφθανει)
𝔐	ηλι ηλι	λ(ε)ιμα	σαβαχθαν(ε)ι

---

[5] Though the authorities ℵ B, with some other witnesses, read ελωι ελωι in Matthew, their reading should be explained on the basis of assimilation to the reading in Mark.

Mark 15:34

ℵ*	ελωι ελωι	λεμα	σαβακτανει
			(corrector, σαβαχθανει)
A	ελωι ελωι	λιμα	σιβακθανει
B	ελωι ελωι	λαμα	ζαβαφθανει
X	ελωι ελωι	λεμα	σαβαχθανει
Δ	ηλει ηλει	λαμα	ζαφθανει
𝔐	ελωι ελωι	λ(ε)ιμα	σαβαχθανι

The form *sabachthani* is not hard to explain, though students will hunt in vain for any commentary that does so.[6] Perhaps either the commentators do not understand the form, or consider it so self-evident that they feel no need to comment. However, for the forthcoming argument we must consider the form. *Sabachthani* contains the Aramaic verb *shəvaq* 'abandon, leave', and its standard pronunciation would, in fact, be *shəvaqtani*. Its representation in Greek is exactly what we would expect. Greek has no *sh* so uses *s* (*sigma*). The indistinct first vowel (*ə*) is naturally represented by *alpha*. It may surprise some to see *taw* with a *dagesh*, i.e. *t*, corresponding to Greek *theta* not *tau*. In fact, however, this is an absolutely regular correspondence. Hebrew *k*, *p* and *t* are frequently transcribed in the Septuagint or New Testament with *kh*, *ph* and *th*, respectively. Thus in Matt 1:3 Perez is Phares (Φαρες) and Tamar is Thamar (Θαμαρ). In Matt 15:22 Jesus is approached by a Canaanite woman (Hebrew Canaanite begins with *k*), but in the Greek she appears as *Khananaia* (Χαναναία). So *th* in *sabachthani* is what we would expect for Hebrew or Aramaic *t*. The less obvious correspondence is between Greek *ch* (χ) and Aramaic *q*, since Hebrew and Aramaic *q* normally corresponds to *k* (κ) in Greek. The combination *kth* (κθ) in Greek is, however, regularly transformed into *khth* (χθ) by assimilation, so that

---

[6]   Some details are given in Willoughby C. Allen, *The Gospel according to Matthew* (ICC; Edinburgh: T & T Clark, 1907), 294-95.

two aspirated consonants occur together.[7] So again the Greek form is what one would predict from the Aramaic.

Having considered the form of the words, we can now consider the phrase as a whole. All are agreed that it is a quotation from Ps 22:1, which begins *'Ēlī 'Ēlī lāmāh ʿᵃzavtānī* (אֵלִי אֵלִי לָמָה עֲזַבְתָּנִי) 'My God, my God, why have you forsaken me?' Leaving aside the address to God it is clear that Jesus quoted this in Aramaic using the Aramaic verb *shəvaq* where Hebrew had *ʿāzav*. Here, however, manuscript D, well known for containing a greater density of Semitisms than most other witnesses, has *Eli eli lama zaphthani* (ηλει ηλει λαμα ζαφθανει) in both Matthew and Mark.[8] This is an almost exact transcription of the Hebrew *ʿᵃzavtānī*. The first consonant (ʿ) naturally cannot be represented in Greek, and with it falls away the following vowel.[9] Hebrew *v* (ב) becomes Greek φ by devoicing to assimilate to the following consonant θ. However, D's reading cannot be original. Whereas D has the same reading in Matthew and Mark, other manuscripts show that the addresses to God are not the same: Matthew has *Eli* and Mark *Eloi*.

Eli *or* Eloi?

This raises a tricky question: which of the forms of address to God is the earlier? And how are the particular forms to be explained? Traditionally the form in Matthew has been viewed as a repre-

---

[7] Another example of assimilation, though this time to remove aspiration can be observed in codex B in Matt 27:46, which reads σαβακτανει, with the two contiguous consonants unaspirated. Compare the reading of ℵ* with σαβακτανει in Mark 15:34, and contrast the reading of A, namely σιβακθανει.

[8] In Matthew this is only the reading of the first hand. A corrector has changed ζαφθανει into σαφθανει.

[9] Or, possibly, the initial *alpha* in *αζαφθανει was omitted by haplography following the final *alpha* in λαμα. See R. H. Gundry, *The Use of the Old Testament in St. Matthew's Gospel: With Special Reference to the Messianic Hope* (Leiden: Brill, 1967), 65.

sentation of Hebrew ʾĒlī found in the original Old Testament text.[10] This raised the problem of why a Hebrew address might stand at the beginning of an Aramaic question. A common answer to this was that Matthew had conformed the wording more to the Old Testament, but that the earlier form was Mark's,[11] whose form ελωι corresponds closely to Biblical Aramaic ʾᵉlāhī (see below).

But according to the text, whatever form he said, Jesus was heard as calling Elijah. In Hebrew Elijah was normally ʾēlīyāhū, but is also recorded simply as ʾēlīyāh (e.g. 2 Kgs 1:3). This latter pronunciation seems to lie behind the spelling of the name as *Elias* (ἠλίας) in the New Testament and Josephus. The Septuagint attests a further pronunciation, namely ēlīū (ηλειου), which might correspond to Hebrew ʾēlīhū. The problem with the view that Matthew changed the pronunciation in order to fit better with the Old Testament is that the form he gives is closer to the name Elijah than Mark's form is. From what we can tell about the pronunciation of Elijah's name, there were three fixed elements which could be represented in Greek with the letters ηλι. What followed the *i*-sound could vary. On the hypothesis therefore that Matthew's Gospel records Jesus' pronunciation we can at least explain why people might think of Elijah's name.

Those who take Matthew's spelling as a secondary development have to suppose that the author conformed the spelling to the Old Testament and *coincidentally* received the bonus that he had conformed the spelling to one which suited the context of talk about Elijah.

The choice with which one is regularly presented that either Matthew's or Mark's form must be the earlier may be a false dichotomy. This emerges when, as Bruce Winter has taught us, we consider the cultural background of the texts.

---

[10] See, for instance, B. M. Metzger, *A Textual Commentary on the Greek New Testament* (2nd ed.; Stuttgart: Deutsche Bibelgesellschaft, 1994), 58.
[11] See, for instance, Craig A. Evans, *Mark 8:27–16:20* (WBC; Nashville: Thomas Nelson, 2001), 497.

The sociolinguistic background to the texts is that the Aramaic of the time was primarily an oral language. This does not mean that Aramaic was not written. The Dead Sea Scrolls show that it was. What it means is that the written forms of the language, rather than oral forms, are not seen as defining the norms of the language.

Giving priority to spoken over written forms of the language will have consequences for how we view any term in the language. Thus while the Semitic word for God which relates to a root ʾl (e.g. Hebrew ʾēl, Akkadian ilu) and the word for God which relates to the root ʾlh (e.g. Hebrew ʾlhym, Aramaic ʾlhʾ) may be seen by historical linguists as separate though related words, we cannot take for granted that the distinction we feel now was felt by all ancient users of these terms. Separate words in our dictionaries they may be, but that does not mean that they were always separate words in a speaker's consciousness. If we are not going to privilege diachronic over synchronic approaches to language, we may therefore have to admit that it might be as legitimate to view Aramaic ʾlʾ and ʾlhʾ meaning 'god', as one word as to admit that they were two.

What might have militated against viewing the forms used by Matthew and Mark as variants of the 'same' word could be the general assumption among scholars that the Aramaic word ʾlʾ meaning 'god' is somewhat artificial, being found mainly in locations like the Targum to Ps 22:1 where it imitates the Hebrew. While it may be true that early Aramaic had no biliteral equivalent of Hebrew ʾēl, only using the word ʾlhʾ (Biblical Aramaic ᵉlāhāʾ) from the triliteral root ʾlh, and though this was the general Aramaic word for 'god', there are occasional occurrences of a biliteral root and a word ʾlh or ʾylʾ (clearly in the emphatic state) meaning 'god'.[12] What is significant about these occurrences is that they are on amulets, and may therefore

---

[12] The form ʾl also occurs in Aramaic texts where it is definite and free-standing; see J. A. Fitzmyer, *A Wandering Aramean: Collected Aramaic Essays* (Missoula: Scholars, 1979), 93.

give better evidence of popular speech than crafted literature would.[13] This opens up the possibility that the forms ʾlhy 'my God', and ʾly 'my God' were not felt to be substantially different words, and thence the possibility that Matthew's ηλι and Mark's ελωι are simply independent transcriptions of the same utterance.

There is of course a certain licence which a third person transcribing a speech may use. To make this point I will need to introduce phonetic transcriptions, the values of which, if not self-evident, can be traced in standard modern English dictionaries. With the help of such transcriptions we may note that a third person transcribing a speech may hear əd'vaɪzəʳ and choose whether to write *adviser* or *advisor*. They may hear a British speaker say ɪn'kwaɪəʳ and write *enquire* or *inquire*, even if some stylistic preferences exist in certain settings.[14] Often the speakers themselves may not even have thought which spelling they prefer, so there is not even an issue of authorial intent involved. The phenomenon of alternative written realisations of the same sound is nothing like as common in English (which has largely standardized spellings) as it was in Koine Greek. Moreover, an even greater number of possible realizations would have existed for representing non-Greek words in Greek.

Now it is not at all beyond the realms of possibility that the phenomenon of alternative written realizations is the phenomenon we have to deal with in Matthew and Mark. To insist that one must be the better or worse transcription may be rather beside the point. A possible scenario is outlined below:

(1) Jesus called on God using a standard Aramaic word.

---

[13] See Joseph Naveh and Shaul Shaked, *Amulets and Magic Bowls: Aramaic Incantations of Late Antiquity* (Jerusalem/Leiden: Magnes/E. J. Brill, 1985), 62, 68, 70, for examples in a form of Syriac and in Jewish Aramaic.

[14] The written realisations would in turn give rise to alternative spoken forms in British and American English.

(2) What he clearly articulated was naturally the initial and final sounds (the vowels *e* and *i*), and the single major consonant between these two, namely *l*.

(3) The vowel sounds which were heard had no fixed value either as short or long vowels since whether a vowel is short or long is not a question of how long it lasts in absolute time (a short vowel in English may be sustained for ten seconds by a performing choir), but of its value within a language system.[15] The same initial vowel was therefore transcribed according to one convention in Matthew as η, and according to another in Mark as ε.

(4) No distinct *o* vowel or consonant *h* was clearly pronounced,[16] but the ω in Mark's ελωι was supplied in the process of converting the spoken form into a written convention, as Mark used the nearest Greek equivalent to the written Aramaic form *'lhy*. *H* could naturally not be written in the middle of a Greek word. Though the vowels in Aramaic *'lhy* are usually transcribed *'əlāhī*, the *ā* (in Masoretic terms, *qametz*) may often have been close to *å* phonetically, and therefore as naturally transcribed into Greek by *omega* as by *alpha*,[17] particularly since if ελαι has been used in Mark's Gospel it would run a greater risk of not being interpreted as trisyllabic.[18] This scenario, or

---

[15] Geert Booij, *The Phonology of Dutch* (Oxford: OUP, 1995), 5, observes that in Dutch both 'the short vowels and the high long vowels /i,y,u/ have an average duration of about 100 msec.' Length of vowels is thus not merely a question of phonetics (and actual time), but of phonology.

[16] It is not unlikely that *h* was often dropped in Galilean Aramaic, though the evidence is meagre; see E. Y. Kutscher, *Studies in Galilean Aramaic* (Ramat-Gan: Bar-Ilan University, 1976), 81. *H* was regularly dropped in certain positions in Qumran Hebrew. Production of an *h*, or at least of a loud *h*, would, moreover, be amongst the most difficult phonetic challenges for someone experiencing the difficulties of inhalation associated with crucifixion. I am grateful to Professor David Short, a physician, and Mrs Rosie Gathercole, a speech therapist, for discussion on this.

[17] An alternative but plausible explanation of the *omega* is found in Macuch, *Grammatik des samaritanischen Aramäisch*, 63.

[18] The issue of whether Jesus pronounced three syllables or two may again be beside the point. Written syllabification represents syllables according to

something like it, is at least possible and should be considered as an alternative to approaches which have only considered privileging one synoptic form over the other. The acceptability of this proposal will depend naturally on the model of synoptic relationships that one adopts.

Sabachthani *and to Leave*

We can now proceed to the final word of the cry, not now to consider its form, but to consider its meaning. What did *shəvaq* mean? Gould comments

> The historical meaning of σαβαχθανεί is not *to leave alone*, but *to leave helpless*, denoting, not the withdrawal of God himself, but of his help, so that the Psalmist is delivered over into the hands of his enemies. So that, while it is possible to suppose that Jesus is uttering a cry over God's withdrawal of himself, it is certainly unnecessary. Such a desertion, or even the momentary unconsciousness of the Divine presence on the part of Jesus, makes an insoluble mystery in the midst of what is otherwise profound, but not obscure.[19]

But why do Matthew and Mark both mention the darkness immediately before Jesus' cry? It seems best to connect the two, and to see in the darkness a withdrawal of divine presence. In fact withdrawal of presence is not alien to the historical meaning of Ps 22. The psalm begins: 'My God, my God, why have you forsaken me, *far away* from my salvation?' Here is distance, as again in v. 11 where we read '*Do not be far* from me because trouble is near because there

---

conventions. The word *twelfth* may be pronounced as disyllabic but is nevertheless monosyllabic within the language system. *Australian* may be pronounced as a single syllable ['Strine'] by some of Bruce Winter's Australian compatriots, but nevertheless contains four syllables when transcribed according to received conventions. 'Strine' has now achieved the level of dictionary entry in the *American Heritage® Dictionary of the English Language* (4th ed.; New York: Bartelby.com, 2002).

[19] Ezra P. Gould, *The Gospel according to Mark* (ICC; Edinburgh: T & T Clark, 1896), 294. The acute accent on σαβαχθανεί is his, but in Aramaic it is the preceding syllable that bears the stress.

is no one helping me.' The context may well be invoked along with the citation.[20]

But consideration of the meaning of *shəvaq* leads to a profound irony. Jesus' cry had two parts: an address to God and a question about why he was abandoned. The first part is misunderstood. Whatever form of address he used to God he is heard as calling Elijah (Matt 27:47; Mark 15:35). Immediately in response to this someone offers him a drink. At this point those standing by tell the man: '*Leave* him. Let's see if Elijah comes ...' (Matt 27:49; Mark 15:36). There is only one obvious verb in Aramaic for 'leave' — the word used in all the early Syriac translations of the Gospels and the word Jesus has just used — *shəvaq*. In response to Jesus' cry 'Why have you *left* me?', the bystanders tell the one person who would have helped to *leave* him, just as the disciples had earlier, thereby conforming to Ps 22:11, 'there is no one helping me'.[21]

Without wanting to read too much into the text, or find connections where the evangelists make none, we may observe that there is one further possible use of the Aramaic word *shəvaq* behind the Greek accounts of the Passion.[22] Luke 23:34, which some weighty authorities omit, records Jesus' words 'Father, forgive them, for they do not know what they are doing'. *Shəvaq* is also the standard Aramaic verb 'to forgive'. It has a similar semantic range to Greek ἀφίημι, the verb used both in Luke 23:34 to mean 'forgive' and in Matt 27:49 and Mark 15:36 to mean 'leave'. Yet, there is no reason to

---

[20] Furthermore, in the near context both Matt 26:31 and Mark 14:27 cite another text, Zech 13:7, specifically to highlight the abandonment of Jesus.

[21] It is important to realize that links discovered by reconstructing the same Aramaic word behind different Greek terms are unlikely to give us direct insight into the intention of the evangelists. However, such reconstruction may lead to the sharper observation of *structural* comparisons and contrasts, which in turn give insight into authorial intent.

[22] It is not impossible that 'Father, into your hands I commend my spirit' (Luke 23:46) represents yet another case of the verb *shəvaq*, referring here to an act of 'leaving' something to someone else. However, this is probably not the most natural Aramaic verb to reconstruct from the Greek.

see a great significance in the choice of vocabulary, unless we use the comparison to reflect that it is at a level deeper than lexical choice that forgiveness and Jesus' cry of abandonment are to be connected.

Jesus and the New Exodus Restoration of Daughter Zion:

Mark 5:21-43 in Context

Rikki Watts

Despite numerous attempts the underlying rationale behind Mark's intercalation of the healing of the haemorrhaging woman and the raising of Jairus' daughter, and its function within his overall theological horizons, have so far eluded scholars. This paper argues that Mark includes them as part of his presentation of Jesus as the agent of Isaiah's new exodus salvation.[1]

Mark's Account

Whether the intercalation is traditional or his own work,[2] Mark presumably includes these stories in this form and at this juncture because they contribute to his larger purpose. Stylistically, the Jairus account utilizes the so-called historic present, making frequent use of καί while the account of the woman employs the imperfect and some fifteen participles; though these distinctions should not be overstated (for instance, the story of the girl has fourteen participles, and both accounts have a similar incidence of parataxis).[3] Nevertheless, commentators have noted a range of similarities between the two. Both stories involve the 'salvation' (vv. 23, 28, 34) of females, either ad-

---

[1]   See Rikki E. Watts, *Isaiah's New Exodus in Mark* (Grand Rapids: Baker, 2000), 176, n. 203.
[2]   E.g. Paul J. Achtemeier, "Toward the Isolation of Pre-Markan Miracle Catenae," *JBL* 89 (1970): 265-91; R. Guelich, *Mark* (WBC; Dallas: Word, 1989), 292; and Joel Marcus, *Mark 1–8* (AB; New York: Doubleday, 1999), 364.
[3]   R. H. Gundry, *Mark* (Grand Rapids: Eerdmans, 1993), 285.

dressed as or called 'daughter' (vv. 23, 34-35), who whether through menstrual disorder[4] or death are regarded as unclean. One has suffered for twelve years, the other is twelve years old (vv. 25, 42). Both Jairus and the woman fall before Jesus (vv. 22, 33), the woman fears but Jairus is told not to (vv. 33, 36). The healed woman is commended for her faith while Jairus is encouraged to believe (vv. 34, 36).[5]

On the other hand, Jairus is a male, a synagogue ruler, a member of a family group, and probably of some means, while the woman, being female, has less status, is impoverished having 'spent all she had', is commonly understood to be permanently unclean (cf. Lev 12:7; 15:19), and if not a widow then is probably to some extent isolated and alone.[6] These features along with the intercalation suggest that the two stories are to be read in the light of one another.[7]

Of the commentators who have given special attention to the linking of these accounts, most agree that the primary point is the importance of faith over against concerns for ritual purity. For Edwards, since the middle element of Mark's intercalations 'nearly always provides the key to the theological purpose of the sandwich', the woman's persistent faith provides 'a powerful lesson'.[8] Marshall, understanding salvation in the larger Old Testament sense of wholeness, sees both accounts as reflecting Mark's opening summation of Jesus' call for repentance and faith in order to experience

---

[4]   On attitudes toward menstrual women, see e.g. Ezek 36:17; CD 4:12–5:17; 11Q19 48:15-17; Josephus, *B.J.* 5.227; *C. Ap.* 2.103-04; *m. Nid. passim*; *m. Zeb.* 4.1.
[5]   E.g. K. Kertelge, *Die Wunder Jesu* (Munich: Kösel, 1970), 110-14.
[6]   E.g. Marcus, *Mark*, 366.
[7]   On Mark's intercalations, see, e.g., J. R. Edwards, "Markan Sandwiches: The Significance of Interpolations in Markan Narratives," *NovT* 31 (1989): 193-216; and T. Shepherd, *Markan Sandwich Stories* (Berrien Springs: Michigan University Press, 1992).
[8]   Edwards, "Markan Sandwiches," 198, 204, 216.

the Kingdom's presence (1:14-15),[9] which in this case means the 're-socialising of those who were marginalised.'[10] Because the language for understanding miracles (6:52; 8:14-21) echoes that of understanding the parables (4:10-12) and because 4:1-34 and 4:35-5:20 are closely linked, Marshall takes the increasingly popular view that these stories function as 'enacted parables',[11] distinguishing between 'insiders' and 'outsiders' through the responses they engender.[12]

For Myers the central issue is the reversal of the honour scale: a synagogue leader must wait for his daughter's visitation while an outcast woman is healed, affirmed as 'daughter', and elevated above the 'faithless' disciples (4:40). The old social order, represented by the young girl, is verging on collapse. 'If Judaism wishes "to be saved …" it must embrace the "faith" of the kingdom' which 'alone will liberate the lowly outcast and snatch the "noble" from death.'[13]

Fisher and von Wahlde, arguing that all four stories (4:35–5:43) are essentially exorcisms[14] representative of all realms of human ex-

---

[9]   C. D. Marshall, *Faith As a Theme in Mark's Gospel* (Cambridge: CUP, 1989), 34-56, 90-110.

[10]   See also M. J. Selvidge, "Mark 5:25-43 and Leviticus 15:19-20: A Reaction to Restrictive Purity Regulations," *JBL* 103 (1984): 619-23, but Jerome H. Neyrey, "The Idea of Purity in Mark's Gospel," *Semeia* 35 (1986): 91-128, suggests that Mark's Jesus was reforming rather than repudiating the purity system.

[11]   Proposed earlier by G. H. Boobyer, "The Redaction of Mark IV.1-34," *NTS* 8 (1962): 59-70. See also M. Boucher, *The Mysterious Parable* (Washington: Catholic Biblical Commission, 1977); with respect to the nature miracles, C. L. Blomberg, "The Miracles As Parables," in *Gospel Perspectives, 4: The Miracles of Jesus* (ed. D. Wenham and C. Blomberg; Sheffield: JSOT, 1986), 327-59; also W. Kelber, *The Oral and Written Gospel* (Philadelphia: Fortress, 1983), 62; and E. S. Malbon, "Echoes and Foreshadowings in Mark 4-8: Reading and Rereading," *JBL* 112 (1993): 211-30.

[12]   Marshall, *Faith As a Theme*, 60-66.

[13]   Ched Myers, *Binding the Strong Man* (New York: Orbis, 1988), 202-03.

[14]   Citing R. E. Brown, "The Gospel Miracles," in *The Bible in Current Catholic Thought* (ed. J. L. McKenzie; New York: Herder & Herder, 1962), 187-90.

istence (nature, exorcism, healing, raising), propose that Mark's collection demonstrates both the need for faith and Jesus' great power in
his apocalyptic defeat of Satan in all of life.[15] But, aside from whether
these stories are truly so representative, faith is not only not mentioned in the exorcism story but is present only in negative terms in
the storm-stilling.

Tolbert suggests that these miracles (4:35–5:43) echo the story of
the sower with 'fear' and 'faith' delineating the distinction between
good and bad soils. 'The four episodes ... are designed primarily to
clarify the distinction between the rocky ground and the good earth,'[16]
while the prominence of 'twelve' suggests some connection with the
disciples (4:10).[17] However, Tolbert seems to confuse faithless fear
with theophanic 'awe' (4:35-41),[18] and, as she recognizes, the fear-
faith polarity is absent from the legion narrative.[19]

Noting the importance of Israel's scriptures for Mark and his
mighty deed stories,[20] numerous scholars have observed parallels (and
differences) between the raising of Jairus' daughter and the Elisha

---

[15] Kathleen Fisher and Urban von Wahlde, "The Miracles of Mark 4:35-
5:43: Their Meaning and Function in the Gospel Framework," *BTB* 11
(1981): 13-16. On the unity of these materials and their connection with the
preceding parables, see David J. Hawkin, "The Symbolism and Structure of
the Markan Redaction," *EvQ* 49 (1977): 98-110; Guelich, *Mark*, 293; D. B.
Peabody, *Mark As Composer* (Georgia: Mercer, 1987), 126-30; Tolbert
(below); F. J. Matera, "'He Saved Others; He Cannot Save Himself': A
Literary Critical Perspective on the Markan Miracles," *Interpretation* 47
(1993): 18; and B. Dale Ellenburg, "A Review of Selected Narrative-critical
Conventions in Mark's Use of Miracle Material," *JETS* 28 (1995): 171-80.

[16] Mary Anne Tolbert, *Sowing the Gospel* (Minneapolis: Fortress, 1989),
171.

[17] Tolbert, *Sowing the Gospel*, 168, n. 58.

[18] See, e.g., T. Dwyer, *The Motif of Wonder in the Gospel of Mark*
(Sheffield: Sheffield Academic Press, 1996); cf. the nuanced approach in
Marshall, *Faith As a Theme*, 70-71.

[19] Tolbert, *Sowing the Gospel*, 161.

[20] E.g. E. K. Broadhead, *Teaching with Authority* (Sheffield: JSOT, 1992),
196; Barry Blackburn, *Theios Aner and the Markan Miracle Traditions*
(Tübingen: Mohr, 1991), 238-62.

and Elijah stories of raising a dead child (1 Kgs 17:17-23; 2 Kgs 4:18-37).[21] Meye, observing parallels with Ps 107's themes of deliverance from (1) hunger and thirst (vv. 4-9; cf. Mark 6:30-44; 8:1-10, 14-21), (2) imprisonment (vv. 10-16; = demon possession; cf. Mark 5:1-20; 6:13; 7:24-30), (3) sickness (vv. 17-22; cf. Mark 5:21–6:5, 13, 53-56; 7:31-37; 8:22-26), and (4) peril at sea (vv. 23-32; cf. Mark 4:35-41; 6:45-52), suggests that the psalm constitutes Mark's 'horizon', not only for the miracles in 4:35–5:43 but up through 8:26.[22] However, Meye's parallels are sometimes vague and their correspondences vary considerably.[23] Derrett[24] contends that Mark's Jesus fulfils the pattern of sacral marriage (Ezek 16:6; Hab 2:4; Hos 2:19-20; Song 2; Zeph 3:17-19; and the story of Ruth) and conforms with Mark's Hexateuchal outline (e.g. storm-stilling, Exod 14:11-22, exorcism/discomfiture of the Egyptians, 14:23-30, ruler of the people, 18:21, 25-26, command to touch not, 19:12, sacred marriage of Israel to Yahweh, 19:10, 14-15, promise of no barren women, Exod 23:26, and blood of the covenant, Exod 24:8). But Derrett's argumentation, and his linguistic and conceptual parallels are too esoteric to be convincing.[25]

A number of common themes emerge. While (1) attention is rightly given to key terms and motifs within the intercalation (e.g.

---

[21] Jesus brings in three disciples with the parents and does not stretch himself over the child; see Guelich, *Mark*, 303. For Blackburn, *Theios Aner*, 245, such raisings are normally 'a prerogative of God'.
[22] Robert Meye, "Psalm 107 As 'Horizon' for Interpreting the Miracle Stories of Mark 4:35-8:26," in *Unity and Diversity in New Testament Theology* (ed. R. A. Guelich; Grand Rapids: Eerdmans, 1978), 1-13.
[23] For Kertelge, *Die Wunder Jesu*, 117-18, Jesus is here a new Moses; cf. J. Bowman, *The Gospel of Mark* (Leiden: Brill, 1965), 147, who suggests a repetition of the plague of blood, but see J. Gnilka, *Das Evangelium nach Markus* (Zürich: Benziger/Neukirchener, 1978), 1:214-15, on the lateness and apparent idiosyncrasy of the Rabbinic tradition to which Kertelge appeals.
[24] Duncan Derrett, "Mark's Technique: The Haemorrhaging Woman and Jairus' Daughter," *Bib* 63 (1982): 474-505.
[25] Watts, *Isaiah's New Exodus*, 9-28.

'faith', 'fear', ritual impurity and status), (2) the integrity of the larger unit (4:35–5:43), (3) its links with the parables chapter, (4) the wider literary context (e.g. 1:14-15; 1:39; 6:52 and 8:14-21, etc.) and (5) the Old Testament background should not be ignored.

A Proposal

I have argued elsewhere that Mark's opening reference to Isaiah (40:3 in Mark 1:2-3), the general Isaianic flavouring of his prologue and account of Jesus' ministry and mighty deeds, along with the three-part structure of his gospel and the content of those three sections, strongly suggest that Mark's story of Jesus is constructed within an Isaianic new exodus horizon.[26] Secondly, Mark's use of miracles to make a larger theological point has long been recognized (e.g. the two healing of the blind stories, the cursing of the fig tree).[27] If so, it is worth asking if these two episodes might also be similarly understood.

The Haemorrhaging Woman

Not only are there a number of linguistic and conceptual parallels with Isa 64:6-9 but these verses are also the only such Old Testament parallel and that in an eschatological setting. In the book's closing stages (63:7–64:11) the prophet offers a final lament, beseeching the Lord to rend the heavens and come down to redeem Israel in a new exodus (63:7–64:3). Then, describing the parlous condition of his people, he says:

---

[26] Watts, *Isaiah's New Exodus*, and especially also, J. Marcus, *The Way of the Lord* (Louisville: Westminster/John Knox, 1992); R. Schneck, *Isaiah in the Gospel of Mark, I-VII* (Vallejo: BIBAL, 1994); M. A. Beavis, "Mark:and Isaiah," in *Fortunate the Eyes That See* (ed. A. B. Beck et al.; Grand Rapids: Eerdmans, 1995), 449-66; and S. E. Dowd, "Reading Mark Reading Isaiah," *LTQ* 30 (1995): 133-43.

[27] Respectively, e.g., E. Best, "Discipleship in Mark: Mark VIII.22-X.52," *SJT* 23 (1970): 323-37 and W. R. Telford, *The Barren Temple and the Withered Tree* (Sheffield: JSOT, 1980).

All of us have become like one unclean, and all our righteous deeds are like a menstrual napkin (כְּבֶגֶד עִדִּים). We all wither away like leaves, and our iniquities, like the wind, carry us off. No one invokes your name, or attempts to take hold of you; for you have hidden your face from us, and have delivered us into the hand of our iniquity. But now, O Lord, you are our father ... now, look, we are all your people. (64:6-7, 9b)

The similarities are striking. The Markan woman is (1) unclean because of her (2) menstrual flow (Lev 15:19). Subject to a worsening μάστιξ of Satan (Mark 5:29, 34; cf. 3:10) and, impoverished through having spent her all on unavailing medical help, she could aptly be described as (3) 'withering away' (v. 26) and (4) Jesus' face is hidden from her (v. 27). However, in Mark's fulfilment of Isaiah's new exodus, this unclean woman, unlike Isaiah's Israel (5) reaches out to this true son of the Father (1:1, 11; 3:11; 5:7).[28] Jesus, turning to look at the one who touched him (vv. 30, 32), addresses the trembling (τρέμουσα) woman (cf. LXX Isa 66:2 — 'this is the one to whom I will look, to the humble and contrite in spirit, who trembles [τρέμοντα] at my word'; cf. 66:5) as (6) 'θυγάτηρ' (cf. Isaiah's 'father'), pronounces her healed, and blesses her with peace (v. 34)[29] — the only use of such language in Mark.

As Westermann remarks on Isa 64:8 — one of only two places in Israel's scriptures where God is explicitly described as Israel's father (the other being Isa 63:16) — 'it is to her Father that Israel turns in straits.'[30] Furthermore, Zion, a synecdoche for the nation/people (Isa 46:13; 59:20; cf. 60:14), is commonly described as θυγάτηρ in Isaiah (1:8; 3:16; 4:4; 10:30, 32; 16:2; 37:22; 52:2; 62:11) whom in the new exodus the Lord blesses with peace (especially Isa 57:19: 'Peace,

---

[28] Ἅπτομαι also means 'to take hold of'; cf. John 20:17; BDAG, 102-03, 2a.

[29] I.e. in restored relationship with God; E. Schweizer, *The Good News according to Mark* (tr. D. H. Madvig; London: SPCK, 1971), 118.

[30] Claus Westermann, *Isaiah 40-66* (tr. D. M. G. Stalker; London: SCM, 1969), 393, 397.

peace, to the far and the near, says the LORD; and I will heal them',
54:10; 60:17; cf. 52:17; 55:12).

It is difficult to accept that these parallels between exiled
Israel/Zion and Mark's unclean woman are accidental, especially
given Mark's overriding new exodus paradigm. It might be objected
that in Isaiah Israel's condition is the result of sin and that Mark
makes no such connection. On the other hand, first-century popular
theology apparently assumed that suffering implied sin[31] and the
LXX's use of μάστιξ likewise implies divine chastening.[32]
Interestingly, *Pss. Sol.* 7:9 describes Israel's present distress as a
μάστιξ, and this in the context of an allusion to Isa 63:17-18 (*Pss.
Sol.* 7:2: '... do not let their feet trample your holy inheritance'; cf.
8:12 where defilement by menstrual blood is a cause of God's
judgment). It seems likely that the onlookers would have assumed the
woman's guilt with her healing implying forgiveness of her sins (Ps
103:3; Jas 5:15).

Consequently, while not taking anything away from the personal
liberation of the woman, the Isaianic parallels suggest that Mark also
sees the woman as a symbol of exiled Israel. Israel too is separated
from her God and unclean. But if she will reach out in faith, Jesus,
son of God, will cleanse the nation of her impurity, reaffirm them as
his 'daughter' people, and bless them with peace.

Jairus' Daughter
Whatever the similarities with the Elisha and Elijah narratives (1 Kgs
17:17-23; 2 Kgs 4:18-37), the only eschatological Old Testament parallel is again found in connection with Isaiah's new exodus and in
close relation to the last great Isaianic lament. Responding to the

---

[31] Cf. Pss 38:3; 103:3; Luke 13:2; John 9:2, and, e.g., *b. Shabb.* 55a citing
Ezek 18:20 and Ps 88:32 (LXX): 'I will visit their lawlessness with a rod,
and their sins with scourges (ἐν μάστιξιν).'
[32] LXX: Tob 13:10; Pss 31:10; 38:1; Jdt 8:27; Tob 11:15; 13:2; etc., and on
the equivalent Hebrew terms (נכה; מכה), note the concentration in the
curse warnings of Deut 28:22, 27, 28, 35, 59, 61.

prophet's cry, the Lord declares concerning Jerusalem that on the day he creates a new heavens and new earth:

> ... no more shall the sound of weeping be heard in it, or the cry of distress. No more shall there be in it an infant that lives but a few days, or an old person who does not live out a lifetime ... (Isa 65:19-20, NRSV)

Mark's Jesus (1) explicitly stills a great commotion of weeping and wailing (Mark 5:38-39), and (2) raises a child from premature death, presumably (3) to live out her days (cf. v. 23). It is also intriguing that both accounts go on to speak of (4) eating (Isa 65:21-22; Mark 5:43).

It might be objected that the MT's 'infant' (עוֹל; LXX ἄωρος) hardly befits a twelve-year-old. One could note that in rabbinic Hebrew עוֹלְהּ means 'girl' (Jastrow) and, whereas παιδίον is usually applied to children under seven years old (Philo, *Opif.* 105; cf. Isa 49:15; Matt 2:20), Mark uses it of a twelve-year-old whose immaturity he seems to stress (ταλιθα 'little girl' [Jastrow], v. 41; κοράσιον, vv. 41, 42). Also, the LXX's ἄωρος is used not only of those who die untimely deaths but especially of those who die unmarried.[33] Nevertheless, the parallelism in Isaiah — 'or an old person who fails to live out their days' (v. 20b) — indicates that deliverance from premature death is not limited to infants and thus includes Mark's young girl (cf. *2 Bar.* 73:3; *Jub.* 23:28). That Mark's account is not set literally in Jerusalem is not really a problem either since, as already noted, in Isaiah the city serves as a synecdoche for the nation and its people.

Given also that names are rare in Mark, it might be significant that he includes one here. Cranfield suggested that Jairus derives from עוּר and means 'may Yahweh awaken', anticipating Jesus' 'awaken-

---

[33]   LSJ, citing *P. Mag. Par.* 1.342; and Epitaphs, *IG* 1².977; cf. *m. Nid.* 5.6; 6.11; *m. Ket.* 4.1 where twelve-year-olds are considered of marriageable age).

ing' of the 'sleeping' girl.[34] On the other hand, if derived from אוּר
Jairus would mean 'He (Yahweh) will enlighten' or 'may he
(Yahweh) enlighten'.[35] If so, then it is noteworthy that Isaiah's new
exodus links the Lord's dawning upon Israel with her healing, the end
of her mourning, and the command to arise:

> Arise, shine; for your light has come, and the glory of the LORD has
> risen upon you. (Isa 60:1) ... But the LORD will be your everlasting
> light, ... and your days of mourning shall be ended (Isa 60:19-20) ...
> Then your light shall break forth like the dawn, and your healing shall
> spring up quickly. (Isa 58:8, NRSV)

Isa 60:1 is particularly interesting since it celebrates the light of the
Lord's glory with a command to (daughter) Zion to 'Arise' (קוּמִי)
which is almost directly repeated in Jesus' words, ταλιθα κουμ(ι)
(Mark 5:41). Jesus' command to Jairus to 'fear not' is also characteristic of God's encouragement in the Isaianic new exodus to his
exiled and fearful people ('fear not' [אַל־תִּירָא; μὴ φοβοῦ] in, for
example, Isa 40:9; 41:10, 13, 14; 43:1, 5; 44:2, 8 [2×]; 51:7; 54:4).

On this reading, the raising of the young woman also symbolizes
what Jesus offers to daughter Zion-Israel. In and through him the
Lord's light will shine upon his people, end their mourning, and enable them to enjoy the new exodus blessings God has promised.

Other Unifying Themes
This daughter Zion imagery might also explain the enigmatic references to 'twelve' (v. 42; cf. v. 25).[36] That Mark nowhere else records

---

[34] C. E. B. Cranfield, *The Gospel according to St. Mark* (Cambridge: CUP,
1959), 183.

[35] Noted in Jerome, *Nom.* 140.2-3; and more recently in, e.g., M. J. Harris,
"'The Dead Are Restored to Life': Miracles of Revivification in the
Gospels," in *Gospel Perspectives, 6: The Miracles of Jesus* (ed. D. Wenham
and C. Blomberg; Sheffield: JSOT, 1986), 305; H. van der Loos, *The
Miracles of Jesus* (Leiden: E. J. Brill, 1968), 509-19; Marcus, *Mark*, 356.

[36] Gundry's suggestion, *Mark*, 275, that this is nothing more than a simple
explanatory detail — in spite of the diminutives the girl was actually old

how long individuals suffered or their age suggests that he sees herein some significance. As noted above, Tolbert proposed a link with the disciples, for whom 'twelve' bespeaks reconstituted Israel. If, as we have suggested, the designation 'daughter' echoes the Lord's address to his afflicted and exiled people, then perhaps Mark is inviting us to see the woman and the girl as symbols of Israel.[37] Isaiah's new exodus salvation is dawning in Jesus who alone can heal daughter Israel of her uncleanness and offer her life.[38]

The response to both mighty deeds is 'awe' and amazement (Mark 5:33,[39] 42). This too is part of the same Isaianic lament. When recollecting the first exodus the prophet appeals to God to do 'awesome things that we did not expect' (Isa 64:3).[40] *1 En.* 1:4-5, similarly reflecting on God's descent on Mount Sinai in mighty power, also speaks of great fear and trembling upon all, declaring that the Lord will show mercy to the righteous, grant them peace (cf. Mark 5:34b), they will belong to him (cf. θυγάτηρ; Mark 5:34a), be prospered and blessed, and 'the light of God shall shine upon them' (v. 8; cf. 'Jairus').[41] Finally, in both of Mark's mighty deeds 'salvation' is the

---

enough to walk around — seems forced. Surely the mere mention of walking implies she was old enough to do so.

[37] Cf. J. Moiser, "'She Was Twelve Years Old' (Mark 5:42); A Note on Jewish-Gentile Controversy in Mark's Gospel," *IBS* 3 (1981): 179-86.

[38] On the use of resurrection imagery for the return from exile, see Ezek 37; cf. Dan 3, 6 and 7.

[39] Guelich, *Mark*, 298; Gundry, *Mark*, 271; Hooker, *The Gospel according to St. Mark* (BNTC; London: A. & C. Black, 1991), 149.

[40] This being standard language for Yahweh's mighty acts; see R. N. Whybray, *Isaiah 40-55* (NCBC; London: Oliphants, 1975), 263; cf. Deut 10:21; Pss 106:22 (which psalm also recalls Israel's rebellion; see below); 145:6; also Exod 15:11; 34:10; cf. Sir 36:1-8. Marshall, *Faith As a Theme*, 70-71, notes that 'the double motif of fear and astonishment pervades the entire gospel' observing that 'at least a dozen different words are used for this theme in more than thirty-four places.'

[41] See further Dwyer, *Motif of Wonder*, 113-15, who also notes that 'fear' ('awe') is a common motif in the Exodus and is integral to the expectation of the new exodus and messianic times.

result (5:23, 28, 34) and this too is obviously a prominent Isaianic new exodus theme (e.g. Isa 59:17; 60:16; 62:1, 11; 63:1, 8, 9).

It might be objected that in Isaiah it is the hostile nations, 'your adversaries', who tremble (Isa 64:1). This is true and Mark seems aware of it (see below). But it is also the case that Israel is amazed (Isa 64:3) and it is this language that Mark employs (Isa 64:2: Aq.: τὰ ἐπίφοβα; Sym. and Th.: φοβερὰ ἃ οὐ προσεδοκῶμεν; cf. Mark 5:33 φοβηθεῖσα).

It is perhaps possible that all of this is mere coincidence. But the number of mutually supportive parallels, the fact that they are uniquely concentrated in the same Old Testament 'text plot',[42] and that they are within an Isaianic new exodus horizon, surely suggest that Mark has highlighted these features to make a theological point.

The Storm-stilling and Gerasene Demoniac
But what of the preceding miracles of the set (4:35–5:20)? If Mark is operating as suggested here, then would not one also expect a similar pattern for the storm-stilling and deliverance of the demoniac? Given that this essay is primarily concerned with 5:21-43 we will confine ourselves to a few brief remarks. First, it is widely recognised that the story of the storm-stilling (4:35-41) echoes God's control of the waters (Pss 18:15; 104:7; 106:9; Job 26:11-12; Isa 51:9-10), most evident during the exodus crossing (Exod 14-15).[43] It is this memory of passing through the sea that undergirds the lament which is at the core of our discussion (Isa 63:11-13). Furthermore, immediately following Jesus' mastering of the sea he 'drowns' the demonic 'legion' therein (Mark 5:13), echoing Pharaoh's watery demise (Isa 43:17; 51:9-11).[44]

---

[42] Using C. H. Dodd's terminology, *According to the Scriptures* (London: Nisbet, 1952).

[43] See the literature cited in Watts, *Isaiah's New Exodus*, 160-63.

[44] Cf. Derrett, "Contributions to the Study of the Gerasene Demoniac," *JSNT* 3 (1979): 2-17; E. C. Hobbs, "The Gospel of Mark and the Exodus" (Ph.D. dissertation, University of Chicago, 1958), 37-39; O. Betz, "The Concept of the So-called 'Divine Man' in Mark's Christology," in *Studies in*

Not only are the Lord's 'adversaries' (= demons) dealt with but the terrified response of 'Legion' echoes their 'troubling' (Isa 64:1; Mark 5:7).

Even Mark 5:1-20's peculiar, even arcane, combination of tomb-dwelling, pigs, and demons is found only in Isaiah, again in connection with the final lament, but as part of God's response (Isa 65:1-7; cf. LXX v. 3: δαιμόνιον).[45] After calming the sea, Jesus delivers this demoniac, even one who did not seek him (Mark 5:7; Isa 65:1) and who lived among the tombs (5:2, 3; Isa 65:4) by night (5:5; cf. Isa 65:4a) in an area populated by pigs (Isa 65:4b; being both unclean and associated with idolatry).[46] And in both the storm-stilling and the exorcism there are again the awe-filled response (4:41; 5:15)[47] and the injunction 'to fear not' (4:40).

On this reading, we have two pairs of stories (4:35–5:20; 5:21-43), each echoing imagery first from the lament (4:35-41; cf. Isa 63:11-13, and 5:25-34; cf. Isa 64:6-7) and then from the Lord's response (5:1-

---

the New Testament and Early Christian Literature: Essays in Honor of Allen P. Wikgren (ed. D. E. Aune; NovTSup 33; Leiden: Brill, 1972), 238-39; Schneck, Isaiah in the Gospel of Mark, 143-45; Watts, Isaiah's New Exodus, 159-60; Marcus, Mark, 348-52.

[45] Notably the detailed monograph on the topic by F. Annen, Heil für die Heiden: Zur Bedeutung und Geschichte der Tradition vom besessenen Gerasener (Mk 5,1-20 parr.) (FTS 20; Frankfurt am Main: Joseph Knecht, 1976) and earlier F. J. Craghan, "The Gerasene Demoniac," CBQ 30 (1968): 529-30; R. Pesch, Der Besessene von Gerasa: Entstehung und Überlieferung einer Wundergeschichte (SBS 56; Stuttgart: KBW, 1972), 30-31; also more recently Schneck, Isaiah in the Gospel of Mark, 137-43. It has further been suggested that Mark's change from μνημείων (v. 2) to μνήμασιν (v. 3) may be due to the influence of LXX Isa 65:4. On this and for a fuller discussion and bibliography, see Watts, Isaiah's New Exodus, 157-59.

[46] On tomb-dwelling and pigs as topoi for idolatry, see Annen, Heil für die Heiden, 133-81.

[47] It might be argued that the demoniac is generally held to be a Gentile whereas Isa 65:1-5 speaks of idolatrous Israelites. But aside from the counter argument that he might be Jewish (see Watts, Isaiah's New Exodus, 164-66) both Isaiah and Mark envisage potential Gentile participation in this salvation (Watts, Isaiah's New Exodus, 319-22).

20; cf. Isa 65:1-7; and 5:21-24, 35-43; cf. Isa 65:19-20) which together form a tightly knit thematic unity: the last great Isaianic lament
has been answered and God has come down among his people and
done 'fearful (awesome) things' they did not expect (Isa 64:3). Why
Mark's particular order? In Isa 63–66 the initial moment of re-
membrance from which the appeal proceeds is God's bringing his
people through the waters at the exodus. Thus Mark relates the storm-
stilling and watery-demise episodes before moving on to two more
accounts symbolizing daughter Zion's restoration. As such it is
entirely in keeping with Mark's Isaianic new exodus motif.

But what of the theme of faith? Marshall is surely right to link this
with Jesus' opening proclamation and his preaching of the
εὐαγγέλιον (Mark 1:14-15): Israel's Isaianic salvation is being fulfilled in Jesus; the path to salvation is through believing (cf. Isa 43:10
and Ps 67:12 LXX, which, recalling the exodus, uses εὐαγγελίζομαι
of the Lord's scattering of his enemies, even those who dwell among
tombs [v. 7]; Mark's *hapax legomenon*, τὴν κατοίκησιν, 5:3, being
the cognate).[48]

Isaiah 63 and Mark
Although Mark begins with Isa 40:3 two key passages suggest that Isa
63-66 is also important for him. At Jesus' baptism and in addition to
the voice from heaven, three motifs stand out: the emergence of 'son
Israel' from the water,[49] the rent heavens, and the Spirit's descent.
This combination is found only in Isa 63:7–64:12.[50] Remembering the
exodus Divine-warrior traditions, the prophet recalls when God led
his sons (63:8) up out of the water (63:11) and sent his Spirit among

---

[48] Watts, *Isaiah's New Exodus*, 96-98.
[49] Cf. Exod 4:22; Isa 63:8; P. G. Bretscher, "Exodus 4:22-23 and the Voice
from Heaven," *JBL* 87 (1968): 301-11.
[50] Cf. I. Buse, "The Markan Account of the Baptism of Jesus and Isaiah
LXIII," *JTS* 7 (1956): 74-75; A. Feuillet, "Le baptême de Jésus d'après
l'Évangile selon Saint Marc (1,9-11)," *CBQ* 21 (1959): 468-90; Marcus,
Way, 49-50; Schneck, *Isaiah in the Gospel of Mark*, 44-47.

them (63:11 and LXX 63:14), and on this basis beseeches God to rend the heavens and do the same again (63:19). For Mark this long-awaited intervention has now begun.

In the Beelzebul controversy, Mark's Jesus, in another allusion to the Divine-warrior (now Isa 49:24-25),[51] warns against blaspheming the Spirit. C. K. Barrett has observed that the 'closest, and perhaps the only, OT parallel' is again Isa 63:10.[52] The prophet recalls how in spite of God's very own delivering presence, Israel rebelled and God became her enemy. Barrett suggests 'this new work of God [in Jesus] was greeted in precisely the same way as the old.'[53] God the Warrior is active in Jesus' exorcisms but again Israel rebels. Furthermore, it is after this Isaianic lament that the Lord unequivocally declares for the first time that his salvation will mean a division among his people (65:8-16).[54]

With these elements of warning and division in mind, it is significant that not only does Mark's Jesus allude to Isa 63 at the very moment when he is emphatically rejected, but this is also the first occasion on which he is explicitly recorded as speaking in parables (3:23). Why is this important? First, immediately after this in 4:1-34 Mark explains the judicial nature of the parables, and particularly their 'dividing' ('insiders' and 'outsiders'; 4:10-11; cf. 3:20, 31) and hardening (cf. Isa 63:17 and 6:9-10)[55] purpose. Secondly, Mark apparently intends these four mighty deeds to be read in connection with Jesus' teaching on parables.

What then of Mark's literary arrangement? In keeping with his opening sentence (Isa 40:3) and baptism scene (Isa 63:19 MT), Mark

---

[51] C. K. Barrett, *The Holy Spirit and the Gospel Tradition* (London: SPCK, 1970), 62; Hooker, *Mark*, 116-17.

[52] Barrett, *Holy Spirit*, 104-05.

[53] Barrett, *Holy Spirit*, 105.

[54] Whybray, *Isaiah 40-55*, 273; Westermann, *Isaiah 40-66*, 399.

[55] While 'hardening' is not explicitly mentioned I would argue, based on the Isa 6 background, that it is certainly implied by the language of Mark 4:12; cf. 6:52; 8:14-21; see Beavis, "Mark:and Isaiah," 114, 90-91.

presents Jesus as both proclaiming and initiating Isaiah's long-awaited new exodus and thus summoning Israel to repentance and faith (1:14-15). But there is opposition (3:20-21, 31). Jesus is accused of being in league with Beelzebul (3:22). Using parables for the first time (3:23), he refutes the charge and, alluding to the Isaianic Yahweh-warrior's deliverance (3:27; Isa 49:24-25; 53:12),[56] warns against blaspheming the Spirit (3:29; Isa 63:10), who had descended upon him at his baptism (1:10; Isa 63:11, 14, 19).

This first mention of parables leads to an explanation of their 'sifting' function (4:1-34, four being told). Mark then records four mighty deed-parables all of which, for those with eyes to see (cf. 6:52 and 8:14-21), demonstrate that in Jesus the Lord's Isaianic redemption of his people has begun. Given the context of warning and division (3:20-35; 4:1-34), these mighty deeds implicitly call for a response of faith. Ironically, those who considered themselves most likely to be 'insiders' find themselves, in the immediately following visit of Jesus to his home village, Nazareth, on the 'outside'. He is unable to do any great δύναμιν, and indeed it is now Jesus' turn to be 'amazed' (ἐθαύμαζεν) because of their lack of faith (6:1-6a).

Conclusion

Echoing the images of Isa 63–66 the intercalated stories of the two women as part of the four mighty deeds of 4:35–5:43 offer further testimony to Mark's contention: the Lord has at last rent the heavens and come down in Jesus to save his people, performing 'awesome things' that they 'did not expect' (Isa 64:3). In Mark 4:35–5:20, as the Yahweh-warrior who now effects the new exodus, Jesus rebukes the waters (Isa 63:11-13) and, drowning the oppressive demonic hosts, delivers the prisoner, even he who dwells among the tombs and did not seek him (Isa 65:1-7). Then in 5:21-43 he 'saves' two 'daughters', one afflicted for twelve years, the other twelve years old. The first (5:25-34) in stirring herself to take hold of him is freed from her 'un-

---

[56] See Watts, *Isaiah's New Exodus*, 146-54.

cleanness' and blessed with peace (Isa 64:6-7). The other (5:21-24, 35-43), while weeping is stilled, is summoned by the one who enlightens to arise from an untimely death to live out her days (Isa 65:19-20). At the same time, both the woman and Jairus testify to the importance of faith (cf. Mark 1:14-15). The message seems clear: Isaiah's new creational, new exodus has come. Deliverance from demonic oppressors has begun. Daughter Zion, wasting away in her uncleanness, even 'dead' in exile, can be cleansed and resurrected, if only she will repent and believe the good news.

Papyrological Perspectives on Luke's Predecessors (Luke 1:1)

Peter M. Head

Introduction

Early in the twentieth century the material realia of the newly discovered documentary papyri and inscriptions provided important evidence for the study of the language and vocabulary of the New Testament. In the pioneering work of Adolf Deissmann and James Hope Moulton, information from a variety of texts in the ancient world was brought to bear on the meaning of words within the New Testament.[1] Against the view that there was a special type of Biblical Greek language, both argued that the language of the New Testament reflected the common language of the people, as also reflected in the papyri. Where Thayer's edition of Grimm's *Lexicon* had listed 767 words attested in the New Testament alone and not at all in the classical tradition, Deissmann was able to show, even in his day, that less

---

[1]   Especially A. Deissmann, *Bible Studies: Contributions Chiefly from the Papyri and Inscriptions to the History of the Language, the Literature, and the Religion of Hellenistic Judaism and Primitive Christianity* (ET; Edinburgh: T & T Clark, 1901; original 1895 and 1897); idem, *Light from the Ancient East: The New Testament Illustrated by Recently Discovered Texts of the Graeco-Roman World* (ET; London: Hodder & Stoughton, 1910; original 1908). J. H. Moulton and G. Milligan, *The Vocabulary of the Greek Testament Illustrated from the Papyri and Other Non-literary Sources* (London: Hodder & Stoughton, 1914-29). Moulton's "Introduction" (pp. vii-xx) remains a useful summary (Moulton died in 1917 after it reached *delta*). See G. H. R. Horsley, "The Origin and Scope of Moulton and Milligan's *Vocabulary of the Greek New Testament*, and Deissmann's Planned New Testament Lexicon: Some Unpublished Letters of G. A. Deissmann to J. H. Moulton," *BJRL* 76 (1994): 187-216.

than fifty of these words remained unattested in the papyri.[2] Moulton
and A. T. Robertson also made pioneering efforts in relation to the
grammar of the Greek New Testament.[3]

In recent years renewed attention to the documentary papyri as an
important resource for the study and interpretation of the Greek New
Testament has emerged. At Macquarie University in Sydney a project
under the leadership of Professor Edwin Judge to revise the famous
work by Moulton and Milligan, *The Vocabulary of the Greek
Testament* (MM), resulted in the research behind the *New Documents
Illustrating Early Christianity* volumes,[4] and is now coming to fruition under the care of Greg Horsley and John Lee.[5] In two other wel-

---

[2] A. Deissmann, *Light from the Ancient East*, 54-142, esp. 73 (in this
section he provides thirty-two examples of such words illustrated from
documentary texts; also some attention is given to idiomatic expressions and
syntax).
[3] J. H. Moulton, *A Grammar of New Testament Greek: Vol. 1,
Prolegomena* (3rd ed.; Edinburgh: T & T Clark, 1908) and *Vol. 2, Accidence
and Word-formation* (Edinburgh: T & T Clark, 1929); cf. also, "New
Testament Greek in the Light of Modern Discovery," in *Cambridge Biblical
Essays* (ed. H. B. Swete; London: Macmillan & Co., 1909), 461-505; A. T.
Robertson, *A Grammar of the Greek New Testament in the Light of
Historical Research* (3rd ed.; London: Hodder & Stoughton, 1919).
[4] G. H. R. Horsley et al., *New Documents Illustrating Early Christianity* (8
vols.; Ancient History Documentary Research Centre, Macquarie University;
Grand Rapids: Eerdmans). See C. J. Hemer, "Towards a New Moulton and
Milligan," *NovT* 24 (1982): 97-123; also G. H. R. Horsley, "Linguistic
Essays," in *New Documents* 5 (1989): esp. 83-92. On p. v of his preface to
the first volume of *New Documents*, Edwin A. Judge wrote: 'The Rev. B. W.
Winter first proposed that we should use the papyrological resources of the
University to revise MM [Moulton and Milligan]'. Anyone who knows
Bruce Winter at all well, will know that he often suggests worthwhile
enterprises. One proposal resulted in my teaching a summer school course on
'The New Testament and Papyrology', where I first began to explore this
subject in a systematic way. The present essay is but a small offering in
gratitude for my friendship with him over the years.
[5] For some recent 'firstfruits' see G. H. R. Horsley and J. A. L. Lee, "A
Lexicon of the New Testament with Documentary Parallels: Some Interim
Entries, 1," *Fil. Neot.* 10 (1997): 55-84; this includes a general discussion of
progress to date and plans for layout, etc., along with specimen entries for

come recent developments the American Society of Papyrologists has
sponsored a well attended group on *Papyrology and Early Christian
Backgrounds* at the annual Society of Biblical Literature Congress
(led since 1998 by David G. Martinez, Associate Professor of
Classics, University of Chicago). Three papyrologists with an interest
in the New Testament have launched a papyrological commentary
series on the New Testament, *Papyrologische Kommentare zum
Neuen Testament*, the first of which by Peter Arzt-Grabner of
Salzburg on Paul's letter to Philemon has recently been published.[6]
Fundamental to both these ventures is the availability of searchable
texts for most published documentary papyri in the Duke Data Bank
of Documentary Papyri (searchable via Perseus).[7]

Luke and Papyrology
The prologue or preface to Luke's Gospel offers, uniquely in the New
Testament, a 'consciousness of authorship',[8] a window into the aims
and intentions of the writer. It is also important for what it reveals

---

words relating to 'teach/teaching' and 'heal/healing'; also G. H. R. Horsley
and J. A. L. Lee, "A Lexicon of the New Testament with Documentary
Parallels: Some Interim Entries, 2," *Fil. Neot.* 11 (1998): 57-84; here they
state that the current aim is a volume treating c. 1,000 words (not an
exhaustive lexicon), and offer specimen entries for 40 words (*alpha-epsilon*)
for which no documentary parallel was noted in MM or BAGD.

[6] *Papyrologische Kommentare zum Neuen Testament* (Vandenhoeck &
Ruprecht). The editors are Peter Arzt-Grabner (Salzburg), Amfilochios
Papathomas (Athens/Vienna) und Mauro Pesce (Bologna). *Philemon* was
published in 2002. For information on the Corinthian correspondence see
http://www.sbg.ac.at/anw/projects/papyri.htm.

[7] Perseus is at http://odyssey.lib.duke.edu/papyrus/texts/DDBDP.html. An
important associated research tool is the *Heidelberger Gesamtverzeichnis
der Griechischen Papyruskunden Ägyptens* (*HGV*; see
http://www.rzuser.uni-heidelberg.de/~gv0/). This aims to be a complete
register of all (published) documentary papyri from Egypt (currently 53,285
records); it also includes a list of 10,570 dated papyri.

[8] H. J. Cadbury, "Commentary on the Preface of Luke," in *The Acts of the
Apostles* (ed. F. J. Foakes Jackson and K. Lake; 5 vols.; London: Macmillan,
1920-33), 2:489.

about the transmission of the gospel tradition in the period leading up to the writing of the gospels. The preface is also designed as a shop window for presenting Luke's complete work to its readers among the wider Graeco-Roman world.

In this paper we want to ask whether papyrological material might make some contribution to understanding the reference in Luke's preface to his predecessors, especially in regard to how Luke intended to characterize them in the first phrase, πολλοὶ ἐπεχείρησαν ἀνατάξασθαι διήγησιν. At first sight it may seem odd to suggest that this most elegantly balanced literary preface with its somewhat formal language might be illuminated from the documentary papyri. But Luke's avoidance of theological terminology and his use of relatively rare and unusual terms has meant that previous studies have compared the documentary papyri with Luke's preface and indeed have made some contribution (most successfully of course when complementing other sources of information about Luke's intention).[9]

A useful example would be Luke's dedication of his work to 'most excellent Theophilus'. It has sometimes been held that the term *Theophilus* is used either adjectivally or symbolically to show that Luke addresses his Gospel to those who are/would be lovers of God.[10] As Origen said:

---

[9] So especially the magisterial work by Cadbury, "Commentary on the Preface of Luke," in *The Acts of the Apostles* (ed. Jackson and Lake), 2:489-510. Cadbury described his aim as 'to consider primarily the actual meaning of the words in the light of fresh inquiry into new lexical material' (p. 489). His work abounds in references to the papyri (alongside a wide range of Greek literature). Although L. Alexander's work focuses mostly on the preface's relationship with literary conventions, her comments also make frequent reference to papyrological evidence; see her *The Preface to Luke's Gospel: Literary Convention and Social Context in Luke 1.1-4 and Acts 1.1* (SNTSMS 78; Cambridge: CUP, 1993).

[10] Evidence for an adjectival usage is found in the papyri, in connection with cities (e.g. *BGU* 937, AD 250; *BGU* 924, III AD); but only once in connection with a person (*P. Lond.* 1674, AD 570).

Someone might think that Luke addressed the Gospel to a specific man named Theophilus. But, if you are the sort of people God can love then all of you who hear us speaking are Theophiluses, and the Gospel is addressed to you.[11]

Nevertheless among a range of other evidence the papyri show clearly that this term was widely used as a proper name for real people.[12] This also fits the ancient literary dedicatory custom.[13] In addition, although some literary and official texts reveal that in certain periods κράτιστε was used for officials of the equestrian rank, the papyri generally reveal such a flexible approach that it is not possible to deduce the precise social standing of Theophilus, even if parallels in Acts might suggest some form of high official.[14]

Papyrological background information does not necessarily solve every problem. A good example of this may be found in Luke's description of his own approach to writing his account, especially his aim 'to write an orderly account'. Here καθεξῆς is used adverbially in

---

[11]   Origen, *Homiliae in Lucam* 1, on Luke 1:1-4; cited from J. T. Lienhard, *Origen: Homilies on Luke, Fragments on Luke* (Fathers of the Church; Washington: Catholic University of America Press, 1996), 9.

[12]   Cadbury cites a range of evidence: *P. Lille* 27 (III BC): a Pisidian; *P. Petrie* I.19.30 (III BC): a Thessalian; *P. Oxy.* 745: a politarch in Egypt (I BC); also commonly used among Jews: MM, *s.v.*, *BGU* 715 (AD 101-102); Cadbury, "Commentary," 507. The prevalence of the name among Jews is noted in *CPJ* I.xix (although only one example is given in the volumes: no. 21 = *P. Gur.* 8 [210 BC from Apollonias in the Fayyum]; three examples from literary texts are noted in T. Ilan, *Lexicon of Jewish Names in Late Antiquity: Part I. Palestine 330 BCE – 200 CE* (TSAJ 91; Tübingen: Mohr Siebeck, 2002), 287-8). L. C. Reilly, *Slaves in Ancient Greece: Slaves from Greek Manumission Inscriptions* (Chicago: Ares, 1978) catalogues four former slaves whose name was Theophilus (no. 1453 = *IG* IX.2.73,16 [from Lamia, I/II AD]; no. 1454 = *IG* IX.2.555,14 [from Larisa, I BC-I AD]; no. 1455 = *Annuario*, 1944-45, no. 174 [from Calymna, II AD]; no. 1468 = *BCH* 66-67 (1942-43), 78, no. 7 [from Delphi, II AD]), referred to in *New Documents* 4 (1987): 178, as noted by Alexander, *Preface*, 133.

[13]   So Alexander, *Preface*, 187-200.

[14]   Alexander, *Preface*, 133. The Duke Data Bank via Perseus turned up 864 results for κράτιστε.

relation to Luke's act of writing (καθεξῆς σοι γράψαι). Although it is sometimes thought (especially in relation to Papias' comments concerning Mark) to relate to chronological order, Luke's own usage elsewhere (in the Greek Bible he alone uses the term, although it is not unknown in contemporary Jewish texts in Greek)[15] suggests something akin to 'consecutively' (cf. Luke 8:1; Acts 3:24; 11:4; 18:23). Until recently no papyrological evidence had been found for this term.[16] Now the term has turned up among the Greek papyri from Kellis, apparently supporting 'consecutively' (*P. Kell.* 23; AD 353).[17] But by this period Greek and Coptic Scriptures are known in Kellis and so the single isolated instance of the use of the term in such a late text is not a particularly secure basis for argument.

Luke's Predecessors: Attempts?

Leaving aside for the moment the 'many', we turn initially to the first verb of the opening clause of Luke's preface, ἐπιχειρέω, 'to set one's hand to', 'endeavour' or 'attempt', often, as here, with a following infinitive expressing the thing attempted.[18] The main question here is one of connotation. Does the use of this term imply either that the attempt itself is problematic or that the attempt implies a lack of successful execution? Origen, for example, took the former view while Eusebius took the latter:

---

[15] *Letter of Aristeas* 193, Cod. M; *T. Judah* 25:1; *Apocalypse of Moses* 8; cf. 1 Clement 37:3; *Martyrdom of Polycarp* 22:3.

[16] An absence noted both by Cadbury ("Commentary," 504) and Alexander (*Preface*, 131).

[17] K. A. Worp, ed., *Greek Papyri from Kellis, 1* (with contributions by J. E. G. Whitehorne and R. W. Daniel; Dakhleh Oasis Project Monograph, 3; Oxford: Oxbow, 1995). *P. Kell.* 23 is a Petition concerning an assault and stealing pigs; lines 4-6 read: ἐποίησα τοὺς λειτουργοὺς πάντας τὴν τύχην ἑαυτῶν τῇ στρατηγικῇ τάξει διδόναι κατὰ τὸ ἔθος καὶ ἕκαστος ἡμῶν *καθεξῆς* ἐκληρώθη εἰς λειτουργείας 'I made all the liturgists declare their status to the office of the strategus according to custom, and each one of us was appointed by lot to his liturgy consecutively.'

[18] See BDAG, 386.

The words 'have tried' imply an accusation against those who rushed
into writing gospels without the grace of the Holy Spirit. Matthew,
Mark, John, and Luke did not 'try' to write; they wrote their Gospels
when they were filled with the Holy Spirit. (Origen, *Homiliae in
Lucam* 1, on Luke 1:1-4 [Lienhard, *Origen: Homilies on Luke*, 5])

Luke himself at the beginning of his treatise prefixed an account of
the cause for which he had made his compilation, explaining that
while many others had somewhat rashly attempted to make a full narrative of the things of which he had himself full knowledge, he felt
obliged to release us from the doubtful propositions of the others and
related in his own gospel the accurate account of the things of which
he had himself firmly learnt the truth from his profitable intercourse
and life with Paul and his conversation with the other apostles.
(Eusebius, *Hist. eccl.* 3.24.15; LCL)

Perhaps these interpretations arose from reflection on the use of the
same term twice in Acts (the only other occurrences in the New
Testament): in Acts 9:29, describing hostile (but unsuccessful)
attempts to kill Paul; and in Acts 19:13, describing the attempts, presumably successful as far as they went albeit presumptuous, by
Jewish exorcists to name the name of Jesus over those who had evil
spirits. Nevertheless the Septuagint is by no means universally negative in phrases containing this verb (e.g. Ezra 7:23; 2 Macc 2:29;
10:15).[19] It seems much more likely that the meaning of the verb and
its connotations are bound up in the whole phrase and the general
context rather than that a negative connotation is inherent in the verb
itself.

The term occurs 82 times in the documentary papyri (according to
the Duke Data Bank), from the third century BC to the sixth century
AD. Many of these occurrences, including those chronologically
closest to Luke, relate to actions that the writer regards negatively, for
example in petitions which spell out a legal charge against someone.

---

[19] It is fair to note that other passages do involve negative and hostile
actions, e.g. 2 Chr 20:11; 1 Esdr 1:26; Esth 9:25; 2 Macc 7:19; 9:2; 3 Macc
6:24; 7:5; 4 Macc 1:5.

However, none of the 82 examples deals with writing or composing.[20] Closer to the Lukan usage is the use of the term among historians to describe their own work or that of others.

Polybius writes that unlike some others, he has 'undertaken to describe the events occurring in all known parts of the world' (ἀναγράφειν ἐπικεχειρήκαμεν..., *Historiae* 2.37.4; cf. 3.1.4: γράφειν ἐπικεχειρήκαμεν).[21] Historians also use this term in the third person to describe other historians, and although the general tone is sometimes negative, there is no evidence that this negativity inheres in this verb. For example, Josephus writes about Justus, son of Pistus, that 'he was not unversed in Greek culture, and presuming on these attainments even undertook to write a history of these events (ἐπεχείρησεν καὶ τὴν ἱστορίαν τῶν πραγμάτων τούτων ἀναγράφειν), hoping by his presentation of the facts to disguise the truth' (*Vita* 40). Later in a long excursus in which Josephus lays out numerous problems with Justus' historical work he writes: 'Justus, having taken upon himself to record the history of this war (συγγράφειν τὰς περὶ τοῦτον ἐπιχειρήσας πράξεις τὸν πόλεμον), has, in order to gain credit for industrious research, not only maligned me, but even failed to tell the truth about his native place' (*Vita* 338). As Josephus goes on to argue, there is nothing problematic about the task itself as it is here expressed, only Justus' lack of veracity and moderation. Elsewhere Josephus writes similarly about the earliest Greek historians (*C. Ap.* 2.13: οἱ μέντοι τὰς ἱστορίας ἐπιχειρήσαντες συγγράφειν). Once again Josephus goes on to

---

[20] E.g. *P. Oxy.* 38 (from AD 49-50): 'Syrus tried to carry off into slavery my infant son Apion' (τοῦ Σύρου ἐπικεχειρηκότος ἀποσπάσαι εἰς δουλαγωγίαν τὸν ἀφήλικά μου υἱὸν 'Απίωνα). The attempt was not ultimately successful as Apion was later recovered to his father.

[21] Alexander, *Preface*, 109-10, notes the basically synonymous use of πειρᾶσθαι in, for instance, 2 Macc 2:23; *Letter of Aristeas* 1, 297, 322, and other sources.

express some reservations about their accuracy, but this does not relate to his use of this verb (and its associated infinitive).[22]

Diodorus Siculus twice uses the term in basically positive expressions of what some other historians have 'undertaken': 'the writers of greatest reputation among the later historians ... have undertaken to record only the most recent events' (*Bibliotheca* 4.1.2; cf. also 1.3.2). Indeed, Polybius also uses the term in the third person, in an extended discussion of the ideal historian (which is also of interest for thinking about Luke):

> It will be well with history either when men of action undertake to write history (οἱ πραγματικοὶ τῶν ἀνδρῶν γράφειν ἐπιχειρήσωσι τὰς ἱστορίας), not as now happens in a perfunctory manner, but when in the belief that this is a most necessary and most noble thing they apply themselves all through their life to it with undivided attention, or again when would-be authors regard a training in actual affairs as necessary for writing history. (Polybius, *Historiae* 12.28.3-5)

Evidence is therefore lacking that the word ἐπιχειρέω is used to indicate that either the attempt or the thing attempted are necessarily viewed negatively by the author. Its use in Luke's preface fits neatly into the broader context of ancient historiography. Whether Luke perceives the action of the 'many' negatively can only be answered internally, and we shall only do that after we have examined the next two words in Luke's preface.

Luke's Predecessors: Compiled?

The verb used to describe the compilation of the narratives is quite a rare term, ἀνατάσσομαι, normally understood as an arrangement of

---

[22] See Cadbury, "Commentary," 494. Alexander, *Preface*, 110, does not agree and takes the expression as expressing modesty and then states that 'it is impossible to escape the derogatory implications when the phrase is used in the third person: one can hardly be modest about someone else'. But she has not demonstrated a concern for modesty among ancient historians, and does not really address the fact that rather similar wording may be used in both positive and critical contexts, without contaminating the verb with a negative or derogatory connotation.

material in orderly sequence.[23] In the relatively few occurrences in the literature the term seems to be used in a variety of different senses. While in Marcus Aurelius it is used about speaking (Marcus Aurelius *Meditationes* 3.5.2), in two places is it clearly used in relation to composition of a text. In *Letter of Aristeas* 144 it is used of Moses' composition of the Torah:

> you must not fall into the degrading idea that it was out of regard to mice and weasels and other such things that Moses drew up his laws with such exceeding care. All these ordinances were made (πάντα ἀνατέτακται) for the sake of righteousness to aid the quest for virtue and the perfecting of character.

In Irenaeus it is used of Ezra's rewriting of the Scriptures after their corruption in the exile:

> God ... inspired Esdras the priest, of the tribe of Levi, to recast all the words of the former prophets (τοὺς τῶν προγεγονότων προφητῶν πάντας ἀνατάξασθαι λόγους), and to re-establish with the people the Mosaic legislation. (*Adv. haer.* 3.21[24].2; ed. Harvey)

Lee and Horsley have recently noted four non-literary occurrences, three in inscriptions (from Kos, Macedonia and Termessos) and one in a documentary papyrus. These authors suggest that the verb means 'set out (information) in writing'.[24] As they later note, this (if generally accepted) 'offers an improved understanding of the much-debated New Testament instance in Luke's preface'.[25] Closer inspection suggests that although the action expressed by the verb does relate broadly to the notion of writing, this attaches more to the general context rather than to the verb itself. The important idea of an orderly presentation is also missing in this definition. So, for example, in their first example, which concerns an inscription listing priests (*LSCG*

---

[23] So BDAG; also Alexander, *Preface*, 110, who regards it as basically equivalent with other compounds of -τάσσειν terms: 'the choice of compounds of -τάσσειν, stressing the ordering of pre-existent material rather than creation *de novo*, is characteristic of the scientific tradition'.

[24] Lee and Horsley, "Some Interim Entries, 2," 62.

[25] Lee and Horsley, "Some Interim Entries, 2," 79.

174.14; 21 BC), the verb relates to two prepositional phrases: the first expresses the location: names are 'set out on a white marble stele' (ἐς δὲ λευκόλιθον ... στάλαν ... ἀνατάξαι); the second expresses the type of list 'all of them with their patronymics in the order in which they served as priests' (κατὰ τάξιν ὡς ἱερατεύκαντι πατριαστεὶ πάντας ἀνατάξαι). Then follows a list of names. The second example also involves listing names (*SEG* 36.681.5; AD 87/88): 'L. Insteius Gemellus the *ephebarkhos* listed the ephebes' (Λ. Ἰνστεῖος Γέμελλος ὁ ἐφήβαρχος ἀνέταξεν τοὺς ἐφήβους), followed by a list of names.

The single occurrence among the papyri occurs at the very end of a rather complex document from AD 122 about a dowry (*P. Fam. Tebt.* 21).[26] Throughout, the scribe has attempted to use a varied vocabulary to express the complicated dowry arrangements of Didymarion. Lee and Horsley render the closing signature of the register as follows:

> [The foregoing points] have been set out in writing through the agency of Lourias (ἀνατέτακται διὰ Λουρίου) also called Apollonios at the office of the village of Tebtunis ...

But the document has already twice affirmed the act of writing with the simple statement: 'Kronion wrote this (Κρονίων ἔγραψα)' (line 29) and 'Lysamichos wrote this (Λυσίμαχος ἔγραψα)' (line 34). It seems more likely, in view of the complexity of the situation, that Lourias is taking credit for the orderliness of the composition rather than the simple act of writing.

Luke's Predecessors: Narratives?
The noun Luke chooses to describe the compilations attempted by the 'many' is διήγησις. This noun occurs only here in the New Testament. Alexander states that in contemporary historiographical literature it was often used (in extension from its use in forensic rhetoric) of the main body of a text as distinct from the preface or an

---

[26] B. A. van Groningen, *A Family-archive from Tebtunis (P. Fam. Tebt.)* (Papyrologica Lugduno-Batava 6; Leiden: E. J. Brill, 1950), 75-78.

excursus (referring to Polybius, *Historiae* 3.36.1; 3.38.4; 3.39.1; 2 Macc 2:32; 6:17; Josephus, *Vita* 336; *Letter of Aristeas* 8).[27] She suggests that Luke's usage does not fit into this 'semi-technical' historiographical mode, but reflects a more general or colloquial usage: 'an account' rather than 'a narrative'. Two texts are taken to support this view: *Letter of Aristeas* 1 and 322 are taken to be more general, 'like Luke's here'; and although the term is uncommon in the papyri, one text (*P. Oxy.* 1468) 'may show a colloquial use not unlike Luke's here'.[28]

In response to Alexander's position (which reflects her general drift away from classifying Luke's preface as influenced by or reflecting the concerns commonly found in historiographical prefaces) I would like to argue that among the texts to which she refers only 2 Macc 2:32 and *Letter of Aristeas* 8 clearly function to distinguish, in 'semi-technical' manner, two parts of the text in question, preface from main body.[29] The others, although used in the context of introducing an excursus or aside, are not used to provide a category distinction between the main body and the excursus (for which no distinct terminology is used). Rather διήγησις is used for the ongoing flow of the story/narrative, which pauses for the moment so that information that is necessary for the reader to understand the story properly can be introduced. Polybius seems quite clear:

> So that my narrative (διήγησις) may not be altogether obscure to readers owing to their ignorance of the topography I must explain whence Hannibal started, what countries he traversed, and into what part of Italy he descended. (*Historiae* 3.36.1)

Without this information,

---

[27] Alexander, *Preface*, 111.

[28] Alexander, *Preface*, 111.

[29] Behind these texts lies Lucian, *Ver. hist.* 55: 'After the preface (τὸ προοίμιον), long or short in proportion to its subject matter, let the transition to the narrative (ἡ ἐπὶ τὴν διήγησιν μετάβασις) be gentle and easy. For all the body of the history is simply a long narrative (ἅπαν γὰρ ἀτεχνῶς τὸ λοιπὸν σῶμα τῆς ἱστορίας διήγησις μακρά ἐστιν).'

The mind here has nothing to lean upon for support and cannot connect the words with anything known to it, so that the narrative
(διήγησις) is associated with nothing in the readers' mind, and therefore meaningless to him. (*Historiae* 3.36.4, not noted by Alexander)

Various types of asides are necessary in order for a reader to understand the narrative (so 2 Macc 6:17; Josephus, *Vita* 336); although too
much information can distract from understanding the narrative. So,
for example, Josephus refrains from listing the names of all the exiled
families who returned to Jerusalem 'lest I distract the minds of my
readers from the connexion of events (τῆς συναφῆς τῶν πραγμάτων)
and make the narrative (διήγησις) difficult for them to follow' (*Ant.*
11.68; cf. Ezra 2:1-70; Neh 7:6-73; 1 Esdr 5:7-46).

Secondly, it does not make any sense to distinguish between *Letter
of Aristeas* 8 on the one hand (as a semi-technical usage) and *Letter of
Aristeas* 1 and 322 on the other (as a more general usage). *Letter of
Aristeas* 1 introduces the trustworthy narrative compiled for
Philocrates (ἀξιολόγου διηγήσεως ... συνεσταμένης); v. 8 reprises
the same term and promises the continuation of this narrative (ἐπὶ τὸ
συνεχὲς τῆς διηγήσεως ἐπανήξομεν), acknowledging implicitly that
this has already begun in the preface; *Letter of Aristeas* 332 then acknowledges that the narrative as promised has now been told.

Thirdly, Alexander suggests that although in general 'the papyri
do not suggest widespread colloquial use',[30] one text 'may show a
colloquial use not unlike Luke's'. In this case I suggest that the first
statement is rather an understatement. Among documentary papyri
available in the Duke Data Bank (searched on Perseus) the term occurs only 12 times, the earliest example being *P. Oxy.* 1468, a legal
petition from AD 258, which is the text Alexander notes. This reads
(*P. Oxy.* 1468.10-11): τὰ δὲ τοῦ πράγματος τοιαύτην ἔχει τὴν
διήγησιν (Grenfell and Hunt: 'The statement of my case is as follows'). This sentence is followed by a blank space indicating a punc-

---

[30]   Alexander, *Preface*, 111.

tuational pause and then by the narrative of the alleged criminal events (concerning slave ownership).[31] Against Alexander this usage would seem to fit perfectly into the pattern of forensic rhetoric rather than a more general or colloquial usage (cf., for example, Aristotle, *Rhet.* 3.16.1; LSJ also refers to Zeno, *Stoic.* 1.23). All the other ten occurrences in the documentary papyri are both later and universally in legal contexts. They do not all occur in connection with a legal case, but quite often in support of loan documentation referring to the arrangements made for the loan (e.g. *P. Oxy.* 4394: 'I acknowledge in conformity with the foregoing statement [διήγησις] that I have received ... [a sum of money]).[32] They reflect a narrative account, but are embedded in forensic contexts.

The first conclusion to be drawn is that if the rather general and colloquial usage proposed by Alexander is not actually attested in the ancient literature then Luke's usage here probably draws upon historiographical terminology to describe these predecessors as 'narratives'.[33] Of all the contemporary evidence probably the closest parallels come in Eusebius' discussion of and excerpts from Papias of Hierapolis (Eusebius, *Hist. eccl.* 3.39.9 and 3.39.14).[34] Here the term διήγησις is used twice. First, '[Papias] had been the recipient of a marvellous recital [διήγησις] attributed to Philip's daughters', which concerned at least two miracles: the resurrection of a corpse in Philip's time and a miracle connected with Justus Barsabbas (3.39.9). Secondly, Eusebius notes that Papias quotes further from 'Aristion's

---

[31] *P. Oxy.* 1468 = B. P. Grenfell and A. S. Hunt, *The Oxyrhynchus Papyri XII* (London: Egypt Exploration Fund, 1916), 197-200. *P. Oxy.* 4122 (AD 305) offers a similar example in another forensic context.
[32] For this or a similar formula see *P. Haun.* 57 (AD 412-415); *P. Heid.* 330 (VI/VII AD); *P. Köln* 322 (VI/VII AD); *P. Lond.* 1007a (AD 558); *P. Münch.* 7 (AD 583); *P. Oxy.* 3955 (AD 611); *P. Oxy.* 4394.197, 218 (AD 494-500); *P. Oxy.* 4397.197, 214 (AD 545).
[33] Alexander notes the absence of this terminology from scientific prefaces.
[34] Noted in BDAG. For other connections between Papias and Luke's preface see R. J. Bauckham, "The Eyewitnesses and the Gospel Traditions," *JSHJ* 1 (2003): 28-60, esp. 31-44.

recitals of the dominical words' (Ἀριστίωνος ... τῶν τοῦ κυρίου λόγων διηγήσεις).[35] Given Papias' general preference for 'the word of a living and surviving voice' (3.39.4) it is probable that these refer to oral narratives, formulated in such a way that they are associated with a named tradent, but not necessarily in each case a long account.[36]

Concluding Reflections

We note firstly the rather obvious point that in dealing with the lexical meaning of various terms the papyrological evidence is only one piece of the jigsaw, and our discussion has illustrated the importance of investigating both the literary and documentary evidence. Since the closest literary evidence came, on several occasions, from the historiographical traditions it is also worth noting that Alexander has underestimated Luke's parallels with the historians and that perhaps more could still be said in favour of Luke's self-perception as a historian.[37]

We noted above that the connotations of various terms were not as clearly negative as some have argued. Various positive connections are drawn between the work of the predecessors and Luke's own compilation, in terms of the events (ἐν ἡμῖν, v. 1), the ultimate source of the traditions (καθώς, v. 2), and the decision to write (κἀμοί, v. 3). These positive connections strongly suggest that Luke is by no means intending to describe his 'predecessors' in a derogatory manner.

If, as both the papyri and Papias suggest, the earlier 'narratives' could have been narrated stories about Jesus, then there is also every

---

[35] ET from BDAG, 245.

[36] See further Bauckham's argument in "The Eyewitnesses and the Gospel Traditions."

[37] Cf. also D. E. Aune, "Luke 1.1-4: Historical or Scientific *Proomion*?" in *Paul, Luke and the Graeco-Roman World: Essays in Honour of Alexander J. M. Wedderburn* (ed. A. Christophersen et al.; JSNTSS 217; London: Sheffield Academic Press, 2002), 138-48; cf. also (as noted by Aune) I. H. Marshall, "Review of Alexander, *Preface*," *EvQ* 66 (1994): 373-76.

reason to accept Luke's description of 'many' who had composed them. Ultimately, of course, Luke affirms that his own narrative stems, not from direct dependence upon his predecessors, but on the apostolic witness which stands behind all the previous attempts 'to compile a narrative of the events which have occurred among us'.

Zechariah Wrote (Luke 1:63)

Alan Millard

'He asked for a writing tablet and ... he wrote, "His name is John"'
(Luke 1:63).[1] Luke's report is chronologically 'the first mention of
writing in the New Testament', as Alfred Plummer observed over a
century ago.[2] There are four other occurrences of writing, using
γράφειν, within the third Gospel, apart from citations of the Hebrew
Bible: 10:20, 'your names are written in heaven'; 16:6, 7, the debtor
instructed by the 'Unjust Steward' to alter his account; 23:38, the
superscription on the cross. Apart from the citations, Matthew uses
γράφειν only for the superscription (27:37); Mark does not use it;
within John's narrative it occurs when Jesus wrote on the ground
(8:6, 8) and for the superscription (19:19-22). The Evangelist places
no special emphasis on Zechariah's action; it was the only way the
new father could confirm his son's name, and, since Elisabeth had
insisted that the name should be John, the reader is left to deduce that
Zechariah had already communicated it to his wife by the same means
and that she had been able to read what he wrote, or had someone else
at hand to read it to her.

Writing by Priests
Zechariah's action is worth noting in any discussion of writing in
Herodian Palestine. That a priest should be able to write is no sur-
prise. Priests are portrayed as reading and writing in the Law (Num

---

[1]   A major concern of Bruce Winter's career has been the study of the New
Testament books in the context of the culture of the first century, a concern
demonstrated in his own works and in the encouragement and stimulus he
has given to others. These paragraphs are offered in appreciation of his
service, especially as Warden of Tyndale House.

[2]   A. Plummer, *Luke* (ICC; 4th ed.; Edinburgh: T & T Clark, 1901), 37.

5:23), the prophet Jeremiah was a priest who wrote (Jer 30:2) and Ezra was a priest and scribe (Ezra 8:1, 2); others were involved in implementing Jehoshaphat's reform, according to 2 Chr 19. Each of the Synoptics represents Jesus consistently treating the priests as able to read by his rhetorical question, 'Have you not read ...?'[3] According to one current authority, all, or most, priests would be able to write and so to read.[4] While there may have been priests who did not need to write as well, it is justifiable to conclude that the majority could.

Zechariah was a priest 'of the order of Abijah', the eighth of the twenty-four priestly courses set out in 1 Chr 24, certainly functioning after the Exile. Rabbinic sources give details of the priestly duties and their organisation. Recently texts have been edited which show how the owners of the Dead Sea Scrolls were very concerned to maintain the system. Among the Scrolls seventeen manuscripts concern the ritual calendar, many including the lists of priestly orders. The authors had to make their own calculations to determine the periods of service for each order because they followed a solar calendar in distinction to the Jerusalem authorities who followed the traditional lunar reckoning. The latter system allowed each of the twenty-four courses to serve for one week in each half of the year, with joint service at certain festivals. The Scrolls show how the twenty-four courses were accommodated in a six-year cycle, with four courses each serving for a third week to complete the solar year. While following the different calendar, the authors were determined to maintain the biblical precedent, giving the names of the priestly families in the same order as in 1 Chr 24:7-19, so Abijah remains the eighth.[5]

---

[3] A. Millard, *Reading and Writing in the Time of Jesus* (Sheffield: Sheffield Academic Press, 2000), 158.

[4] E. P. Sanders, *Judaism, Practice and Belief 63 BCE-66 CE* (London: SCM, 1992, corrected reprint 1998), 170-82.

[5] S. Talmon and J. Ben-Dov, "Calendrical Documents and Mishmarot," in *Calendrical Texts, Qumran Cave 4, XVI* (ed. S. Talmon, J. Ben-Dov and U. Glessmer; Discoveries in the Judaean Desert 21; Oxford: Clarendon, 2001), 1-166.

Zechariah and his family lived 'in the hill country of Judaea', the expression indicating the toparchy of Jerusalem.[6] Other priests 'are found living together as a number of families or in larger communities throughout the length and breadth of the land' according to rabbinic sources, as far north as Sepphoris in Galilee, the home of the High Priest of 5 BC, Joseph ben Elam.[7] If there were 7,200 priests, as Joachim Jeremias calculated,[8] then there was a considerable number of men who could write scattered across the land. Each priest served at the Temple for only two weeks in the year, so all of them would have been in their homes for most of the time. E. P. Sanders thought it 'probable' that priests acted as magistrates and drew up legal deeds, opining that in small villages in Judaea and Galilee there may have been only one magistrate and one legal expert to prepare such documents.[9] Luke's report of Jesus reading from a scroll of Isaiah in the synagogue at Nazareth, while not involving a priest, implies that a relatively small place owned a copy of Isaiah and if Isaiah, almost certainly the scrolls of the Torah, which was even more central. While this is a deduction without first-hand evidence, it contrasts with the view recently expressed by Catherine Hezser that some villages lacked their own Torah scrolls, so visiting rabbis would have brought their own with them. She based that conclusion on the story of Rabbi Meir in the second century writing out the text of Esther from mem-

---

[6]   E. Schürer, *The History of the Jewish People in the Age of Jesus Christ*, II (rev. and ed. G. Vermes, F. Millar and M. Black; Edinburgh: T & T Clark, 1979), 191.

[7]   S. Safrai, "The Temple and the Divine Service," in *The World History of the Jewish People*, 1st series, 7. *The Herodian Period* (ed. M. Avi-Yonah; Jerusalem: Massada Publishing, 1975), 284-337; see 291; cf. "The Temple," in *The Jewish People in the First Century*, 2 (ed. S. Safrai and M. Stern; Assen: Van Gorcum, 1976), 865-907; see 870; J. Jeremias, *Jerusalem in the Time of Jesus* (London: SCM, 1969), 194, n. 146.

[8]   Jeremias, *Jerusalem*, 199-204.

[9]   Sanders, *Judaism*, 170-71, 180.

ory when he was in a place which did not have a copy of the book.[10] However, the book of Esther held a unique position in Jewish thought and its absence cannot be taken as a sign that there were no other biblical scrolls in the village; certainly the absence of the canonical form of Esther from the Dead Sea Scrolls does not signify the absence of all Scripture from that collection!

Writing Tablets

The writing tablet which Zechariah requested is denoted by the word πινακίδιον. That is a diminutive of the common word for a flat piece of wood, a plank or board, πίναξ, used for a writing tablet from Homer onwards and borrowed by Mishnaic Hebrew (*m. Aboth* 3:17, etc.). Such wooden writing tablets, the inner surfaces coated with wax, were used from at least 2,000 BC onwards in Babylonia and Assyria and also in Egypt and the Levant. They were called *lē'um* in Akkadian and *luaḥ* in West Semitic and Hebrew, words which have the same range of meaning as πίναξ. Of the few occurrences of πινακίδιον in Classical Greek, we may note its use by the author of *On Marvellous Things Heard* for a tablet on which an oath could be written then thrown into a sacred pool in Sicily where it would either float or sink (*Mir. ausc.* 834b.12-14) and by Isocrates, c. 400 BC, as part of the necessary equipment of a student.[11] In Roman times too, Epictetus, near the end of the first century AD, includes it with writing implements and little notebooks, γράφεια, τιτλάρια, among the equipment of school children (*Dissertationes* 3.22.74).

Zechariah only needed a surface large enough to write two words: *šmh yḥnn* or *yḥnn šmh*, so a small tablet would be very suitable for

---

[10] C. Hezser, *Jewish Literacy in Roman Palestine* (Tübingen: Mohr Siebeck, 2001), 467, 479.

[11] *Fragmenta* 14; a similar saying is attributed to Antisthenes, living at about the same time, by Diogenes Laertius, *Vitae Philosophorum* 6.3. See G. Matthieu, E. Brémond, *Isocrate* IV (Paris: Les Belles Lettres, 1962), 235. I am grateful to my colleague Alexei Zadorojnyi for supplying the occurrences of πινακίδιον from the *Thesaurus Linguae Graecae*.

him. Among examples of writing tablets from the Roman world some
as small as 7.2 × 4.5 cm have been unearthed. Such tablets are only
preserved in unusual circumstances (as buried wood usually rots)
unless, exceptionally, they are made of other materials. Even when
the boards are found, the wax has often perished, so that the messages
once written are lost except in those cases where a sharp stylus has
scratched the wood. Those examples, and others that do retain the
wax, reveal that the texts written on them were normally mundane
and ephemeral, exactly like Zechariah's.[12] From Herodian Palestine
no wooden writing tablets survive. From a little later, with documents
from the Bar Kochba Revolt (AD 132-35), have come two pieces of
writing tablets with some wax, but without any trace of writing.[13]
Besides those, the same finds have produced one example of the
wafer thin folded wooden slats which were used as writing materials
across the Roman world and are amazingly exemplified by the hundreds found at Vindolanda on Hadrian's wall, from the same period.[14]

Writings Preserved

The majority of the other documents from the Bar Kochba period are
written on papyrus, the common writing material, made in Egypt and
exported around the Mediterranean world. Most of the documents can
be dated early in the second century, but some are older; one bears a
date in the second year of Nero's reign (AD 55/56). Some books
among the Dead Sea Scrolls were written on papyrus, too, and the
value of the papyrus is shown by fragments of pieces which were re-
used for writing legal deeds and letters.[15]

---

[12] See Millard, *Reading*, 26-29.
[13] P. Benoit, J. T. Milik and R. de Vaux, *Les Grottes de Murabba'at*
(Discoveries in the Judaean Desert 2; Oxford: Clarendon, 1961), 44.
[14] See Millard, *Reading*, 29, 30.
[15] E. Tov, *The Texts from the Judaean Desert*, 39: *Indices* (Oxford:
Clarendon, 2002), 211-13, lists examples, among them one of the calendrical
texts with an account on the back (see there, n. 40).

Leather was the alternative material for books and documents. Egyptian scribes had used it already in the second millennium BC and it was introduced into Babylonia as the Aramaic alphabet gained currency there in the seventh century BC. Papyrus was known there, but had to be imported and so was not always readily available; leather sheets were an acceptable substitute. The situation is nicely revealed by the letters which Arsames, the Achaemenid governor of Egypt, resident in Babylon, sent to his officials in his province. Later leather scripts are found at Dura-Europus where it appears that leather was the normal writing material prior to the Roman conquest.[16] The predominance of leather in the Dead Sea Scrolls may suggest the strength of the eastern custom in that Jewish community whose members came from many places, some bringing their books with them.

The small numbers of written documents from first-century Palestine demands assessment in a wider context. In her study of literacy through the whole period of Roman Palestine, Hezser has concluded that the meagre number of documents surviving there when compared with the thousands from Roman Egypt indicates that the use of written records in daily life was uncommon.[17] Yet the comparison is faulty. The texts taken to the remote caves in the Judaean Desert by refugees during the Bar Kochba Revolt were evidently precious to their owners, or related to current concerns — it is hard to imagine people in those circumstances carrying papers which had no value to them, or for which they would have no use. On the other hand, most of the papyri from Egypt have been recovered from rubbish heaps; they were wastepaper. Even that Egyptian rubbish is only available to modern scholarship because the water supplies of the towns that dumped it dried up long ago, leaving them dry and the papyri dehydrated.

The number of papyri in modern collections runs into the hundreds of thousands, yet they are only a proportion, certainly a small propor-

---

[16] See Millard, *Reading*, 66.
[17] Hezser, *Jewish Literacy*, 488.

tion, of all the documents written in Graeco-Roman Egypt. The ancients themselves will have destroyed a far greater quantity. Moreover, it is worth remembering that no papyrus documents survive at all from the administrative offices, business centres and great households of the Roman capital of Egypt, Alexandria, just as none survive from the heart of the Empire, Rome, or its other major cities. Had dehydrated rubbish heaps from those cities been available to archaeologists, the amount of material in modern museums would be multiplied many times. How different would be the task of Roman historians reconstructing classical history and society if that were so, or, better still, if the archive buildings still stood with their contents intact! Similarly, were there access to documents from Herod's Jerusalem, how much wider and deeper would be knowledge of the complicated first-century politics and religion there! In all these cases a far wider range and variety of texts would be accessible than the Bar Kochba documents preserve.

Writing in Palestine

Hezser draws attention to the fact that 'a great number of papyrus letters have been found in Egypt but practically none in Palestine',[18] although, while the actual numbers differ greatly, the proportion of letters to other documents in the papyri from Palestine may be little different from the proportion in Egypt.[19] The circumstances in which most of the letters were deposited in Palestine inevitably affects their content, for they were selected by the refugees, presumably for their relevance to their affairs. The presence of many legal documents but no letters in the archives of the two ladies, Babatha and Salome Komiase, found in the Judaean desert caves, cannot indicate whether letter-writing was limited to 'political, military and religious leaders and some businesspeople' or 'practiced by a much broader section of

---

[18] Hezser, *Jewish Literacy*, 488.
[19] For a list of papyri from the region, see H. M. Cotton, W. E. H. Cockle, F. G. B. Millar, "The Papyrology of the Roman Near East: A Survey," *JRS* 85 (1995): 214-35.

society' because those archives are the result of deliberate choice.[20] In contrast, the letters from Graeco-Roman Egypt exist by chance, having been discarded with other rubbish or left behind in abandoned houses.

Again, when comparison is made between the 'tens of thousands' of inscriptions known from Roman Italy and the 'few hundred' of the Roman period from Palestine, the overall situations need to be scrutinized. There are 'approximately 500-1000 Jewish epitaphs from Roman Palestine (excluding the ossuary inscriptions)' which 'seems to be a meager output'.[21] The Jewish epitaphs belong to the period after the Fall of Jerusalem, the ossuary inscriptions to the century prior to AD 70. Yet the ossuary inscriptions should not be discounted, for they served the same purpose of identification as the simplest Roman epitaphs.

The Jewish tombs of the Herodian period around Jerusalem contained numerous stone ossuaries and hundreds have been recovered bearing the names of the deceased whose remains they contained. In some cases the names were engraved with care by specialists before the ossuaries were placed in the tombs, on them the Jewish or Greek letters are even and easily legible. In other cases the names were scratched on the boxes when they were apparently already in the tomb chambers, the writers using sharp points, perhaps nails. Those examples show widely varying competence in writing, the cramped situations sometimes causing the names to be scribbled vertically and in various positions on the containers. Instead of incising the letters, some people wrote them with charcoal and it is likely that more existed than have survived because the charcoal is easily rubbed off. There were ossuaries made of wood which have perished, with any inscriptions they may have borne. Each inscribed ossuary has to be counted as an inscription from Roman Palestine. They marked the

---

[20] Hezser, *Jewish Literacy*, 289.
[21] Hezser, *Jewish Literacy*, 289, 373.

burials of people of consequence and so are comparable with the funerary inscriptions of Roman Italy.

They may be fewer in number because Palestine was a smaller country and also because the custom of inscribing memorials to the dead was not usual there. The names on the ossuaries were basically for identification, not commemoration. In the same way, the erection of statues to honour living dignitaries was alien to Jewish society, so inscriptions of that sort would not be found in Palestine prior to the Roman occupation. For comparisons to be justified and productive, the circumstances of each case have to be taken into account.

Potsherds were the scrap paper for every part of the ancient world where writing was done in ink. Messages could also be scratched on them. Normally people would use them for short and ephemeral notes, or for immediate records of transactions that would be entered into ledgers soon afterwards and the sherds discarded. The length of text to be written could determine the size of potsherd chosen, but the handwriting need be no smaller than the script on a scroll.[22] A marriage deed drafted on a potsherd found at Marisa, dated 176 BC, and the deed of gift on another found at Qumran illustrate that.[23] Where sites have lain undisturbed until recent times, ostraca may be found in groups, as at Masada; where the sites have been inhabited continually, they will appear haphazardly, sometimes disturbed by later activities. Again, the relatively small number discovered from the Herodian era does not indicate little use was made of them. The two examples cited can be taken as survivors of a much larger body.

Another comparison Hezser made to suggest literacy existed at a lower level in Palestine than in Italy concerns graffiti on house walls: 'Whereas almost every major Roman street would have been flanked

---

[22] As assumed by Hezser, *Jewish Literacy*, 130.

[23] E. Eshel and A. Kloner, "An Aramaic Ostracon of an Edomite Marriage Contract from Maresha," *IEJ* 46 (1996): 1-22; F. M. Cross and E. Eshel, "Ostraca from Qumran," *IEJ* 47 (1997): 17-28, re-edited by A. Yardeni, "A Draft of a Deed on an Ostracon from Khirbet Qumran," *IEJ* 47 (1997): 233-37.

by houses covered with graffiti, the only comparable Jewish graffiti to speak of has [sic] been found at Herodion'.[24] Visitors to Pompeii cannot but be aware of the graffiti; visitors to the Holy Land will not notice any, except in parts of Herodion. That is not because none were written on house walls, but because the plaster does not remain on the walls which would display them if they were written. Therefore no valid comparison can be made on this matter.

The report about Zechariah, the role of the debtor in the parable of the Unjust Steward and the other references to writing in the Gospels deserve to be set alongside the varied material remains and information drawn from Josephus, other writers and rabbinic sources in any consideration of the extent and use of writing in Roman Palestine. The references may be few, but that should not be taken to reflect a restricted currency of writing. No known ancient author composed an account of spinning and weaving in Roman Palestine, and yet those skills were an ordinary part of daily life. References to them only occur where appropriate in various narratives (e.g. Matt 6:28). In the same way, no known ancient author composed an account of writing or education in Roman Palestine. The references that do occur are incidental — present because they are a necessary part of the narrative, reflecting a normal activity.

Conclusion

Unless there is clear evidence, it may not be assumed that writing was restricted to small, elite circles in the principal cities. Many people never needed to write and rarely needed to read. Some could do the latter in a limited way; most writing was done by professional scribes or other educated professionals, like the priests. Yet the distribution of such people across the land meant that no one was likely to be far from someone who could read or write for him.

---

[24] Hezser, *Jewish Literacy*, 500; cf. 413-16.

Atonement Theology in Luke-Acts:

Some Methodological Reflections

David Peterson

Many contemporary scholars reflect the position of Conzelmann,[1] who argued that Luke sees no soteriological significance in the death of Jesus and makes no connection with the forgiveness of sins.[2] Atonement is not part of the primitive kerygma in Acts, which is dominated by a theology of triumph and glory. Tyson echoed a similar perspective when he concluded that:

> The conviction of divine necessity constitutes Luke's main contribution to the theological discussion of Jesus' death. But he seems uninterested in piercing through to an understanding of the theological reason for the death or in analyzing what it was intended to accomplish.[3]

Dibelius is another key figure in this debate. He explored the background of Jewish martyrdom tradition and proposed that Luke presented the death of Jesus as a model of martyrdom.[4] Talbert developed this view and considered its apologetic significance for Luke and his readers, in the light of both Jewish and Graeco-Roman

---

[1] This article is contributed with gratitude for Bruce Winter's fellowship and encouragement in many areas of ministry together over a period of 38 years, in Australia and England.
[2] H. Conzelmann, *The Theology of St. Luke* (tr. G. Buswell; New York: Harper & Row, 1960), 200-01. G. Herrick, *The Atonement in Lucan Theology in Recent Discussion*, 1997, http://www.bible.org, helpfully shows the influence of Conzelmann's work on subsequent thinking about this topic.
[3] J. B. Tyson, *The Death of Jesus in Luke-Acts* (Columbia: University of South Carolina, 1986), 170.
[4] M. Dibelius, *From Tradition to Gospel* (tr. B. L. Woolf; New York: Charles Scribner's Sons, 1971).

perspectives on martyrdom.[5] But this whole approach has been challenged by Karris, who proposed that Luke's model had its background in the motif of justice and was more precisely that of the innocently suffering righteous one.[6]

On a different track, Danker drew attention to the well-known Graeco-Roman preoccupation with great benefactors and proposed that Luke presented the passion of Jesus as 'a beneficent process'.[7] Moessner saw Luke drawing on 'living Deuteronomistic traditions of the unrelenting obduracy of Israel throughout its history to receive God's pleaders of repentance'.[8] This enabled Luke to present a theological interpretation of the inescapable enigma that Israel as a whole had rejected its 'messianic fulfiller of salvation'.

Carroll's examination of Luke's crucifixion scene identified several of the themes already noted. Jesus died as 'Prophet par excellence and Christ of God'. This continued and completed the agenda laid down by God and by Scripture: Jesus' death was the unjust murder of an innocent man, 'whose fate does not impugn the gospel he preached, nor that which proclaims him Lord'; Jesus' death was an exemplary martyr's death, providing a model for Christians; salvation occurs at the cross 'because Jesus, who embodies salvation, is present, still offering repentance and a share in God's kingdom to

---

[5]   C. H. Talbert, "Martyrdom in Luke-Acts and the Lukan Social Ethic," in *Political Issues in Luke-Acts* (ed. R. J. Cassidy and P. J. Scharper; New York: Orbis, 1983).
[6]   R. J. Karris, "Luke:23:47 and the Lucan View of Jesus' Death," in *Reimaging the Death of the Lukan Jesus* (ed. D. D. Sylva; Frankfurt: Anton Hain, 1990), 68-78, reprinted from *JBL* 105 (1986): 65-74.
[7]   F. W. Danker, "Imaged through Benefice," in *Reimaging* (ed. Sylva), 57-67.
[8]   D. P. Moessner, "The 'Leaven of the Pharisees' and 'This Generation': Israel's Rejection of Jesus according to Luke," in *Reimaging* (ed. Sylva), 79-107 (105-06).

sinners'.[9] Carroll's approach shows that the issue is quite complex, even for an assessment of the Third Gospel alone.

Richard provided something of a companion study, evaluating Luke's treatment of the death of Jesus in Acts. Richard's approach is methodologically challenging and offers the beginning of a helpful way forward. He lists all the references to the death of Jesus in Acts, in the order of their appearance, and briefly seeks to analyse the function of each in the development of Luke's narrative.[10] Only occasionally does he explore the theological significance of each reference in its context. A more thorough treatment of this topic would explore the relevance of related terms and concepts. When Richard dwells on the theological potential of a passage, his exploration is weak because it is too contextually bound and not seen as part of the unfolding narrative presentation of this theme. So, for example, with reference to the citation from Isa 53 in Acts 8:32-33, he concludes without discussion that Luke is interested 'not in the atoning death of Jesus but in the fulfilment of scripture in the obedient passion (silence), death (humiliation), and resurrection (taking up from the earth) of the Servant.'[11]

Richard concludes that the death of Jesus along with his resurrection is 'invariably related by Luke to the plan of God for the salvation of humanity'.[12] Luke has not opted for the resurrection at the expense of the cross, but is preoccupied with the theme of Christ's continuing activity as saviour, both as the one enthroned at God's right hand and 'the one who lives and acts within the community as proclaimer of salvation, directly and through intermediaries (Acts 13:38 and 26:23).'[13] 'Luke astutely makes direct and indirect references to all

---

[9]   J. T. Carroll, "Luke's Crucifixion Scene," in *Reimaging* (ed. Sylva), 108-24 (123-24).
[10]   E. Richard, "Jesus' Passion and Death in Acts," in *Reimaging* (ed. Sylva), 125-52 (134-50).
[11]   Richard, "Jesus' Passion and Death in Acts," 146.
[12]   Richard, "Jesus' Passion and Death in Acts," 150.
[13]   Richard, "Jesus' Passion and Death in Acts," 151.

aspects of the Christ-event, including the passion and death, to under-score the continuity both of God's plan and of its realization on the human stage.'[14]

Narrative and Theological Development

Despite many valuable insights, none of the essays noted so far, nor their proposed backgrounds, seems adequate in terms of the structure and flow of Luke-Acts as a whole. They are representative of the approaches to this topic that continue to be taken by a variety of scholars. Some propose diverse parallels with Jewish or Graeco-Roman literature. Such studies seem to be selective in the use of background material and are not concerned with the total extent and shape of the relevant data in Luke-Acts. Some ignore the narrative development in Luke's two volumes and simply focus on the potential significance of particular references to Jesus' suffering and death. Even when narrative development is noted, as in Richard's study, this is not sufficiently linked with an examination of the way Luke's theology of the cross is signalled by the use of key terms and scriptural allusions.

Hence one may argue that a satisfying treatment of this subject would entail a thorough investigation of the narrative development of the theme of Jesus' death in Luke-Acts, coupled with a study of the way Luke develops a theology of salvation, especially through the speeches that are a significant part of his presentation. This raises the fundamental question of how we are to identify Luke's theology.[15]

Scholars often ascribe certain atonement references to Luke's sources and categorise them as 'non-Lukan'. However, narrative criticism sidesteps the issue of sources (which is problematic in Acts anyway) by focusing on the finished text. Such expressions become Lukan by virtue of their inclusion in Luke's narratives. As Marguerat

---

[14]   Richard, "Jesus' Passion and Death in Acts," 152.
[15]   Cf. I. H. Marshall, "How Does One Write on the Theology of Acts?" in *Witness to the Gospel: The Theology of Acts* (ed. I. H. Marshall and D. Peterson; Grand Rapids/Cambridge: Eerdmans, 1998), 3-16.

and Bourquin argue, 'if we want to grasp the theology of the narrator, we must essentially question his narrative strategy.'[16] They also note that a narrator can provide explicit and implicit commentary on the things recorded. Implicit commentary is provided when 'the narrator speaks "tacitly" through the words and actions of the characters through the plot.'[17]

What follows is not a precise application of the techniques of narrative criticism. Some observations about Luke's narrative strategy are offered, with particular reference to the placement and content of certain speeches. At the same time, the aim is to discover what Luke might be saying to his readers through the words and actions of his characters about the atoning significance of Jesus' death. With Tannehill,[18] I want to argue for the narrative unity of Luke-Acts, while acknowledging with Parsons and Pervo that Luke and Acts are sufficiently different to suggest two distinct literary genres.[19]

Two Farewell Discourses
Green rightly insists that an atonement theology is foundational to Luke's soteriology. But he begins by conceding that Jesus' words in Luke 22:19-20 and Paul's in Acts 20:28 are not Lukan theology.

Inasmuch as Jesus' eucharistic words speak of his death inaugurating the New Covenant, which is based on a definitive forgiveness of sins (Jer 31:34), there can be no doubt that they 'root human

---

[16] D. Marguerat and Y. Bourquin, *How to Read Bible Stories: An Introduction to Narrative Criticism* (tr. J. Bowden; London: SCM, 1999), 22. Cf. M. A. Powell, *What Is Narrative Criticism? A New Approach to the Bible* (London: SPCK, 1990).
[17] Marguerat and Bourquin, *How to Read Bible Stories*, 106.
[18] R. C. Tannehill, *The Narrative Unity of Luke-Acts: A Literary Interpretation* (2 vols.; Minneapolis: Fortress, 1986, 1990).
[19] M. C. Parsons and R. I. Pervo, *Rethinking the Unity of Luke and Acts* (Philadelphia: Fortress, 1993), 37-40. In my opinion they exaggerate the differences to establish their point here.

salvation in the death of Jesus'.[20] However, the absence of vv. 19b-20 from part of the Western textual tradition leaves some scholars in doubt about the originality of this reading.[21] In my judgement, the overwhelming preponderance of external evidence supports the longer reading and the shorter reading could be due to some scribal accident or the desire to eliminate the second mention of the cup. However, even if the longer reading is taken as authentic, the presence of 'non-Lukan expressions' in these verses, possibly echoing the liturgical tradition of the Pauline churches (cf. 1 Cor 11:24b-25), makes some scholars sceptical about the influence of this theology on Luke's own presentation.[22] So Green concludes that 'Luke has neither exploited the redemptive themes of the Last Supper nor made this material his own by integrating it more fully into his narrative.'[23]

This is a weak conclusion, given the fact that Luke's narrative then uniquely records a quotation from Isa 53:12 by Jesus (Luke 22:37). This is preceded by amazingly emphatic words, insisting that this Scripture must be fulfilled in him (τοῦτο τὸ γεγραμμένον δεῖ τελεσθῆναι ἐν ἐμοί), and it is followed by the affirmation, 'for what is written about me has its fulfilment' (καὶ γὰρ τὸ περὶ ἐμοῦ τέλος ἔχει). Although there is debate about whether the specific reference ('and he was counted among the lawless') is a pointer to the fact that the whole passage from Isa 53 should be understood as being fulfilled in the events of the cross, this seems most likely from the unfolding

---

[20] J. B. Green, "The Death of Jesus, God's Servant," in *Reimaging* (ed. Sylva), 1-28 (3-4).

[21] Cf. B. M. Metzger, ed., *A Textual Commentary on the Greek New Testament* (2nd ed.; Stuttgart: Deutsche Bibelgesellschaft, 1994), 148-50, for the divided opinion of the committee preparing the 4th revised edition of the United Bible Societies' *Greek New Testament*.

[22] Green, "The Death of Jesus, God's Servant," 4-7, rightly observes that the community meals in Acts do not seem to have the specifically redemptive focus of the meals mentioned in 1 Cor 11:17-34.

[23] Green, "The Death of Jesus, God's Servant," 4.

of Luke's passion narrative.[24] Indeed, the phrase 'he was numbered amongst the transgressors' shows that 'he was occupied with the fact that he, who least deserved it, was to be punished as a wrongdoer.'[25]

The outcome of the cross and resurrection is then shown in Luke 24 to be that 'repentance and forgiveness of sins are to be proclaimed in (Jesus') name to all nations, beginning from Jerusalem' (24:47). So the sequence of Luke's Gospel at its climax is clear. The theological significance of Jesus' death is first disclosed at the Last Supper (even if the wording in 22:19-20 has been influenced by that of the Pauline churches). It is linked both to the fulfilment of the Passover (vv. 15-18) and the fulfilment of Jeremiah's prophecy of the New Covenant about the forgiveness of sins (vv. 19-20). The Son of Man then goes forward to his death 'as it has been determined' (κατὰ τὸ ὡρισμένον, v. 22). This divine determination is linked to the fulfilment of Isa 53, which is then illustrated in the narrative to follow. The scriptural necessity of the Messiah's death and resurrection is then specifically articulated in the teaching of Luke 24:26, 44-46, and made the basis for the challenge to preach the promised forgiveness of sins.

Turning to Paul's address to the Ephesian elders in Acts 20:17-35, Green notes that there is once again a textual problem with regard to the key verse. The manuscript evidence for 20:28 is fairly evenly divided between 'the church of God' (τὴν ἐκκλησίαν τοῦ Θεοῦ) and 'the church of the Lord' (τὴν ἐκκλησίαν τοῦ κυρίου). The former is probably the original on the basis of being the 'harder' reading.[26] This decision has implications for whether the following expression (ἣν

---

[24] Green, "The Death of Jesus, God's Servant," 22-23, actually makes this point, but he does not satisfactorily incorporate this insight into his overall argument. Cf. W. J. Larkin, Jr., "Luke's Use of the Old Testament," *JETS* 20 (1977): 326-36, for a detailed treatment of the way Luke's Passion narrative reflects the fulfilment of Isa 53 more extensively.

[25] R. T. France, "The Servant of the Lord in the Teaching of Jesus," *TynB* 19 (1968): 26-52 (31).

[26] Cf. Metzger, *Textual Commentary*, 425-27.

περιεποιήσατο διὰ τοῦ αἵματος τοῦ ἰδίου) should be translated 'which he purchased with the blood of his own (Son)' or 'which he purchased with his own blood'. Either way, Green argues that Luke is 'parroting' the phraseology of others: 'He has not developed this motif. He has not "owned" it.'[27]

However, in a later article, he makes the interesting observation that, 'the specifically covenantal language employed in 20:28 (περιποιέομαι, 'to acquire'; cf. Exod 19:5; Isa 43:21) and 20:32; 26:18 (ἁγιάζω, 'to sanctify'; cf. Deut 33:3) reminds us of Luke's record of Jesus' last meal with his disciples wherein he grounds the "new covenant" in his own death (Luke 22:19-20).'[28] Here we have the basis for establishing a profound biblical-theological framework for Luke's soteriology. Apart from the parallels between these fare-well speeches in Luke and Acts, there are verbal and thematic links between Acts 20:28, 32 and other texts in Luke-Acts. Green himself goes on to explore the extent to which Servant Christology undergirds Luke's thinking and more will be said about this below. Even what has been said so far should make us cautious about concluding that the salvific effect of the cross is 'not woven fully into the fabric of Luke's theology of the cross.'[29]

Furthermore, we need to consider the place of the speech to the Ephesian elders within the structure and flow of Acts. It is the only recorded message to a group of Christian 'insiders' (though cf. 14:22) and clearly addresses those with some theological knowledge and leadership potential. Luke-Acts is written so that Theophilus and those he represents 'may know the truth concerning the things about which you have been instructed' (Luke 1:4). Readers are expected to have some understanding of the significance of the terms used in

---

[27] Green, "The Death of Jesus, God's Servant," 7.
[28] J. B. Green, "'Salvation to the End of the Earth' (Acts 13:47): God As Saviour in the Acts of the Apostles," in *Witness to the Gospel* (ed. Marshall and Peterson), 83-106 (99).
[29] Green, "Salvation to the End of the Earth," 99.

Acts 20. The similarities between this speech and the theology of Paul's letters have often been noted, though there are various 'Lukanisms' present as well.[30] For the readers, there has been at least some preparation to understand this terminology in the light of Luke's presentation so far.

The warning of 20:28-31 has the effect of alerting readers to the danger of false teaching and division in the ongoing life of the church. Within this context, the image of the church as the people purchased to belong to God through the shedding of Christ's blood is striking. It shows the preciousness of the church to God and therefore the importance of leaders and people persevering as 'the sanctified', faithful to the end. The encouragement of 20:32 is specifically that 'the message of his grace' will be sufficient to sustain leaders in their task of enabling Christ's flock to enter the inheritance secured for them by Christ's sacrifice. Like Jesus' words at the Last Supper, this speech offers a significant challenge about the future, linked to a certain understanding of the atoning work of Christ. This theme is thus highlighted by key figures towards the end of both Luke and Acts.

The Means of Salvation in Acts
Green proposes that three texts in Acts are programmatic for explaining how salvation through Christ is made available. The first is in 5:30-32. Peter proclaims that Jesus' resurrection and exaltation to the right hand of God as 'Prince' (ἀρχηγός) and 'Saviour' (σωτήρ) make it possible for him to offer repentance and forgiveness of sins (cf. 2:38; 3:19-20, 26; 11:18). His death is mentioned in the accusation that the religious authorities 'hanged him on a tree' (κρεμάσαντες ἐπὶ ξύλου, 5:30; cf. 10:39; 13:29; 1 Pet 2:24, where similar language is found). This unusual way of describing his cruci-

---

[30] Cf. B. Witherington, *The Acts of the Apostles: A Socio-rhetorical Commentary* (Grand Rapids/Carlisle: Eerdmans/Paternoster, 1998), 610-11. Unlike Jesus' words at the Last Supper, Paul's speech in Acts 20 does not envisage a death, but rather the problems created by his departure from their midst.

fixion seems to be an allusion to Deut 21:22-23 (κεκατηραμένος ὑπὸ θεοῦ πᾶς κρεμάμενος ἐπὶ ξύλου). An implicit commentary on Jesus' death is thus provided, suggesting that he was cursed by God.

The penal character of 'hanging on a tree' would have been understood by the high priest and his associates. Does Luke assume from his use of the term on three occasions in Acts that it will have this meaning for his readers too? The raising of Jesus in this sequence of thought proclaims his vindication and ability to save from God's judgement even those who condemned him to death. While there may not be an articulated theology of Christ becoming a curse for us here (cf. Gal 3:13-14), such an atoning dimension to his death could easily be argued or assumed from the cumulative effect of the argument in 5:30-31. 'These allusions serve to locate Jesus' death firmly in the necessity of God's purpose. The ultimate disgrace, the curse from God, is antecedent to exaltation.'[31]

Green's second text is Acts 10:43. Here the witness is less direct, but quite similar. Jesus' ability to forgive sins in this verse is said to be in accordance with the testimony of 'all the prophets'. Green argues that the solution to this puzzling allusion to the prophets is 'Luke's consistent view that at his exaltation Jesus received the title "Lord" and with it the divine prerogative to offer salvation.'[32] That may indeed be so in the case of 2:33, which is the third text to which Green draws attention and which in its context is showing how the prophecy from Joel cited in 2:21 is fulfilled in and by the exalted Lord Jesus Christ. Here, however, two observations are in order.

---

[31] Green, "Salvation to the End of the Earth," 101.
[32] Green, "The Death of Jesus, God's Servant," 9. Green expounds this 'exaltation-soteriology' on pp. 9-11 and then seeks to relate this to a number of other New Testament texts where the salvific character of Jesus' resurrection in tandem with the cross is highlighted (pp. 11-12). He then shows parallels with the literature of Late Judaism, where exalted human beings carry out soteriological functions (pp. 12-18).

First, it should be remembered that the presentation of the gospel in Acts is generally more Christological than soteriological.[33] Christ is proclaimed as Saviour and the benefits of his saving work are offered to all, but the process by which he achieves that salvation is not always explained. Nevertheless, we have enough indications from Luke to know how the process with respect to the cross was understood and expounded, by both Peter and Paul. I will develop this argument shortly. Secondly, we must ask what Scriptures could be included in the testimony of 'all the prophets', other than those with strictly Christological significance (such as we find in the sermons in Acts 2 and 13). To begin to answer this question, we must look carefully at the sermon in Acts 3.

Peter's Sermon in Acts 3
Peter's sermon on the occasion of the healing of the lame man is not merely a restatement of his Pentecost address. It is more soteriological in content and complements the earlier sermon in significant ways. Luke reveals more of the breadth and depth of the apostolic gospel in this second sermon. The healing 'in the name of Jesus Christ' (3:6, 16) is a further sign of the Messianic salvation. Forgiveness of sins is offered once more to the crowd (3:19), and possibly also the Holy Spirit in terms of 'times of refreshing' from the presence of the Lord (3:20), paralleling the twofold offer of 2:38. However, the miracle appears to point more broadly to the renewal of all things contingent upon Christ's return, which is described as 'the time of universal restoration that God announced long ago through his holy prophets' (3:21; cf. Isa 35; 65:17-25).

Even the offer of forgiveness is couched in different terms: 'so that your sins may be wiped out' (εἰς τὸ ἐξαλειφθῆναι ὑμῶν τὰς

---

[33] By way of comparison, it is interesting to note that Paul first presents the gospel in Rom 1:3-4 in Christological terms, but then from 1:16-17 and more extensively from 3:21 onwards, he presents the gospel in soteriological terms.

ἁμαρτίας).[34] This is linked to a simple statement that God has ful-filled 'what he had foretold through all the prophets, that his Messiah would suffer' (3:17). Here the focus is on *Christ's death alone*, though the resurrection has been previously highlighted (3:13, 15). Could any particular text from the prophets be the background in this context? Many commentators have suggested a deliberate echo of Isa 52:13 in the wording of v. 13 ('God glorified his servant Jesus'). The verse which introduces the fourth Servant Song in the Septuagint reads, ἰδοὺ συνήσει ὁ παῖς μου καὶ ὑψωθήσεται καὶ δοξασθήσεται σφόδρα. Acts 3:13 reads, ἐδόξασεν τὸν παῖδα αὐτοῦ Ἰησοῦν. An echo of the same theology could possibly be found in 3:26, where Peter speaks about God having 'raised up his servant' (ἀναστήσας ὁ θεὸς τὸν παῖδα αὐτοῦ). Although the term τὸν παῖδα αὐτοῦ and the parallel expressions in 4:27, 30 are not necessarily pointers to the full servant theology of Isa 53, the use of ἐδόξασεν seems to indicate a deliberate allusion to that passage in Acts 3:13-18. Peter begins where the fourth Servant Song begins, with the exaltation of the Servant. However, the emphasis in 3:13-15, 17 is also on the unjust suffering by which he became the Saviour, able to offer a definitive forgiveness of sins and all the promised blessings of eschatological salvation.

It is reasonable to conclude that Isa 52:13–53:12 is the basis of Peter's thinking in Acts 3:13-15, 17-19, and that Jesus is envisaged as fulfilling the pattern of redemptive suffering set out in that prophecy. In terms of the flow of Luke's narratives, the announcement of its imminent fulfilment in Luke 22:37 shows us how we are to under-stand the events in the Passion narrative. Then, in Peter's second ser-mon, there is an explicit interpretation of these events and their out-come in language echoing that specific prophecy.[35] The narrative in

---

[34] In Acts 3:19 the meaning of this verb is similar to Ps 51[50]:9 ('blot out all my iniquity'; cf. Ps 109[108]:14) and Isa 43:25 ('I am he who blots out your transgressions'; cf. Jer 18:23).

[35] Rejection of Jesus as 'the Holy and Righteous One' could be a deliberate allusion to Isa 53:11. From 7:52 and 22:14 it seems that ὁ δίκαιος was a

Acts 8:26-38 shows us how the fourth Servant Song could be used evangelistically and reinforces the view that it is the primary reference when Peter says, 'In this way God fulfilled what he had foretold through all the prophets, that his Messiah would suffer' (3:18).

Green similarly argues that 'the Servant-theme makes up something of the sub-structure of Luke's two-part narrative.'[36] So, for example, he proposes that δίκαιος in Luke 23:47 is not simply a declaration of Jesus' innocence but 'an intentional allusion to the fate of Jesus as the Suffering Servant of Yahweh', as proclaimed in Acts 3:13-14. Luke's portrayal of Jesus on the Mount of Olives (Luke 22:39-46) marks him out as the Isaianic Servant and not simply as a martyr.[37] The Servant Christology Luke develops embraces Jesus' whole ministry, but focuses especially on his death and resurrection. 'The seminal Servant-text in this regard is Is. 53:11, which relates the thought, "following his suffering, my righteous one will justify many".'[38]

In Acts 3, this Servant Christology is then linked with the coming of the prophet like Moses (3:22-23; cf. Deut 18:15, 18-19), to bring the people of Israel back to the God of the covenant, and with the fulfilment of the Abrahamic promise to make Israel a source of blessing to the nations (3:25). Mention of the Servant being sent first to Israel, 'to bless you by turning each of you from your wicked ways' (3:26) is reminiscent of Isa 49:5-6. This sermon as a whole shows a well-considered, integrated biblical theology. Servant Christology is at its

---

messianic designation, derived from prophetic expectations (e.g. Isa 32:1; 53:11; Jer 23:5; Zech 9:9; cf. *1 En.* 38:2; 53:6; *Pss. Sol.* 17:35). ὁ ἅγιος is probably a synonym here (cf. Luke 4:34 par.; John 6:69; 1 John 2:20; Rev 3:7), even though it is not used in exactly the same way elsewhere in Acts (cf. 4:27, 30).

[36] Green, "The Death of Jesus, God's Servant," 19.

[37] Green, "The Death of Jesus, God's Servant," 21-22.

[38] Green, "The Death of Jesus, God's Servant," 24. Green notes the parallel with Rom 4:25 here. The remainder of his article explores the way the Servant theme 'interpenetrates Luke's larger interests, albeit implicitly'.

heart and, consistent with the Isaianic Songs, the Servant's ministry is linked to the notion of a definitive covenant renewal, so that God's salvation can reach the end of the earth. At the heart of that renewal, according to Isa 53, is the atoning work accomplished by the death of the Servant himself.

Paul's Sermon in Pisidian Antioch
The similarities between the sermon attributed to Paul in Acts 13:16-41 and Peter's Pentecost sermon have often been noted. In particular, the resurrection of Jesus proclaims his messiahship in terms of the fulfilment of Ps 2:7, Isa 55:3 and Ps 16:10 (Acts 13:33-37). Through this exalted Saviour, forgiveness of sins is proclaimed to Jews and 'devout converts to Judaism' alike (13:38, 43). However, Paul goes beyond Peter in explaining here that 'by this Jesus, everyone who believes is set free from all those sins from which you could not be freed by the law of Moses' (13:39).

Barrett is reluctant to ascribe 13:38-39 to Paul, believing that Luke betrays here 'a less than full understanding of his theology'.[39] The expression πᾶς ὁ πιστεύων δικαιοῦται ('everyone who believes is set free') certainly sounds very Pauline (cf. Rom 6:7, δεδικαίωται ἀπό). Moreover, as Barrett points out, there is a close relationship between Paul's understanding of justification and forgiveness (cf. Rom 4:5-7). But the preceding clause is the odd one (ἀπὸ πάντων ὧν οὐκ ἠδυνήθητε ἐν νόμῳ Μωϋσέως δικαιωθῆναι). It could mean that the law of Moses offered forgiveness and freedom from the penalty for sin in some cases, but Jesus provides complete salvation from sin. If this is so, the reference will be to the sacrifices which could atone for sins committed inadvertently, but could not deal with deliberate sin.[40] More likely, it means that Jesus sets people free from the consequence of all sin, in a way which the law could not. Either way, the

---

[39] C. K. Barrett, *A Critical and Exegetical Commentary on the Acts of the Apostles* (ICC; Edinburgh: T & T Clark, 1994), 1:651.
[40] Cf. Witherington, *Acts*, 413.

contrast points to the inability of the law to deal with sin in the way that Jesus has, through his death and resurrection.

This means that Luke has given us a sermon from Peter and a sermon from Paul in which some atonement theology appears to be present. In Acts 3, the forgiveness of sins is linked explicitly with the Messiah's suffering, 'foretold through all the prophets'. From various verbal clues it appears that Isa 53 is specifically in mind and is central to the background. In Acts 13, the forgiveness of sins through Jesus brings a freedom from sin which the law of Moses could not provide.

Concluding Reflections

Luke reports an interpretation of Jesus' death that regularly portrays it as the fulfilment of Scripture. In some contexts, Jesus is specifically identified with the Servant figure of Isaiah's fourth Servant Song. This background seems to provide a framework for viewing Jesus' death redemptively. When the offer of forgiveness is announced, it is normally preceded by a declaration of Jesus' innocence, followed by the proclamation of his shameful death on the cross and his vindication through resurrection (Acts 5:30-31; 10:39-43; 13:28, 38). Sometimes there is even the hint that he was cursed by God because he hung upon a tree (5:30; 10:39; 13:29). The suffering of an innocent person like this, to bring salvation to others, is reminiscent of the penal and substitutionary death of the Servant set forth in Isa 53.[41]

The quotations from Isa 53 in Luke 22:37 and Acts 8:32-33 do not make explicit reference to vicarious atonement. However, they draw attention to the *key aspects* of Jesus' suffering (the innocent one suffering the death of a transgressor, led like a sheep to the slaughter), suggesting that these events should be understood in terms of the Book of Isaiah's redemptive theology.

The farewell scene in the Upper Room (Luke 22:14-38) provides a theological basis for interpreting the events to follow and a justifica-

---

[41] Cf. D. Peterson, ed., *Where Wrath and Mercy Meet: Proclaiming the Atonement Today* (Carlisle: Paternoster, 2001), 19-24, on Isa 53.

tion for the claim that forgiveness of sins can be proclaimed in the name of the exalted Christ (24:44-47). From the standpoint of narrative unity, this points the readers of Luke's second volume towards a redemptive view of Jesus' death, even if this is not always articulated in the recorded sermons.

Although Acts 20:28 is presented as Paul's teaching, from what I have argued above, there is no reason to doubt that Luke was comfortable with its note of vicarious atonement. Indeed, Luke's inclusion of this theology in Paul's farewell discourse to the Ephesian elders suggests its importance for his readers. The rhetorical function of Paul's exhortation is both to warn about the future of God's flock and to assure leaders of the basis on which it will be sustained and preserved. This is Luke's opportunity to address Christian readers directly about their future, as his second volume draws to a close.

In Acts 20, as in Jesus' discourse in the Upper Room, the shedding of the Messiah's blood is the means by which the New Covenant is inaugurated and the Messiah's people are sanctified for their share with him in his eternal inheritance. This is the heart of 'the message of his grace' (v. 32), which is able to sustain the church in the face of persecution and false teaching. In other words, atonement theology in Luke 22 and Acts 20 is not simply the basis for the proclamation of forgiveness but also for the forming and maintaining of the eschatological people of God.

In terms of narrative development, particularly the placement of key speeches, and in terms of theological development, particularly the introduction and interweaving of important Old Testament themes, Luke presents a view of Jesus' death that involves vicarious atonement. Although the resurrection is prominent in Luke's presentation of the early preaching and the atoning significance of Jesus' death is not always stressed, the differences of emphasis in the various sermons show that Luke was seeking to present a comprehensive and cumulative picture of early Christian thinking about the saving significance of those great events.

'I Suppose' (οἶμαι):

The Conclusion of John's Gospel in Its Literary and Historical Context

Andreas J. Köstenberger

Introduction

Discussions of the authorship of the Fourth Gospel continue un-abated, and commentators leave no stone unturned in their quest to solve this enigma of Johannine studies. One of several issues that have yet to receive adequate attention is the fact that the Gospel concludes with a first person reference, 'I suppose' (οἶμαι). It is widely held that the final two verses of the Gospel, perhaps together with the last chapter in its entirety, were added by the Church or some later redactor. This appears to find support by the third person reference to 'this disciple who witnesses to these things' and the first person plural verb οἴδαμεν ('we know') in the penultimate verse. This conclusion also nicely undergirds a variety of source and redaction-critical theories surrounding the composition of the Fourth Gospel. The Johannine community, it is argued, here comes to the fore as the community responsible for the final version of the Gospel. Some view John 21:24-25 more narrowly as an authentication of the preceding Gospel by its recipients. Others draw more far-reaching inferences from these final verses, holding that the Johannine community was responsible for the body of the Gospel as well. According to these interpreters, John's Gospel tells the story of Jesus in terms of the history of this Johannine community.

These views would perhaps be less assailable if it were not for the presence of the first person verb οἶμαι ('I suppose') in the concluding verse of the Gospel. As Morris acknowledges, if John 21:24-25 were added by a later group, one would expect the first person plural to continue through v. 25.[1] The stubborn fact is that it does not. In an important recent study H. M. Jackson has adduced considerable primary evidence to suggest that both the third person singular and the first person plural references in the penultimate verse should be understood within the framework of ancient conventions of self-reference.[2] Specifically, Jackson has plausibly shown that John 21:24 most likely is cast in the third person in order to affirm the credibility of the author's own witness.[3] In the second part of the verse, the author shifts to the first person plural — an 'associative collective' where the 'you' subsumed under the 'we' are the book's Christian readers but where the 'I' included in the 'we' is the author[4] — and in v. 25 to the first person singular, striking a more informal, familiar

---

[1] Leon Morris, *The Gospel according to John* (NIGTC; rev. ed.; Grand Rapids: Eerdmans, 1995), 775, n. 64.

[2] H. M. Jackson, "Ancient Self-referential Conventions and Their Implications for the Authorship and Integrity of the Gospel of John," *JTS* 50 (1999): 1-34.

[3] 'This is the disciple', 'his testimony' (cf. 19:35; see also 17:3 where Jesus is portrayed as referring to himself as 'Jesus Christ'). Compare Thucydides' practice of introducing himself in the third person (Thucydides, *Hist.* 1.1.1 and 5.26.1) and of referring to himself as 'Thucydides' (*Hist.* 4.104.4: 'Thucydides, the son of Oloros, who composed this history'; this is true also of Julius Caesar, *B Gall.*, who regularly refers to himself in the third person as 'Caesar'). Cf. Jackson, "Ancient Self-referential Conventions," 27 (see also ibid., 28-30 on Josephus).

[4] Jackson, "Ancient Self-referential Conventions," 23-24. Cf. D. A. Carson, *The Gospel according to John* (Grand Rapids: Eerdmans, 1991), 684, who refers to 1:14; 3:2, 11; 20:1; 1 John 1:2, 4, 5, 6, 7; 3 John 12; and 2 Cor 12:2-4; Adolf Schlatter, *Der Evangelist Johannes* (2nd ed.; Stuttgart: Calwer, 1948 [1930]), 376, with reference to 3:2 and 20:2; and Daniel Wallace, *Greek Grammar beyond the Basics* (Grand Rapids: Zondervan, 1996), 397, who lists the present passage as a (debatable) example of the exclusive 'we', 'in which the first person plural restricts the group to the author and his associates.'

tone in order to underscore his personal involvement and in order not to appear unduly detached from the events recorded earlier.[5]

In light of Jackson's findings it can therefore no longer be confidently maintained that the references to 'this disciple' and the phrase 'we know' in John 21:24 provide compelling grounds for signalling a shift of authorship from the person responsible for the bulk of the Gospel to the authenticating community in 21:24-25. In what follows I will seek to build on Jackson's findings and attempt to supplement them with some primary data concerning the term οἶμαι.[6] I will argue that, even apart from Jackson's study, the first person singular reference in John 21:25 is best understood as a final expression of authorial modesty by the author of the entire Gospel.[7] After a survey of the state of scholarship on John 21:24-25 representative instances of οἶμαι in contemporaneous extrabiblical Greek literature will be cited. This will be followed by an evaluation of the significance of this data for an assessment of the authorship of John's Gospel.

State of Research

John 21:24-25 from the Same Hand As the Rest of the Gospel
The view that 21:24-25 come from the same hand as the rest of the Gospel and particularly from the apostle John is a decided minority

---

[5]   Jackson, "Ancient Self-referential Conventions," 8.

[6]   The term οἶμαι (elsewhere also attested in the uncontracted form οἴομαι), though not in the first person singular, is used elsewhere in the New Testament only in Phil 1:17 and Jas 1:7. For lexical entries see Louw and Nida, § 1.369; BDAG, 701; and LSJ, 1208-09, who note that the term occurs already in Homer with the meaning 'think, suppose, believe', which suggests that the word's denotation has remained constant in ancient Greek. While the lexical meaning of οἶμαι is thus not disputed, its rhetorical import requires further study. In the study below we will follow the syntactical analysis in BDAG, 701, and limit ourselves to the study of syntactical parallels to the usage of οἶμαι or οἴομαι followed by an accusative and infinitive.

[7]   Compare the oblique self-reference 'the disciple Jesus loved' in the second half of the Gospel (13:23; 19:26; 20:2; 21:7, 20).

view in modern Johannine scholarship. This has not always been the case. As is acknowledged by the church historian Eusebius, Origen wrote in his commentary on John's Gospel, 'Why must I speak of John who leaned on Jesus' breast, who has left one Gospel while confessing that he could compose so many that the world could not contain them?'[8] Clearly, Origen considered the apostle John ('the one who leaned on Jesus' breast', John 13:23; cf. 21:20) to be the writer of the final verse of John's Gospel.

In recent years the position has been articulated by Carson, who, while noting that certainty is impossible, states that 'I suppose' is probably an 'overt self-reference', especially if v. 24 constitutes a self-reference as well.[9] Yarbrough, too, maintains that 'we' in v. 24 may be another way of saying 'I' or, alternatively, John may here serve as a spokesman for a larger group.[10] Schlatter proposed that John may have dictated the preceding text in the presence of his collaborators, hence the expression 'we' in v. 24 may refer to those around the apostle who could authenticate his witness as those who had heard his message.[11]

---

[8] Origen, *Comm. in Johannem* 5.3 (quoted in Eusebius, *Hist. eccl.* 6.25.9-10). Elsewhere Origen speaks of John the author of Revelation as the one who 'thought that not even the world itself could contain the books that could be written' (*Comm. in Johannem* 13.33). Origen quotes or refers to John 21:25 several more times in his commentary.

[9] Carson, *John*, 685-86.

[10] Robert W. Yarbrough, *John* (Everyman's Bible Commentary; Chicago: Moody, 1991), 212, citing Schlatter.

[11] Schlatter, *Evangelist Johannes*, 376. For a vigorous refutation of the view that 21:25 represents an addition by a later editor see further John Chapman, "'We Know That His Testimony Is True,'" *JTS* 31 (1930): 386-87, who contends that it is 'quite inconceivable' that an interpolator composed this 'very Johannine' verse. The main burden of Chapman's essay is to argue that 'we know' in 21:24 constitutes a 'plural of authorship' (pp. 376-86).

John 21:24-25 a Later Addition, Vv. 24 and 25 from the Same Hand
But many differ, contending that 21:24-25 represents a later addition.
Regarding the question of precisely who was responsible for this addition, however, commentators disagree. A minority of scholars who
consider 21:24-25 to be a later addition hold this was done during the
apostle's lifetime and with his knowledge. Zahn suggests that ch. 21
was written by a disciple or friend of the apostle who was given a
certain amount of freedom in the composition of this material. Zahn
explains the shift from the first plural in 21:24 to the first singular in
21:25 by proposing that the person who wrote both verses in v. 25
ventures a highly subjective opinion only in his name, while v. 24
reflects the common experience of the entire group.[12] Morris similarly
contends that the 'we know' in 21:24 is a genuine plural indicating
the authentication of the preceding Gospel by others 'though perhaps
including' the apostle himself.[13]

Most, however, believe that it was the Johannine circle in Ephesus
or some later editor or ecclesiastical redactor who added the final two
verses (or the entire last chapter) after John's death. Interestingly, this
is Schlatter's view in his more popular *Erläuterungen* (though not in
his scholarly commentary; see above).[14] This is also the view of
Barrett (though he is adamant about the unity between 21:24-25 and
the rest of ch. 21), Bernard (though he strongly defends the unity of
vv. 24 and 25), as well as Bultmann, Brown and Lindars.[15] According

---

[12] Theodor Zahn, *Das Evangelium des Johannes* (6th ed.; KNT; Leipzig:
Deichert, 1921), 705-07; idem, *Introduction to the New Testament*
(Edinburgh: T & T Clark, 1909), 3:251. Interestingly, Zahn (*Evangelium*,
707) claims v. 25 is 'awkward, but genuinely Jewish', while Schlatter
(*Evangelist Johannes*, 376) writes that the verse is 'a bit more Greek than the
preceding text'. The primary data cited below seem to support Schlatter.
[13] Morris, *John*, 775.
[14] Adolf Schlatter, *Das Evangelium des Johannes* (Erläuterungen zum
Neuen Testament 3; Stuttgart: Calwer, 1962 [1899]), 307.
[15] C. K. Barrett, *The Gospel according to St. John* (2nd ed.; Philadelphia:
Westminster, 1978), 583; J. H. Bernard, *A Critical and Exegetical
Commentary on the Gospel of John* (ICC; Edinburgh: T & T Clark, 1928),

to Bernard, in v. 24 the writer associates others with himself while in v. 25, the 'editorial reflection or colophon', he speaks only for himself.[16]

Though they may differ on their specific source or redaction-critical proposals, Bultmann, Brown and Lindars all see 21:24-25 as a later addition subsequent to the apostle's death. Bultmann views the 'we' of v. 24 as an appeal to the consciousness of the community of which the author — a later ecclesiastical redactor — is a part. In a rather glaring instance of assertion without argument, Bultmann states categorically that the 'rhetorical οἶμαι v. 25 naturally has nothing to do with οἴδαμεν.'[17] Is Bultmann's abruptness an indication that he senses in the shift from the first person plural to the first person singular in 21:24-25 an unwelcome difficulty for his hypothesis?

Lindars is only slightly less dogmatic than Bultmann when he maintains that the 'I suppose' does not conflict with the 'we' in v. 24, 'being merely a stylistic device.'[18] But Lindars does not elaborate as to the nature of this 'stylistic device' and its implications for the interpretation of 21:24-25. He proceeds to assert that vv. 24-25 were penned by a later editor who, attempting to conclude in terms grander than 20:30-31, managed only to produce 'an exaggerated literary conceit, which is not to be taken seriously.' The reader is referred to 20:30-31 for the proper conclusion of John's Gospel.[19]

714; Rudolf Bultmann, *The Gospel of John* (tr. George R. Beasley-Murray et al.; Oxford: Blackwell, 1971), 717; Raymond E. Brown, *The Gospel according to John* (AB; Garden City: Doubleday, 1970), 1129; and Barnabas Lindars, *The Gospel of John* (Grand Rapids: Eerdmans/London: Marshall, Morgan & Scott, 1972), 642.

[16] This is akin to Zahn's solution (see above).
[17] Bultmann, *John*, 718, n. 1.
[18] Contrast the dogmatism of Bultmann and Lindars on this issue with F. F. Bruce's humble acknowledgment that the authorship of the final postscript is 'uncertain' and his admission that he does not know how the 'I' in 'I suppose' relates to the 'we' of 'we know'. See Bruce, *The Gospel of John: Introduction, Exposition and Notes* (Basingstoke: Pickering, 1983), 410.
[19] Lindars, *John*, 642.

Lindars' language is echoed by Schnackenburg, who states that v. 25 'betrays' a different hand than v. 24 and who calls v. 25 an 'affected sentence' by an 'ambitious writer'. If this writer belonged to the editorial circle, Schnackenburg maintains, he was not its most capable member. Similar to Lindars, Schnackenburg refers the reader to the (in his view) far superior ending of 20:30-31.[20]

Brown, too, acknowledges the shift from the 'we' to the 'I', though his conclusions are neither as dogmatic nor as negative as those of Bultmann, Lindars and Schnackenburg. Brown entertains the possibility that v. 25 may have been added by someone other than the redactor only to reject it. According to Brown, it is best to see v. 25 as the redactor's last thought or perhaps afterthought. Without adducing evidence, Brown proposes that the 'I' of v. 25 may be 'explicable as a rhetorical device in a literary hyperbole'. Vv. 24 and 25 were likely written by the same person.[21]

John 21:24-25 a Later Addition, Vv. 24 and 25 from Different Hands
In contrast to these writers, some (though perhaps not the majority) maintain that vv. 24 and 25 were added at different times by two different groups or individuals. Westcott contends that vv. 24-25 are separate notes attached to the Gospel prior to its publication. He believes that when compared with 19:35, 21:24 turns out not to be written by the fourth evangelist but was probably added by the Ephesian elders. The change of person in v. 25, so Westcott, marks a change of authorship from the Ephesian elders to an unspecified later hand. Westcott ventures the concluding suggestion that v. 25 may contain words of John as reported by those who had heard him.[22] Closely aligned with Westcott's view is Ridderbos, who believes the

---

[20] Rudolf Schnackenburg, *The Gospel according to St. John* (New York: Crossroad, 1990), 3:374.

[21] Brown, *John*, 2:1129.

[22] B. F. Westcott, *The Gospel according to St. John* (Grand Rapids: Eerdmans, 1975 [1881]), 306.

'we' of v. 24 represents the 'Church's confession', while v. 25 comes 'again from another hand' (citing the 'I suppose' in v. 25).[23]

Michaels provides a fairly complex redaction-critical reconstruction of the background of 21:24-25.[24] According to Michaels, the 'we' are the writers of the Gospel in its final form (presumably the leaders of the church to whom the beloved disciple belonged during his lifetime). One of them then added the final postscript on behalf of the group, with the apparent purpose of defending the Gospel against the charge of incompleteness or the criticism that some of the audience's favourite stories about Jesus had been omitted. The 'I' of the 'I suppose' allows the scribe who added v. 25 to stand out temporarily among the 'we' of v. 24. Somewhat similarly to Michaels, Brodie holds that the 'we' is the entire body of believers, while the 'I suppose' reflects 'a detail that gives the impression of an individual' doing the actual writing, one who was inspired by the memory of the beloved disciple and set his message in writing.[25]

Whitacre, too, maintains that v. 24 contains the testimony of John's disciples. He lists several possible scenarios for the authorship of v. 25 (though acknowledging that 'there can be no certainty on this matter'): a further redactor; the 'I' as part of the hyperbole (citing Brown); the beloved disciple (Carson), or a later scribe (that is, neither the beloved disciple nor any of his disciples). Whitacre tentatively favours the final option.[26]

Much more radical is Wilckens, who, echoing Lindars' and Schnackenburg's negative assessments (see above), views v. 25 as a failed attempt at providing an addendum (*verunglückter Zusatz*). He believes v. 24 is the original conclusion (by the church) while v. 25

---

[23] Herman Ridderbos, *The Gospel of John* (Grand Rapids: Eerdmans, 1997), 672.

[24] J. Ramsey Michaels, *John* (NIBC; Peabody: Hendrickson, 1989), 363-64.

[25] Thomas Brodie, *The Gospel according to John* (New York: OUP, 1993), 596.

[26] Rodney A. Whitacre, *John* (IVPNTC; Downers Grove: IVP, 1999), 500.

was added by a later hand.[27] Even more negative than Wilckens is the nineteenth-century German commentator Heinrich August Wilhelm Meyer, who considers v. 25 to be apocryphal, calling the passage '*un-Johannean*' owing to the occurrence of οἶμαι, particularly in the first person singular, and labelling the verse's concluding hyperbole an 'absurd and tasteless *exaggeration*.'[28]

Finally, some do not comment on the first person singular reference in v. 25 at all. Among these is Borchert, who affirms that the 'we' of v. 24 constitutes a 'community confession' and the 'authenticating colophon' by the Johannine community.[29] Witherington believes the 'we' is the fourth evangelist, who is not the beloved disciple but one of his disciples.[30] One further issue is the omission of v. 25 from the original of Codex Sinaiticus. The verse was added by the first hand. Commentators are widely agreed that the omission was probably accidental.[31]

---

[27] Ulrich Wilckens, *Das Evangelium nach Johannes* (NTD; Göttingen: Vandenhoeck & Ruprecht, 1998), 331.

[28] H. A. W. Meyer, *Critical and Exegetical Handbook to the Gospel of John* (tr. William Urwick; Edinburgh: T & T Clark, 1884), 555.

[29] Gerald Borchert, *John* (NAC; Nashville: Broadman & Holman, 2002), 342.

[30] Ben Witherington, *John's Wisdom* (Louisville: Westminster John Knox, 1995), 357.

[31] E.g. Barrett, *John*, 588. John 21:25 is a critical plank in David Trobisch's thesis of a Canonical Edition of the New Testament; see Trobisch, *The First Edition of the New Testament* (Oxford: OUP, 2000). On the basis of his assessment that John 21:23 'indicates that the beloved disciple had died before this text was written' (p. 54), Trobisch contends that a 'voice different from the author of the Fourth Gospel' speaks in John 21:24 (p. 96). Trobisch also sees a break between 21:24 and 25 and views 21:25 as 'an editorial note to the readers' of the Canonical Edition (pp. 7, 97, 103), maintaining that '[t]he first person singular ("I suppose") indicates that the publishers of the canonical Gospel collection assumed that they were well known to their readership' (p. 98). In light of the elaborate connections between the two chapters Trobisch does not think that John 21 is simply an appendix to a book ending with John 20. Rather, he views John 21 'as the product of the final editors of this Gospel, who not only added a chapter but also revised

Assessment of State of Research

We conclude our assessment of previous research on John 21:24-25 with the following preliminary observations.

(1) None of the major commentaries surveyed above engages extrabiblical instances of οἶμαι in roughly contemporaneous Greek literature. We will attempt to fill this lacuna in the study below.

(2) Commentators struggle to explain the shift from the first plural to the first singular in 21:24-25 in a variety of ways. Solutions range from viewing v. 24 as the original conclusion and v. 25 as a later scribal addition to understanding the individual in v. 25 as a member of the community referenced in v. 24, to labelling the first person verb in v. 25 as a 'rhetorical device' of some sort. This considerable degree of interpretative diversity suggests that the last word on this issue has not yet been spoken. Also, it seems necessary to explore further the possibility that οἶμαι may represent some kind of stylistic or rhetorical device.

(3) At times commentators cite the different style and/or vocabulary of 21:24-25 in relation to the preceding Gospel. An investigation of this issue is beyond the scope of the present essay. In light of the limited data and the fact that arguments from vocabulary statistics are rarely conclusive, however, this point seems to be less significant, especially since we are dealing here with a concluding statement.

---

the manuscript produced by the "beloved disciple"' (pp. 150-51, n. 32, apparently following H. Thyen; similarly, Martin Hengel, *Die johanneische Frage* [WUNT 67; Tübingen: Mohr-Siebeck, 1993], 272). Trobisch acknowledges, however, that the final chapter 'could be the work of author or publisher alike' (ibid.).

While detailed interaction with Trobisch's work is beyond the scope of this essay, the present study does not seem to support his above-stated conclusions. Rather, ch. 21, including 21:23-25, should most plausibly be viewed as penned by the author of the Fourth Gospel within a literary framework that reads 21:23 as still written during the beloved disciple's lifetime; takes the third person singular verb in 21:24 as an authorial self-reference and the first-person plural verb as associating the author with his readers; and interprets 21:25 as a final expression of authorial modesty.

(4) At times one senses a certain amount of impatience with the data, a glibness in dismissing the relevance of the first person singular verb, or detects strained efforts at resolution. One of the reasons for this may be that the first person plural in v. 24 (suggesting community authorship) fits better with certain redaction-critical reconstructions than the first person singular in v. 25 (indicating an individual author). No one approaches a given text without presuppositions, but the implications of the first person singular verb in v. 25 for the Gospel's authorship should be faced regardless of one's preconceived notions in this regard.

Οἶμαι in Its Ancient Literary and Historical Context

We turn now to an investigation of the usage of the term οἶμαι in extrabiblical literature.[32] While very rare in the Christian canon, the expression occurs not infrequently in extrabiblical Greek writings that are roughly contemporaneous with the New Testament.[33] The word is used particularly by historians such as Diodorus of Sicily, Dionysius of Halicarnassus, Josephus and Plutarch.[34] While an effort has been made to look at all first-century BC and AD examples, the following examples must of necessity remain illustrative rather than exhaustive.[35] In what follows we will provide a sampling of some of the

---

[32] Thanks are due to Corin Mihaila for his research assistance on the extrabiblical instances of οἶμαι.

[33] It does so in both its contracted and its uncontracted forms. For the purposes of the present study we surveyed occurrences of this term in extrabiblical Greek writings in the first century BC and the first century AD. Only present-tense instances in the first person singular were considered.

[34] BDAG, 701 distinguishes between two syntactical patterns: with a following infinitive; and followed by an accusative and infinitive. Since the occurrence in John 21:25 follows the latter pattern, our investigation is limited to instances of οἶμαι plus an accusative and infinitive.

[35] Initial data were accessed through the *Thesaurus Linguae Graecae* database. Searches for οἶμαι in both its contracted and uncontracted forms were run for the first century BC and AD. These data were then manually evaluated for the presence of the syntactical construction found in John 21:25, namely a following accusative and infinitive. Since there was a

more relevant instances of οἶμαι in the period in question to allow the reader to form his or her opinion as to the meaning as well as rhetorical impact of the expression. These data will then form the basis for a concluding attempt at applying the observations gleaned from a look at the primary data to the interpretation of John 21:25.

Diodorus of Sicily

The historian Diodorus of Sicily reports a given speech concluding with the following words: ἱκανά μοι τὰ ῥηθέντα· λόγων γὰρ πλειόνων οὐκ οἶμαι ὑμᾶς προσδεῖσθαι ('But I have said enough; for *I cannot think* you have need of further words'; *Bibliotheca* 8.12.15; c. 30 BC).[36] We observe that the person venturing the opinion is the same as the one who has delivered the preceding speech. The term οἶμαι is used at the conclusion of an extended utterance by the speaker himself.

Dionysius of Halicarnassus

A similar example comes from Dionysius of Halicarnassus (writing during Augustus' reign), who reports a speech by one senator, Titus Larcius, to his fellow senators, which contains the following reference: οἶμαι δὲ μηδὲν ἡμᾶς δεῖν ἐν τῷ παρόντι σκοπεῖν, εἰ μή ... ('*It is my opinion*, therefore, that we ought to consider nothing else at present than [by what means these evils are to be removed from the state] ...'; *Hist.* 6.35.2). Again, the term in question is found in the context of a concluding statement that is inextricably tied to the person of the speaker.

Three more relevant passages in Dionysius' writings may be cited. The first two are found in his *Roman Antiquities*. In *Ant. Rom.* 4.74.2,

---

sufficient number of examples in major writers translated into English, there was no need to look further into material by minor writers not translated into English. In many cases these documents are in any case spurious or uncertain in dating.

[36] English renderings of classical works cited here are from the Loeb Classical Library.

we read, ἔτι πρὸς τούτοις, ὃ πάντων οἴομαι τῶν εἰρημένων χρησιμώτατον ἔσεσθαι ('There is one thing more which *in my opinion* will be of greater advantage than all that I have mentioned'). In *Ant. Rom.* 5.48.1, Dionysius writes, ἐν ἀρχῇ γὰρ τοῦ λόγου τοῦδε τὰ πολλὰ εἴρηται· ὃ δ' ἁπάντων ἐστὶ τῶν τοῦ ἀνδρὸς ἐγκωμίων θαυμασιώτατον καὶ οὔπω τέτευχε λόγου, τοῦτ' οἴομαι δεῖν μὴ παρελθεῖν ('[I need not relate all the achievements of this man for which he deserves to be both admired and remembered,] because most of them have been already narrated in the beginning of this Book; but *I think* I should not omit one thing which most deserves admiration of all that can be said in his praise and has not yet been mentioned'). One final example from this writer comes from Thucydides, *Hist.* 49.3: ἱκανῶς δ' οἴομαι καὶ διὰ τούτων φανερὸν πεποιηκέναι τὸ προκείμενον, ὅτι ... ('I think that the above examples illustrate clearly enough my thesis ...').

In several other instances, the word οἶμαι is not part of an opening or concluding statement but contained in the body of a speech or piece of writing, but nonetheless forms an integral part of the extended utterance of which it is a part and clearly conveys the point of view of the speaker or writer of the entire discourse unit (e.g. *De Isaeo* 17.53; *Hist.* 1.30.1; 3.9.6; *Ant. Rom.* 4.4.7).

Josephus
An interesting example comes from the writings of the Jewish historian Josephus, who concludes his discussion of the covert murders committed by the *sicarii* as follows: διὰ τοῦτ' οἶμαι καὶ τὸν θεόν ... ἀποστραφῆναι μὲν ἡμῶν τὴν πόλιν ('This is the reason why, *in my opinion*, even God Himself ... turned away from our city [and, because He deemed the temple to be no longer a clean dwelling place for Him, brought the Romans upon us and purification by fire upon the city ...; for He wished to chasten us by these calamities]'; *Ant.* 20.166; c. AD 93/94). A similar reference is found in Josephus' *Jewish War*: ὥστ' ἐγὼ πεφευγέναι μὲν ἐκ τῶν ἁγίων οἶμαι τὸ θεῖον

('*My belief*, therefore, is that the Deity has fled from the holy places'; *B.J.* 5.413; c. AD 75-79).

In *Against Apion*, Josephus intersperses the following comment in his discussion: ὅτι μὲν οὖν καὶ ἑτέροις τοῦτο πολλοῖς συμβέβηκε ..., οἶμαι, γιγνώσκειν τοὺς πλέον ταῖς ἱστορίαις ἐντυγχάνοντας ('That many others have ... met with the same fate, is a fact of which, *I imagine*, all habitual readers of history are aware'; *C. Ap.* 1.220; c. AD 93/94). In another passage in his *Jewish War* Josephus writes, οἶμαι πάντας ἥκειν πεπεισμένους οἴκοθεν ... ('[However, of the abandoned character of these conspirators against liberty and that it would be impossible to conceive any adequate punishment for what they have done,] *I feel sure* that you were all convinced when you left your homes ...'; *B.J.* 4.185).

Plutarch

The prolific Greek historian Plutarch (born before AD 50; died after AD 120) provides several relevant instances of the use of οἶμαι, only a few of which can be cited here. We begin with an instance where Plutarch uses οἶμαι in an editorial statement similar to John 21:25: Τὰ μὲν οὖν ἄγαν περιβόητα καὶ ὅσων οἶμαί σε βεβαίως βιβλίοις ἐντυχοῦσαν ἱστορίαν ἔχειν καὶ γνῶσιν ἤδη παρήσω ('Those incidents which are so often recited, and those of which *I assume* that you, having kept company with books, have assuredly record and knowledge, I will pass over for the present; but with this exception: [... Since, however, many deeds worthy of mention have been done by women ... it may not be a bad idea to set down first a brief account of those commonly known]'; *Mulier. virt.* 243D.7).

Elsewhere Plutarch writes, τὰς δὲ λέξεις οὐκ οἴομαί σε δεῖσθαι νῦν ἀκούειν ἐμοῦ καταλέγοντος ('*I don't think* you need to hear me now recite the passage word for word, for the third book concerning Justice can be had everywhere'; *Comm. not.* 1070D.12). Introducing a subject, he begins another passage with the following words: Οὐκ ἂν ἀηδῶς δ' οἶμαί σε προακοῦσαι περὶ τῆς ἀκουστικῆς αἰσθήσεως ...

('*I think* you may not find unwelcome some preliminary remarks about the sense of hearing'; *De recta ratione audiendi* 37F.11).

The following passages illustrate this writer's usage of the term οἶμαι conveying a sense of authorial modesty in venturing a variety of opinions on a wide range of subjects:

> τρυφὴν γὰρ οἶμαι καὶ παιδιὰν πρὸς ᾿Αντίοχον διαναυμαχεῖν ... ('For *I think* it was the merest child's play to win a seafight against Antiochus'; *Lys.* 4.4);

> οἶμαι δὲ καὶ τῇ πρὸς τοὺς πολεμίους ἐπιεικείᾳ διαφέρειν τὸν ἄνδρα τοῦ ἀνδρός ('*I think* also that in merciful behaviour towards their enemies the two men were different'; *Ages.* 3.2);

> Οἶμαι δὲ καὶ τὰς τελευτὰς τῶν ἀνδρῶν ἐμφαίνειν τινὰ τῆς ἀρετῆς διαφοράν ('*I think*, too, that the way in which the men died makes manifest a difference in their high excellence'; *Cleom.* 3.1);

> ὃ καὶ Σερτώριον οἶμαι παθεῖν ἤδη τῆς τύχης αὐτὸν ἐπιλειπούσης ... ('And this, *I think*, was the case with Sertorius when fortune at last began to forsake him'; *Sert.* 10.7);

> οὕτως οἶμαι καὶ τοὺς θεοὺς εὐεργετεῖν τὰ πολλὰ λανθάνοντας, αὐτῷ τῷ χαρίζεσθαι ('So, too, *I imagine* the gods confer their benefits, for the most part, without our knowledge, since it is their nature to take pleasure in the mere act of being gracious and doing good'; *Adol. poet. aud.* 63F.4).[37]

Preliminary Observations

While limitations of space precluded a comprehensive citation of all roughly contemporaneous instances of οἶμαι in extrabiblical Greek literature, the above examples are more than sufficient to provide

---

[37] Other pertinent references in Plutarch include *Quomodo adul.* 63F.4; *Consolatio ad Apollonium* 107A.4; *Sept. sap. conv.* 147E.9; 148.E.8; 160A.9; *Alex.* 326E.6; 333E.7; *Is. Os.* 351E.1; *De E apud Delphos* 392A.1; 399E.2; 404D.8; *Def. orac.* 429D.4; *De sera* 551E.9; *Exil.* 600A.7; 602D.9; *An seni* 792E.6; *Praec. ger. rei publ.* 799A.6; 799E.4; *De Herodoti malignitate* 869C.11; *Fac.* 932F.4; *De primo frigido* 953B.7; *Soll. an.* 963C.7; 987B.1; *De animae procreatione* 1012D.7; *Lat. viv.* 1130A.9.

comparative data that should prove helpful in interpreting the term's use in John 21:25. While not all of the above references are found in conclusions, at least two relevant observations can be made.

First, the term generally seems to convey the notion of authorial modesty in commending a claim or a comment made by the writer to his or her audience. It is often (though not always) part of discourse found at the beginning or conclusion of a section or at points of transition.

Secondly, the first person singular instances of οἶμαι surveyed above regularly constitute an integral part of the authorial perspective. If John 21:25 constitutes a later addition to an original Gospel by another hand, this would appear to be without precedent in extrabiblical Greek literature.

Conclusion

By way of brief summary, then, the term οἶμαι is a literary term frequently used by historians reflecting authorial modesty in stating a claim or opinion. It is commonly part of authorial discourse, not infrequently at the beginning or conclusion of a literary unit or at points of transition. In its extrabiblical instances the term regularly forms an inextricable part of the author's argument that cannot be easily separated from the larger context by source or redaction-critical means.

Applied to the ending of John's Gospel, it would seem therefore that there is no known ancient precedent for a later editor or group of editors using οἶμαι in the context of authenticating the message of an original author or witness. This primary evidence would appear to render redaction-critical proposals unlikely that separate the last one or two verses of John's Gospel from the rest of the Gospel and assign different authorship to these. At the very least, this would suggest that John 21:24-25 should be viewed as part of ch. 21 as a whole.

In light of the links between ch. 21 and the preceding Gospel, the findings of the present study strengthen the possibility that 21:24-25 are an integral part of the authorial message of the entire Gospel, whereby the first person singular form οἶμαι would suggest a single author rather than a group of authors, editors or redactors.[38] If so, the 'I' of v. 25 would seem to be included in the 'we' of 21:24, and the third person reference to 'the disciple' in v. 24 may well constitute an authorial self-reference by the 'I' of v. 25 as well.[39]

---

[38] If the apostle John did in fact live to a ripe old age as tradition has it, there seems to be no compelling need to posit complicated theories of communities or individuals editing or redacting the apostle's material (or traditions going back to the apostle) in any case, since John would still have been alive at the time the Gospel was written and thus could very likely have been its author (including the final two verses).

[39] Incidentally, the converse of an authorial 'we' (where the author includes himself as well as his audience), namely a communal 'I', is hardly an option for the first person singular verb οἶμαι in John 21:25. I know of no instance where a community refers to itself as 'I' in biblical literature or elsewhere. However, this seems to be the type of 'rhetorical device' hinted at by some commentators (such as Brown or Lindars; see survey above).

Ὁμοθυμαδόν in Acts

Co-location, Common Action or 'Of One Heart and Mind'?

Steve Walton

'When *I* use a word,' Humpty Dumpty said in rather a scornful tone, 'it means just what I choose it to mean — neither more nor less.'[1]

And there's the rub in studying ancient authors: what exactly do they mean in the choice of a particular word in a particular literary context? Today's scholars are alert to the dangers of the 'intentional fallacy' — since we do not have access to the minds of authors, especially ancient ones, except through their writings, any construction of 'the author's intention' is necessarily a reading of the text.[2] But this should not be seen as a counsel of despair, as if it implies that we can say nothing about what ancient authors meant; rather, it alerts us to a potential difficulty, a difficulty that can be ameliorated by careful study of the wider ancient settings, historical, cultural and literary, as well as the actual use of the word under examination in the author's own writings.[3]

---

[1] Lewis Carroll, *Through the Looking-Glass* (London: Andrew Dakers, n.d.), 104 (ch. 6). An interesting sidelight on the word study which follows is that the 'Alice' of Carroll's story was based on Alice Liddell, daughter of Henry G. Liddell, an editor of the major Greek lexicon, LSJ, and Carroll was C. L. Dodgson, Fellow of Christ Church, Oxford, where Liddell was then Dean (I owe this observation to Dr Christopher Stray and Dr David Gill).

[2] See, e.g., William K. Wimsatt, Jr, *The Verbal Icon: Studies in the Meaning of Poetry* (Lexington: University of Kentucky, 1954), 3-18 (this section written in collaboration with Monroe C. Beardsley).

[3] In this, Bruce Winter has demonstrated fine skills, not least in his work on Roman Corinth, which helpfully illuminates issues in the Corinthian correspondence; see Bruce W. Winter, *After Paul Left Corinth: The*

Meet the Word

In the New Testament ὁμοθυμαδόν is found almost exclusively in the Book of Acts (1:14; 2:46; 4:24; 5:12; 7:57; 8:6; 12:20; 15:25; 18:12; 19:29),[4] with the single exception of Rom 15:6.[5] A sharp division exists in scholarship over its meaning in Acts.

The word is formed from three components: ὁμός, θυμός and an adverb termination -δόν.[6] The first is straightforward, meaning 'one and the same, common'. The second is more complex, for θυμός denotes intense feeling, and can be a positive characteristic, expressed as 'passionate longing',[7] or a negative one, expressed by 'anger',

---

Influence of Secular Ethics and Social Change (Grand Rapids: Eerdmans, 2001). I offer this brief study in warm tribute to a fine Christian scholar and friend whose example, encouragement and wise counsel have been of considerable help at key stages of my own work.

[4] There are also variant readings including ὁμοθυμαδόν at 2:1 and 20:18. The former includes the word in C³ E Ψ 33 1739ˢ and 𝔐, in place of ὁμοῦ 'together', but it is absent in the best and earliest witnesses (ℵ A B C*, etc.). The fact that it is found in place of ὁμοῦ perhaps suggests that the early scribal tradition considered ὁμοθυμαδόν to contain at least the idea of co-location, and perhaps more. Similarly, at 20:18 the word is found in E 2464 and a few others, but it is omitted in the major witnesses (ℵ B C Ψ 33 1739) and 𝔐. Thus it seems very unlikely that either verse should be counted among our list of uses of ὁμοθυμαδόν in Acts. For the full range of readings, see Reuben J. Swanson, ed., *New Testament Greek Manuscripts, Variant Readings Arranged in Horizontal Lines against Codex Vaticanus: The Acts of the Apostles* (Sheffield: Sheffield Academic Press, 1998), ad loc.

[5] Luke T. Johnson, *The Acts of the Apostles* (SP; Collegeville: Liturgical, 1992), 34, followed by Ben Witherington, *The Acts of the Apostles: A Socio-rhetorical Commentary* (Carlisle/Grand Rapids: Paternoster/Eerdmans, 1998), 113, erroneously asserts that this word is peculiar to Luke-Acts in the New Testament.

[6] BDAG, 706. A. T. Robertson, *A Grammar of the Greek New Testament in the Light of Historical Research* (London: Hodder & Stoughton, 1914), 295-96 and MM, 445, note that forming adverbs using this accusative ending is typical in the Hellenistic period.

[7] BDAG, 461 art. θυμός, § 1, cites only extra-biblical sources for this sense with any certainty, notably Plato, *Crat.* 419e, θυμὸς ἀπὸ τῆς θύσεως καὶ ζέσεως τῆς ψυχῆς ('[the word] θυμός is derived from the raging and boiling of the soul').

'wrath' or 'rage'.[8] Thus etymology leads us to expect senses denoting shared passion, both positive and negative. Etymology is, of course, to be handled with considerable care. Barr rightly states, 'the etymology of a word is not a statement about its meaning but about its history'[9] — and we may even express caution about Barr's implied confidence in recovering a word's history through its etymology. Hence usage is properly the focus of this debate.

The majority view stems from Hatch, who claims that the sense of the word shifts from classical use for 'with one accord' to a weakened sense of 'together' in the LXX and New Testament.[10] First, Hatch asserts (without evidence) that the classical usage can always be translated in line with the etymological sense. Then he examines LXX usage and claims: (1) it is used to translate Hebrew words meaning simply 'together'; (2) those same Hebrew words are elsewhere translated by Greek words or phrases which are simply about co-location; (3) there are contexts where the etymological sense is impossible. Finally, he roundly asserts (without discussion) that in the New Testament there is never any reason for assuming that the word means other than 'together'.

Cadbury adds an examination of the Acts uses,[11] claiming that: (1) the word is used generally of association of time, place or action; (2) the riots mentioned in Acts 7:57; 18:12; 19:29 'do not imply regulated purpose'.

A minority argues, on the contrary, that the classical sense continues in the New Testament, irrespective of whether the LXX uses

---

[8]   BDAG, 461 art. θυμός, § 2.
[9]   James Barr, *The Semantics of Biblical Language* (Oxford: OUP, 1961), 108; cf. the warning of D. A. Carson, *Exegetical Fallacies* (Carlisle/Grand Rapids: Paternoster/Baker, 1984), 26-32, concerning the 'root fallacy'.
[10]   Edwin Hatch, *Essays in Biblical Greek* (Oxford: Clarendon, 1889), 63-64.
[11]   Henry J. Cadbury, "Lexical Notes on Luke-Acts. I," *JBL* 44 (1925): 214-27, citing 216-18.

the word with a weakened sense.[12] Abbott claims that only in Acts 5:12, and perhaps 15:25, is the sense 'together' necessary. Moulton and Milligan cite uses in second-century BC papyri in support of the sense 'unanimously'.[13]

Commentators on and translators of Acts divide: some agree with Hatch;[14] others follow Abbott.[15] So here is a word which invites further investigation. Generally, the lexica refer to few actual uses of the word in their discussions,[16] and so we shall seek to track usage through literary and non-literary sources up to New Testament times, and then to re-examine Acts in the light of our discoveries.

Pre-Christian Graeco-Roman Usage
Literary usage can be traced back to the fifth century BC. A search of the *Thesaurus Linguae Graece* CD-ROM finds the following uses up to Christian times (excluding LXX):

---

[12]   T. K. Abbott, *Essays Chiefly on the Original Texts of the Old and New Testaments* (London: Longmans, Green & Co., 1891), 96; so also MM, 448.
[13]   *P. Tebt.* I.40; *P. Paris* 63 (= *P. Petrie* III.26). Cadbury, "Lexical Notes on Luke-Acts," 217-18, criticises Moulton and Milligan's selective quotation of the latter, and argues that the subject is impersonal, and that therefore ὁμοθυμαδόν must be rendered 'alike'.
[14]   E.g. C. K. Barrett, *A Critical and Exegetical Commentary on the Acts of the Apostles* (2 vols.; ICC; Edinburgh: T & T Clark, 1994, 1998), 1:88-89 (repeating Hatch's arguments); F. J. Foakes Jackson and K. Lake, eds., *The Beginnings of Christianity, Part I: The Acts of the Apostles* (5 vols.; London: Macmillan, 1920-33), 4:54; with ESV, GNB, NEB, NIV, NRSV, REB and RSV.
[15]   E.g. Joseph A. Fitzmyer, *The Acts of the Apostles: A New Translation and Commentary* (AB; New York: Doubleday, 1998), 215; Jacob Jervell, *Die Apostelgeschichte* (MeyerK; Göttingen: Vandenhoeck & Ruprecht, 1998), 119, n. 71; Johnson, *Acts*, 34, 59, 140; with AV, NJB, NLT, Phillips.
[16]   See the all-too-brief entries in LSJ, 1224; BDAG, 706; BAGD, 566; MM, 448; *EDNT* 2:511; Louw and Nida, § 31.23; *TDNT* 5:185-86; *NIDNTT* 3:908-09; *TLNT* 2:580-81. The latter is the most useful discussion, including references.

BC	5th century	5^{17}
	4th century	5^{18}
	3rd century	2^{19}
	2nd century	24^{20}
	1st century	13^{21}
AD	1st century	14 (of which 11 NT)^{22}

The earliest uses focus on a shared, usually unanimous, decision or common action. Thus Aristophanes writes of common action:[23]

> οὐδὲν ποιοῦμεν ὦνδρες ἀλλ᾽ ὁμοθυμαδὸν ἅπασιν ἡμῖν αὖθις ἀντιληπτόν

> This won't do, friends. Come! *all together*! Everyone to the work and with a good heart for the business. (*Pax* 484)

Similarly, Xenophon highlights common action against the Lacedaemonians:

> Θηβαῖοι δὲ καὶ πάντες οἱ ἀποστάντες ἀπὸ Λακεδαιμονίων μέχρι μὲν τούτου τοῦ χρόνου ὁμοθυμαδὸν καὶ ἔπραττον καὶ ἐσρατεύοντο ἡγουμένων Θηβαίων.

> Up to this time the Thebans and all who had revolted from the Lacedaemonians had been acting and carrying on their campaigns *in full accord*, under the leadership of the Thebans. (*Hell.* 7.1.22)

---

[17] Aristophanes, *Pax* 484; *Av.* 1015; Plato, *Leg.* 805a; Xenophon, *Hell.* 2.4.17; 7.1.22.

[18] Demosthenes, *In Philippum* 4.59; *Orationes* 14.37; Dinarchus, *In Aristogitonem* 20; *In Philoclem* 7; Crantor, *Frag.* 13.

[19] *Letter of Aristeas* 178; Mantheo, *Frag.* 54, extant only as a quotation in Josephus, *C. Ap.* 1.227-87 (= 1.26-31).

[20] 21 uses in Polybius (see n. 25 below); Diogenes; *Sibyline Oracles* 3.458 (this reference taken to be from an early section of the *Oracles*); *T. 12 Patr.* 8.6.10.

[21] Diodorus Siculus, *Bibliotheca Historica* 13.112.3; 19.22.4; 31.39.1; Dionysius of Halicarnassus, *Ant. rom.* 6.41.2; 7.22.3; Isidorus (Aegyptius), *Hymni in Isim* 4; Philo, *Conf.* 58; *De vita Mosis* 1.72, 136; *Flacc.* 123, 132, 144; *Legat.* 356.

[22] Aside from the New Testament uses, Josephus, *A.J.* 15.277; 19.357 and his quotation of Mantheo (n. 19 above).

[23] Translations cited are from LCL unless otherwise stated.

Demosthenes uses ὁμοθυμαδόν in conjunction with acting ἐκ μιᾶς γνώμης ('from one mind'), which suggests that here ὁμοθυμαδόν denotes something different from simple agreement:[24]

> For they are convinced that if you offer a *whole-hearted* and unanimous opposition to Philip [ἂν μὲν ὑμεῖς ὁμοθυμαδὸν ἐκ μιᾶς γνώμης Φίλιππον ἀμύνησθε], you will beat him and they will have no further chance of earning his pay. (*Orationes* 10.59.2)

A mass of examples — twenty-one in total — is found in Polybius in the second century BC.[25] Almost all are in military or political settings, and here unanimity of decision or action is the consistent theme.[26] Typical examples include:

> αὐτοί τε φρᾶς ὁμοθυμαδὸν ἔδωκαν παρακληθέντες εἰς τὴν τῶν Ῥωμαίων πίστιν
>
> They [the Corcyreans] *unanimously* accepted the Romans' invitation to place themselves under their protection ... (*Historiae* 2.11.5)

> ἐνεχείρησαν ὁμοθυμαδὸν ἐν τούτοις τοῖς καιροῖς πρὸς τοὺς κατὰ τὴν Ἰταλίαν πολεμίους ...
>
> They [the Romans] threw *their whole effort* into the struggle with their enemies in Italy ... (*Historiae* 2.22.11)

> ἤδη τῶν πραγμάτων οὐκέτι διδόντων ἀναστραφὴν ἠνάγκαζε τὰ περιεστῶτα καταφεύγειν ὁμοθυμαδὸν ἐπὶ τὸν Ἀντίγονον.
>
> Circumstances now no longer permitting delay, they were compelled by their position to appeal *with one voice* to Antigonus. (*Historiae* 2.51.4)

> τὸ δὲ πέρας, ἀναχωρήσαντες εἰς τὴν παρεμβολὴν καὶ συνεδρεύσαντες μετὰ τῶν χιλιάρχων οἱ περὶ τὸν Ἄππιον, ὁμοθυμαδὸν ἐβουλεύσαντο πάσης ἐλπίδος πεῖραν λαμβάνειν πλὴν τοῦ διὰ πολιορκίας ἑλεῖν τὰς Συρακούσας.

---

[24] *Contra* Heidland in *TDNT* 5:186.

[25] Polybius, *Historiae* 1.8.4, 1.45.4, 1.80.7; 2.11.5, 2.22.11, 2.51.4; 3.13.4; 4.25.5, 4.53.6, 4.79.7; 5.16.7, 5.71.1; 6.6.11; 8.7.5, 8.31.4; 10.37.3; 11.16.2; 15.19.7; 16.31.4; 23.16.9; 27.8.7; 28.4.13.

[26] The uses in Diodorus Siculus and Dionysius of Halicarnassus (both first century BC) are very similar.

At last Appius retired to his camp and called a council of his military tribunes, at which it was *unanimously* decided to resort to any means rather than attempt to take Syracuse by storm. (*Historiae* 8.7.5)

In most passages ὁμοθυμαδόν *could* simply be rendered 'together' (as Hatch asserts for the New Testament), for generally in Polybius ὁμοθυμαδόν denotes an agreed decision or action. However, for an ancient author a person is known by actions, for they reveal character,[27] and so the split between outward agreement and inner oneness (as we would put it) may be our late modern construct, rather than an appropriate tool for analysing the ancients' thinking.

With Philo we approach the New Testament period and culture more closely. He comments on Exod 19:8:

> Wonderful then indeed is the symphony of voices here described, but most wonderful of all, exceeding every harmony, is that united universal symphony in which we find the whole people declaring *with one heart* [ὁ λαὸς ἅπας ὁμοθυμαδὸν εἰσάγεται λέγων], 'All that God hath said we will do and hear.' (*De confusione linguarum* 58)

The appearance in this sentence of other words indicating shared speech, and Philo's exaltation of the people's words in Exod 19:8 above other kinds of shared speech, suggests that ὁμοθυμαδόν here denotes a kind of shared expression which comes (as we might say) from the heart of the people. His usage elsewhere is similar, notably in commenting on shared grief in *De vita Mosis* 1.136:[28]

> ὥστε συνέβη καὶ διὰ τὴν κοινοπραγίαν τοῦ πάθους ἀπάντων ἀρθρόως ὁμοθυμαδὸν ἐκβοησάντων ἕνα θρῆνον ἀπὸ περάτων ἐπὶ πέρατα κατὰ πάσης τῆς χώρας συνηχῆσαι.

> And so, since in this general disaster the same emotion drew from all a *united* outcry, one single dirge of wailing resounded from end to end of the whole land.

---

[27] See Plutarch, *Alex.* 1.1.
[28] Similar to the use of shared rejoicing in *T. Naph.* 6.10.

Hatch's assertion concerning classical usage, that 'it can always be translated "with one accord"'[29] is thus a maximising reading of the texts, for while ὁμοθυμαδόν clearly denotes shared feeling or mind in some cases, in others it is used simply for a unanimous decision or united action, behind which Hatch presumes a shared mindset stands.

Non-literary usage appears to be confined to a small number of occurrences in inscriptions[30] and papyri. The epigraphical uses occur in similar political/military settings to those in Polybius. Among the papyri, *P. Tebt.* I.40 line 8 (c. 117 BC) uses the phrase 'having received information that the inhabitants of the village are ὁμοθυμαδόν holding fast to your protection,'[31] a setting where some phrase expressing unanimity seems to be required.

Septuagintal Usage

Three main senses can be identified among the 36 uses in the LXX.[32] First, the word is at times used simply for co-location and can there be rendered 'together', such as in 3 Macc 6:39:[33]

μεγαλοδόξως ἐπιφάνας τὸ ἔλεος αὐτοῦ ὁ τῶν πάντων δυνάστης ἀπταίστους αὐτοὺς ἐρρύσατο ὁμοθυμαδόν

on which the Lord of all most gloriously revealed his mercy and rescued them all *together* and unharmed. (NRSV)

Secondly, the word is used to denote shared action which suggests a shared purpose, such as in the sequence in Jdt 15:2, 5, 9:[34]

---

[29] Hatch, *Essays*, 63.

[30] *SIG*³ 742:14 (not, as frequently cited, 13) [an Ephesian inscription c. AD 85]; 1104:29 (not, as frequently cited, 28) [an Athenian inscription, c. 37 BC].

[31] Translation from George Milligan, *Selections from the Greek Papyri* (Cambridge: CUP, 1912), 28.

[32] Cf. Spicq's (different) threefold analysis in *TLNT* 2:580-81; and that of J. Lust, E. Eynikel and K. Hauspie, eds., *A Greek-English Lexicon of the Septuagint* (2 vols.; Stuttgart: Deutsche Bibelgesellschaft, 1992, 1996), 2:331, suggesting 'with one accord, with one mind' and 'together' as possible translations.

[33] Similar examples include Job 6:2; 9:32.

[2] Overcome with fear and trembling, they did not wait for one another, but *with one impulse* all rushed out and fled by every path
[ἀλλ' ἐκχυθέντες ὁμοθυμαδὸν ἔφευγον ἐπὶ πᾶσαν ὁδόν] across the
plain and through the hill country ... [5] When the Israelites heard it,
with one accord they fell upon the enemy [πάντες ὁμοθυμαδὸν
ἐπέπεσον ἐπ' αὐτούς], and cut them down as far as Choba. Those in
Jerusalem and all the hill country also came, for they were told what
had happened in the camp of the enemy. The men in Gilead and in
Galilee outflanked them with great slaughter, even beyond Damascus
and its borders ... [9] When they met her, they all blessed her *with one
accord* [εὐλόγησαν αὐτὴν πάντες ὁμοθυμαδόν] and said to her, 'You
are the glory of Jerusalem, you are the great boast of Israel, you are
the great pride of our nation!' (NRSV)

V. 2 portrays the Assyrian army fleeing in panic when they hear of
the death of Holofernes, their commander. V. 5 describes the Israelites' pursuit and killing of the enemy as they fled, and leads to the
people blessing Judith, who killed Holofernes (v. 9). In each case
united action is denoted, and each time it comes from shared motiva-
tion and purpose.

Thirdly, there are places where the etymological sense seems to be
present. Three examples seem clear:

> καὶ συνήχθη πᾶν τὸ πλῆθος ὁμοθυμαδὸν ἐπὶ τὸ εὐρύχωρον τοῦ
> πρὸς ἀνατολὰς τοῦ ἱεροῦ πυλῶνος
>
> the whole multitude gathered *with one accord* in the open square be-
> fore the east gate of the temple. (1 Esdr 9:38, NRSV)

Here ὁμοθυμαδόν is unlikely simply to denote common location,
since the use of πᾶν τὸ πλῆθος ('the whole multitude') and ἐπὶ τὸ
εὐρύχωρον ('in the open square') already emphasises that everyone
was there. Ὁμοθυμαδον is therefore likely to add a further point of
common purpose, which is that they wish Esdras the priest to read the
law to them (v. 39).

> All the people were greatly astonished. They bowed down and wor-
> shipped God, and said *with one accord* [προσεκύνησαν τῷ θεῷ καὶ

---

[34]   Similar examples include 3 Macc 4:6; 5:50; Jdt 7:29.

εἶπαν ὁμοθυμαδόν], 'Blessed are you our God, who have this day humiliated the enemies of your people.' (Jdt 13:17, NRSV)

The setting here is of Judith's return to Bethulia with the head of Holofernes, the enemy commander, whom she killed after getting him drunk. Again there are cotextual indicators of common location and shared experience, so that when they speak it is unlikely that the author is thinking of choral speech — rather, the setting suggests united worship, both in words and in heart and mind.

> his three friends, having heard all the evil things which had come upon him, each came from his own country to him, Eliphaz the king of the Temanites, Bildad the prince of the Shuhites, Zophar the king of the Meunites and they came to him *with a united purpose*, in order to console and care for him [παρεγένοντο πρὸς αὐτὸν ὁμοθυμαδὸν τοῦ παρακαλέσαι καὶ ἐπισκέψασθαι αὐτόν]. (Job 2:11 LXX, my tr.)

Here the idea of common location is present, but it is expressed by παρεγένοντο ἕκαστος ἐκ τῆς ἰδίας χώρας πρὸς αὐτόν ('they each came from their own country to him') and παρεγένοντο πρὸς αὐτόν ('they came to him'). The genitive infinitives which follow, τοῦ παρακαλέσαι καὶ ἐπισκέψασθαι, express the purpose of their coming. Thus it seems most likely that ὁμοθυμαδόν here denotes a shared mood or purpose among Job's three friends.[35]

It is notable that, among the LXX passages considered, most have no Hebrew original with which to be compared (only in Job is this so). So Hatch's argument that ὁμοθυμαδόν usually translates יַחְדָּו or יַחַד, both normally meaning 'together', is mistaken, for three reasons. First, the wider LXX usage needs to be considered, including those works extant only in Greek. Secondly, it is unwise to assume that the LXX translators always intended to convey the same nuance in Greek as is found in the Hebrew text: there are numerous places

---

[35] In agreement with Lust, Eynikel and Hauspie, eds., *Lexicon* 2:331. Jdt 4:12 may provide a further example of this usage.

where they paraphrased or expanded the Hebrew original.[36] Thirdly, the Hebrew Bible can use יַחְדָּו to express more than physical co-location; for example, in Jer 5:5 (where LXX has ὁμοθυμαδόν) it denotes the shared action of rich people all over Israel. The further step in Hatch's argument, to claim that other uses of יַחְדָּו and יַחַד are translated by Greek phrases denoting co-location, is irrelevant: for Hatch's argument to have any possibility of standing up, there must be *no* places where ὁμοθυμαδόν in the LXX is likely to have the stronger sense of shared heart or mind — and we have seen that this is not so.

And So to Acts ...

In the light of Graeco-Roman and LXX uses, we turn to New Testament usage, which principally means Acts. Uses here divide between those of Christian groups (1:14; 2:46; 4:24; 5:12; 15:25, and perhaps 8:6, concerning the Samarian crowds listening to Philip) and non-Christian opponents of the church (7:57; 18:12; 19:29, and perhaps 12:20 of the people of Tyre and Sidon jointly approaching Herod). As with the LXX, they seem to fall into three groups.

First, there is at least one case where physical co-location is the focus, namely 2:46, where Luke contrasts the daily gathering of believers ὁμοθυμαδόν in the temple with their breaking bread κατ᾽ οἶκον ('from house to house').

Secondly, shared action is the focus in other cases. Acts 12:20 seems to belong here:

> Now Herod was angry with the people of Tyre and Sidon, but they came to him in unity [ὁμοθυμαδὸν δὲ παρῆσαν πρὸς αὐτόν] and, after persuading Blastus, the king's chamberlain, they asked for peace because their country was fed from the king's country. (my tr.)

---

[36] For a helpful introductory discussion, see Karen H. Jobes and Moisés Silva, *Invitation to the Septuagint* (Grand Rapids/Carlisle: Baker Academic/Paternoster, 2000), 86-102; more fully on Job, Donald H. Gard, *The Exegetical Method of the Greek Translator of the Book of Job* (JBLMS 8; Philadelphia: SBL, 1952).

The joint mission from Tyre and Sidon which comes to Herod seeking reconciliation with him is not merely 'together' in location, but also in its action — this is a united approach to Herod. So while the idea of shared location is present, there is also unanimity, similar to the political contexts in Polybius.

Acts 8:6 may also belong here:

> The crowds listened to the things Philip said ὁμοθυμαδόν, as they heard them and saw the signs which he performed. (my tr.)

The very fact that 'the crowds listened[37] to the things Philip said' shows that they were all together in one place. Their listening is characterised as ὁμοθυμαδόν, 'united' — we might almost say 'as one person' in order to convey that they were unitedly focused on listening to Philip.[38] It may be that there are hints of a shared commitment of heart and mind, but they are not clear enough to place 8:6 in our third category.

Acts 18:12 presents a united attack by the Corinthian Jews on Paul during Gallio's proconsulship:

> But when Gallio was proconsul of Achaia, the Jews attacked Paul in unison [ὁμοθυμαδὸν οἱ Ἰουδαῖοι τῷ Παύλῳ] and brought him to the tribunal.

This certainly pictures more than these people appearing in the same place at the same time. They have a shared commitment to get rid of Paul and this finds expression in their united legal proceedings before the proconsul. As with 8:6, it is clear that there is shared passion behind their shared action,[39] but it may be too much to say that ὁμοθυμαδόν expresses that shared passion here.

---

[37] προσεῖχον is fronted for emphasis.
[38] Gerhard Schneider, *Die Apostelgeschichte* (2 vols.; HTK; Freiburg: Herder, 1980, 1982), 1:488, n. 40, suggests that it approximates to 'alle miteinander'.
[39] Rudolf Pesch, *Die Apostelgeschichte* (2 vols.; EKK; Zürich: Benzinger, 1986), 2:150, cleverly puns 'now he uses *einmütig* (unanimous) in a negative sense as *einwütig* (united in rage).'

In 19:29 ὁμοθυμαδόν characterises the rush of the crowds into the Ephesian theatre:

> And the city was filled with confusion; they rushed ὁμοθυμαδόν into the theatre after seizing Gaius and Aristarchus, who were Macedonians and Paul's travel companions. (my tr.)

There is certainly more here than shared time and place; this is united action, perhaps stemming from united concern. Fitzmyer suggests 'with one impulse'.[40] Pesch wishes to see the crowd as united in rage,[41] but it is hard to be sure how far below the surface of the text this united passion is to be located. Hence, 19:29 straddles the boundary between our second and third categories.

Thirdly, the shared action in at least some cases stems from a shared attitude of heart or mind. Often there are cotextual indicators of shared location already present, which suggest that ὁμοθυμαδόν is adding more to the notion of shared time or space.

Acts 1:14 is an example with such indicators:

> These all were devoting themselves ὁμοθυμαδόν to prayer with the women and Mary the mother of Jesus and his brothers.

'These all' refers to the apostles, who were listed in v. 13, where they are said to be in the upper room οὗ ἦσαν καταμένοντες, 'where they were *staying*'.[42] Further, in v. 15 it is 'during those days' that Peter stood up among the brothers and sisters to speak, which again implies that the people referred to in v. 14 are in the same place at the same time. Thus for Luke to use ὁμοθυμαδόν simply to add yet another word for shared space and time would be overkill — it seems highly likely that here our word denotes a shared commitment of heart and mind to prayer.[43]

Acts 4:24 suggests a similar conclusion:

---

[40] Fitzmyer, *Acts*, 659.
[41] Pesch, *Die Apostelgeschichte*, 2:180.
[42] BDAG, 522.
[43] So Ernst Haenchen, *The Acts of the Apostles* (Oxford: Blackwell, 1971), 154, n. 1; Jervell, *Die Apostelgeschichte*, 119, n. 71.

Those who heard lifted up their voice ὁμοθυμαδόν to God: 'Sovereign Lord, you are the one who made the heavens and the earth and the sea and everything in them.' (my tr.)

Here it is clear from Luke's statement that Peter and John 'went to their own people' (ἦλθον πρὸς τοὺς ἰδίους, v. 23) that the believers are in one place. It seems unlikely that Luke is portraying choral speech by using ὁμοθυμαδόν,[44] and so we might paraphrase, 'Those who heard lifted their voice in united concern to God' — the shared passion here being a united concern for the mission of God among the Jewish people,[45] which finds expression in the prayer which follows (vv. 24b-31).

Acts 5:12 also presents the body[46] as sharing a location:
... they all [ἄπαντες] were ὁμοθυμαδόν in Solomon's Portico.

In the context of 4:32-37, which present the principle of shared possessions, modelled by the positive example of Barnabas, and 5:1-11, which narrate the negative example and disloyalty of Ananias and Sapphira, Luke's choice of ὁμοθυμαδόν here surely highlights the believers' shared commitment to life together.[47]

Acts 7:57 is less clear cut:
After crying out with a loud voice, they covered their ears and rushed ὁμοθυμαδόν upon him [sc. Stephen]. (my tr.)

Certainly ὁμοθυμαδόν denotes united action, for it modifies the verb ὥρμησαν ('they rushed'). The earlier part of the sentence highlights that their united attack on Stephen arose from what they heard from him: 'after crying with a loud voice, they stopped their ears.' The idea of shared passion,[48] here negative in expression, lies behind their

---

[44] *Contra* Pesch, *Die Apostelgeschichte*, 1:175.

[45] Cf. Fitzmyer, *Acts*, 307.

[46] Probably the whole community of believers and not only the apostles, with Jervell, *Die Apostelgeschichte*, 200-01; *contra* Johnson, *Acts*, 92.

[47] So also Haenchen, *Acts*, 242, n. 3: 'Here ... [ὁμοθυμαδόν] doubtless retains its full meaning.'

[48] Johnson, *Acts*, 140, sees an ironic echo of the unity of heart and mind in the Christian community.

shared action, and that may be the most we can say here. Thus 7:57 lies between our second and third categories of use.

Acts 15:25 is similar to 7:57:

> It seemed good to us, having come to unanimity [γενομένοις ὁμοθυμαδόν], to choose men to send to you, with our beloved Barnabas and Paul.

Here, the idea of unanimity of decision is present at the end of the Jerusalem meeting as well as shared place and time.[49] They have spent time together in the same location and now present their agreed findings to the churches addressed in the letter.[50]

We may finally note that the only other New Testament use, Rom 15:6, also shows this nuance of shared passion:

> [5] ὁ δὲ θεὸς τῆς ὑπομονῆς καὶ τῆς παρακλήσεως δῴη ὑμῖν τὸ αὐτὸ φρονεῖν ἐν ἀλλήλοις κατὰ Χριστὸν Ἰησοῦν, [6] ἵνα ὁμοθυμαδὸν ἐν ἑνὶ στόματι δοξάζητε τὸν θεὸν καὶ πατέρα τοῦ κυρίου ἡμῶν Ἰησοῦ Χριστοῦ.

> [5] May the God of steadfastness and encouragement give to you to share the same mind with each other according to Christ Jesus, [6] so that in unity of heart, from one mouth you may glorify the God and Father of our Lord Jesus Christ. (Rom 15:5-6, my tr.)

Here there are strong cotextual indicators of unity: Paul prays that the believers will share the same mind (τὸ αὐτὸ φρονεῖν ἐν ἀλλήλοις, v. 5) and speak with one voice (ἐν ἑνὶ στόματι, v. 6) in glorifying God. In the ἵνα clause (v. 6, expressing purpose), ὁμοθυμαδόν surely provides the inward dimension of unity in worship as ἐν ἑνὶ στόματι provides the outward, hence my rendition as 'unity of heart'.[51] This seems very clearly to belong in our third category.

---

[49] *Mart. Pol.* 12.3 echoes 'it seemed good to them unanimously', but there of the crowd unanimously shouting for Polycarp's execution.

[50] Barrett, *Acts*, 2:742, sees both physical location and unanimity here.

[51] With C. E. B. Cranfield, *A Critical and Exegetical Commentary on the Epistle to the Romans* (2 vols.; ICC; Edinburgh: T & T Clark, 1975, 1979), 2:738; Thomas R. Schreiner, *Romans* (BECNT; Grand Rapids: Baker, 1998), 750; *contra* Heinrich Schlier, *Der Römerbrief* (HTK; Freiburg: Herder,

Conclusions

In sum, then, we may say that the picture is more complex than either Hatch or Abbott suggests, but overall ὁμοθυμαδόν is used rather more with at least some sense of unity of thought or action than merely in the sense of shared location. Luke uses it to highlight a major theme, the unity of the earliest Christians. That said, we may also observe that, even with this word which Luke favours using and which suits his theological purpose (in emphasising the unity of the believing community), he can and does use it with a variety of nuances, including using it to indicate the unity of the opposition to the believers. This observation highlights the danger of a one-dimensional redaction-critical approach which does not permit an author such variety of use and sense: real authors are more subtle and varied in their use of language than those posited by more extreme forms of redaction criticism.

We may bring our findings together in a proposal for a revised (somewhat expanded!) entry for BDAG:

> ὁμοθυμαδόν (ὁμός 'one and the same, common', θυμός 'passion', and adv. termination) adv. (Aristoph., X. et al. On its formation s. BDF § 122; Mlt-H. 164; Rob. 295-6)
>
> **(1) located in the same place at the same time,** *together* Acts 2:46 (contrasted w. κατ' οἶκον). This mng. *together* (NRSV et al.) is claimed in 5:12 and elsewhere (so EHatch, Essays in Biblical Greek, 1889, 63f; HCadbury, JBL 44, 1925, 216-18), but seems unlikely (so JKAbbott, Essays Chiefly on the Original Texts of the OT and NT, 1891, 96; M-M).

1977, reprint 2002), 422; James D. G. Dunn, *Romans* (2 vols.; WBC; Dallas: Word, 1988), 840-41, who both see ὁμοθυμαδόν as simple 'unanimity', highlighting only the political usage in pre-Christian times — although Dunn does recognise an outward/inward contrast, as we suggest above. N. T. Wright, "The Letter to the Romans," in *The New Interpreter's Bible* (ed. Leander E. Keck; Nashville: Abingdon, 2002), 10:395-770, citing 746, sees this inward dimension as the shared mind of v. 5. Since, for ancients, the heart is the seat of the thoughts and will, 'unity of heart' is an appropriate rendition for ὁμοθυμαδόν here.

(2) sharing in the same action or decision, *unitedly, unanimously, with one impulse, as one person* (X. 7.1.22, Aristoph. *Pax* 484; Polyb. 2.11.5; 2.22.11; 2.51.4; 8.7.5; Jdt 15:2, 5, 9; SIG³ 742,14 [I. AD]; 1104,29 [I. BC]; P. Tebt. I.40 [II. BC]) freq. in political or military contexts) Ac 12:20; 20:18 v.l.; γενόμενοι ὁμ. *unanimously* Ac 15:25. In addition, Ac 8:6; 18:12; 19:29 may fit here or in sense **(3)** below.

(3) shared passion or commitment, *with one heart/mind/purpose* (Demosth. 10.59.2; Philo, Mos. 1.136, Conf. 58, 1 Esdr 9:38; Jdt 13:17; Job 2:11 LXX; MPol 12:3) Ac 1:14; 2:1 v.l.; 4:24; 5:12; prob. 7:57; 15:25; perh. 8:6; 18:12; 19:29; W. ἐν ἑνὶ στόματι δοξάζειν τὸν θεόν Ro 15:6.—DELG s.v. θυμό. M-M. TW. Spicq.

The Italian Cohort in Acts 10:1

Irina Levinskaya

Acts 10 tells the story of the conversion in Caesarea of a Roman centurion, Cornelius, in the early AD 40s.[1] The question whether the army
in Judaea consisted of local regiments only, or included also auxiliary
units introduced from abroad, is controversial. Many scholars have
regarded it as impossible for Roman troops to be in Judaea under
Agrippa, i.e. between AD 41 and 44, and doubted Luke's story of a
conversion of an officer of a Roman auxiliary cohort on these
grounds.[2] But even if the years 41-44 are ruled out, the conversion
can still stand since a date before AD 41 fits well into Luke's chronological scheme. On the other hand, Speidel thinks that there could
have been Roman troops in Judaea even in Agrippa's time: 'Roman
troops stationed in client states, side by side with native irregulars are
not unusual: they are known, for example, in the Bosporan kingdom
and in Palmyra. Indeed the very army of the procurators must have
remained in Palestine when the country was given over to king
Agrippa I from AD 41 to 44. Client states were considered integral
parts of the Roman empire, and Agrippa II is known to have been

---

[1] I am most grateful to Joyce Reynolds who kindly read and commented
on a draft of this paper and made the English sound more natural than
anything I am able to produce now or (I am afraid) shall be able to produce
in the future. The article has also benefited considerably from her vigorous
criticism, though we are not agreed on all points.
[2] See, for instance, E. Schürer, "Die σπεῖρα Ἰταλική und die σπεῖρα
Σεβαστή (Act. 10,1. 27,1)," *ZWT* 18 (1875): 424; R. M. Grant, *A Historical
Introduction to the New Testament* (London: Collins, 1963), 145; E.
Haenchen, *Die Apostelgeschichte* (KEK; 7th ed.; Göttingen: Vandenhoeck &
Ruprecht, 1977), 346, n. 2.

especially subservient'.[3] He argued also that documentary evidence revealed Luke's account to have been 'more accurate and reliable than has often been admitted'. I believe that there is no reason at all to reject Luke's story about a Roman centurion, but every reason to accept that we do not at present know all that we should like of its context. My discussion will, I hope, introduce readers to some of the complexities of Roman military and administrative history relevant to the biblical story while illustrating the ease with which failure to pursue details can lead us astray. I also believe that it is appropriate to present an article discussing at length the minor details of the background of the Book of Acts in this *Festschrift* to Bruce Winter, who is one of the most energetic proponents of communicating the fruits of the labours of ancient historians and epigraphists as well as the results of archaeological discoveries to New Testament studies.

Of Cornelius himself we have no information except in Acts.[4] According to Acts 10:1 Cornelius served in an Italian cohort (ἐκ σπείρης τῆς καλουμένης Ἰταλικῆς). In modern commentaries on this verse his cohort is identified with *cohors II Italica*, known from several inscriptions. The degree of confidence in this identification varies — from the *undoubtedly* of Fitzmyer[5] to *wahrscheinlich* in Haenchen[6] — but I know of no commentaries where something

---

[3] M. P. Speidel, "The Roman Army in Judaea under the Procurators: The Italian and the Augustan Cohort in the Acts of the Apostles," *Ancient Society* 13/14 (1982/1983): 239.

[4] Most auxiliary centurions were promoted from the ranks, but there are exceptions and some were appointed from civilian status; see J. F. Gilliam, "The Appointment of Auxiliary Centurions (P Mich. 164)," *TAPA* 88 (1957): 155-68. The name Cornelius is also uninformative; it became widespread after P. Cornelius Sulla in 82 BC freed 10,000 slaves who took their names from his *gens*. In *CIL*, vols. II(3)-XV, there are about 2,600 inscriptions in which members of the *gens Cornelia* are mentioned; see A. Lussana, "Osservazioni sulle iscrizioni di una gens romana," *Epigraphica* 13 (1951): 33-43.

[5] J. A. Fitzmyer, *The Acts of the Apostles: A New Translation with Introduction and Commentary* (AB; New York: Doubleday, 1997), 449.

[6] Haenchen, *Die Apostelgeschichte*, 333.

different is proposed. This identification was first put forward by Bormann[7] and was accepted by Cichorius in his classic article on Roman cohorts.[8] Meanwhile we know two auxiliary cohorts in the Roman army whose names included the word *Italica*.[9] Both were citizen cohorts (*civium Romanorum*) and so belonged to a privileged section of the auxiliary troops. The soldiers of such cohorts were, at least when these were originally raised, Roman citizens,[10] and to a certain extent, they might be equated with legionaries, since,

---

[7]   E. Bormann, "Die älteste Gräberstrasse von Carnuntum," *Archaeologisch-epigraphische Mittheilungen aus Oesterreich-Ungarn* 18 (1895): 219.

[8]   C. Cichorius, "Cohors," *RE* 4 (1900): 231-356, esp. 304.

[9]   I know of only one article, written by an expert on the Roman army, in which the possibility of the identification of the first Italian cohort with the one in which Cornelius served is explicitly admitted: D. L. Kennedy, "Milliary Cohorts: The Evidence of Josephus, *B.J.* III.4.2 (67) and of Epigraphy," *ZPE* 50 (1983): 253-63, esp. 258; cf. also Speidel, "The Roman Army in Judaea," 237, n. 12, who seems to consider that the *cohors I Italica* may possibly have been stationed in Judaea in the same period.

[10]   Citizen cohorts in the Roman army belonged to two groups: (1) true citizen cohorts ([a] cohorts with the addition *voluntariorum*, such as for instance *cohortes voluntariorum civium Romanorum*; [b] *cohortes ingenuorum*; [c] *cohortes classicae*), which were raised early in the first century (mostly after the Pannonian revolt of AD 6 and Varus' defeat in Germany), but sometimes even earlier; see P. A. Brunt, "C. Fabricius Tuscus and an Augustan Dilectus," *ZPE* 13 (1974): 181; cf. M. P. Speidel, "Citizen Cohorts in the Roman Imperial Army: New Data on the Cohorts Apula, Campana, and III Campestris," *TAPA* 106 (1976): 340-41; and (2) titulary citizen cohorts which, from the Flavian period onwards, received this title as a distinction for gallant action (Speidel, "Citizen Cohorts," 340). Gradually the difference between privileged auxiliary cohorts and others ceased to exist; see K. Kraft, *Zur Rekrutierung der Alen und Kohorten an Rhein und Donau* (Dissertationes Bernenses, ser. 1, fasc. 3; Bern: A. Francke, 1951), 86: 'Seit Traian ist kein Unterschied mehr zwischen Bürgerkohorten und normalen Auxilien in der zivilen Rechtstellung ihrer Soldaten festzustellen'. In the military diploma of AD 93 (*CIL*:XVI, 38) we have a direct statement that *peregrini* were enrolled in the citizen cohorts: ... *qui militant in cohorte III Alpinorum et in VIII voluntariorum civium Romanorum qui peregrinae condicionis probati erant.*

according to Tacitus, *Ann.* 1.8, Augustus left to their soldiers a donative equal to that of legionaries: *legionariis aut cohortibus civium Romanorum trecentos nummos viritim dedit.*

The name suggests that both cohorts were raised in Italy,[11] but when and under what circumstances we do not know. Holder thinks that this occurred 'probably some time before the Pannonian Revolt of AD 6'.[12] He suggested this date having in mind the *cohors Apula*, another Italian cohort, which was recruited in Apulia long before AD 6. Cheesman thought that the *cohortes Italicae* formed a fresh series some time after the Pannonian Revolt and the Varian disaster.[13] Both these dates are equally possible, but there is no documentary or literary evidence for either. As to the recruits to the Italian cohorts, Cheesman thought that, as these cohorts are attested in service only in the East (in Syria and Cappadocia), they could represent 'the remainder of the 4,000 oriental freedmen whom Tiberius enrolled to put down the brigands in Sardinia (Tac. *Ann.* 2.85)'.[14] Tacitus was

---

[11] The auxiliary cohorts were usually named from the ethnicity of the people from whom they were originally recruited to the Roman army, either in the genitive plural (*Afrorum, Belgarum, Hispanorum*) or in adjectival form (*Alpina, Hispana, Apamena*). Sometimes geographical names, for instance *Dacica, Macedonica, Syriaca*, which were derived from the name of the province where they had been stationed, were added to their main name. For more details see Cichorius, "Cohors," 232-34.

[12] P. A. Holder, *Studies in the Auxilia of the Roman Army from Augustus to Trajan* (BAR International Series 70; Oxford: BAR, 1980), 66.

[13] G. L. Cheesman, *The Auxilia of the Roman Imperial Army* (Oxford: Clarendon, 1914), 66, n. 2.

[14] The expression which Tacitus used (*quattuor milia libertini generis ea superstitioni infecta*) is not very clear, and has given birth to a number of interpretations. I agree with Merrill (accepted in the translation in LCL: 'of freedmen stock'), who argued that *libertini generis* was not actually a periphrasis for *libertinorum*, but the 'scornful class appellation' for both freedmen and their descendants; see E. T. Merrill, "Expulsion of Jews from Rome under Tiberius," *CP* 14 (1919): 366-67. For a different point of view see M. Williams, "The Expulsion of the Jews from Rome in AD 19," *Latomus* 48 (1989): 770-72; see also E. M. Smallwood, *The Jews under Roman Rule from Pompey to Diocletian: A Study in Political Relations*

describing the measures taken by the Romans against votaries of Jewish and Egyptian cults. The passage is full of ambiguities, though comparison with other accounts of this event[15] shows that only Jews were sent to Sardinia. Cheesman gave no arguments in favour of his remarkable idea except that, if any of these unfortunates had survived, 'the Eastern provinces would have been the natural place to send them to'.[16] Natural they may have been, but natural things do not necessarily happen. Besides, it actually does not seem very natural. Why would the cohorts, if their soldiers had been the surviving representatives of the *taeterrima gens* (as Tacitus called Jews) expelled by Tiberius from Italy (according to Tacitus) or (more likely) from Rome (according to Suetonius, Dio Cassius and Josephus), have been called *Italica* and have belonged to the elite auxiliary troops of *civium Romanorum*?[17]

Cheesman mentioned freedmen in the light of Mommsen's account of the Italian citizen cohorts. The full name of the Italian cohorts included the word 'volunteers' — *voluntariorum*. Its meaning is problematic. Mommsen, followed by many, considered that volunteers of the citizen cohorts were freedmen.[18] It is known from quite a

---

(Studies in Judaism in Late Antiquity 20; 2nd ed.; Leiden: Brill, 1981), 207-08. Sardinia was notorious for its bad climate; cf. Livy, *Ab urbe condita* 23.34.11: *gravitas caeli*; Pomponius Mela, *De chorographia* 2.123: *ut fecunda, ita paene pestilens*; Pausanias, *Graeciae descriptio* 10.17.11: ἀὴρ θολερὸς καὶ νοσώδης. According to Tacitus, the Roman senate cynically reasoned that even if all Jews succumbed to the pestilent climate, the loss would be cheap (*vile damnum*).

[15] Suetonius, *Tib.* 36.1; Josephus, *A.J.* 18.81-84; cf. also Dio Cassius, *Historia Romana* 57.18.5a; Seneca, *Epistolae morales* 108.22.

[16] Cheesman, *The Auxilia*, 66, n. 2.

[17] Surprisingly, Cheesman's interpretation was accepted by T. R. S. Broughton, "The Roman Army," in *The Beginnings of Christianity, 5: Additional Notes to the Commentary* (ed. K. Lake and H. J. Cadbury; London: Macmillan, 1933), 442.

[18] Th. Mommsen, *Res gestae divi Augusti* (2nd ed.; Berlin: Weidemann, 1883), 72, n. 1; Th. Mommsen, *Römisches Staatsrecht* (3 vols.; 3rd ed.;

number of ancient sources that, under Augustus, there were levies of freedmen after the Pannonian Revolt and the Varian disaster. Velleius Paterculus, *Res gestae divi Augusti* 2.111.1, says that in AD 6 'levies were held, from every quarter all the veterans were recalled to the standards, men and women were compelled, in proportion to their income, to furnish freedmen as soldiers'[19] (*habiti itaque delectus, revocati undique et omnes veterani, viri feminaeque ex censu libertinum coactae dare militem*). According to Suetonius, *Aug.* 25, 'except as a fire-brigade at Rome, and when there was fear of riots in times of scarcity, he [Augustus] employed freedmen as soldiers only twice: once as a guard for the colonies in the vicinity of Illyricum, and again to defend the bank of the river Rhine.' These freedmen were kept in separate units (Augustus 'kept them under their original standard' — *sub priore vexillo habuit*), did not serve alongside free-born soldiers, and were not armed in the same way.[20] In 2.113 Velleius, describing Tiberius' army in Illyricum in AD 7, mentioned more than ten thousand veterans, and in addition a large number of volunteers (*pluribus quam decem veteranorum milibus, ad hoc magno voluntariorum numero*). If we compare all three passages it seems a natural conclusion that 'freedmen' of the first passage in Velleius are called 'volunteers' in the second and that since they were kept in separate units, the *cohortes voluntariorum* of the documentary sources are the best candidates for them. This is explicitly said by Macrobius, *Sat.* 1.11.32, according to whom Augustus recruited in Germany and in Illyricum quite a number of cohorts of freedmen, which he called 'volunteer cohorts': *Caesar Augustus in Germania et Illyrico cohortes libertinorum complures legit, quas voluntarias appelavit.*

Leipzig: S. Hirzel, 1887), 3:449, n. 3; 679, n. 1; cf., for instance, Cheesman, *The Auxilia*, 65; E. Ritterling, "Legio," *RE* 12 (1925): 1233, 1237.

[19] Tr. F. W. Shipley, LCL.

[20] Cf. also Dio Cassius, *Historia Romana* 55.31.1-2, who gave a slightly different turn to the event: according to him Augustus took the slaves from their owners on payment of their value and cost of their maintenance for six months. The same *dilectus* is also referred to by Pliny, *Nat.* 7.45.149.

The same equation of freedmen and volunteers can be found in *Scriptores Historiae Augustae, vita Marci Antonini philosophi* 21.6: *... et servos, quemadmodum bello Punico factum fuerat, ad militiam paravit, quos voluntarios exemplo volonum appelavit.*

The equation of volunteers with freedmen was, however, firmly rejected by Kraft whose examination of the term *voluntarius* led him to the conclusion that it always denoted a free citizen: '"voluntarius" im inerrömischen Gebrauch nirgends einen Freigelassen, sondern freie römische Bürger bedeutet.'[21] He also argued that the texts of Macrobius and of *Scriptores Historiae Augustae* were unreliable, and that the freedmen mentioned by Suetonius were used for short term duties only and that their units did not become permanent parts of the Roman army. He showed that, throughout the first century, the soldiers of voluntary cohorts had been recruited from free-born citizens. His arguments were supported by P. A. Brunt, who thought that the existence of a *cohors Apula* some time before the levies of AD 6 and 9/10 was 'proof that Roman citizens could serve in separate cohorts as well as legions' and gave 'an additional reason for believing with Kraft that the citizen cohorts under consideration were recruited in the same way as legions'.[22] Another piece of evidence which supports Kraft's theory was suggested by M. Speidel, who published a career inscription of a Roman soldier who was discharged as a *voluntarius* after he had served longer than the regular term: *missus voluntarius honesta missione.* Speidel thinks that the usage of *voluntarius* as a military *terminus technicus* which denotes soldiers who volunteered to continue their service after completion of their term 'sheds light on the disputed origin of the *cohortes voluntariorum*: they may have been formed from men of the legions, or from the *auxilia*, who were willing to put off their discharge.'[23] All these arguments make a

---

[21] Kraft, *Zur Rekrutierung der Alen und Kohorten*, 90.
[22] Brunt, "C. Fabricius and an Augustan Dilectus," 181.
[23] M. P. Speidel, "The Captor of Decebalus: A New Inscription from Philippi," *JRS* 60 (1970): 151.

strong case in favour of free-born recruitment to the citizen cohorts. On the other hand, I find it difficult to dismiss completely the definite connection made by Roman historians of different generations, between the recruitment of slaves (who were immediately liberated) and the idea of free choice which was denied to free men subjected to the levy.[24] The antiquarian comparison of volunteers and *volones*, made by Macrobius, is based on this paradox. I am tempted to argue that *cohortes voluntariorum* may have consisted both of freedmen and of free-born citizens (for instance, soldiers of the legions who volunteered to put off their discharge), who quite possibly served in separate centuries of the auxiliary citizen cohorts.

Epigraphical and Other Evidence for the Italian Cohors
The earliest reference to an Italian cohort is generally considered to be in an inscription from Pisidian Antioch which W. H. Ramsay interpreted as the epitaph[25] of the first priestess of *Dea Iulia Augusta*, under which name Livia Drusilla, widow of Augustus, was consecrated by Claudius.[26]

Ramsay presents the inscription as follows:

```
        [D.?              M.?]
        [Caristaniae Fronti]-
        nae I]uliae sa[cer-
        d]o[ti] deae Iu[liae
        Au]gustae ma[ndatu
  4     T. Vo]lumni Varro[nis
        II]vir. quaest. III
```

---

[24] The most explicit example is Livy, *Ab urbe condita* 22.57.11: *vellentne militare*.

[25] No one as far as I know has questioned this interpretation, although Joyce Reynolds with whom I discussed it suggested that it might be useful to reconsider Ramsay's supplements.

[26] W. H. Ramsay, "Early History of Province Galatia," in *Anatolian Studies, Presented to W. H. Buckler* (ed. W. M. Calder and J. Keil; Manchester: Manchester University Press, 1939), 206-08.

p]ontif. praef. coh.

. Ç.R̲.] Italic. trib. mil.

8   l]eg. VȮI Claudiae

piae fidelis

[CC?   DD?]

[To the Di Manes ?]. To [Caristania Frontina Iu]lia, the priestess of the goddess Iu[lia Au]gusta on the [order of Titus Vo]lumnius Varro, duumvir, quaestor 3 times, pontifex, prefect of the Italian cohort [of Roman citizens], military tribune of Legion VII Claudian Faithful Loyal.[27] [Colonia Caesarea dedicated this ?].

Ramsay dated the lettering of the inscription to the period between AD 14 and 81: 'The lettering is post-Augustan, and earlier than Domitian.' But since the legion in which Volumnius Varro served as a military tribune had received the title Claudia Pia Fidelis in 42[28] and 'the priestess was nominated in 41' he thought that the inscription was probably engraved about AD 65-75. This date is insecurely founded,[29] but it is not my concern here. I am interested in establish-

---

[27] It is interesting to note that the civil and military appointments which Volumnius Varro held are listed in reverse order: the civil, which start from the highest municipal office (*duumvir*) followed by the less important (*quaestor*), are in descending order, while the military are in ascending: prefect of a cohort and then tribune of a legion. Varro's municipal offices are mentioned first, which does not mean that he necessarily held them before he started his military service, though more often the holders of equestrian military appointments were recruited from those who had reached the level of *duumvir*; see E. Birley, *Roman Britain and the Roman Army: Collected Papers* (Kendal: T. Wilson, 1953), 133.

[28] Dio Cassius, *Historia Romana* 60.15.4: 'He first rewarded the soldiers in various ways, especially by causing the legions composed of citizens (the seventh and the eleventh) to be named Claudian and Loyal and Patriotic by the senate' (tr. E. Cary on the basis of the version of H. B. Forster, LCL). Ramsay placed this in AD 43, but the right date is AD 42; see Ritterling, "Legio," 1617.

[29] The cult of Iulia Augusta was introduced in AD 41, but it was only Ramsay's guess that the Iulia of the inscription was the first priestess. The inscription (whether or not it was an epitaph as Ramsay thought), could have been engraved at any time between AD 42 and 81 if Ramsay was right about

ing an approximate date for Volumnius Varro's service in the Italian cohort. He could have been a tribune of Legion VII at any time between AD 42 (or even earlier since theoretically he could become a tribune before this legion received its honorary titles) and Domitian's reign. There was no fixed term for equestrian tenures of command, but a period of three or four years was quite a usual practice;[30] so that Volumnius Varro could have been prefect[31] of an Italian cohort any time between the mid 30s and the end of the 70s[32] and could even have been a commander when Cornelius was a centurion.

The possibility that the cohort of this inscription was the one in which Cornelius served was mentioned by Saddington.[33] He based his

---

the dating of the lettering. This *ante quem* in Domitian's reign has not been noticed and the equestrian *militiae* of T. Volumnius Varro are commonly dated to the Claudian-Neronian period; see, for instance, H. Devijver, *Prosopographia militiarum equestrium quae fuerunt ab Augusto ad Gallienum*, 2 (Leuven: Universitaire Pers Leuven, 1977), V 130, and Holder, *Studies in the Auxilia*, 251, E 90.

[30] Birley, *Roman Britain*, 137-38.

[31] The commanders of the *cohortes voluntariorum* were normally *tribuni*; the exceptions are very rare and are usually dated to a later period: the *cohors VIII voluntariorum* was commanded by a *tribunus* before Domitian, but from the middle of the second century by a *praefectus*; in the *cohors XXIV voluntariorum* a similar change took place at the end of the second or at the beginning of the third century; see M. Le Glay, "Le commandement des *cohortes voluntariorum* de l'armée romaine" with *Addendum*: J. F. Gilliam, "Another Prefect in a *cohors voluntariorum*," *Ancient Society* 3 (1972): 209-22. With the Italian cohorts (no matter whether the cohort of this inscription was the first or the second) the change was in the opposite direction: it was in the later period that they were under command of tribunes. Le Glay in his list of citizen cohorts (both *cohortes voluntariorum* and *cohortes ingenuorum*) does not mention this inscription.

[32] Ramsay claimed that T. Volumnius Varro 'served two equestrian militiae after 41' since he thought that Volumnius Varro 'nominated Julia Caristania priestess of Julia Augusta' in AD 41 as 'duumvir and pontifex' (Ramsay, "Early History," 208.

[33] D. B. Saddington, "The Roman *auxilia* in the East: Different from the West," in *Limes XVIII: Proceedings of the XVIIIth International Congress of Roman Frontier Studies Held in Amman, Jordan (September 2000)*, 2 (ed.

opinion on the traditional notion that Cornelius' cohort was the second Italian and on the interpretation of this inscription by Kraft, who suggested that there should be restored a numeral *II* instead of a title *civium Romanorum*.[34] Kraft argued that the title *civium Romanorum* was extremely rare in the inscriptions before the Flavians and proposed that since the second Italian cohort was attested as being stationed in the East it was possible that it was also mentioned in this inscription. This proposition cannot be accepted on epigraphical grounds. Both Kraft and Saddington, who refers to Ramsay's reading of the inscription as an 'emendation', did not take into account that Ramsay in his publication of the inscription marked the letters *C* and *R* with underdots which means that he saw traces of letters which he took to be *C* and *R* on the stone. Kraft's suggestion has not been generally accepted and it has usually been assumed that the Italian cohort of this inscription was the first.[35]

Ramsay shows one space unfilled before his hypothetical *C.R.* in the beginning of line 7, but one cannot be sure that his drawing is precise — significantly he made no suggestion as to which cohort figured in the inscription, though the restoration of its number would be obvious were he sure that there was space for only one letter. One might have hoped that there would have been some guidance on this

---

Ph. Freeman et al.; BAR International Series 1084 (II); Oxford: BAR, 2002), 880.

[34] Kraft, *Zur Rekrutierung der Alen und Kohorten*, 195.

[35] See, for instance, J. Spaul, *Cohors²: The Evidence for and a Short History of the Auxiliary Infantry Units of the Imperial Roman Army* (BAR International Series 841; Oxford: Archaeopress, 2000), 27, who notes, however, that Volumnius Varro 'may have commanded the *cohors II Italica*', but thinks that 'it seems more likely that he commanded the unit which was stationed in Cappadocia'. This remark seems to show that Spaul considers the *cohors I Italica* to have been stationed in Cappadocia. But on p. 26 of his work he contradicts himself and claims with a wrong reference to M. P. Speidel, that the '*cohors I Italica* was serving in Syria in mid-first century'. Spaul aimed to update and replace the article by Cichorius (see n. 8), but at least in the part on Italian cohorts which I have checked, made a number of mistakes on some of which I shall comment later.

point from the indications that Ramsay gave about the variable widths of the letters.[36] He registered that some letters, such as *DOQ* were very broad, some — *ERL* — comparatively narrow. Thus in line 6 we have fourteen letters (thirteen preserved plus one which can be easily restored), among which one letter repeated twice (*O*) is wide and two (*E* and *R*) are narrow. We have also a narrow letter *I* in this line. In line 7 in which the Italian cohort is mentioned, we have thirteen letters fully preserved and traces of two more. There are no wide letters in this line and two of them (*R* and *L*) repeated twice are narrow. The narrow letter *I* is repeated in this line four times. The longest surviving line, line 4, has sixteen letters (ten are preserved and six are plausibly restored) of which three are narrow and two are broad. In this line the letter *I* is repeated twice. There was then room for the figure *II* in line 7. If Volumnius Varro served in the second Italian cohort the line will have had seventeen letters which makes it equal in length only to the line in which Ramsay restored the name of the priestess, but shorter if we take into consideration the width of the letters.[37] To sum up, I think that theoretically either of the Italian co-

---

[36] Unfortunately the inscription perished immediately after Ramsay had copied it. He told a sad and, alas, quite familiar story about its destruction. The block of local limestone on which it was inscribed was incorporated into the wall of a house. Ramsay spent three hours copying it, standing on a ladder lent by the owner, until light failed. 'Next morning,' writes Ramsay, 'I returned, hoping to make a squeeze. The lord of the mansion (νοικοκύρις) gave the ladder with a quaint smile. Ascending, I found that the stone was covered with a layer of mortar. Then I understood that smile' (Ramsay, "Early History," 207).

[37] B. Levick and S. Jameson, "C. Crepereius Gallus and His *Gens*," *JRS* 54 (1964): 99, n. 9, considered that the restoration of the name can hardly be right, given that it 'requires 17 letters in the second line of the inscription against an average 14½ in the eight other full lines', but since on Ramsay's restoration of the name one letter (*O*) is broad and two (*R*, twice and *E*) are narrow and there is also a narrow letter *I* repeated three times, it is at least possible on grounds of space, though questionable in view of our complete lack of information about the lady. There is no valid evidence for the introduction of a lady with the name *Caristania Frontina Iulia*. All that we know of the subject's name is that it included *Iulia*. Ramsay's restoration is

horts could have been mentioned in this inscription but given the lack of a photograph or squeeze it seems imprudent to restore a figure.[38] All that we know about the Italian cohorts from this inscription then is that between the mid 30s and the early years of Domitian's reign one of them was stationed in an unknown place, and was under the command of a *praefectus*.

Let us look now at the other evidence presently available about the Italian cohorts. I shall start with the second cohort.

The earliest evidence is in the epitaph of a certain Proculus, found at Carnuntum (Petronell in modern Austria);[39] he had served as an *optio* (that is, a junior officer who assisted a centurion and, if needed, could take command of a *centuria* in place of a centurion) in the second Italian cohort of Roman citizens:

> Proculus Rabili f(ilius) Col(lina) Philadel(phia) mil(itavit)[40] optio coh(ortis) II Italic(ae) c(ivium) R(omanorum) (centuria) Fa[us]tini, ex vexil(lariis) sagit(tariis) exer(citus) Syriaci stip(endiorum) VII, vixit an(nos) XXVI, Apuleius frater f(aciundum) c(uravit).

> Proculus, son of Rabilus, of the tribe Collina,[41] from Philadelphia, served as an *optio* of the second Italian cohort of Roman citizens, from the century of Faustinus, a member of the vexillation of archers in the Syrian army, served for seven years, lived 26 years; his brother Apuleius undertook the making (of this tomb).

---

unjustified. Also unjustified is her treatment by Spaul, *Cohors²*, 27, n. 3, who accepted Ramsay's restoration of her name and stated that she was the wife of Volumnius Varro — which is theoretically possible, but wholly unproved.

[38]   Thus Devijver, *Prosopographia*, V 130, was absolutely right in rejecting any identification and in asking *quae cohors* instead.

[39]   Bormann, "Die älteste Gräberstrasse," 218-19; *CIL* III, 13483a = *L'année épigraphique* 1896, 27 = Dessau, *ILS* 9168.

[40]   I accept the reading by Speidel, "The Roman Army in Judaea," 235. Bormann suggests *mil(es)*.

[41]   Claudius, Nero and the Flavian emperors assigned new citizens to the tribe *Quirina*, but there are other examples of Philadelphians and also inhabitants of Gerasa and Gadara who were assigned to the tribe *Collina*. See B. Isaac, "The Decapolis in Syria: A Neglected Inscription," *ZPE* 44 (1981): 73.

The generally accepted date of the inscription, AD 69/70, is due to Bormann who connected it with the expedition of C. Licinius Mucianus from Syria to Italy (Tacitus, *Hist.* 2.83). The subject had served for seven years when he died, so started his military career in AD 62/63.

Thus from this inscription we know that a task force drawn from the second Italian cohort was described as belonging to the Syrian army. If the unit in which Proculus served belonged to the army led by Mucianus to Italy, there is no difficulty in assuming that soldiers from the Judaean army were described as part of the Syrian army, since Mucianus' 'Syrian army' is not the army garrisoning *in* Syria, but the army which Mucianus brought *from* Syria. Besides, as Speidel argued, 'Syria was the most important command in the Orient and various other armies contributing to its bowmen task force could be subsumed under its name. The Italian cohort could have been stationed in Judaea despite the fact that one of its soldiers was designated as *vexillarius sagittarius* of the Syrian army.'[42] It was with this inscription in view that Bormann identified the Italian cohort of the Book of Acts with the *cohors II Italica*. But it is worthwhile to remember that we have no evidence for the location of *cohors I Italica* at this time. Meanwhile, the inscription supplies us with interesting information. First, this cohort had an attachment of archers; secondly, at least some of its soldiers were enrolled locally. Proculus was a Roman citizen as indicated by his *tribus*, but as his father's Arab name suggests he was possibly not born a citizen, but received his citizenship on enrolment. His father's name also shows that the Philadelphia of this inscription is Amman in Jordan.[43]

---

[42] Speidel, "The Roman Army in Judaea," 236-37.
[43] Approximately at the time when Proculus started his military service other recruits from Amman were also enrolled in the Roman auxiliary forces, probably because of the Parthian campaigns of Corbulo; see Speidel, "The Roman Army in Judaea," 236.

The cohort is attested in Syria by the diplomata *CIL* XVI, 35 of AD 88 and *RMD* 4 of AD 91. The diplomata also show what the earlier evidence does not: by these years the unit included non-citizens since some of its soldiers received their citizenship on discharge like soldiers of non-citizen auxiliary cohorts.

The second Italian cohort is also mentioned in an epitaph of its tribune, C. Paccius Firmus from Rome, with a date unspecified within the first and second centuries.[44]

In the middle of the second century, the second Italian cohort was still stationed in Syria as appears from a diploma of AD 157, where it is mentioned among other cohorts under the command of the legate of Syria, Attidius Cornelianus.[45]

Another inscription which mentions an Italian cohort was found at *Forum Sempronii* in Umbria.[46] This cohort is unnumbered, and some scholars have identified it with the second Italian cohort[47] and some with the first,[48] though none has given explanation for their preference. It records the gratitude of the community to the family of Lucius Maesius Rufus for the supply of grain to the city. His *cursus honorum* runs as follows:

> L(ucio) Maesio L(ucii) f(ilio) Pol(lia) Rufo proc(uratori) Aug(usti), trib(uno) mil(itum) leg(ionis) XV Apollinaris, trib(uno) coh(ortis) mil(liariae) Italic(ae) Volunt(ariorum) quae est in Syria, praef(ecto) fabrum bis.

---

[44] *CIL* VI, 3528.

[45] *CIL* XVI, 106 = *ILS* 9057.

[46] *CIL* XI, 6117.

[47] Devijver, *Prosopographia*, M 7; E. Birley, "Alae and Cohortes Milliariae," Corolla memoriae Erich Swoboda dedicata, *Römische Forschungen in Niederösterreich* 5 (1966): 65; Cichorius, "Cohors," 304; Holder, *Studies in the Auxilia*, 68; L. Boffo, *Iscrizioni greche e latine per lo studio della Bibbia* (Brescia: Paideia, 1994), 299-300.

[48] H.-G. Pflaum, *Les carrières procuratoriennes équestres sous le Haut-empire Romain*, 3 (Paris, Paul Geuthner, 1961), 985, n. 117 ter; A. Degrassi, "Epigraphica III," *Memorie Accad. Naz. Lincei, classe di Scienze mor. stor. e filologiche*, ser. 8a, 13 (1967): 22. Kennedy, "Milliary Cohorts," 257, thinks that both cohorts are possible.

> To Lucius Maesius Rufus, the son of Lucius, from the tribe Pollia,
> procurator of Augustus, military tribune of the legion XV Apollinaris,
> tribune of the milliary Italian cohort of volunteers which is in Syria,
> twice prefect of engineers.

The title *civium Romanorum* is absent here, but instead, for the first
time, the Italian cohort is called a voluntary unit (*voluntariorum*) and
milliary (*milliaria*). Cichorius, who considered this cohort to be the
second, derived its full name from this inscription, adding 'of *civium
Romanorum*'.[49] This restored full name, which has never been attested by documentary evidence, has found its way into the majority
of commentaries on the Book of Acts. The identification of the cohort
mentioned in this inscription with either of the Italian cohorts deserves discussion.

The inscription has no date. Pflaum thought it was produced some
time between the Flavian period and the beginning of the reign of
Septimius Severus. He considered the *terminus ante quem* of the *cursus honorum* to be determined by the words *quae est in Syria*, since in
AD 194, Septimius Severus divided Syria into two parts (*Syria Coele*
and *Syria Phoenice*), and the designation *Syria* ceased to be used.[50]
Devijver gave the same date for the inscription, but he thought that it
more probably belonged to the beginning of the second century than
to the end.[51] The proposal in *PIR²* M 79 to date it instead in the
Flavian period is offered without serious arguments merely on the
grounds that Maesius Rufus could have served in the second Italian
cohort which at this time *ad exercitum Syriacum pertinebat*.

The date at which milliary units were first formed is controversial.[52] The unresolved scholarly debate is reflected in the latest edition
of the *Oxford Classical Dictionary*: here *s.v.* "cohors" we are told that
'cohortes milliariae ... were used from the Neronian period onwards'

---

49 Cichorius, "Cohors," 304.
50 Pflaum, *Les carrières procuratoriennes*, 985.
51 Devijver, *Prosopographia*, M 7.
52 I am planning to discuss this issue elsewhere.

while *s.v.* "auxilia" that 'Probably in the Flavian era larger regiments (milliary) were created.' The earliest documentary evidence for the existence of milliary cohorts dates to AD 85 when two such cohorts (*I Britannica milliaria* and *I Brittonum milliaria*) were mentioned in military diplomas for Pannonia.[53] After AD 85 milliary cohorts regularly appeared in the diplomata. Birley argues that 'in diplomas which attach the title to some units, we shall be justified in holding that the units not so styled were not milliary'.[54] In each of the diplomata of AD 88 and 91 there was one cohort which was styled milliary, but not the second Italian. According to Birley this means that it was not milliary at the time when the diplomata were produced; but Maesius Rufus served in a *milliary* Italian cohort.[55] If it was not the second as the diplomata testify, then it should be the first. Holder firmly rejected this possibility on the grounds that the first Italian cohort was at this time stationed in Cappadocia.[56] But was it?

The first Italian cohort is mentioned in three inscriptions and quite possibly also by Arrian.[57]

---

[53] *CIL* XVI, 31.

[54] Birley, "Alae et Cohortes," 61.

[55] It was also not called *milliaria* in the later diploma of AD 157, though in this diploma only an *ala* was styled milliary, but none of the cohorts were.

[56] Holder, *Studies in the Auxilia*, 68, n. 12.

[57] The reader who consults a recent book by J. Spaul will be surprised to find there much more evidence for the first Italian cohort than anywhere else. The explanation is simple: Spaul decided to identify *cohors I Italica* with the *cohors I Flavia civium Romanorum*. He justifies this by the following arguments: 'It is highly unlikely that Vespasian, Titus or Domitian raised a citizen unit which would use the numeral *I* as a matter of right. But if one of the Flavian emperors wished to decorate a citizen unit, the gift of citizenship would be inappropriate, but the gift of the Imperial family name would indicate the special devotion of the unit to the Imperial dynasty.' This is a bizarre argument, as is Spaul's statement that 'the inscriptions which mention *I Italica* all seem to belong to the first century, while the inscriptions which mention *I Flavia* date from AD 88 onwards.' This sentence is written at the bottom of a page, at whose top two pieces of evidence for *cohors I Italica* from the middle of the second century are given.

The first inscription is an epitaph to P. Valerius Priscus from Urci in *Hispania Citerior*, who died at the age of 65. He held his appointment in the *militia secunda* as *tribunus cohortis I Italicae miliariae Voluntariorum civium Romanorum in Cappadocia*. The inscription is dated to the middle of the second century. Valerius Priscus' *militia prima* was with the *cohors Apamenorum saggitariorum* which was then stationed in Cappadocia. We know that this cohort was in Egypt in AD 145,[58] but not when it was first stationed there. We know that Valerius Priscus served in this cohort some time before AD 145 (but not how long before). He served his *militia tertia* as prefect of a milliary *ala I Numidica* in Africa, and ended his military career as prefect of *ala I Hispanorum Auriana* which was stationed in Raetia and is known to have been among the troops in this province between AD 107 and AD 156/157. Before the reign of Trajan command of an *ala milliaria* could follow immediately after the military tribunate, whereas later it followed that of an *ala quingenaria*.[59] Thus Valerius Priscus' military career can be dated to the time before Hadrian and it is clear that the first Italian cohort was stationed in Cappadocia at the beginning of the second century.

The second inscription is for C. Nasennius Marcellus Senior who served his *militia prima* and *militia secunda* in the same regiments as Valerius Priscus but a few decades later.[60] It is assumed by scholars that the first Italian cohort (*cohors I Italica civium Romanorum voluntariorum*) was then in Cappadocia,[61] but this is not mentioned in his epitaph explicitly.

---

[58] *P. Lond.* 178 in F. G. Kenyon, *Greek Papyri in the British Museum*, 2 (London: British Museum, 207); A. Degrassi, "Epigraphica III," 21; *L'année épigraphique* 1974, 226.

[59] Birley, *Roman Britain*, 149.

[60] *CIL* XIV, 171 = Dessau, *ILS* 2741.

[61] See, for instance, H. Devijver, *De Aegypto et exercitu Romano sive prosopographia militiarum equestrium quae ab Augusto ad Gallienum seu statione seu origine ad Aegyptum pertinebant* (Studia Hellenistica 22; Leuven: Universitaire Stichting van België, 1975), 78, 86.

The first Italian cohort is also mentioned in a Greek honorary inscription from Samos[62] which E. Ritterling dated to the time of Trajan or Marcus Aurelius.[63] The cohort's number is restored, but I believe with certainty. From this inscription we know the *cursus honorum* of a certain Gaius Flavianus who served his *militia prima* as a prefect of *cohors I Numidarum*, his *militia secunda* as tribune of *cohors I Italica* (χειλί[αρχος σπείρης πρώτη]ς Ἰταλικῆς)[64] and his *militia tertia* as prefect of *ala II Gallorum*.

Finally, the first Italian cohort is thought to have been mentioned by Arrian in his *Acies contra Alanos*. Arrian was Hadrian's legate of Cappadocia in AD 131-37, and his work is a literary version of the orders of march which were issued by him in AD 135 to repel the incursion of the Alans. The Italian cohort (or the Italians, as he sometimes referred to this regiment) was among his Cappadocian troops: πεζοὶ δὲ ἐπὶ τούτοις τετάχθων ... οἵ τε Ἰταλοὶ καὶ Κυρηναίων οἱ παρόντες (*Acies* 3); προτετάθων δὲ αὐτῶν οἱ τῆς σπείρας τῆς Ἰταλικῆς πεζοί. πάντων δὲ ἡγείσθω Πούλχερ, ὅστις καὶ τῆς σπείρας τῆς Ἰταλικῆς ἄρχει (*Acies* 9); καὶ οἱ τῶν Ἰταλῶν ἱππῆς (*Acies* 13).

This survey of evidence for the first Italian cohort shows that we do not know for certain where it was stationed before the second century. Holder's assumption that it cannot be the cohort of Maesius Rufus' inscription since it was at that time stationed in Cappadocia is not sound.

---

[62] Spaul, *Cohors²*, 27, names Chios as the provenance of this inscription with a reference to *IGR* IV, 964. He remarks that Dessau, *ILS* 8865, gives it as Samos; in fact all scholars (including E. Fabricius, "Alterthuemer auf der Insel Samos," *Mitteilungen des deutschen archäologischen Institutes in Athen* 9 [1884]: 262; *IGR* IV, 964; as well as Dessau) give it as Samos.

[63] E. Ritterling, "Zur Erklärung von Arrians Ἔκταξις κατ' Ἀλανῶν," *Wiener Studien, Zeitschrift für Klassische Philologie* 24 (1902): 362, n. 2.

[64] Cichorius, "Cohors," 305, thought that Flavianus might have possibly served in the *legio I Italica* rather than in the first Italian cohort, but, as Ritterling, "Zur Erklärung," 362, n. 2, pointed out, the size of the lacuna is not big enough for the restoration λεγεῶνος.

Holder also finds suspect the suggestion that the cohort which is mentioned in this inscription (in his view the second) was *milliaria*. The post of Maesius Rufus in the Italian cohort is abbreviated as *trib. coh. mil. Italic. Volunt. quae est in Syria*. Holder claims that this is an error for *trib. mil. coh. Italic. Volunt.*, 'since the title *milliaria* is not abbreviated as "mil." and does not appear in that position in other inscriptions'.[65] Both assumptions are mistaken. The word *milliaria* was abbreviated as *mil.* and did appear in that position.[66] But despite the fact that Holder's arguments are wrong, he is right in denying a milliary status to the second Italian cohort. The only inscription which describes an Italian cohort as milliary refers in my opinion to the first Italian cohort.

To sum up. First, there is no foundation for the choice of the second Italian cohort as the one mentioned in the Book of Acts: either of the Italian cohorts is equally possible. Secondly, the name of the Italian cohorts should not be given in a commentary to the Acts in the extended form which includes *milliaria*. There is no evidence that milliary cohorts existed as early as the AD 40s and we have no reliable grounds for believing that the second Italian cohort was one thousand men strong even later when such cohorts did exist.

---

[65] Holder, *Studies in the Auxilia*, 66.
[66] See, for instance, *CIL* III, 8353: *tr(i)b(unus) coh(ortis) I mil(iariae) Delm(atarum)*.

Before Paul Arrived in Corinth:

The Mission Strategies in 1 Corinthians 2:2 and Acts 17

Conrad Gempf

Introduction

Bruce Winter's important work on 1 Corinthians[1] revolves around the question that arises when one considers the variety and seriousness of difficulties that Paul is required to deal with in 1 Corinthians: Why did he not deal with these matters when he was there with them? To some extent, the problems must have arisen or developed *after* Paul's 18-month stay in the city.[2] In the process of elucidating the situation, Winter brings much of the cultural background of the Roman colony of Corinth to light. In the Introduction to his work, he was careful to distinguish between the 'cultural and historical background' of the city and its people (and therefore Paul's addressees) from the 'theological background' of Paul himself.[3]

Winter helpfully extends our notion of cultural background forward in time to consider social and cultural events in the ongoing experience of the community in Corinth. We might usefully extend the Pauline background slightly backward in time to consider events in Paul's own experience just prior to his coming to Corinth. In particular, there is a theory once very popular and espoused by Sir

---

[1]   Bruce Winter, *After Paul Left Corinth: The Influence of Secular Ethics and Social Change* (Grand Rapids: Eerdmans, 2001).

[2]   Winter, *After Paul Left Corinth*, 2-4.

[3]   Treating the former in the volume *After Paul Left Corinth*, while intending to treat the latter in a future volume; see Winter, *After Paul Left Corinth*, xii.

William Ramsay which has never been convincingly answered but on which some of Winter's work throws new light.

Before Paul went to Corinth, Acts tells us, he was in Athens. As Paul himself does sometimes reflect on one community in light of another (cf. 1 Cor 11:16; 2 Cor 9:2), there seems nothing inherently implausible about a theory that suggests that Paul himself would be fine-tuning his own methods and strategies in light of his experiences. It does not seem impossible, for instance, that the fiasco of miscommunication at Lystra (Acts 14:8-13) is part of the reason why Paul thereafter sticks to major metropolitan centres.[4] At the very least, it seems clear that Luke does not confine himself to incidents in which Paul shines.[5]

In a wonderful display of intertextuality, Ramsay presented a theory that fitted two cities and New Testament books into place with the satisfying 'click' of a jigsaw puzzle piece deftly chosen. In Athens, Paul spoke with great eloquence and learning to the Athenian philosophers (Acts 17:22-31). The harvest of souls was meagre. Then Paul went to Corinth. From his own letter we find that when he came to them he made a conscious decision to 'know nothing among you except Jesus Christ, and him crucified' (1 Cor 2:2). For Ramsay, this was no coincidence:

> It would appear that Paul was disappointed and perhaps disillusioned by his experience in Athens. He felt that he had gone at least as far as was right in the way of presenting his doctrine in a form suited to the current philosophy; and the result had been little more than naught.

---

4 Conrad Gempf, "Mission and Misunderstanding: Paul and Barnabas in Lystra (Acts 14:8-20)," in *Mission and Meaning: Essays Presented to Peter Cotterell* (ed. A. Billington et al.; Carlisle: Paternoster, 1995), 58-59.

5 Even apart from Lystra and the Eutychus incident (Acts 20:7-9), Luke's Paul is someone who does not even get along with someone whose nickname is 'Son of Encouragement' (Acts 15:39) and who must apologize for his temper (Acts 23:3-5).

When he went on from Athens to Corinth, he no longer spoke in the
philosophical style.[6]

Ramsay points to the general character of 1 Corinthians as well as to
2:2 in particular: 'nowhere throughout his writings is he so hard on
the wise, the philosophers, and the dialecticians.'[7] There seems also
to be a clue in the Acts account of Paul's work in Corinth. When Acts
18:5 reports that 'Paul was devoting himself completely to the word,
solemnly testifying to the Jews that Jesus was the Christ,' Ramsay
sees significance there. He writes that this picture of Paul emphasises
a 'specially marked character in the Corinthian preaching'.[8]

As we shall see in the next section, this idea was only partially answered by academic argument,[9] but rather effectively shelved for
other reasons entirely. The time is ripe for a re-examination, however.

Athens and the 'Failure' of Worldly Wisdom
In discussing other ideas of Ramsay concerning the book of Acts,
Colin Hemer expressed the view that what caused them to fall out of
currency was not any defect in their reasoning or any decisive rebut-
tal, but a shift in the wind of academic fashion.[10] Specifically, an increased interest in the theological leanings and redactional activities
of the New Testament writers caused a pendulum swing away from

---

[6]   William Ramsay, *St Paul the Traveller and the Roman Citizen* (London:
Hodder & Stoughton, 1895), 252.
[7]   Ramsay, *St Paul the Traveller*, 252.
[8]   Ramsay, *St Paul the Traveller*, 252-53.
[9]   I am thinking primarily here of N. B. Stonehouse, *Paul before the
Areopagus and Other New Testament Studies* (London: Tyndale Press,
1957), 32-36, a work which will be summarised in the next section. Litfin
notes a few other scholars who have taken sides on the question; see Duane
Litfin, *St Paul's Theology of Proclamation: 1 Corinthians 1-4 and Greco-
Roman Rhetoric* (SNTSMS 79; Cambridge: CUP, 1994), 238, n. 73 (without,
oddly, mentioning either Ramsay or Stonehouse).
[10]   C. J. Hemer, *The Book of Acts in the Setting of Hellenistic History* (ed.
Conrad Gempf; WUNT 49; Tübingen: Mohr, 1989), 2. Cf. W. W. Gasque, *A
History of the Criticism of the Acts of the Apostles* (Tübingen: Mohr, 1975).

what came to be regarded as naïve historicism. This swing, coupled with the clinging to modernist ideals that, somehow, real history would be objective and detached, created an environment in New Testament studies where it was unacceptable to view Acts as an attempt at history in even the broadest sense. Any discussion about whether Paul changed his mission strategy between Acts 17 and 18 would be a discussion about Luke's imagination rather than Paul. And because it was no longer possible to read statements in 1 Corinthians as pertaining to matters written up in Acts, the question lost its poignancy and had no relevance to what were judged to be the main interests of scholars.

There were some who persisted in the then unfashionable notion that Acts was of interest to Pauline studies. Among them was Bruce who wrote that Ramsay's theory 'has little to commend it'.[11] He offers no argument, other than a footnote referring the reader to Ned Stonehouse, one of the few to tackle Ramsay's theory head on. His primary reasons for rejecting the idea were that (1) Luke's presentation of Paul is that of a masterful orator not a failure; (2) the results attained in Athens, even if disappointing, are not emphasised by Luke nor need they be caused by Paul's method; and (3) the speech is not Paul's only mission work there — the preaching in the synagogue and in the market place is portrayed as being about 'Jesus and the resurrection', a fairly good summary of the message which Paul (and the other preachers in Acts) delivered with good effects elsewhere.[12]

In the main, however, the matter was not discussed until scholarly fashion began changing in the past twenty years. For while New Testament studies concerned itself with inward-looking theology and redaction, and even while it began its still-continuing fascination with narrative method, classicists and archaeologists continued to ac-

---

[11] F. F. Bruce, *The Book of the Acts* (rev. ed.; NICNT; Grand Rapids: Eerdmans, 1988), 344.

[12] Stonehouse, *Paul before the Areopagus*, 32-36.

cumulate masses of inscriptional and other non-literary evidence, including, inevitably, materials that had direct relevance to the period of
the first century and even to the specific places and peoples in the
biblical texts. Works like the Hemer volume and the Acts in Its First
Century Setting volumes did much to restore the credibility of Acts
and marked a change in the tide of academic fashion.[13]

Thus in the works of more recent writers who take the historical
background more seriously, Ramsay's theory has occasionally re-
emerged. Murphy-O'Connor, for example, composed a popular
commentary on 1 Corinthians at about the same time as a book on the
texts and archaeology of Corinth. In the commentary, he wrote:
'[Paul] had come to Corinth in a depressed state. After his failure at
Athens (Acts 17:32-33), he had to face the cynical weakness of a
great port-city ... Yet he refused the artifices of rhetoric and logic, and
simply proclaimed Jesus as the Crucified Lord.'[14] Similarly, even
Witherington is attracted to it, dismissing it as a major factor in his
Acts commentary ('... this is probably reading too much into the
text'[15]), yet of two minds in his Corinthians commentary: 'I doubt

---

[13] Hemer, *Book of Acts*. The five Acts in Its First Century Setting volumes,
published jointly by Eerdmans and Paternoster, beginning in 1993 under the
series editorship of Bruce Winter, with I. H. Marshall and David Gill as
consulting editors, consolidated a wealth of information from the non-
literary as well as the literary sources. Note that it is not merely conservative
answers that went out of fashion and are coming back in, but the perception
that someone working with the text should *ask* about the value of traditions,
as opposed to merely describing the theology. Works from other viewpoints
that show this same shift include Gerd Lüdemann, *Early Christianity
according to the Traditions in Acts* (London: SCM, 1989, orig. 1987) and,
more recently, the 2003 University of Chicago Ph.D. by Clare K. Rothschild
soon to be published as *Luke-Acts and the Rhetoric of History: An
Investigation of Early Christian Historiography* (Tübingen: Mohr, 2004).
[14] Jerome Murphy-O'Connor, *1 Corinthians* (Wilmington: Glazier, 1982),
17. Cf. Jerome Murphy-O'Connor, *St Paul's Corinth: Texts and
Archaeology* (Wilmington: Glazier, 1983).
[15] Ben Witherington, *The Acts of the Apostles: A Socio-rhetorical
Commentary* (Carlisle: Paternoster, 1998), 533.

that Paul resolved to follow this strategy because of his experience in Athens ... Perhaps Paul did feel that he had indulged in too much accommodation, since he does not mention Christ crucified in the Acts account.'[16]

There are still some, it must be said, who doubt that Paul ever gave such a speech in Athens or who maintain the posture of 'it doesn't matter'[17] but it is now acceptable once again to ask the question about the real results of Paul's visit to Athens and whether he or Luke would have regarded it as a failure.

The fact that the Athens speech was a particularly appropriate construct for that city and that particular audience is clear. For instance, in marked contrast to the earlier mission speech of Paul in Pisidian Antioch, there is no direct reference to the Old Testament; instead we find quotations and allusions to pagan literature.[18] This appropriateness goes beyond the content of the speech. Paul's method and demeanour and the other details of the story are often seen as being reminiscent of a philosopher/rhetor.[19]

---

[16] Ben Witherington, *Conflict and Community in Corinth: A Socio-rhetorical Commentary on 1 and 2 Corinthians* (Grand Rapids: Eerdmans, 1995), 121, n. 3.

[17] Soards manages to have it both ways at once, apparently endorsing the old liberalism of Dibelius and Haenchen in the text, while admitting that the point is widely debated. In treating the speeches themselves, his approach is much closer to 'it doesn't matter'. See Marion Soards, *The Speeches in Acts: Their Content, Context and Concerns* (Louisville: Westminster/John Knox, 1994), 8-9; 95-100.

[18] Even if, as Gärtner suggests, these come from typical Jewish critiques of pagan religion. Cf. Bertil Gärtner, *The Areopagus Speech and Natural Revelation* (Uppsala: Gleerup, 1955), 197, 222 and *passim*.

[19] Most obvious perhaps is the charge of preaching foreign gods (17:18), perhaps deliberately reflecting the charge against Socrates (Xenophon, *Mem.* 1.1.1). It is difficult to weigh how evocative Luke means for the setting in the agora, the verb for carrying on a dialogue and other touches to be. See Abraham Malherbe, *Paul and the Popular Philosophers* (Minneapolis: Fortress, 1989), 151, and the literature there cited; also p. 163, n. 90, where the primary focus is on the defence speeches, but is applicable to the

At the same time, we must be careful not to overstate the extent of Paul's accommodation in Athens. Careful study of the conventions and nuances of actions in the highly competitive arena of public speaking suggests that Luke's description of the Athens speech might have been intended to cast Paul as a competent amateur playing by other rules rather than as a seasoned and polished professional orator.[20]

Since Paul never mentions the Athens incident in his writings,[21] our only source for reckoning whether it was enough of a failure to make Paul change his strategy is Luke's book of Acts.[22] Barrett is dismissive: 'we may be confident that Luke did not intend to describe a lapse on the part of his hero.'[23] But as mentioned in our introduction above, Luke shows more than once that he is willing to display his hero Paul in less than the best possible light.

Ramsay writes that the fruit of Paul's rhetorical efforts 'had been little more than naught'.[24] A few people became followers, Acts

---

Areopagus as well. See also, however, Bruce Winter, "On Introducing Gods to Athens: An Alternative Reading of Acts 17:18-20," *TynB* 47 (1996): 71-90.

[20] So, for example, is Luke's explicit statement that Paul *stood* to tell the Athenians about their religiosity and ignorance a breach of the convention of the seated preliminary which included self-recommendation and praise of the audience? On the preliminaries, see Bruce Winter, "The Entries and Ethics of Orators and Paul (1 Thessalonians 2:1-12)," *TynB* 44 (1993): 55-74, esp. 58-59; Bruce Winter, *Philo and Paul among the Sophists* (2nd ed.; Grand Rapids: Eerdmans, 2002), 144-47.

[21] Unless, as suggested by Ramsay et al. the renunciations of 1 Corinthians are oblique references — the very point in question here.

[22] This is unfortunate as there is no way for us adequately to test the conjecture that part of the reason for the silence was embarrassment at his failure. The omission cannot be counted in favour of such a conjecture either, of course. Not only would that be an argument from silence, but it is atypical for Paul's letters to mention his visit to any city other than the one to which he is currently writing.

[23] C. K. Barrett, *The First Epistle to the Corinthians* (2nd ed.; London: Black, 1971), 63.

[24] Ramsay, *St Paul the Traveller*, 252.

17:34 tells us: 'Dionysius, a member of the Areopagus, also a woman named Damaris, and a number of others.' This is not quite as negligible as Ramsay would have us believe. Later in the book a speech has to be judged a remarkable success when one of those sitting in judgement even grudgingly refers to Paul's persuasiveness (Acts 26:28). Here in Athens, one of the judges, one of the elite, is converted and so are a number of others, despite Paul's blunt and non-Athenian reference to bodily resurrection. As Litfin writes: 'there had been fruit with even this elite and hostile audience.'[25]

The response, in fact, does not appear markedly different to responses in other cities, but rather conforms to the pattern set there. In Philippi, there were Lydia and the brothers (Acts 16:40), in Thessalonica, 'a large number of God-fearing Greeks and not a few prominent women' and in Athens we have a prominent man, a perhaps prominent women and 'a number' of others. Witherington, with characteristic wryness, remarks: 'Athens is one of the few places on this journey where Paul is not in fact run out of town!'[26] The fact is that Luke is everywhere vague about Paul's harvests. Many times, it is true, Luke uses words to convey 'many' or 'large numbers' but not always.[27] If we compared them to Peter's early efforts, when thousands became baptized followers in Acts 2:41

and again in 4:4, all of Paul's results seem meagre. It does not seem that Luke was making such comparisons nor meaning for us to do so.

Corinth and the Rejection of Worldly 'Wisdom'
For Ramsay, Acts 18:5 — 'Paul devoted himself exclusively to preaching, testifying to the Jews that Jesus was the Christ' — seemed to indicate clearly that Paul renounced the embellishments of rhetoric

---

[25] Litfin, *St Paul's Theology of Proclamation*, 238.

[26] Witherington, *Acts of the Apostles*, 533.

[27] A prime example is the mission in Philippi already mentioned. Luke and Paul clearly think it was successful, yet we only hear of a few specific individuals (and their households) being saved (Acts 16).

and philosophy. He writes 'This strong expression, so unlike anything else in Acts, must, on our hypothesis, be taken to indicate some specially marked character in the Corinthian preaching.'[28] If we granted, however, that it referred to the method of preaching, it is difficult to see how we could know whether that change was due to a failure among the philosophers, or merely to the change in audience. Luke just as clearly, after all, signposts that Paul here is witnessing to Jews. Luke could just as easily be making a positive contrast, commending Paul's flexibility (of which he himself was so proud, as we shall see below). Could it not just as likely be paraphrased: 'Among the Athenians, Paul knew how to act, but he was not addicted to such an approach, and when he was back among Jews, he used methods appropriate to them'?

The most likely interpretation of Acts 18:5, however, is that the emphasis on Paul's devotion to the preaching when Silas and Timothy arrived concerns not the change of heart they found in him, but rather a change of practical and financial circumstances which their arrival effected. It is not that they found him wholeheartedly preaching Jesus — in contrast with Acts 17. Rather, their arrival allowed him to preach Jesus full-time, in contrast with 18:3-4. Before their arrival, Paul stayed and worked with Aquila and Priscilla and reasoned in the synagogue only on the Sabbath.

Thus the only indicators of the supposed change of heart come from the Corinthian correspondence rather than Acts. When he came to them, it was not with 'eloquence or superior wisdom', rather he 'resolved to know nothing' but Jesus Christ crucified, 'not with wise and persuasive words', so that their faith 'might not rest on human wisdom' (1 Cor 2:1-5).

Superficially, we see Paul visiting two Greek towns and using a different mission strategy in each. Were this the case, attributing the difference to the results of the first attempt might seem reasonable.

---

28 Ramsay, *St Paul the Traveller*, 252-53.

But Athens and Corinth are very different places and have very different atmospheres. Murphy-O'Connor recognizes this, but (following Strabo) seems to favour Corinth:

> [Athens was] an old sick city whose past was infinitely more glorious than its present ... a mediocre university town dedicated to the conservation of its intellectual heritage ... Corinth, on the contrary, was a wide-open boomtown. San Francisco in the days of the California gold rush is perhaps the most illuminating parallel ... All its wealth was new money ... In opposition to the complacency of Athens, Corinth questioned ... New ideas were guaranteed a hearing.[29]

This argument displays a certain romanticism about American history, and, more importantly, a very modernist conception of the values of 'new thinking' as opposed to 'ancient wisdom'. The Romans had little interest in the avant-garde as such, but designed, built and extrapolated in the trajectories set out by ancient Greece. In our day, slogans such as 'New! Improved!' might be regarded as positive, but in Paul's day, the best things and ideas were the old things and ideas, the ones with pedigree. The fascination with Judaism (as a philosophy, rather than as a practice), on which Paul (and Josephus and Philo) traded heavily, was precisely due to its antiquity — if it is that old, older than Socrates, there must be something to it.[30] Indeed, when writing to the Corinthians, Paul expects that practices which he opposes will be perceived by his audience as inferior because they are 'innovations' (1 Cor 14:36; 11:16; 4:17; 7:17; 1:2). Our perspective

---

[29] Jerome Murphy-O'Connor, *Paul: A Critical Life* (Oxford: Clarendon, 1996), 108-09.

[30] So, for example, Josephus rants about the Greeks, knowing the Romans' obsession with their philosophies and histories as if they had a long pedigree. Josephus argues by stating that he regards Greek things as having happened only yesterday compared with Jewish history (Josephus, *C. Ap.* 1.2). Unfortunately, we have no surviving writings of Gentile proselytes or even God-fearers, but Tacitus seems to give some backhanded evidence. He writes of various practices of the Jews which he finds disagreeable and then writes that some of them have at least 'the defence of antiquity', while others are merely despicable (Tacitus, *Hist.* 5.5).

on the effects of visiting Athens and Corinth in the first century must be tempered by first-century values.

Murphy-O'Connor is absolutely correct, however, that the distinctions between the cities were stark. Paul's Corinth was not, really, a Greek city at all, but a totally rebuilt Roman colony. Despite the obvious early intentions to imitate Rome rather than Greece,[31] there are suggestions that new Corinth soon tried to use ancient Greek Corinth's reputation to its advantage, putting a thin veneer of Greek civilization and heritage over a new colony of freedmen and opportunists.[32] And Corinth was the best place for such people with ambition. In his monograph on leadership in Roman Corinth, Clarke calls it 'a climate which lent itself to social mobility ... it was in Corinth [unusually] that positions of city government were open to people of this socially mobile class of freedmen.'[33]

Even if Murphy-O'Connor is right about Athens being old and sick, the one claim to greatness Athens still had was precisely its

---

[31] See Winter, *After Paul Left Corinth*, esp. 8-11.

[32] As Winter argues, it is wrong to see Corinth as 'a Greek city with a Roman façade'. Cf. Winter, *After Paul Left Corinth*, 10-11 and 18-19, citing p. 11. I am arguing for the reverse: a Roman colony with a thin Greek veneer that is perhaps more traded upon than Winter allows. One amusing but characteristic example of this selective veneer is the bronze trade. Ancient Corinthian bronze was legendary for its quality. The shoddier workmanship coming out of the new town may still have been proudly stamped with the equivalent of 'Genuine Corinthian Bronze'. See Pliny, writing at about the time of Paul, *HN* 34.7: 'for ages there had no longer been any famous artists in metalwork [in Corinth]; yet these [more recent] persons designate all the specimens of their work as Corinthian bronzes.' He then goes on to provide methods for distinguishing the genuine old product. Also writing around the time of Paul, the satirist Petronius ridicules this phenomenon in writing of a character called Trimalchio who claimed to have acquired genuine Corinthian bronze vases by the simple expedient of buying them from a man named Corinth! (Petronius, *Sat.* 50).

[33] Andrew D. Clarke, *Secular and Christian Leadership in Corinth: A Socio-Historical and Exegetical Study of 1 Corinthians 1-6* (Leiden: Brill, 1993), 10.

learned intellectualism.[34] Paul's Corinth, though not alone in this regard, was also apparently noted for its pretensions in this realm. Dio Chrysostom's famous passage about Diogenes in Corinth displays the comically inappropriate non-philosophical thuggery that characterised the Corinthian would-be 'postgraduate students' and against a backdrop which contrasts humorously with a university setting:

> One could hear crowds of wretched sophists around Poseidon's temple shouting and reviling one another, and their disciples, as they were called, fighting with one another, many writers reading aloud their stupid works ... many fortune-tellers interpreting fortunes, lawyers innumerable perverting justice and peddlars, not a few, peddling whatever they happened to have.[35]

Any speaker with common sense nestled amongst the 'jugglers', facing such students, would be ill-advised to reuse the written transcript prepared for the setting of the Areopagus or an audience of educated true Epicureans and Stoics. But Paul may have been concerned not only with what will 'play' to this different audience, but may have been concerned deliberately to avoid catering to their self-deceits.

Much of Winter's work is concerned with the understanding and characterisation of these first-century sophists found in Corinth.[36] They differ from the Athenian philosophers in some very important ways.

---

[34] Gill documents first-century BC changes in the Athenian landscape, notably the addition of a new Odeion in the agora. He writes, 'This served as a hall for lectures and reflects the continuing role of Athens as a centre for philosophy.' See David Gill, "Achaia," in *The Book of Acts in Its Graeco-Roman Setting* (ed. D. Gill and C. Gempf; The Book of Acts in Its First Century Setting, 2; Grand Rapids: Eerdmans, 1994), 441-42.

[35] Dio Chrysostom, *Orationes* 8.9.

[36] See in particular, Winter, *After Paul Left Corinth* and Winter, *Philo and Paul.*

The sophists of the first century shared superficial characteristics with their fifth century BC counterparts.[37] There remains the dedication to excellence in oratory and the travelling. But many sophists of Paul's time were more akin to entertainers or trial lawyers than educators.[38] Their goal was often acceptance and admiration (or financial gain, which in the ancient world could be cashed in for status and admiration) rather than education and edification. They were 'declaimers' rather than 'debaters'. Malherbe, using Dio, describes them:

> Sophists ... [who] delivered such speeches [for demonstration] felt no real involvement in the occasion on which they were delivered ... lacked substance ... preaching for their own gain and glory.[39]

Seneca is one of many ancient writers who despaired of such ineffectual employment of otherwise admirable rhetorical skill: 'Why do you tickle my ears? Why do you entertain me? There is other business at hand; I am to be cauterized, operated upon, or put on a diet. That is why you were summoned to treat me!'[40] It is difficult to read such an indictment without thinking of Paul's harangues to the Corinthians who, unlike Seneca, wanted entertainment and thrived on tickling, but needed cauterizing as badly as anyone. Although the juxtaposition can be overstated, it remains largely true that 'in contrast with philosophers, sophists are shown [in Plutarch, as often in Dio and Philo] to be motivated by selfish ambition and to care little for their audience or their disciples' welfare.'[41]

---

[37] For the statistics of the revival of the term sophists in the first century, see Winter, *After Paul Left Corinth*, 32.

[38] Although, as Winter points out, it is probably going too far to see 'sophist' purely as a pejorative term in the primary sources, though it has come to be that now. See Winter, *Philo and Paul*, 55-58 and the literature there cited.

[39] Malherbe, *Popular Philosophers*, 39, and the ancient literature there cited.

[40] Seneca, *Epistolae morales* 75.6-7.

[41] Winter, *Philo and Paul*, 139.

This also helps to explain Paul's apparent ambivalence about Apollos.[42] It is doubtful that he saw Apollos as a charlatan interested only in his own glory or gain. But at the same time, Apollos' eloquence and style may have communicated the wrong message to the Corinthians, reassuring them where they needed challenging, tickling them where an incision was required.[43] Although he does not mention 1 Corinthians in this context, Malherbe writes about the necessity in such a climate for philosophers to describe themselves 'in negative and antithetic terms' exactly as Paul does in his letter.[44] Barrett perceptively writes 'He is not contrasting his evangelistic method in Corinth with that which he employed elsewhere, but with that which others employed in Corinth.'[45]

---

[42] It is clear that Paul attempts to portray Apollos as having an equal ministry before God (1 Cor 3:5-9, but is there a discordant note in v. 10?) and yet himself as having a unique relationship with them of which Apollos can have no part (1 Cor 4:14-16). There also may be a deliberate tension between Paul's determination to come to see them (1 Cor 4:19) and stay with them for a good long time (1 Cor 16:5-7) on the one hand and his description of Apollos's casual attitude about going to Corinth on the other. 'Now concerning our brother Apollos, I strongly urged him to visit you with the other brothers, but he was not at all willing to come now. He will come when he has the opportunity' (1 Cor 16:12).

[43] Winter, *Philo and Paul*, 176-78, focuses on the Corinthians' attitude toward Apollos rather than Paul's — *they* 'pitted Paul against Apollos' (p. 178). The chapter on Christian sophists argues that after Apollos's refusal to return (1 Cor 16:12) the Corinthians recruited other Christian rhetors and it is they rather than Apollos himself to whom Paul responds in 2 Corinthians. If Apollos was, however, the embodiment of a strategy Paul deliberately chose to avoid, it is difficult to escape the question of Paul's attitude towards him.

[44] Malherbe, *Popular Philosophers*, 48. Malherbe, however, refers to 1 Thessalonians, which, as we will mention again in the final section of this paper, is not without significance to our topic.

[45] Barrett, *1 Corinthians*, 64.

Conclusion and Suggestion: Mission Wisdom and Flexibility

For most readers of the New Testament, the spotlight is on Paul. Therefore, when modern readers like Ramsay or ourselves look at the mission to these two cities, the things that tend to dominate our attention are the differences in how our hero seems to have acted. It is only by diligently working to attend to the historical background that we begin to see the matters which would have dominated Paul's attention: the difference between the genuine philosophers of the ancient city of classical Greek learning on the one hand, and the 'wannabes' caught up in rhetorical brawls in this new Roman colony. The juxtaposition created in travelling from Athens to Corinth must have been like visiting Beijing one day and London's Chinatown the next. The difference between the two cities and the teachers plying their trades must have been so pronounced (and so ironic) that it would have been more remarkable for Paul to have made the mistake of teaching the same way to both cities!

It was to these very Corinthians that Paul most clearly trumpeted the flexibility of his practice and strategy, albeit speaking in terms of Jew and Gentile, weak and strong; 'I have become all things to all people so that by all possible means I might save some' (1 Cor 9:19-23). And by comparing his letter to Corinth with that to the Galatians, we can see this to be no idle boast. To the libertarian Corinthians, he argues repeatedly for constraints on their actions and for disciplined order to their worship. To the Galatians, having the opposite problem, he pleads 'it is for freedom that Christ has set us free' (Gal 5:1). It is clear that even within the body of the undisputed epistles, what Paul said and how he argued were heavily tailored to the needs and character of his intended audience. As Judge wrote, Paul reacted to what was at hand, 'exploiting the material rather than subjecting [him]self to it'.[46]

---

[46] Edwin Judge, "St. Paul and Socrates," *Interchange* 14 (1973): 110, as cited by Mark Strom, *Reframing Paul: Conversations in Grace and Community* (Downers Grove: IVP, 2000), 185.

And this ability to exploit what he found also points to likenesses in the approaches to Corinth and Athens. Strom wrote that, in Corinth, Paul's refusal to emulate the sophists' eloquence and persona was a decision to 'set himself on a collision course with the contemporary conventions'.[47] Ramsay thought this to be unique: 'nowhere ... is [Paul] so hard on the wise, the philosophers, and the dialecticians.'[48] But this is not so clearly the case. I have argued elsewhere that it is no mistake that both sections of the Acts 17 speech to the 'lovers of wisdom' — the philosophers — begin with explicit reference not to the audience's great knowledge, but to their ignorance (Acts 17:23, 30).[49] To praise and then temporarily excuse the learned because of their ignorance is, if anything, sharper than to attack human wisdom outright. By his deliberate provocations and by his decision to explain that he meant bodily resurrection, Luke's Paul in Athens, no less than Paul in 1 Corinthians, deliberately set himself on a collision course with the 'learned people' in favour of what looked like foolishness.

Ramsay argued that Paul changed his pattern after the failure in Athens; Witherington feels it, on balance, more likely that 'Paul adjusted his missionary strategy due to the situation he found in Corinth.'[50] Another theory worth testing further might be that Paul did not change his strategy in Corinth, but rather, it was Athens that was the exception.[51] This is precisely what is hinted at, though not

---

[47] Strom, *Reframing Paul*, 16.

[48] Ramsay, *St Paul the Traveller*, 252, although Ramsay *does* specifically say 'nowhere in his writings', it is clear from the rest of his paragraph that he thinks it true of Acts as well.

[49] Conrad Gempf, "Athens, Paul at," in *Dictionary of Paul and His Letters* (ed. Martin Hawthorne et al.; Leicester: IVP, 1993), 51-54.

[50] Witherington, *Acts of the Apostles*, 533, although we have noted his ambiguity on the matter earlier.

[51] Barrett argues for something like this, but only because he regards the Athens strategy to be a fabrication of Luke's. See C. K. Barrett, *A Critical*

articulated, in the recent work on Paul's entry to Thessalonica. In 1 Thess 2:1-12, though perhaps less forcefully than in 1 Cor 2:1-5, Paul also talks about his 'unplugged' approach there in terms that must now be seen as a deliberate contrast with the sophists. If before Paul went to Corinth, he went to Athens, it is also true that before Paul went to Athens, he went to Thessalonica (Acts 17:1). 'Paul's initial comings to Thessalonica *and* Corinth are described in terms that are clearly intended to show his deliberate renunciation of entry conventions and ethics of orators.'[52] There are ample reasons for Paul's taking up his anti-sophistic approach in both cities, but the proper question is not so much whether the failure at Athens made him design a new strategy for Corinth, but rather, if Acts can be trusted, what made him alter his usual approach for Athens. Ramsay's apparent 'new departure' might turn out to be neither new nor a departure, and Paul's practices seem understandable in the context of what we now know about the cultural situations of the cities themselves.

---

and Exegetical Commentary on the Acts of the Apostles, Vol. II (ICC; T & T Clark, 1998), 825, and Barrett, *1 Corinthians*, 63-64.

[52] Winter, "Entries," 73 (emphasis mine). See also Winter, *Philo and Paul*, 150-55.

'Beloved Brothers' in the New Testament and Early Christian World

Alanna Nobbs

'Beloved' and 'Beloved Brothers'

The adjective ἀγαπητός is used from the very beginnings of Greek literature:[1] 'and now again my well-loved son (παῖδ' ἀγαπητόν) have the storm-winds swept away from our halls without tiding', laments Penelope in the Odyssey.[2] The adjective is found in other Classical authors,[3] frequently characterising the love appropriate for an only child;[4] it is used thus in the Septuagint[5] and other Jewish Greek[6] texts. Its connection with μονογενής[7] probably first endeared it to New Testament authors: it is used prominently of Jesus (the 'beloved son')

---

[1] Papyri are abbreviated according to J. F. Oates et al., eds., *Checklist of Editions of Greek, Latin, Demotic and Coptic Papyri, Ostraca and Tablets* (5th ed.; Oakville: American Society of Papyrologists, 2001). This paper has benefited through discussions with Dr Malcolm Choat, who is preparing a full treatment of the archive of Theophanes.

[2] Homer, *Od.* 4.727 (Murray, LCL); cf. *Od.* 4.817, 5.18.

[3] See LSJ, 6.

[4] See *DGE*, fasc. 1 (1989), 15.

[5] Gen 22:2, 12; Amos 8:10; Zech 12:10.

[6] See esp. Philo, e.g. *Leg.* 3.209; *Migr.* 140. Many other 'Jewish' apocrypha such as the *Testaments of the Twelve Patriarchs* and the *Apocalypse of Esdras* have been manifestly subject to Christian editing, and no conclusions can be based upon usage found within them. By the phrase 'Jewish Greek' is meant here Greek written by Jews, rather than the separate Greek dialect imagined by some scholars; cf. G. H. R. Horsley, "The Fiction of Jewish Greek," in his *New Documents Illustrating Early Christianity*, 5 (North Ryde, N.S.W.: Ancient History Documentary Research Centre, Macquarie University, 1989), 5-40.

[7] Hesychius, *s.v.* ἀγαπητός (ed. Schmidt, vol. 1, 14).

in the Gospels.[8] It is first applied to the noun 'brother' (ἀδελφός) in Codices Vaticanus and Alexandrinus of the Book of Tobit.[9] With Paul, ἀγαπητὸς ἀδελφός emerges as an epistolary salutation, as the plural ἀγαπητοί becomes a term for the Christian community. The semantic sense of the Pauline usage is not new, yet Paul invests the term with a new conception.[10] The ἀγαπητοί are 'beloved in Christ', bonded together as a community by this ἀγάπη. It is the community at Corinth whom Paul first addresses as 'beloved brethren';[11] Onesimus and Tychicus are the first to be called a 'beloved brother' by Paul,[12] and it was this phrase which became the most widely used version within the Christian community.

In early Christian epistolography, the collective ἀγαπητοί is commonplace as an address, thus frequently in Clement of Rome's first letter to the Corinthians and Ignatius of Antioch's letters to the Magnesians, Trallians and Smyrnaeans, as well as in his letter to Polycarp. Somewhat surprisingly, ἀγαπητὸς ἀδελφός takes longer to enter post-Pauline Christian epistolography: we wait until the third century for imitations of the familiar Pauline letter openings which also incorporate the phrase: Ὠριγένης Ἀφρικανῷ ἀγαπητῷ ἀδελφῷ ἐν θεῷ Πατρὶ διὰ Ἰησοῦ Χριστοῦ τοῦ ἁγίου παιδὸς αὐτοῦ εὖ πράττειν ('Origen to his beloved brother Africanus in God the father through Jesus Christ his holy son, be well');[13] the bishops in the synod to condemn Paul of Samosata send their greetings 'to the beloved brethren in the Lord' (ἀγαπητοῖς ἀδελφοῖς ἐν κυρίῳ).[14]

---

[8] E.g. Matt 3:17; Mark 1:11; Luke 3:22.
[9] Tob 10:13: καὶ Ἔδνα εἶπεν πρὸς Τωβίαν, Ἀδελφὲ ἀγαπητέ. Codex Sinaiticus reads Ἀδελφὲ ἠγαπημένε; is the reading in A and B the result of Christian editing?
[10] O. Wischmeyer, "Das Adjectiv ΑΓΑΠΗΤΟΣ in den paulinischen Briefen: Eine traditionsgeschichtliche Miszelle," NTS 32 (1986): 476-80.
[11] 1 Cor 15:58.
[12] Eph 6:21; Col 4:7, 9; Phlm 16.
[13] PG 11, 48B.
[14] Eusebius, Hist. Eccl. 7.30.2.

Around the same time, Hippolytus addresses Theophilus as ἀγαπητὸς ἀδελφός at the outset of his treatise on the Antichrist (*de Antichristo* 1). The phrase, by then, had passed into the general Christian epistolographic discourse. It is around the same time that it appears in the papyri.

Literary uses of ἀγαπητὸς ἀδελφός are all by Christian writers. However, the situation in documentary texts is less clear. The central question is whether use of the phrase stayed entirely within the Christian domain. In the usage of Paul and the sub-Apostolic authors, the formulation serves to indicate the shared relationship of the sender and recipient of a letter 'in Christ'. But did its use remain exclusive in this way? Would a Christian use the phrase of a non-Christian? Would non-Christians have used it?

In papyri, ἀγαπητὸς ἀδελφός begins to be used only in the late third century,[15] most noticeably in a series of 'letters of recommendation', written to introduce travellers to other Christian communities.[16] The writers, presumably Christian leaders in their own communities, address their correspondents as 'beloved brother' while asking for the bearer to be accorded hospitality, and sometimes further instruction.[17]

---

[15] Cf. the discussion in Horsley, *New Documents Illustrating Early Christianity*, 4 (North Ryde, N.S.W.: Ancient History Documentary Research Centre, Macquarie University, 1987), 252-54.

[16] See *P. Alex.* 29; *SB* 16.12304; *SB* 10.10255; *PSI* 3.208; *PSI* 9.1041: all are to be dated in the late third or early fourth century, including *P. Alex.* 29, which should probably be dated thus (with the editio princeps) rather than the early third century as suggested by M. Naldini, *Il cristianesimo in Egitto* (2nd ed.; Fiesole: Nardini, 1998), no. 19. On these 'letters of recommendation' see T. M. Teeter, "Letters of Recommendation or Letters of Peace?," in *Akten des 21. Internationalen Papyrologenkongresses* (ed. B. Kramer et al.; Stuttgart/Leipzig: Teubner, 1997), 954-60; K. Treu, "Christliche Empfehlungs-Schemabriefe auf Papyrus," in *Zetesis: Album Amicorum* (ed. Th. Lefevre et al.; Fs. E. de Strycker; Antwerp/Utrecht: Nederlandsche Boekhandel, 1973), 629-36.

[17] *PSI* 9.1041 recommends Leon, who is a 'catechumen in the beginning of the Gospel'; *P. Oxy.* 36.2785, a letter of recommendation addressed to an ἀγαπητὸς πάπας, recommends a 'catechumen in Genesis'.

In the fourth century the adjective becomes regularly applied to other nouns, such as 'child' (τέκνον), 'son' (υἱός), 'father' (πατήρ), and the terms for Christian leaders ἄπα and πάπας.[18] As Tibiletti notes, ἀγαπητὸς ἀδελφός is found in securely Christian settings, but does not emerge clearly in pagan letters of the period.[19]

All the letters from the third and fourth century in which ἀγαπητὸς ἀδελφός is used are marked by other elements as written by Christians: the contractions of κύριος and θεός (known as *nomina sacra*, 'sacred names') which the early Christian scribes developed,[20] or the 'in the Lord/in God' (ἐν κυρίῳ/ἐν θεῷ) formula given theological currency by Paul.[21] It seems a perfectly reasonable supposition that, as the use of ἀγαπητὸς ἀδελφός corresponds with the spread of Christianity through Egypt,[22] it forms an indicator of Christianity in and of itself. Yet the fourth-century papyri give pause for thought.

The Archives of Theophanes and Abinnaeus
The most troubling is the archive of Theophanes. This consists of public papers, private letters, itineraries, accounts and memoranda belonging to Theophanes, a resident of the Nile metropolis Hermopolis Magna in the first quarter of the fourth century. He was a *scholasticus*,[23] and in this capacity may have been on the staff of the Prefect of Egypt.[24] He also held several positions in the Hermopolitan

---

[18] References are given in Horsley, *New Documents*, 4:252.

[19] G. Tibiletti, *Le lettere private nei papiri greci del III e IV secolo d.C. tra paganesimo e cristianesimo* (Milan: Vita e Pensiero, 1979), 44-45.

[20] C. H. Roberts, *Manuscript, Society and Belief in Early Christian Egypt* (Schweich Lectures; London: OUP for the British Academy, 1979), 26-48.

[21] Cf. D. Timms, "The Pauline Use of *en Christo*: Re-examining Meaning and Origins: A Linguistic Analysis" (unpublished Ph.D. dissertation, Macquarie University, 2000).

[22] See in general C. W. Griggs, *Early Egyptian Christianity from Its Origins to 451 C.E.* (2nd ed.; Leiden: Brill, 1991).

[23] See the letters of introduction written for him, *P. Ryl.* 4.623 and P. Lat Arg I.

[24] See the discussion of C. H. Roberts, *P. Ryl.* 4.104ff.

administration.[25] Most prominently, he undertook a journey to Antioch, delivering and receiving letters as he went, carrying letters of introduction to the provincial governors of Syria, and keeping meticulous daily accounts. This journey can be roughly dated to between AD 317 and 323.[26]

In the private letters to and mentioning Theophanes edited by B. R. Rees in *P. Herm.* he emerges as a leader of the circle to which he belonged. Some of this group clearly worshipped Hermes Trismegistus, who is mentioned by name; polytheistic terminology is also used in the letters.[27]

The general consensus of those who have studied the archive is that the private letters are not from a Christian milieu. Both C. H. Roberts and Rees, the original editors, regard Theophanes and the others mentioned in the letters as cultivated pagans. Roberts describes the family's cultural background as 'thoroughly pagan and Hellenic'.[28] Rees sees Theophanes as a member of a pagan circle priding itself on its standards of education and on its pagan associations. That they, or at least some of them, are involved in the worship of Hermes Trismegistus is clear from the use of polytheistic terminology:

> the inexorable water of the cult of the God Hermes who protects (*P. Herm.* 2.11-12);

> may Hermes Trismegistus and all the Gods grant you permanent happiness (*P. Herm.* 3.20-25).

In *P. Ryl.* 4.624, Theophanes' sons write to him, telling him that from him they have 'learnt to think little of those who think differently' (τῶν ἄλλως φρονούντων, 1.18). Roberts saw 'some division of feeling in which Theophanes is involved ... an allusion perhaps to the

---

[25] He is recorded as being a gymnasiarch and *exactor*; see *CPR* 17A.18.3n.
[26] Roberts, *P. Ryl.* 4.105.
[27] See in particular *P. Herm.* 2-3, *SB* 12.10803.
[28] *P. Ryl.* 4.105.

Christians, perhaps to the party of Constantine'.[29] Rees felt it was 'almost certainly an allusion to Christians'.[30] This fitted well with the assertion, articulated by both Rees and Roberts,[31] that the archive is best placed in the context of preparations for the civil war between Constantine and Licinius. The phrase 'those who think differently' has no parallel in the papyri.[32] Where it is used in literary sources (e.g. Sozomen, *Hist. Eccl.* 4.28.7, 6.23.10, 6.27.10), it is in reference to heresies within the established church. However, Moscadi disallowed the political and religious connotations which Roberts and Rees attached to the phrase; for him, the sons were simply referring to those who disagreed with their own high opinion of their father.[33]

Naldini and Moscadi opt for a Christian interpretation of at least some of the letters. Naldini does so primarily because *P. Herm.* 4 is addressed 'to our beloved brother (ἀγαπητὸς ἀδελφός) Theophanes'.[34] To this Moscadi adds the senders' names, Leon and Joannes.[35] Apart from *P. Herm.* 4, ἀγαπητὸς ἀδελφός appears in none of the private letters in the archive, and beyond this use there is little in *P. Herm.* 4 to suggest any religious affiliation. Ἀδελφός is used extensively throughout the letters edited by Rees, either alone or in conjunction with κύριος. This 'family' terminology is employed even in those letters which specifically mention the worship of Hermes and contain polytheistic references; so it can hardly be regarded as a sure indication of a Christian brotherhood.

---

[29] *P. Ryl.* 4.624.18n.

[30] *P. Herm.* 2.33n.

[31] B. R. Rees, "Theophanes of Hermopolis Magna," *BJRL* 51 (1968): 164-83; C. H. Roberts, "A Footnote to the Civil War of A.D. 324," *JEA* 31 (1945): 113.

[32] But cf. Gal 5:10; Phil 3:15.

[33] A. Moscadi, "Le lettere dell'archivio di Teofane," *Aeg* 50 (1970): 88-154, at 108.

[34] Naldini, *Il Cristianesimo*, no. 38.

[35] Moscadi, "Le lettere dell'archivio di Teofane," 130.

E. Wipszycka points out that Naldini and Moscadi, in regarding some of the letters as being from a Christian milieu, have based their hypotheses on criteria which are far from sure. She dismisses the use of ἀγαπητὸς ἀδελφός as being no more certain than the use of the formula εὔχομαι παρὰ τῷ κυρίῳ θεῷ.[36] She notes that the name Leon has been attested since the Ptolemaic period and that the Joannes of *P. Herm* 4, given his association with a Hermetic circle, may call himself by that name as a consequence of the influence of the Jewish religion on the philosophical and religious interests of his circle.[37] However, she later retracted her argument on the latter point, admitting Joannes was a decidedly Christian name.[38] More recently, Bagnall has argued that there is no evidence for Theophanes' own religion, and that *P. Herm*. 4, 5 and perhaps 6 are written by Christians.[39]

Depending on how one views the archive, we either have a non-Christian using the term, or a Christian using the term of a probable non-Christian. For the first editor of the letters, Rees, this meant that the phrase ἀγαπητὸς ἀδελφός was not a secure indicator of Christianity; others echoed his judgment.[40] Yet need a hard and fast rule be applied? Evidence of Christianity elsewhere in the archive of Theophanes indicates that the beliefs of this circle may have been more diverse than Rees was prepared to admit. Nor can influence

---

[36] 'I pray before the Lord God'; see especially the 'Archive of Paniscus', *P. Mich.* 3.214-21 (Coptus, 297).

[37] E. Wipszycka, "Remarques sur les lettres privées chrétiennes des iie-ive siècles (à propos d'un livre de M. Naldini)," *JJP* 18 (1974): 203-21, at 214.

[38] E. Wipszycka, "La christianisation de l'Egypte aux ive-vi^e siècles: Aspects sociaux et ethniques," in her *Etudes sur le christianisme dans l'Egypte de l'antiquité tardive* (Rome: Institutum Patristicum Augustinianum, 1996), 63-105, at 85, n. 34.

[39] Roger S. Bagnall, *Egypt in Late Antiquity* (Princeton: Princeton University Press, 1993), 271-72.

[40] E. A. Judge and S. R. Pickering, "Papyrus Documentation of Church and Community in Egypt to the Mid-fourth Century," *JbAC* 20 (1977): 47-71, at 69; Wipszycka, "Remarques," 214.

between traditions be totally excluded; non-Christians may have picked up the terminology from Christian acquaintances, even if they did not use it in the sense of 'the brotherhood of Christ' with which Paul clothed it.[41]

The slightly later archive of Abinnaeus, a cavalry commander in the Fayum in the 340s and 350s, provides another test case. Several of his correspondents address him as ἀγαπητὸς ἀδελφός.[42] The writers in every case seem clearly Christian. But the editors were moved to wonder whether Abinnaeus would have been so addressed were he not himself also a Christian.[43] There is nothing in the archive which speaks to the question of Abinnaeus' own beliefs: a statue of Fortune stood prominently in his camp at Dionysias, but this need not reflect what Abinnaeus believed. The editors of the archive sat somewhat on the fence, but seemed inclined to believe Abinnaeus himself was not a Christian. Later commentators, however, have generally seen him as a Christian.[44] If the archive is read this way, the salutation ἀγαπητὸς ἀδελφός retains its force as expressing a communal bond between the commander and his various correspondents.

Was, then, 'beloved brother' a phrase which truly indicated common membership of a Christian brotherhood, or is it the only clear example to date of an epistolary phrase passing from primarily Christian usage to more common currency? If so, it needs to be recognised that this would mark the assimilation of Christian vocabulary to a common religious milieu, in the same way as phrases such as παντοκράτωρ or ὕψιστος θεός show the process the other way.

---

[41] A. M. Nobbs, "Formulas of Belief in Greek Papyrus Letters of the Third and Fourth Centuries," in *Ancient History in a Modern University* (ed. T. W. Hillard et al.; Fs. E. A. Judge; Grand Rapids: Eerdmans, 1998), 2:233-37, at 234-35; cf. Horsley, *New Documents*, 4:254-55.

[42] *P. Abinn.* 6, 7, 8, 19, 32.

[43] *P. Abinn.*, Intro. pp. 30-33.

[44] See esp. T. D. Barnes, "The Career of Abinnaeus," *Phoenix* 39 (1985): 368-74.

Equality or Mutuality?

Paul's Use of 'Brother' Language

Andrew D. Clarke

Introduction

The hermeneutical gap which exists between first-century and twenty-first-century readers is one which is widely underestimated. Despite regular warnings to 'Mind the Gap!', too often readers of the New Testament take a leap without fully accounting for the differences in culture and society which separate the original recipients of Paul's letters from ourselves. While Christians have fundamentally regarded the New Testament as a historical source, it is too often interpreted unhistorically. Use of the social sciences has increased our sophistication in investigating the New Testament texts as crucial sources of sociological, and not just theological, data, but Bruce Winter has nonetheless repeatedly argued that investigation of the social dimensions of the Pauline communities *must* be founded on an adequate appreciation of the prevailing cultural context of antiquity.

One particular contribution of Bruce Winter's scholarship has been his specific reminder that exegetes should read the Pauline texts regarding the family and family relationships in the light of their appropriate first-century context. He has written widely on women, wives and widows from this perspective, and demonstrated the essential importance of interpreting the New Testament data in the light of the prevailing expectations and practices of which Paul's first readers would have been aware.[1]

---

[1]   Cf. in particular his "Providentia for the Widows of 1 Timothy 5:3-16," *TynB* 39 (1988): 83-99; "The 'New' Roman Wife and 1 Timothy 2:9-15: The Search for a *Sitz im Leben*," *TynB* 51 (2000): 285-94, and *Roman Wives,*

In this chapter I shall focus attention on the extensive use and nature of 'brother' (ἀδελφός) language in the Pauline epistles, and by extension on the nature of the relationships between Paul and his correspondents. In the course of the chapter I shall first provide an overview of Paul's use of ἀδελφός language, and highlight the difficulties inherent in translating the collective term 'brothers' (ἀδελφοί); I shall then outline a widely-held assumption regarding this language; and, finally, I shall describe a contrasting reading of 'brother' language, supported by examples of ἀδελφός language in the documentary papyri and a literary discourse written by a late first-century Greek author.

'Brothers' in the Pauline Epistles

The metaphor of the family was extensively used by Paul as a motif to describe the ways in which individuals within the Christian communities should view their relationships. His use of the 'father' metaphor, and the father-child relationship in regard to those in communities which he had founded or certain named individuals is a key element of this.[2] Similarly, we should further note Paul's use of 'household' (οἶκος and οἰκία) language as the context of church meeting, a metaphor for the church and as a model of community organisation.[3] In a recent article, David Horrell has argued that such household language, whilst occurring throughout the Pauline tradition, is notably more pervasive in Colossians, Ephesians and the Pastoral Epistles, where its use is more explicit as a model for structuring social relationships within the communities.[4]

Roman Widows: The Appearance of New Women and the Pauline Communities (Grand Rapids: Eerdmans, 2003).

[2] Cf. Corinth, Thessalonica, Philippi, Timothy, Titus, Onesimus; 1 Cor 4:14, 17; 2 Cor 6:13; Phil 2:22; 1 Thess 2:7, 11; 1 Tim 1:2, 18; 2 Tim 1:2; 2:1; Titus 1:4; Phlm 10.

[3] E.g. Rom 16:5; 1 Cor 16:19; Col 4:15; 1 Tim 3:5, 15.

[4] David G. Horrell, "From ἀδελφοί to οἶκος θεοῦ: Social Transformation in Pauline Christianity," JBL 120 (2001): 293-311.

In addition to this metaphorical or fictive parent-child relationship, and possibly as a further aspect of the οἶκος or οἰκία metaphor, however, Paul also widely uses the term 'brother' (ἀδελφός). He uses it in this metaphorical sense some 112 times in Romans, 1 and 2 Corinthians, Galatians, Philippians, 1 Thessalonians and Philemon; with rather fewer instances in Ephesians, Colossians, 2 Thessalonians and the Pastoral Epistles.[5] To present that frequency in a more accessible perspective, this address is used in the early and indisputably Pauline epistles approximately once per page of the Nestle-Aland (27th ed.) text. In the vast majority of these occurrences, that is some 69 times, we find the word in the vocative plural, in order to address those in the churches,[6] even those with whom he considers that he has a father-child relationship. The vocative singular only rarely occurs in the corpus.[7] The feminine singular form, ἀδελφή, is used five times in the Pauline epistles, and once in the plural form in the Pastoral Epistles. In all, it emerges that Paul's favourite term of address to his correspondents is ἀδελφός.

In a very significant recent article, Arzt-Grabner has drawn attention to the range of uses of the term 'brother' in the Greek and Latin documentary papyri. These include the following metaphorical uses: 'a husband, a near or distant kinsman, a friend or acquaintance, an equal in rank or office, a colleague in the administration or in a craft, or a business partner',[8] although he underlines that it is often difficult, from the limited context, to determine whether the term is being used metaphorically or not.[9] In the Pauline letters, it is clearer that the term is used almost exclusively in a fictive kinship sense, and may thereby reinforce the sense of a relationship analogous to that of

---

[5] 20 times in these other letters. Statistics provided by David Horrell.

[6] This includes seven occurrences in 2 Thessalonians, and none are recorded in Ephesians, Colossians, Philemon or the Pastoral Epistles.

[7] Phlm 7, 20.

[8] P. Arzt-Grabner, "'Brothers' and 'Sisters' in Documentary Papyri and in Early Christianity", *Rivista Biblica* 50 (2002): 187.

[9] Arzt-Grabner, "'Brothers' and 'Sisters' in Documentary Papyri," 188.

natural siblings. The term 'brothers' is now used in contemporary, European, Christian contexts for the most part to a far lesser degree than appears to have been the case in Paul's extant correspondence with congregations and individuals. Accordingly, both our unfamiliarity with the term in such a context and an awareness that words tend not to have a narrow and fixed semantic range prompt investigation into the connotation of 'brothers' in Paul's correspondence. Our next question must, therefore, concern the implied nature of this relationship which is circumscribed by the description 'brothers'. It could, for example, be descriptive of a shared relationship to a fictive progenitor (they have the same fictive father); it could be descriptive of the affection between the parties (they are, or should be, 'brotherly'); and it could also express the relative status between the parties (they share, or should share, a relationship of parity within the fictive family). 'Brother' in its Pauline contexts could clearly, therefore, be taken in a number of these senses, and, unsurprisingly has been by interpreters. We are at an advantage where a particular sense is clearly defined, and are necessarily at a loss where no such hermeneutical context is explicitly described.

We may note that the NRSV translates the vocative plural ἀδελφοί most commonly as 'brothers and sisters'. This expression presents an inclusivity which the gender-specific term 'brother' lacks, but loses the simplicity and brevity of the collective term. However, the NRSV also adopts a number of other translations for this same term, most of which also avoid a restrictive male referent, but each of which contains different other emphases.

The NRSV translates the term ἀδελφοί as 'beloved' in a number of places.[10] This is a clear attempt to avoid any gender-specificity to the noun in that it does not appear to exclude a relationship with

---

[10]   Phil 1:12; 3:13; 1 Thess 5:4, 14, 25; and 2 Thess 3:6. Note, however, that on two occasions the same term 'beloved' is used to translate the composite phrase ἀδελφοί μου ἀγαπητοί (1 Cor 15:58; Phil 4:8).

female members which the term 'brothers' might do. In so doing, however, it also avoids any explicit reference to a fictive sibling relationship. Clearly, the term 'beloved' characterises numerous familial and non-familial relationships. Furthermore, it makes no statement about any hierarchy between the parties. Love can be a characteristic of hierarchical relationships or egalitarian relationships. On the other hand, 'beloved' does particularly highlight the quality of love, but in a somewhat archaic fashion.

In contrast, in a number of other places, the same term is translated in the NRSV as 'friends'.[11] This again avoids the tension of gender-specific language, but it may well also suggest a different level of affection from 'beloved'. In addition, as with the term 'beloved', it makes no comment about the relative status between the parties. Accordingly, both translations detail level of affection, but neither determines social structure nor implies shared fictive father or mother figures.

On one occasion each, the NRSV translates the term ἀδελφοί as 'members of God's family' and 'members of God's church'.[12] Here the predominant note is a shared membership of the community of believers, and a reasonable assumption, without further information, is that this is on equal terms. Gender specificity is avoided in both translations, and one of the translations presupposes a fictive familial, and presumably loving, relationship.

Finally, the NRSV also translates the term ἀδελφοί as 'brothers' in a couple of instances.[13] Here Paul appears to be referring to a specific group of fellow believers, all of whom are male, for example the apostles.

These attempts by the NRSV to give specific content to the one term ἀδελφοί ('brothers and sisters', 'beloved', 'friends', 'members

---

[11] Rom 7:4; 1 Cor 14:26, 39; 2 Cor 11:9; Gal 4:12, 28, 31; 5:11; 6:1; Phil 4:21.
[12] Gal 1:2; 1 Tim 6:2.
[13] 1 Cor 9:5; 2 Cor 8:23.

of God's family', 'members of God's church' and 'brothers') highlight both the difficulties in translating the term and the interpretative
assumptions which a choice of words entails. In what sense did Paul
use the term? How might his readers and hearers have understood the
address? And most problematic, how is it that Paul could address the
same people, in the same letter, as both 'brothers' and those whom he
'fathered'?[14]

Egalitarianism or Hierarchy?

It is this latter issue which, I believe, is the major sticking point in
recent scholarship. If 'brothers' implies a relationship of equals, how
is it that Paul, as a brother, can also exercise authority over such
equals? The article by Horrell referred to above helpfully identifies
this as an anomaly. In particular, he argues that, just as οἶκος and
οἰκία language becomes more pervasive during the later decades of
the New Testament period, so also we find that ἀδελφός language
becomes less widespread. The implication drawn from this is that this
change reflects a social transformation in early Christianity. The
earlier period contrasts with the later in terms of hierarchical structure. It is assumed, although not clearly demonstrated, that fictive
brother language is egalitarian language, while fictive household language presupposes a more clearly structured community organisation.
In the following lengthy quotation, Horrell draws attention to this tension. He seeks to describe the early model as egalitarian, yet rightly
acknowledges that it includes some individuals who exercise authority. The result is an egalitarianism tempered by the exercising of
charismatic domination by a few.

> We might then broadly characterize this change as one from the
> model of an egalitarian community of ἀδελφοί toward the model of a
> hierarchical household-community ... It would be misleading, how-
> ever, not to qualify that conclusion somewhat, for the genuine Pauline
> letters both assume and urge the recognition of certain people — pri-
> marily Paul himself — as being in positions of power and authority.

---

[14] 1 Cor 1:10; 4:15.

> If the Pauline churches develop, as they seem to do, from a loosely organized sectarian-type movement where the language of brotherhood predominates, into one that is more structured and 'churchlike', which mirrors the conventional household hierarchy in its own internal organization, then we should perhaps speak of changes in the form of authority and power, rather than implying that we simply move from egalitarianism to authoritarianism.[15]

The problem is very clearly identified by Horrell, and it necessarily leaves us with the untidiness of an Orwellian egalitarianism which is diluted by authority invested in or accorded to a few individuals. The problem is all the greater for other scholars who interpret Paul's own exercising of power to be that of domination in an authoritarian fashion.[16] A range of implications can be drawn. It may be that Paul's use of egalitarian language is disingenuous. This may be analogous to the widespread social custom of a Graeco-Roman patron publicly addressing his client as 'friend' (*amicus*), when the relationship is self-evidently one of hierarchy, and fuelled by debt, not affection. Or possibly it parallels the Westminster parliamentary etiquette of addressing a colleague as 'honourable friend' when you clearly believe him or her to be neither. An alternative conclusion is that of Horrell who determines that the situation is more complicated than that of a simple egalitarianism.[17] The thrust of his reconstruction is that there is a period of transformation from egalitarianism to stratified hierarchy, where the egalitarianism is diluted by the existence of authority figures. Thus he writes:

---

[15] Horrell, "From ἀδελφοί to οἶκος θεοῦ," 310.

[16] Cf., for example, E. A. Castelli, *Imitating Paul: A Discourse of Power* (Literary Currents in Biblical Interpretation; Louisville: Westminster, 1991); and E. Schüssler Fiorenza, *In Memory of Her: A Feminist Theological Reconstruction of Christian Origins* (London: SCM, 1983).

[17] Cf. his careful argument refuting a simple 'discipleship of equals', summarized in his, *The Social Ethos of the Corinthian Correspondence: Interests and Ideology from 1 Corinthians to 1 Clement* (Edinburgh: T & T Clark, 1996), 124-25. I am grateful to David Horrell for his constructive comments on an earlier draft of this paper.

> [It] should not be taken to imply that Paul's vision is unambiguously
> of an egalitarian community. It seems to me that that *is* essentially
> what Paul implies with the designation ἀδελφοί, but that is not the
> only designation Paul uses, either of himself or of his congregations.
> ... What seems clear, nonetheless, is that the frequent use of ἀδελφός
> language reflects both an established designation for the members of
> the Christian assemblies and Paul's efforts to ensure that social re-
> lationships ἐν ἐκκλησίᾳ are structured in a manner appropriate to
> their description as groups of equal siblings. Yet distinctions can be,
> and are, made among the ἀδελφοί (cf. Gal 6:6; 1 Thess 5:12), and
> Paul certainly does not restrict himself to a role as an ἀδελφός among
> equal siblings.[18]

It seems to me that it is by exploring this final sentence of the quotation that we could find a resolution to the conundrum. Specifically, I
want to propose that it is not necessary to assume that ἀδελφός language carried connotations of egalitarianism in the first century. It
was noted above that the NRSV occasionally translated the vocative
plural ἀδελφοί as 'beloved' and 'friends' — and in so doing it
focused particularly on affection, and avoided connotations of status
distinction or, indeed, common fictive parenthood. I want to suggest
that the popular concept of egalitarianism in social organisation today
can inadvertently colour investigation into Paul's use of ἀδελφός language. Paul's apparent authoritarianism is frowned upon in a post-
modern culture which is suspicious of dominant authorities. It is,
therefore, attractive to be able to highlight elements of egalitarianism
in the ἀδελφός language, and contrast this against residual notions of
hierarchy in the Pauline letters. It seems to me rather, that Horrell
rightly draws attention to the 'brotherly' characteristics of 'affection,
mutual responsibility and solidarity', but need not incorporate also the
notion of equality:

> The prominence of this kinship description would seem to imply that
> Paul both assumes and promotes the relationship between himself and
> his addressees, and among the addressees themselves, as one between

---

[18] Horrell, "From ἀδελφοί to οἶκος θεοῦ," 303.

equal siblings, who share a sense of affection, mutual responsibility, and solidarity.[19]

Indeed, Arzt-Grabner draws attention to a number of first and second-century sources which use the clearly unequal phrase 'my lord brother' (κύριέ μου ἀδελφέ) as a referent to an older brother, together with some later papyri which *may* apply the phrase 'to the brother and lord' (τῷ ἀδελφῷ καὶ κυρίῳ) in a metaphorical sense.[20] A further mid-first-century Latin ostracon from Egypt describes a colleague as more like a twin brother than a friend, thereby clarifying both familial closeness and equality:

> Ego te non tamquam amicum habeo sed tamqua[m] fratrem gemellum qui de uno ventre exivit ('I do not have you like a friend, but like a twin brother, who has come out of the same womb')[21]

Arzt-Grabner also highlights some first-century business correspondence between the gymnasiarch of Arsinoe and a certain Apollonius.[22] Whilst the former addresses Apollonius in affectionate terms as 'brother' and 'dearest' (φιλτάτῳ) in a number of letters,[23] it appears that Apollonius addresses the gymnasiarch more formally (γυμνασιάρχῳ),[24] which suggests that the relationship is recognized to be unequal, but nonetheless the more senior gymnasiarch condescends to use more familiar terminology.

The following inscription from the late second or early third century highlights how one brother, Saturnilus, writes to his older brother Sempronios in the following remarkable terms:

---

[19] Horrell, "From ἀδελφοί to οἶκος θεοῦ," 299.
[20] Arzt-Grabner, "'Brothers' and 'Sisters' in Documentary Papyri," 188-89.
[21] Arzt-Grabner, "'Brothers' and 'Sisters' in Documentary Papyri," 192, citing C. Epist. Lat. 74, 6-9 (available on the Duke Databank of Documentary Papyri).
[22] Arzt-Grabner, "'Brothers' and 'Sisters' in Documentary Papyri," 195.
[23] *BGU* I 248; 249; II 531; III 850 (available on the Duke Databank of Documentary Papyri).
[24] *BGU* II 594; 595 (available on the Duke Databank of Documentary Papyri).

For you know, brother, that I regard you not only as a brother but as a father and lord and god (ὡς πατέρα καὶ κύριον καὶ θεόν).[25]

In the light of this papyrological evidence, it becomes clearer that 'brother' language, whether describing a metaphorical or natural relationship, does not necessarily include notions of equality. Furthermore, Paul's 'mixed-metaphor' use of ἀδελφός language alongside father-child language may not be as problematic as at first appears.

Plutarch and Brotherly Love
Additional literary support for this contention can be found in Plutarch's work *Concerning Brotherly Love*.[26] Betz suggests that 'Plutarch's treatise is the only *systematic* presentation of what antiquity had to say about the ethics of "brotherly love"',[27] and yet, until recently, Plutarch's analysis has been almost entirely ignored by New Testament scholars.[28]

---

[25]   Arzt-Grabner, "'Brothers' and 'Sisters' in Documentary Papyri," 195, citing *P. Mich.* III 209 (available on the Duke Databank of Documentary Papyri).

[26]   In Latin it is called *De fraterno amore*, and in Greek it is called περὶ φιλαδελφίας.

[27]   H. D. Betz, "De fraterno amore (*Moralia* 478A-492D)," in *Plutarch's Ethical Writings and Early Christian Literature* (ed. H. D. Betz; Leiden: Brill, 1978), 232.

[28]   A number of works have recently been published which explore the relationship between Plutarch's analysis and the New Testament data in more detail, although the particular debate regarding hierarchy and egalitarianism has not been a key focus: Reider Aasgaard, *'My Beloved Brothers and Sisters!' A Study of the Meaning and Function of Christian Siblingship in Paul, in Its Greco-Roman and Jewish Context* (Oslo: University of Oslo, 1998) [forthcoming with Continuum]; R. Aasgaard, "Brotherhood in Plutarch and Paul: Its Role and Character," in *Constructing Early Christian Families: Family As Social Reality and Metaphor* (ed. H. Moxnes; London: Routledge, 1997), 166-82; S. S. Bartchy, "Undermining Ancient Patriarchy: The Apostle Paul's Vision of a Society of Siblings," *BTB* 29 (1999): 68-78; Karl Olav Sandnes, *A New Family: Conversion and Ecclesiology in the Early Church with Cross-cultural Comparisons* (Studies in the Intercultural History of Christianity; Bern: Peter Lang, 1994). Cf. also H.-J. Klauck, "Brotherly Love in Plutarch and in 4 Maccabees," in *Greeks,*

Concerning Brotherly Love, written probably in the final years of the first century, details at length what he considers ought to be the characteristics of brotherly love. Plutarch does not presuppose that brothers always acted according to these ideal principles; indeed his complaint was precisely that true brotherly love was an unfortunate rarity. Specifically, he opens his discourse by declaring that the qualities of brotherly love are more commonly lacking than evident.

> [A]ccording to my observation, brotherly love is as rare in our day as brotherly hatred was among the men of old; when instances of such hatred appeared, they were so amazing that the times made them known to all as warning examples in tragedies and other stage-performances; but all men of to-day, when they encounter brothers who are good to each other, wonder at them no less than at those famous sons of Molionê, who, according to common belief, were born with their bodies grown together; and to use in common a father's wealth and friends and slaves is considered as incredible and portentous as for one soul to make use of the hands and feet and eyes of two bodies.[29]

He argues at length that the ideal of brotherly love is one of mutual dependence and support.

> Nature from one seed and one source has created two brothers, or three, or more, not for difference and opposition to each other, but that by being separate they might the more readily co-operate with one another. For indeed creatures that had three bodies and an hundred hands, if any such were ever really born, being joined together in all their members, could do nothing independently and apart from one another, as many brothers, who can either remain at home or reside abroad, as well as undertake public office and husbandry through each other's help if they but preserve that principle of goodwill and concord which Nature has given them.[30]

Romans and Christians: Essays in Honor of Abraham J. Malherbe (ed. D. L. Balch, E. Ferguson, W. A. Meeks; Minneapolis: Fortress, 1990), 144-56, which also draws on Johannine material. See also the major volume Klaus Schaefer, *Gemeinde als 'Bruderschaft'* (Frankfurt: Lang, 1989).

[29] Plutarch, *Mor.* 478C.
[30] Plutarch, *Mor.* 478E.

He argues that brotherly love is a fundamental strength within a household, indeed it generates love:

> through the concord of brothers both family and household are sound and flourish.

> Excellent and just sons will not only love each other the more because of their parents, but will also love their parents the more because of each other.

> Now as regards parents, brotherly love is of such sort that to love one's brother is forthwith a proof of love for both mother and father.[31]

Indeed, Plutarch might well reject the NRSV's translation of ἀδελφοί as 'friends', in that he argues that the affection between friends is but a pale imitation of what can truly exist between brothers.

More notably for our own concern in the present chapter is the space which Plutarch devotes to the relationship of an inferior brother to his superior, and of the superior brother to the inferior.[32] In chs 12–15 of the discourse we find an extensive discussion of the concept of equality and inequality between brothers. He begins by addressing how the superior brother should act towards his inferior sibling. Life is such that inequalities exist, but they should be handled so as not to create division.

> All manner of inequality is dangerous as likely to foster brothers' quarrels, and though it is impossible for them to be equal and on the same footing in all respects (for on the one hand our natures at the very beginning make an unequal apportionment, and then later on our varying fortunes beget envies and jealousies, the most shameful diseases and plagues, ruinous not only for private houses, but for whole states as well); against these inequalities we must be on our guard and must cure them, if they arise. One would therefore advise a brother, in the first place, to make his brothers partners in those respects in which he is considered to be superior; ... in the next place, to make manifest to them neither haughtiness nor disdain, but rather, by defer-

---

[31] Plutarch, *Mor.* 478F, 480E, F.
[32] Cf. Aasgaard, "Brotherhood in Plutarch and Paul," 171-72.

ring to them and conforming his character to theirs, to make his superiority secure from envy and to equalize, so far as this is attainable, the disparity of his fortune by his moderation of spirit.[33]

This is then developed by a specific address to the inferior brother (*Mor.* 485C-E). The inferior brother who is ambitious should seek to compete in areas in which his superior brother does not partake. Envy is thus neutralized by choosing a non-contentious area so that brothers can both excel, while not competing. His argument is widely supported by examples from nature, from mathematics and from history.

A further moment of crisis which can radically threaten the relationship between brothers is when the father dies and the inheritance is to be divided (*Mor.* 483C-484B). Plutarch notes that inheritance does not treat brothers as equals — indeed, that such differences in status can often mark clear tensions in the relationship between brothers. This is one of the key moments at which the inequality between brothers is painfully brought to the fore.

The case is clear. For Plutarch, brotherly love is to be highly valued, and one of its biggest threats comes from the inevitability that nature produces inequalities between brothers. Nonetheless, at all costs, brotherly love should win the day.

Conclusion

Such a brief treatment of the issue can no more than highlight the single point that interpreters of the New Testament can all too easily superimpose on the text concerns which are alien to the original environment. While there is a widespread suspicion of hierarchical structures in the church today, it is tempting to adopt the ἀδελφός language in Paul and imbue it with notions of equality which are common to sibling relationships in Western societies today.[34] A closer

---

[33] Plutarch, *Mor.* 484C-D.

[34] I am grateful to David L. Baker and Paul Ellingworth for their suggestion that we could contrast many other languages (mainly Far Eastern, including Chinese, Indonesian, Thai) where one must specify a senior or junior

look at papyrological and literary sources, however, demonstrates that ἀδελφός language does not presuppose egalitarianism. Indeed, it is precisely this relationship between brothers which can bring into sharp and painful relief the distinctions in status which nature and inheritance have endowed. It is brotherly love which holds together the relationship between brothers, notwithstanding such inequalities. Brotherly love is concerned with mutuality, rather than equality. Arzt-Grabner concludes from the documentary papyri: 'In both senses — the literal and the metaphorical — "brother" expresses closeness, solidarity and some kind of bond or engagement.'[35] In the light of this background evidence, it is then important that we revisit the place of ἀδελφός language in the broader equality/hierarchy debate concerning the Pauline communities.

---

brother, and cannot simply refer to a brother regardless of comparative status.
[35] Arzt-Grabner, "'Brothers' and 'Sisters' in Documentary Papyri," 202.

'For the Husband Is Head of the Wife':

Paul's Use of Head and Body Language

I. Howard Marshall

In 1 Cor 11:3 Paul creates a set of relationships in which God is the head of Christ,[1] Christ is the head of each man and the man (*sc.* husband) is the head of the woman (*sc.* wife). In Eph 5:22-33[2] there is teaching about the mutual relationships of husbands and wives. Wives are to be subject to their husbands as to the Lord, and a basis for this is given in that the husband is the head of the wife, as Christ is the head of the church (he being the saviour of the body), but as the church is subject to Christ, so should wives be to their husbands in every respect. Similarly, the love of husbands for their wives is to be analogous to that of Christ for the church, and Christ's love for the church is then developed in a manner that is partly dependent on the marriage metaphor: Christ cleanses the church so that it might be glorious and free from blemish, like, we may assume, a bride coming in purity to her husband. In a related metaphor or comparison husbands are to love their wives like their own bodies, just as Christ loves his body, the church. Then comes a quotation about a man leaving his parents to become one flesh with his wife, and this is applied to the relationship between Christ and the church. Finally husbands are re-

---

[1]   I am grateful for this opportunity to thank Bruce for his friendship and to express my appreciation of his work in shedding fresh light on the New Testament from the Graeco-Roman world.

[2]   I take Paul to be the author of Ephesians and Colossians, but I do not think that my argument depends on this assumption.

minded to love their wives like themselves and wives to reverence[3] their husbands.[4]

What led Paul to develop this understanding of the husband-wife relationship?[5] How did Paul come to believe that there was an analogy between husband-wife and God-man or Christ-church and that what is true of the latter relationships should also be true of the former? And how did he come to employ the terms 'head' and 'body' in this connection? Can any fresh light be shed on these questions?

Body Language in the Earlier Letters
Paul's use of 'body' language with reference to the church has been thoroughly explored with regard to both its origins and its significance, but some things still remain obscure.[6]

The earliest explicit expression of 'body' language by Paul in relation to the church is in 1 Corinthians. In ch. 12 the main purpose of the metaphor is to explain the relationships between the different members of the church who mutually support one another by their different functions, and all are valuable and necessary, even though Paul does allow that some gifted persons (apostles, prophets and teachers) are more important than others. The ears, nose and eyes are

---

[3]   The softer meaning is probably justified in the context of a loving husband rather than a tyrant or a God against whom we have sinned.

[4]   The instructions in Col 3:18-19 lack the imagery of headship and the analogy with Christ and the church.

[5]   For a major discussion of origins and interpretation see M. Barth, *Ephesians* (AB; Garden City: Doubleday, 1974), 183-210, 651-753.

[6]   For a full survey of earlier discussion see E. Best, *One Body in Christ* (London: SPCK, 1955); cf. E. Best, *Ephesians* (ICC; Edinburgh: T & T Clark, 1998), 189-96. The essentials are in A. T. Lincoln, *Ephesians* (WBC; Dallas: Word, 1990), 66-72. See now G. L. O. R. Yorke, *The Church As the Body of Christ in the Pauline Corpus: A Re-examination* (Lanham: University Press of America, 1991); G. W. Dawes, *The Body in Question: Metaphor and Meaning in the Interpretation of Ephesians 5:21-33* (Leiden: Brill, 1998); C. Stettler, *Der Kolosserhymnus: Untersuchungen zu Form, traditionsgeschichtlichem Hintergrund und Aussage von Kol 1,15-20* (Tübingen: Mohr Siebeck, 2000), 199-234.

treated as individual members of the body, and the head itself is treated like any other member (1 Cor 12:21). Even so, the body is the body of Christ (1 Cor 12:27), and Paul can say 'Just as it is with the [human] body, so also it is with Christ' (1 Cor 12:12), as if Christ were identical with the body as a whole.[7]

The specific *development* of the metaphor here is best explained by reference to the comparison, well-attested elsewhere in the ancient world between a political community and a body.[8] What is debatable is whether this political metaphor explains the *origin* of Paul's application of it to the church. Coincidentally Christian language also included the use of the term body for the body of Christ crucified on the cross and represented by the loaf of bread in the Lord's Supper. In 1 Cor 10 Paul makes the point that the bread broken at the Lord's Supper is, i.e. 'represents', the body of Christ, and in parallelism with 'the blood of Christ' this must refer symbolically to his crucified body.[9] But he immediately draws the further point that because there is one loaf, from which all of us partake, the 'many' are 'one body'. The relevance of this to the immediate issue, namely the incompatibility of eating the Supper and food sacrificed to idols, is explained by Fee: the point is not the *unity* of the church but the *solidarity* that results from the union of the members which forbids being partners in associations with demons.[10] Here, then, it would seem that the concept of the church as a body is already in Paul's mind and he can draw on it to say that the participation of believers in

---

[7]   Stettler, *Der Kolosserhymnus*, 219, interprets the phrase as 'so also Christ is one', although he is at work in the various limbs and organs in different ways. The same metaphor recurs in Rom 12:3-5, where Christians form one body 'in Christ'. Similar points about not thinking too highly of their own gifts but simply getting on and using them for mutual benefit are made. Again, nothing is said about the functions of the body vis-à-vis Christ.
[8]   A. C. Thiselton, *The First Epistle to the Corinthians* (NIGTC; Grand Rapids/Carlisle: Eerdmans/Paternoster, 2000), 990-95.
[9]   The manner of this representation need not be discussed here.
[10] G. D. Fee, *The First Epistle to the Corinthians* (NICNT; Grand Rapids: Eerdmans, 1987), 469.

eating the one loaf constitutes them as a solidarity or is a meaningful symbol of their existing solidarity. If 1 Cor 11:29 refers to not recognising that the congregation gathered round the table is the body of Christ in which every member must be honoured and no social divisions should be allowed to split it, then again an existing usage of the term must be presumed to be familiar to the readers.

Clearly the fact that Jesus made the loaf a symbol of his body played a role in the development of the metaphor of the church as his body. Once the church was understood as the body of Christ it was natural to see the one loaf from which all ate as symbolical not only of the physical body of Christ but also of the church which was already understood to be *his* body (1 Cor 12:27).[11] But the Lord's Supper is unlikely to have been the originating factor. In the sayings at the Last Supper the reference is unmistakably to his body given for them, and the parallelism with the blood makes this reference quite unambiguous. Some other influence is needed to account for the development of a secondary understanding of the bread as the church.

It is possible that the Christian use of the metaphor developed from the political metaphor that lies behind 1 Cor 12. But it is generally held that the basic element to be explained is the understanding of the church as the body *of Christ*, and that this cannot have arisen from the political metaphor that Paul exploits in 1 Cor 12. Already in 1 Cor 6:15 the bodies of individual believers are 'limbs and organs' (REB) of Christ, and in Rom 12:5 individual members form one body 'in Christ', i.e. by virtue of their union with Christ. Resort is then made to Paul's theology of union with Christ and baptism into Christ.[12] But those who go down this route offer no explanation as to

---

[11] C. Stettler (in correspondence) asks whether the symbolism of 'one body' attaches to the partaking of one loaf or to the loaf itself.

[12] See especially P. Stuhlmacher, *Biblische Theologie des Neuen Testaments* (Göttingen: Vandenhoeck & Ruprecht, 1992), 1:358-59. He links together the Eucharistic tradition, the Adam-Christ typology and the concept of Jesus as the crucified and resurrected Messiah-Son of Man. G. Strecker, *Theology of the New Testament* (Louisville: WJK, 2000), 182-86, is sceptical

how *body* language arose out of this theology. For myself I see no real difficulty in saying that the believers form a unity like a political association in virtue of their common faith in Christ and their incorporation as his people.[13] To call them 'the body of Christ' is no different from calling them 'the church of God' (1 Cor 1:2) or 'the churches of Christ' (Rom 16:16).[14] Consideration should be given to the hypothesis of C. Chavasse, as developed by Stettler, that the origin lies in the concept of the bride as the body of her husband since husband and wife form one body (or 'one flesh', Gen 2:24; cf. 1 Cor 6:16) and occasionally the wife is said to be her husband's flesh.[15]

However the development took place, the significant point is that the concept of the body of Christ is already a fully established part of Paul's theological vocabulary in his earlier letters and must form at least part of the background to the later usage, whether from Paul himself or a follower.

Body Language in Colossians and Ephesians

The body metaphor reappears in Colossians and Ephesians. There is continuity. Once again the body is the body of Christ and it consists of members who must show concern for one another (Col 3:15; Eph 4:16, 25; 5:30). The mutual love, which, in the light of 1 Cor 13, is implicit in 1 Cor 12 and 14, becomes explicit (Eph 4:16). But new

---

of the Eucharistic origin and thinks that the derivation of the idea owes more to the 'in Christ' concept and baptism. G. B. Caird, *New Testament Theology* (Oxford: Clarendon, 1994), 175, holds that three sources may all have contributed something to Paul's thought: the political usage; the tradition of the Eucharistic words; and the Hebrew use of 'flesh' (which lies behind the use of 'body') to signify 'kinship, both of the family and of the nation'.

[13]   Cf. Fee, *1 Corinthians*, 600-03.

[14]   It may be pure chance that Paul only uses the phrase 'churches of Christ' (cf. Gal 1:22) rather than 'church of Christ'. He prefers to speak of the church/churches of God (for the plural see 1 Cor 11:16).

[15]   Stettler, *Der Kolosserhymnus*, 214-20. However, to say that husband and wife form one body is not quite the same as saying that the wife is the body of the husband, and the interpretation of the passages cited in support of the wife being seen as her husband's flesh is not unproblematic.

features enter. The body grows (Col 2:19; Eph 4:16). What concerns us most here is that the head is now identified as Christ and differentiated from the rest of the body. It is associated with supremacy (Col 1:18b) but is also the source from which the body is supplied with nourishment and so enabled to grow (Col 2:19). In Ephesians great emphasis is similarly placed upon the supreme place of Christ in the universe, but in the opening prayer he is said to be 'head over everything for the church' rather than 'head over the church' (Eph 1:22) and his fullness overflows into the church (Eph 1:23). Certainly the church is also said to be subject to Christ (Eph 5:24), but the initial thought is of the way in which the supremacy of Christ over the universe is for the good of the church. Somewhat awkwardly Christ is the head because other powers are placed beneath his feet![16]

How did the metaphor develop in this way? The 'political' aspect of the metaphor, while not totally absent, is somewhat sidelined, and the main emphasis is more on the relationship of head and body with the head being both supreme and also the source of whatever it is that causes the body to grow as this 'substance' spreads through a body composed of connected parts. Can this development be explained?

Many scholars have found it difficult to envisage the development of two different uses of the body concept within the mind of one Christian thinker, namely Paul. I suggest that such a development is perfectly conceivable. The idea of the headship of Christ was already familiar to Paul. It emerges, as we shall see, in 1 Cor 11:3, where we have the familiar statement that Christ is the head of every, i.e. each, man. If Christ is the head of every man, then the move to his being head over all things and of the church is a simple one.

If the starting point of Paul's thought in Colossians was in fact the concept of the head, it is then because the idea of 'head' was already in his mind that Paul developed a fresh use for the body metaphor. In Col 2:10 the primary thought in Paul's mind is that of the headship of

---

[16] Cf. G. Howard, "The Head/Body Metaphors of Ephesians," *NTS* 20 (1973-74): 350-56.

Christ; he is thinking of the superiority of Christ over 'every power and authority'. Already in the Old Testament 'head' language can be used to express the superiority of God over everything (1 Chr 29:11).[17] What is needed to enable Paul to make the transition from the thought of the dominion of Christ as head to the thought of his headship of the church (Col 1:18)? He already knows that the church is the body of Christ and believers are his limbs and organs (1 Cor 6; 12). He also is familiar with the metaphor of the head, and he has applied it to Christ in 1 Cor 11:3 where he says that the head of every man is Christ. Are any further ingredients needed? He can be presumed to be aware of the relation of head and body in ancient physiology. So Paul can develop a consistent picture in which Christ is the head of his body; this means that he holds the pre-eminent position (Col 1:18), and that nourishment flows from him to every part of the body so that it grows (2:19). There is also a stress on the fact that there is only one body of Christ, and therefore believers should live in peace and unity because they all belong to this one body (3:15).

Similar thoughts reappear in Ephesians. Again we have the thought of the cosmic headship of Christ (Eph 1:22). There is the same thought of the nourishment of the church and the need for the parts to hold together (4:16; cf. 5:30). There is the same use of the picture of the one body (4:4).

It seems that the usage is plastic and flexible. Christ is the head of the universe in that he is supreme over all the powers within it, and he exercises this headship for the benefit of the church. The universe is not his body, but the church is his body, in that he is the source of its life. The church is subject to Christ who is its head; here he is the saviour of the body, a term wide enough to encompass his deliverance of it by his self-giving to death and his continuing sustenance of it.

---

[17]   Cf. Ps 18:44; Hos 2:2 MT of the king.

So the original 'body' metaphor has been expanded by assigning a special position to the head, by picking up the metaphor of sustenance from the head, by recognising the authority of the head over the members, and also by picking up the idea of Christ as head over the universe because it has been placed under his feet. These developments were possible because the metaphorical usages were there to hand. It is dubious whether ancient mythology regarding the cosmos and the god who creates or controls it had any influence.[18]

Husband and Wife

What now of the use of the language of headship with respect to the husband and wife? The application of the term 'head' to a husband seems to be unprecedented. Here I rely with confidence on Wayne Grudem's *Thesaurus Linguae Graecae* search which did not find any texts making this application. Until fresh evidence to the contrary is forthcoming, we may cautiously conclude that this application is not attested in Greek before we find it in Paul.[19]

However, two relevant texts may be noted. First, Barth cites Aristotle:

---

[18] One of the main arguments for this view lies in the apparent awkwardness of the apposition 'the body [namely] the church' in Col 1:18, which has suggested that an original understanding of the body as the universe has been replaced by an understanding of the church as the body. See, however, P. T. O'Brien, *Colossians, Philemon* (WBC; Waco: Word, 1982), 48-50; N. T. Wright, "Poetry and Theology in Colossians 1.15-20," *NTS* 36 (1990): 444-68; and especially Stettler, *Der Kolosserhymnus*, 86-94, 231-34, who argues that the second strophe of the passage begins with v. 18a rather than 18b, and that parallels for understanding 'body' as a designation for the world are lacking.

[19] Grudem's researches were concerned primarily with establishing the significance of the term 'head' in ancient literature. I am grateful to him for confirming to me that his investigations did not reveal any texts where the term is applied to a husband (email, February 2003). Thus the conclusion reached earlier by M. Barth, *Ephesians*, II, 617-18, still stands.

> The rule of the household is a monarchy, for every house is under one head (*Pol.* 1255b).[20]

Here we have the term 'head' being used as a self-standing metaphor for exercising the function of a ruler without any correlative use of the term 'body' to signify the area ruled. But it is easy to see that the statement could be particularised to indicate that the wife is under the head of the household, who would normally be her husband.

In a second passage from Plutarch a wife is compared with a body to be governed by her husband:

> And control ought to be exercised by the man over the woman, not as the owner has control of a piece of property, but, as the soul controls the body (σῶμα), by entering into her feelings and being knit to her through goodwill. As, therefore, it is possible to exercise care over the body without being slave to its pleasures and desires, so it is possible to govern a wife, and at the same time delight and gratify her.[21]

Here the analogy is of the soul inhabiting the body and not of the head controlling the body. Again, then, we have no precise parallel to Paul's usage. But it is clear that the prevalence of this kind of thinking was congenial to the development of the headship language to apply to the husband-wife relationship.

Therefore, it would seem that the conditions were right for somebody to apply the language of head and body to husband and wife, and that somebody may well have been Paul who must accordingly be given the credit for the introduction of the idea in Greek literature.

How, then, did Paul develop his particular form of expression? Two roots seem probable.

---

[20] Barth, *Ephesians*, 618; cf. Lincoln, *Ephesians*, 369; C. S. Keener, *Paul, Women and Wives: Marriage and Women's Ministry in the Letters of Paul* (Peabody: Hendrickson, 1992), 146-47.

[21] Plutarch, *Mor., Conj. Praec.* 142.33 (Babbitt, LCL). (I am grateful to James Hering for drawing my attention to this passage.) Plutarch lived c. AD 50-120, and therefore his writings are certainly later than those of Paul but they could be contemporary with a post-Pauline school.

The first is that Paul was responding to a situation at Corinth in which women were not covering their physical heads in the church meeting. If this behaviour was indicative of a loose woman, then we can understand that it was seen as disrespectful to her metaphorical 'head', i.e. her husband, and therefore Paul saw the need to correct the behaviour.[22]

The second is the existing understanding in the Hellenistic world of the householder (normally a married man) as head of the household and of him as 'governing' his wife. I propose that the failure of some women to cover their physical heads was the catalyst that led to the application of the term 'head' to describe the role of the husband in relation to the wife.

Thus we have the combination of the problem of wives failing to cover their (physical) heads and the social climate in which the householder was the 'head' of the household producing an interesting coincidence of language. It is astonishingly similar to the way in which the use of the term 'body' in the Lord's Supper to refer to the physical body of Christ symbolised by the bread facilitated the secondary application of the term to the church and so helped to strengthen the concept of the church as the body of Christ.

However, this is not the whole story. Here, as in the later discussion in Ephesians, the discussion of husbands and wives is placed in the context of a higher level of relationship. 'The head of every man is Christ ..., and the head of Christ is God.'[23] Commentators generally seem to be so taken up with the husband-wife relationship here that they give little or no attention to the theological statements in v. 3. It

---

[22] Paul is probably thinking particularly of Christian men rather than unbelievers and specifically of men who are husbands, since the situation is focused on Christian husbands and wives. It can be safely excluded that the thought is that any man is the head of any woman, but it could be that the father of an unmarried daughter is seen as her head in the context of a patriarchal society.

[23] By the time we get to v. 7 Christ has dropped out of the picture and the man is the image and glory of God.

tends to be overlooked that the application of the metaphor to the relation between Christ and the husband (or man) also occurs here for
the first time. How is this to be explained? Are there any parallels? It
is tempting to assume that Paul brings in this fact so as to create a
forceful analogy: just as the man must honour his head, Christ, so the
woman must honour her head, her husband. The apparent afterthought
'and God is the head of Christ' is likewise a fresh theologoumenon,
based on the parallel in 1 Cor 3:23, and fitting in with the declaration
that Christ is subject to God in 15:27-28. It serves to strengthen further the call to honour the person who functions as head. By bringing
in the analogy of husband-Christ, Paul is able to ground more firmly
his argument that the wife must treat her physical head differently
from the way in which the man treats his physical head.

In v. 7 it is the man who is the image and glory of *God*; this point
is from Genesis, and hence it is not said that the man is the image and
glory of *Christ*, although Paul may imply this. The woman is the
glory of her husband. This implies that she herself is a 'glorious'
being, and therefore she brings lustre to her husband, in the same way
as the created universe, being originally 'good', and especially hu-
mankind, is intended to add to the glory of God. Paul, it seems to me,
is not denying that the woman is also the image and glory of God. To
do so would go against Gen 1:27, which clearly affirms that both
male and female are made in the image of God. But the Genesis narrative goes on to describe how the first woman was made from the
first man, and is his helpmeet. Consequently, she has a relationship to
him that must be preserved, so that he is not dishonoured. It would
seem possible to me that Paul can affirm this additional relationship
of the wife to the husband without denying her prior relationship to
God.

The reason why the relationship is discussed in an asymmetrical
fashion is that there does not appear to have been any comparable
cultural practice by men which would dishonour their wives. Consequently, Paul can go on to affirm the mutual dependence of husband

and wife in vv. 11-12, and affirm that 'everything', i.e. both of them, is from God.

The result of this development in 1 Cor 11 is that Paul has produced a use of the term 'head' which is independent of the body metaphor.

In 1 Corinthians the thought of origin is present and honour is due to the originator. Paul can say that the woman comes from the man and not vice versa, evidently on the basis of Gen 2; but then he retracts by adding that the man is through the woman, and everything is from God. Although the physical head is in view, it seems to be symbolic of the metaphorical head, and the body of which the head is a part or over which it exercises direction (or whatever) plays no part whatever in the thought. Granted that the thought of super-ordination is expressible by the metaphor, it seems clear that the correlative motifs of subordination and obedience do not play any significant part in this passage.

When we come to Ephesians, it seems more likely that Paul takes over the picture of the church in relation to Christ as its head, and uses it to draw up a parallel and paradigm for the wife-husband relationship. But in fact he does not apply the term 'body' to the wife,[24] although there is probably a parallel between Christ as the saviour of the 'body', namely the church, and the husband in his role of loving care for his wife. From the relationship he draws the responsibility of the wife to be subject and of the husband to love in a way that is parallel to Christ's self-giving love for the church. The way in which Paul develops the thought of Christ and the church beyond what was required by the context confirms that this was a topic that had already been developed for its own sake; it is already present in 2 Cor 11:2, and finds further expression in non-metaphorical terms in Titus 2:14 where Christ redeems 'us' (i.e. the church) from iniquity and cleanses us to be his own special people for himself (cf. Heb 9:14). So Christ

---

[24] M. Barth's interpretation of v. 28 that husbands are to love their wives 'for they are their bodies' has not been upheld by subsequent commentators.

cares for the church, i.e. for us, 'because we are members of his body'. Husbands, then, are to love their wives like their own bodies; but while the church is said directly to *be* the body of Christ, the wife is to be valued *like* her husband's physical body ('as himself', v. 33). The result is that the passage as a whole begins with the relation of the wife to the husband, but is then absolutely dominated by the relation of Christ to the church, so much so that Paul has to remind himself (cf. the strong πλήν after his ecclesiological digression) of what his opening theme was, and to insert the closing point about the wife reverencing her husband.

The outcome of this discussion is to suggest that in Eph 5 Paul begins with the concept of Christ as head of his body, the church, and then applies the analogy of the head to the husband-wife relationship, but without identifying the wife as the body to her 'head'. He was able to do so because of the existing understanding of the husband or householder as the head of both wife and family and because the concept of Christ as head of the body was already developed and indeed very much in mind in this letter.

Much in this study has been tentative and speculative. Nevertheless, it seems very probable that Paul is the originator of 'head' language with regard to Christ in relation to the church and the husband in relation to his wife. This indeed, is the major conclusion of this study. In our desire to read the New Testament against its background, we must be prepared to give credit to the authors for being the first on occasion to conceive of fresh ideas that are not paralleled in the contemporary world. That appears to be the case on the evidence so far available for the use of this particular metaphor with reference to the husband-wife relationship.

The Appeal to Convention in Paul

E. A. Judge

Does Paul Endorse Convention in 1 Corinthians 11:16?

English 'convention', like Latin *consuetudo* and Greek συνήθεια, accentuates by its prefix a custom that is the conscious practice of a collectivity.[1] But for which collectivity does Paul use the term συνήθεια in 1 Cor 11:16? Does it refer to the circles whose practice Paul criticises?[2] Or is Paul classifying the traditions (παραδόσεις) he handed on to them (1 Cor 11:2) as a convention held both by himself and 'the churches of God' (11:16, sc. the non-Pauline churches)?

The latter view is implied by the RSV translation ('we recognise no other practice'), matched by the NIV and other recent versions, and going back at least to Moffatt's ('no other standard of worship',

---

[1]   See D. K. Lewis, *Convention: A Philosophical Study* (Cambridge, Mass.: Harvard University Press, 1969), ch. 3, for other types of customary life (norms, rules, imitation, agreement, social contract, conformity), and, for the way morality differs, see E. Turiel, *The Development of Social Knowledge: Morality and Convention* (Cambridge: CUP, 1983). For the classical and historical usage see L. Koep, "Consensus," *RAC* 3 (1955): 294-303; J. Ranft, "Consuetudo," *RAC* 3 (1955): 379-90; G. Funke, "ἕξις, ἔθος, ἦθος, συνήθεια, νόμος und 'zweite Natur' im klassischen Denken," *Archiv für Begriffsgeschichte* 3 (1958): 78-79; idem, "Gewohnheit," *Historisches Wörterbuch der Philosophie* 3 (1974): 597-616.

[2]   The difficulty in imagining where they might have got it from has perhaps deflected attention from this identification. A. Wire, *The Corinthian Women Prophets: A Reconstruction through Paul's Rhetoric* (Minneapolis: Fortress, 1990), 129: 'perhaps someone like Apollos brought it from elsewhere'. The need to explain why men should have been led to veil themselves has prompted a far-reaching analysis of dress practice amongst both men and women by B. W. Winter, *After Paul Left Corinth: The Influence of Secular Ethics and Social Change* (Grand Rapids: Eerdmans, 2001), 121-41.

1901). The gratuitous term 'other' gives it away.[3] The classic translators and commentators from Jerome and Luther onwards have however correctly understood that the demonstrative adjective τοιαύτην
ties the term συνήθειαν to the practice Paul is criticising (AV, 'we
have no such custom'). In conflict situations Paul regularly uses
τοιοῦτος (whether adjective or pronoun) as a distancing term ('such a
person as that'). (He is of course therefore hardly proposing here to
abandon his own 'custom' for the sake of peace.) Moreover τοιοῦτος
in Paul is always rhetorically backward-looking. He can therefore
hardly intend by συνήθεια any 'custom' of disputatiousness which he
will exemplify in the following passage (1 Cor 11:17-22).[4] E. E. Ellis
has carefully analysed the reasons for taking 1 Cor 11:3-16 as 'a pre-
formed tradition' inserted into the letter after it was already drafted.
He is of course very alert to the consciously didactic (as distinct from
habitual) character of such a 'tradition', but still slips into seeing v. 16
as 'an implicit identification of the teaching ... as a customary usage'.[5]

Paul uses συνήθεια in 1 Cor 8:7 of the 'practice' of idolatry. In
John 18:39 Pilate uses it for the Jewish 'custom' under which he
might release a prisoner at the Passover. C. B. Welles drew attention
to the fact that Moulton and Milligan's *Vocabulary* had not picked up
the association of the term with a cultic sanctuary, 'a late Hellenistic

---

[3]   This telling point has already been noted by G. D. Fee, *The First Epistle
to the Corinthians* (NICNT; Grand Rapids: Eerdmans, 1987), 524, n. 3; 530,
n. 9, but both Fee (530, 'he argues for maintaining a custom') and Wire (31-
33), 'Argument from Universal Church Practice') easily slip back into the
habit of making Paul treat his own 'tradition' as a convention, not apparently
allowing for the critical distinction between these two very different ways of
depending upon inherited patterns.
[4]   As argued, with the help of the alternative ms reading of participle and
verb in v. 17, by A. P. Stanley, *The Epistles of St. Paul to the Corinthians*
(2nd ed.; London: Murray, 1858), 206.
[5]   E. E. Ellis, "Traditions in 1 Corinthians," *NTS* 32 (1986): 481-502, at
493, the word 'implicit' clearly recognising that Paul does not call his
'tradition' a 'custom'.

180   E. A. JUDGE

development' seen also in Josephus and Philo.[6] Inscription no. 68 in Welles is a letter, perhaps of Attalus III, guaranteeing the right of asylum to a Lydian temple on condition that no change be made to its existing συνήθεια, or 'practice'. When the Samians petitioned Augustus for the benefit of freedom (from taxation) such as the Aphrodisians uniquely enjoyed, he replied that, even though his wife was backing their request and he would himself have liked to grant it, it would be unjust 'without good cause' to break his συνήθεια, since that would be to act at random (εἰκῇ).[7]

Here we witness the conscious creation of an administrative practice (or tradition?) out of what began as a military revolution (the Aphrodisians had taken his side in the war even though under his opponent's control). Might not Paul also, one must ask, have spoken of the arrangements in his new *ekklesiai* as 'his' συνήθεια? But in fact he spoke rather of παραδόσεις (1 Cor 11:2). Yet might not τοιοῦτος ('of such a kind') have been taken all the same to imply that these traditions constituted another kind of συνήθεια? And indeed the pericope is packed with what seem to be conventional appeals to propriety: what 'dishonours' one's head (vv. 4-5), what would be 'disgraceful' (v. 6), what one 'ought' to do (v. 10), what is 'appropriate' (v. 13), what is 'degrading' according to 'nature itself' (v. 14). But all of this is deployed to prop up a didactic 'tradition' defended by argument, and not resting upon the security of convention.

The Earliest Pauline Pattern of Personal and Church Life

The pericope that ends with Paul's rejecting their συνήθεια began with his praising them because 'you remember me in everything', πάντα μου μέμνησθε (1 Cor 11:2). The sole instance of this verb in the Pauline homologoumena, it is glossed by the following clause about their keeping the traditions he had handed on to them. It also no

---

[6]   C. B. Welles, *Royal Correspondence in the Hellenistic Period* (New Haven: Yale University Press, 1934), 274, 366.
[7]   J. M. Reynolds, *Aphrodisias and Rome* (London: Society for the Promotion of Roman Studies, 1982), no. 13.

doubt echoes the much more explicit formula of v. 1, to which it has been appended: 'Be imitators (μιμηταί) of me, as I am of Christ'. He had explained earlier (1 Cor 4:16-17) how this was to be attained: he had sent Timothy 'to remind you of my ways in Christ, as I teach them everywhere in every church'. The 'ways' are no convention, but a path (ὁδός) for life consciously set through teaching and reinforced by reminders. This is the Pauline substitute for the literal 'following' of Jesus by the first disciples. Paul could hardly claim to be a 'follower' in the manner that they had been.[8] Writing from Corinth at an earlier stage he had laid out, for the Thessalonians he had recently left, the way the new pattern of imitation was to be opened up.

(1) πάντοτε (1 Thess 1:2), 'always' in the sense of being 'uninterruptedly' (ἀδιαλείπτως) repeated, becomes the characteristic mark of Paul's thanksgivings as he recalls the response of his converts. Only the frustrated letters (2 Cor and Gal) fail to begin with such assurance. In 2 Thess 1:3 it is expressed as an obligation (ὀφείλομεν), a fitting thing (ἄξιον), in view of their abundant care for each other. In 2 Cor 1:11 he turns it around so that they work at it together in thanksgiving for the favour done to him. Paul only twice uses the classical adverb ἀεί, of a state or condition that 'always' applies (2 Cor 4:11; 6:10). The Atticists disapproved of πάντοτε, recommending instead διὰ παντός (2 Thess 3:16, a formal benediction) or ἑκάστοτε (never in Paul). But he revels in the familiar term, weaving its pointed sound through the plosive crescendo of the first letter.[9] Here the conventional themes of plain good or evil are magnetised around the central commitment to thanksgiving. Conventional people of the time guarded themselves by a daily sacrifice at home. But those who have

---

[8] E. A. Judge, "The Teacher As Moral Exemplar in Paul and in the Inscriptions of Ephesus," in *In the Fullness of Time: Biblical Studies in Honour of Archbishop Donald Robinson* (ed. David Peterson and John Pryor; Sydney: ANZEA, 1992), 185-201.

[9] On the alliterative structure of 1 Thess 5:15-24, and much else of cultural interest, see A. J. Malherbe, *The Letters to the Thessalonians* (AB; New York: Doubleday, 2000), 106-07, 327-40.

died with Christ, who was sacrificed 'once for all' (Rom 6:8-10), give themselves ἀδιαλείπτως to thanksgiving (1 Thess 5:18), being whole and blameless (v. 23). Paul's thanksgiving was inspired not so much by their intellectual response, as by its effect on their lifestyle. He recalls the 'work' produced by their faith (1 Thess 1:3), the 'labour' of their care, and the 'endurance' of their hope. This is the 'fulfilment' (πληροφορία, v. 5) of 'the word'. But they came to it because they knew what kind of men (οἷοι) Paul and Silvanus and Timothy had shown themselves to be when living amongst them. And this had been done deliberately, 'for your sake' (δι' ὑμᾶς).

(2) μιμηταί (1 Thess 1:6), 'imitators', seems a rather shallow term for the deep experience of bonding that Paul has in mind. It is not the conventional imitation of an ethical model, as in 3 John 11, 'do not imitate evil but imitate good'. The verb in 1 Thessalonians (uniquely) is not imperative (setting a standard for future behaviour) but aorist (recognising something that had already happened). What the apostles had demonstrated 'for your sake', you also had already experienced. Its validity however stems from the fact that at the same time you had become imitators 'of the Lord'. Paul's later formula ('as I am of Christ', 1 Cor 11:1) makes the Lord's experience the guiding principle. But what specifically is this experience?

(3) θλῖψις (1 Thess 1:6), 'affliction', establishes the bond, yet it is not any ordinary suffering, but rather the persecution that falls upon those who accept 'the word' and are glad to suffer because the Holy Spirit empowers them (v. 5). This pattern is spelled out in 1 Thess 2:13-16. They had become 'imitators of the churches of God ... in Judaea' because they suffered from their own countrymen the same things as had been done to the Lord Jesus and the prophets there. It had been 'set down' for us (κείμεθα, 3:3). With time the political confrontation is left behind, but the bonding with Christ in his sacrifice remains as the mainspring for a life (or 'walk') of self-giving (Eph 4:32–5:2 in the context of 4:25 to Eph 5:5): 'forgiving one another, as God in Christ forgave you. Therefore be imitators of God

... and walk in love, as Christ loved us and gave himself up for us'. 'We rejoice in our sufferings' (Rom 5:3) because 'suffering produces endurance' and 'God's love has been poured into our hearts through the Holy Spirit' (v. 5).

(4) This τύπος (1 Thess 1:7), or 'imprint', then becomes a 'pattern' for life supplied from the one community to others. Not only did the word of the Lord 'echo' from them across Macedonia and Achaea, but their trust in God was reported everywhere, so that the apostles needed to say no more (v. 8). To the Philippians Paul advises watching those who 'walk' in a certain way, that is according to the 'pattern' set by him and his 'fellow-imitators' (Phil 3:17). The 'pattern' for 'imitation' can then be applied to a particular case, as with the principle of depending upon one's own earned income (2 Thess 3:7-9), thus exemplifying a rule: 'If anyone will not work, let him not eat' (v. 10). Later it can be generalised: 'Present yourself in everything as a "pattern" of good works' (Titus 2:7). Even though 'affliction' was 'set down' for us (1 Thess 3:3) there is no quiescent fatalism here, but rather thanksgiving and joy (v. 9), the vitality of life itself (v. 8), aroused by the good news (v. 6) of their 'standing fast' in the Lord (v. 8). This particular term, first attested in Paul and typically imperative in mood, converts the perfect stem of the verb into a new present form (στήκω). It signifies the moral commitment that follows from personal decision, upheld by the Lord (Rom 14:5). It is the opposite of servility (Gal 5:1). One must be ready to 'stand fast' in trust (1 Cor 16:13), in one spirit (Phil 1:27), in the Lord (Phil 4:1). The Thessalonians have 'turned to God from idols ... to wait for his Son from heaven' (1 Thess 1:9-10), yet they are not held in a static pattern, but rather are on the move.

(5) περιπατεῖν (1 Thess 2:12), 'to walk about', picks up an everyday term as a metaphor for one's lifestyle in relation to other people. It would have been familiar to some as used of the walking ministry of Jesus and his followers. To others it may have been reminiscent of the way philosophers taught, walking up and down with their stu-

dents. Paul of course was the nurturing teacher of the Thessalonians (v. 7), concerned not only with the gospel (v. 8) but with moral behaviour (v. 10). The focus has passed now from 'imitation' to walking 'worthily' (ἀξίως) of God who is calling them into his kingdom (v. 12). What this means in practice is not explained. Paul needed only to allude to what he had said during his recent visit. That had been received by them as a word from God himself (v. 13). Later there will be talk of acting 'worthily' of the gospel of Christ (Phil 1:27), of the saints (Rom 16:2), of one's calling (Eph 4:1), or of the Lord (Col 1:10). Paul returns to the theme of 'walking' in 1 Thess 4:1, and then begins to itemise what this means. It relates to social matters. But they are in particular 'to keep quiet' (1 Thess 4:11). ἡσυχάζειν in the papyri is the posture of those who petition the authorities for justice against oppression. This is perhaps reflected in the 'peaceful and quiet life' sought through prayers on behalf of the public authority (1 Tim 2:2). But in 1 Thess 4:11 Paul's point is that one should earn one's own livelihood by working, and thus not be socially dependent on other people's patronage (cf. 2 Thess 3:6, 12). That Paul is undermining the social status system is hinted at in the oxymoron: 'keeping quiet' is to be their 'ambition', for which they should 'strive' (φιλοτιμεῖσθαι).

(6) To walk εὐσχημόνως (1 Thess 4:12), 'respectably', in regard to 'those outside', is now the focus (contrast 2:12). As with the English word, the term implies both good conduct and social esteem. The conduct wins esteem, while esteem confers the goodness upon it. (The same double-sidedness arises with other words, e.g. 'decently'.) Paul appeals to both aspects, 'decent' or proper behaviour in one's sexual life (1 Cor 7:35-36; 12:23-24; Rom 1:27) and 'respectability' in the eyes of others (1 Cor 14:40; Rom 13:13). The high social status that came to be indicated by the term appears with the prominent women enlisted against Paul at Pisidian Antioch (Acts 13:50), and for him at Berea (Acts 17:12). A late first-century oracle promises the

enquirer an improved livelihood, but especially living 'respectably'.[10]
A correspondent (*P. Hamb.* 1.37) addresses the second-century
Claudius Antoninus as a 'true philosopher', but especially as 'respectable', a view inspired by the correspondent's 'remembering' (cf.
1 Cor 11:2) his 'gentlemanliness' (καλοκαγαθία) and 'character'
(ἦθος). Neither quality is cited however by Paul as the basis for 'respectability'.

(7) At the very end of the letter (5:27) Paul places the
Thessalonians under oath (ἐνορκίζω) to have it read to 'all the brethren', whom he has already bound with 'a holy kiss' (5:26). It is meant
to establish a norm. This is clarified in the second letter. They are to
'stand', and 'grasp' (κρατεῖτε) the 'traditions' (παραδόσεις) which
they have been 'taught', whether orally (διὰ λόγου) or by letter 'from
us' (Paul, Silas and Timothy), the authors of both letters (2 Thess
2:15). These 'traditions' are emphatically not customs but explicit
instructions enjoined on them 'in the name of the Lord Jesus Christ'
(2 Thess 3:6). The 'traditions' are held in a consciously personal way,
sealed in direct contact (the 'holy kiss'), and envisaged through 'remembering' (1 Cor 11:2) the apostle. They are to 'imitate' him
(2 Thess 3:7). Such apostolic 'instructions' (παραγγελίαι) were delivered 'through the Lord Jesus' (1 Thess 4:2), and are derived from
him and his example (Eph 5:1-2; Acts 20:35). Tertullian denounced
custom as based on ignorance if it contradicted the truth which Christ
located in himself (*Virg.* 1.1-2). But Augustine stated that there were
also customs not found in the written tradition which are rated on a
par with that because they are preserved universally in the church
(*Bapt.* 2.7.12).

---

[10] P. Vindob. Salomons 1; in *New Documents Illustrating Early
Christianity*, 2 (ed. G. H. R. Horsley; North Ryde, N.S.W.: Ancient History
Documentary Research Centre, Macquarie University, 1982), 8.

Social Obligation in Paul

The English auxiliary verbs (e.g. 'should', 'ought' and 'must') are regularly used to soften the direct imperatives that confront us with someone else's demand. They shift the obligation to some un-identified principle which does not need to be justified. The Pauline letters however are strong on imperatives (sometimes relaxed by auxiliary verbs in modern translations). Where they do use Greek auxiliary verbs (or nouns) of obligation there is typically an explicit argument to justify it. We are obliged (ὀφείλομεν) to give thanks (1 Thess 1:3; 2 Thess 2:13), because God's grace is seen in the converts' behaviour. A man ought (ὀφείλει) not to veil his head and a woman ought to do so (1 Cor 11:7, 10), because that expresses God's purpose in their creation. We are not 'debtors' (ὀφειλέται) to the flesh (Rom 8:12), because of the indwelling Spirit. To love the other is the only debt you still have (ὀφείλειτε) to him (Rom 13:8), because love fulfils the law. Your debts (ὀφειλάς) under the social order (tax, duty, respect, Rom 13:7) you have already paid. We who are strong are obliged (ὀφείλομεν) to build up the weak (Rom 15:1-3), since Christ did not please himself. It was because they were debtors (ὀφειλέται) to them (Rom 15:27) that gentile believers shared their goods with 'the poor among the saints' in Jerusalem. In three cases the obligation is presumably self-evident, since it is not argued (1 Cor 7:36; 9:10; 2 Cor 12:14). There are a dozen passages in the homologoumena where Paul uses the impersonal verb δεῖ ('it must be that ...'). But it is always only a summary way of citing the didactic 'tradition' he has been arguing for. It is entirely remote from any sense of an unidentified, inherent, primal 'necessity'. Contrast the neo-Platonic principle of Plotinus (*Enn.* 4.[28]39):[11]

> ... the Reason-Principle of the universe ... in perfect adaptation of law to custom ... is made to thread its way in and out ... and all coalesces by a kind of automatism. (11-17)

---

[11]　Tr. S. McKenna; Library of Philosophical Translation.

> ... intentions are not to be considered as the operative causes ... it is a
> matter of the inevitable relation of parts ... the life of the Cosmos does
> not look to the individual but to the whole. (25-33)

Such a principle undergirded a hierarchical society and justified the exclusion of beggars from its ideal state.

Honour and shame set the axis of social life for ancient cultures, but are upended by Paul in major confrontations. Yet in some ways he does exploit their terms. As with 'respectability' (point (6) above), 'honour' (τιμή) is endorsed (Rom 13:7), yet in it we are to prefer one another (Rom 12:10). Like 'glory' (δόξα) it is a prized social reward (Rom 2:7), the only credible form of immortality according to Cicero, but Paul defers it until the final day of judgement (Rom 2:10). He makes bolder use of its opposite, 'dishonour' (ἀτιμία), but for the pathological passions (Rom 1:26) and for his own mock 'boasting' (2 Cor 11:21) in the inverted tests of true apostleship (2 Cor 6:8). At that point Paul is concerned that his ministry not be 'discredited' (μωμηθῇ, 2 Cor 6:3; 8:10). In general the varied terminology of 'good' and 'bad', 'fitting' and 'unfitting' is used by Paul not with reference to any aesthetic or social criterion (in spite of the temptation to which translators of Phil 4:8 may succumb), but typically of moral discrimination. It may well coincide with socially conventional judgement, but behind it all lies the challenging focus on the test which God will apply, surfacing in such terms as δοκιμή ('testedness', a form appearing first in Paul) and ἀδόκιμος ('rejected').

One's formal position in civil or domestic life is, however, positively endorsed. It has been assigned by God (1 Cor 7:17; cf. 2 Cor 10:13). I call this 'rank' as distinct from 'status'.[12] Rank must be accepted as an obligation. But status avoids responsibility and takes advantage of wealth or education. It is the same within the church. The Spirit assigns different ministries in the one body (1 Cor 12:4-12). There is a rank order (v. 28; cf. Rom 16:7), but in status those thought

---

[12] E. A. Judge, *Rank and Status in the World of the Caesars and St Paul* (Christchurch: University of Canterbury, 1982).

less respectable are treated with greater respect (1 Cor 12:23). Paul may occasionally seem to go for something like philosophical detachment. He wants people to be 'undistracted' (ἀμερίμνους, 1 Cor 7:32). God provides 'total self-sufficiency' (αὐτάρκειαν, 2 Cor 9:8). Paul has learned to be 'self-sufficient' whatever his circumstances (Phil 4:11). But always he means only to clear the way for his utterly unphilosophical and overwhelming commitment to the lost cause of Christ in his sufferings (Phil 3:10). Those who 'mind earthly things' are 'enemies of the cross of Christ' (vv. 18-19). But our 'commonwealth' (πολίτευμα, v. 20) is 'in heaven'.

This alternative citizenship leaves the civil order intact. Even Nero, whose sword hung over Paul's neck, is answerable to God (Rom 13:1-5). But within the church all social status is to be sacrificed. This is the only bodily victim that is now given up to please God (Rom 12:1). The offering consists in a transformation of attitudes ('the mind') that breaks with those that rule this age, 'putting to the test' (δοκιμάζειν) here and now what we know to be the 'final' (τέλειον) will of God (v. 2). Paul goes on directly to specify the problem: it is self-promotion in social relations (v. 3). He had fought this with the Galatians. Those who 'thought they were something' (Gal 2:6) had been imposing the old rules to create a power base: 'they make much of you ... so that you may make much of them' (Gal 4:17). 'They want to make a fine impression ... so that they will not be branded with the cross of Christ' (Gal 6:12). With the Thessalonians Paul had confronted those who were happy to live off the largesse of benefactors (the conventional means of self-promotion for both giver and receiver). Instead he set a (for them) humiliating standard, manual work (1 Thess 4:11; 2 Thess 3:11-12). In Corinth Paul had alienated the well-to-do patrons of the church by refusing to accept their support, and by rejecting the cultivated platform display expected of a civilised authority.[13]

---

[13] Peter Marshall, *Enmity in Corinth: Social Conventions in Paul's Relations with the Corinthians* (Tübingen: Mohr, 1987).

In pulling down the props of established status, Paul takes care not to ensnare them with a 'noose' (βρόχος) of his own. Nothing was to disrupt their 'bonding' (τὸ εὐπάρεδρον) with the Lord (1 Cor 7:35). As for their relations with each other, they are presented as a deliberate 'construction' (οἰκοδομή, 1 Cor 14:12, 26), in which their 'meeting' (ἐκκλησία) is conceived as itself a building under way (a Pauline innovation?). Although the foundation stones were laid, each person contributed to the new structure his particular gift. This paradox, validating conventional rank in the old order, but turning status upside down within it as a foretaste of the new, has been historically one of the transforming forces of our civilisation.[14]

---

[14] E. A. Judge, "Cultural Conformity and Innovation in Paul," *TynB* 35 (1984): 3-24.
An earlier version of the present paper was read to the New Testament Seminar at the Divinity School, Cambridge, on 12 November 1991.

'With What Kind of Body Do They Come?' (1 Corinthians 15:35b):

Paul's Conception of Resurrection Bodies

Brian S. Rosner

Introduction

The study of the background to the New Testament is a growth industry. Hoards of fascinating comparative studies drawing on both new and previously known materials promise to shed shafts of light in every direction. On the other hand, a lack of consensus on almost any given issue or text continues to dog genuine progress in our understanding of the intersection of the New Testament with its world. Everyone seems to have their parallels and is convinced of their critical nature for New Testament exegesis and history, while at the same time conflicting hypotheses abound.

To take one example, if the majority of commentators detect the influence of the Old Testament and ancient Jewish sources on Paul's idea of bodily resurrection, scholars such as Porter and Martin have asserted Paul's indebtedness here to Graeco-Roman pagan teaching.[1] This essay considers this specific test case in an attempt to move the discussion forward with reference to a number of general questions: Which of the two broad categories of background is decisive for understanding the origin of Paul's teaching? To which dimensions of the task of interpretation do the respective backgrounds contribute? What is the interpretative gain afforded by such investigations?

---

[1]   S. E. Porter, M. Hays and D. Tombs, eds., *Resurrection* (Sheffield: Sheffield Academic Press, 1999); D. B. Martin, *The Corinthian Body* (New Haven: Yale University Press, 1995).

Whereas the subject of resurrection bodies is touched on tangentially in 1 Thess 4:13-17, Rom 8:18-23, Phil 3:20-21, 1 Cor 6:13b-14 and 2 Cor 5:1-5, we shall concentrate on 1 Cor 15, Paul's most explicit and detailed discussion.

The historical situation which gave rise to Paul writing this chapter is difficult to pinpoint with absolute certainty. The precise role of a spiritual elite in Corinth, the prevalence of an overrealised eschatology, the influence of Jewish wisdom speculation and the importance of sociological factors can be differently assessed. Nonetheless, common to all mirror readings of the chapter is the recognition, based on 15:12 ('some of you say there is no resurrection of the dead'), that some within the Corinthian congregation were sceptical about the concept of a future resurrection of believers. It is not that this group did not believe in any post-mortem existence, since in 15:29 Paul speaks of a 'baptism on behalf of the dead', which though problematic for us was apparently quite acceptable to them. Rather, the notion of *bodily* resurrection seems to have been in dispute.[2] If in 15:1-34 Paul contends that the resurrection of the dead is central to the gospel, in 15:35-58 he explains how the *bodily* resurrection of believers is neither unintelligible nor inconceivable. Indeed, the double question of 15:35, along with Paul's word of stern rebuke in 15:36, indicates that it was the very possibility of the body's involvement in the afterlife which some in Corinth denied. 'With what kind of body do they come?' (15:35) is at the heart of the dispute.

Indications within the chapter itself advise we look for three potential influences on Paul's teaching concerning the resurrection

---

[2]   Peter Lampe, "Paul's Concept of a Spiritual Body," in *Resurrection: Theological and Scientific Assessments* (ed. Ted Peters et al.; Grand Rapids: Eerdmans, 2002), 105, asserts uncontroversially: '[W]ithout the bodily aspect there is no legitimate usage of the word "resurrection", according to Paul.' In Rom 8:23 Paul describes the effects of the resurrection in terms of τὴν ἀπολύτρωσιν τοῦ σώματος ἡμῶν, 'the redemption of our body'.

body: Paul's citation of a Greek proverbial saying from a lost play of Menander in 15:33b suggests a Graeco-Roman background (see under 'Graeco-Roman Background' below); the phrase, 'according to the Scriptures' repeated in 15:3-4, and numerous quotations of and allusions to the Old Testament throughout the chapter point to a biblical and Jewish background (see under 'Biblical and Jewish Background' below); and the linking of the resurrection of believers to that of Jesus Christ, 'the last Adam', in 15:45-49, suggests the possible influence of Jesus tradition (see under 'Jesus Tradition' below). Paul's identity itself throws up these three backgrounds; respectively, Paul was a Roman citizen, a Jew and an apostle of Jesus Christ.

Graeco-Roman Background

Attitudes to death and the afterlife in Greek and Roman thought, as evidenced both in literary traditions and in inscriptions, express a variety of viewpoints.[3] On the negative side, Epicureanism regarded death as the cessation of existence, based on an atomistic physics which posited the dissolution of even the soul into its constituent elements at death. A host of epitaphs reinforce this sentiment, counseling passers-by to observe 'how quickly we mortals return from nothing to nothing'. A common epitaph employed the (not so comforting) refrain, *non fui, fui, non sum, non curo,* I was not, I was, I am not, I care not.[4]

The belief that individuals continued a shadowy existence in their tombs represented an only slightly preferable alternative to complete annihilation.[5] Even the collective version of such an afterlife, the

---

[3] I am indebted to Mark Stephens' excellent study, "'This Mortal Body Shall Put on Immortality': Paul's View of Resurrection Bodies in Historical Context" (unpublished B.A. honours thesis, Macquarie University, 2000), for alerting me to many of the primary and secondary sources in this and the following section.

[4] Both cited in K. Hopkins, *Death and Renewal* (Cambridge: CUP, 1983), 230.

[5] Hopkins, *Death and Renewal*, 233-35.

equally shadowy Hades, was in no sense a place of bliss.[6] Blessed immortality was reserved for only a few in the Elysian Fields or the Islands of the Blest.[7]

Among the more positive beliefs was the widely-held notion of the immortality of the soul. Based on a body/soul dualism, death was conceived of as the release of the immortal soul from the strictures of the mortal body. Plutarch, for instance, saw the soul attaining the realm of the gods only by freeing itself from the attachment to the senses, becoming 'pure, *fleshless*, and undefiled'.[8]

Of interest for our purposes is the fact that the vast majority of Graeco-Roman traditions deny the body a place in conceptions of the afterlife. Two possible exceptions to this generalization, namely translation and raisings from the dead, in fact turn out to prove the rule. Translation stories, in which exceptional individuals are snatched from the jaws of death and transferred to a place of bliss, do seem to be bodily in nature since the whole person, including the body, disappears.[9] However, most of the translations involve the *circumventing* of death, with the individual being removed before they die. Vital to Paul's conception of the afterlife in 1 Cor 15 is the resurrection of *the dead* (οἱ νεκροί) — the defeat of death (θάνατος), not its avoidance.

---

[6]   Lucian, the second-century satirist, in *De luctu* 9, comments that the dead in Hades exist 'in the form of shadows that vanish like smoke in your fingers. They get their nourishment, naturally, from the libations that are poured in our world and the burnt-offerings at the tomb, so that if anyone has not left a friend or kinsman behind him on earth, he goes about his business as an unfed corpse, in a state of famine.' Cited in Dale B. Martin, *The Corinthian Body* (New Haven: Yale University Press, 1995), 109-10.

[7]   Peter G. Bolt, "Life, Death and the Afterlife in the Greco-Roman World," in *Life in the Face of Death* (ed. Richard N. Longenecker; Grand Rapids: Eerdmans, 1998), 68-70.

[8]   Plutarch, *Romulus* 28.6. Italics added.

[9]   Peter G. Bolt, "Mark:16:1-8: The Empty Tomb of a Hero?," *TynB* 47 (1996): 34.

Raisings from the dead, which can be found in mythical, philosophical and historical types of literature, also seem to be less than true parallels to Paul's notion of resurrection, in that they are only temporary restorations to mortal bodily existence.[10] In fact, when the terminology of resurrection is used, it turns up in statements concerning its inherent impossibility, as for example in Aeschylus' *Eumenides*: 'When the dust hath drained the blood of man, once he is slain, there is no return to life (ἀνάστασις).'[11]

A specific version of the continuance of the soul in the afterlife of interest to 1 Cor 15 is astral immortality, the idea that following death human beings become stars or some kind of heavenly body.[12] Death was conceived of as the casting off of the 'lower' or 'earthly' substance, the body, and the ascension of the soul, which consists of fire, ether or spirit (πνεῦμα), to its proper celestial home. Some scholars have taken Paul's references to celestial bodies in 15:40-41 as implying the same belief.[13] But this is to read too much into Paul's analogy, which simply makes the point that bodily diversity exists within the creation itself. He does this to lay the groundwork for the argument that the glory of the present bodies and the glory of resurrected bodies will be different (15:42a). Dan 12:2-3, where the raised are said to 'shine like the brightness of the sky, ... like the stars forever and ever', a key Old Testament text on resurrection (see below), is, as

---

[10] Cf. A. J. M. Wedderburn, *Baptism and Resurrection: Studies in Pauline Theology against Its Greco-Roman Background* (Tübingen: Mohr Siebeck, 1987), 183.

[11] Aeschylus, *Eum.* 647-48, mentioned in Wedderburn, *Baptism and Resurrection*, 181.

[12] See Alan Scott, *Origen and the Life of the Stars* (Oxford: OUP, 1991) and Martin, *The Corinthian Body*, 117-19.

[13] See, e.g., Adela Yarbro Collins, "The Empty Tomb in the Gospel according to Mark," in *Hermes and Athena: Biblical Exegesis and Philosophical Theology* (ed. E. Stump and T. P. Flint; Notre Dame: University of Notre Dame, 1993), 113.

Richard Hays contends,[14] a more likely source for Paul's reference here. The metaphor of the risen righteous ones shining like stars in both Daniel and 1 Cor 15 is used to depict their glorious state.

Not unrelated is Dale Martin's assertion that Paul's use of earthly and heavenly terminology in 15:40-41 reveals his indebtedness to a hierarchical conception of matter, as found in some Graeco-Roman thought.[15] Paul begins at the lower end of the spectrum, with 'earthly bodies', and moves on to higher 'heavenly bodies'. However, the way Paul introduces his comments points to his reliance on the biblical tradition of creation.[16] The bodies mentioned in 15:39-41 correspond to three of the days of creation in reverse order, the sixth and fifth in verse 39 and the fourth in verses 40-41.

The two examples above, astral immortality and a hierarchical conception of matter, indicate that the case for Paul's dependence in 1 Cor 15 on Graeco-Roman views is difficult to establish, especially when compared with the main alternative hypothesis of biblical and Jewish influence (see further below). Indeed, as N. T. Wright puts it, 'Christianity was born into a [Graeco-Roman] world where its central claim [resurrection] was known to be false. Many believed that the dead were non-existent; outside Judaism, nobody believed in resurrection.'[17]

However, it is not that Graeco-Roman background is irrelevant to 1 Cor 15. Its main interest lies in helping us to appreciate not so much Paul's thinking as the thinking and behaviour of those to whom he wrote. In recent New Testament scholarship this point is nowhere

---

[14] Richard B. Hays, *First Corinthians* (Louisville: John Knox Press, 1997), 271.

[15] Martin, *The Corinthian Body*, 125-26.

[16] Cf. Raymond F. Collins, *First Corinthians* (SP; Collegeville: Liturgical, 1999), 563.

[17] N. T. Wright, *The Resurrection of the Son of God: Christian Origins and the Question of God, Vol. 3* (London: SPCK), 35. Unfortunately Wright's major study of resurrection appeared too late to be used for this essay, apart from this passing reference.

better illustrated and confirmed than in Bruce Winter's prodigious stream of publications. With reference to 1 Corinthians alone, in Part One of *After Paul Left Corinth*,[18] Winter argues: (1) that the divisions addressed in chapters 1–4 arise from a competitive spirit inherent in the educational model of the Sophists; (2) that the reason that the affair in chapter 5 between a man and his father's wife was so scandalous resides in Roman jurisprudence concerning adulterous incestuous affairs; (3) that the lawsuit in 6:12-20 arose from the culturally ingrained pursuit of status by defeating adversaries in vexatious litigation; (4) that the gluttony, drunkenness and debauchery in which guests indulged after private banquets help explain the context of 6:12-20; (5) that the problem of veils in 11:1-16 has to do with wives discarding their veils which served as a sign of their married status; and (6) that the puzzling reference to Jesus and curses in 12:3 can be understood as Paul's response to Corinthian Christians who were attempting to pull down their adversaries by means of curses in Jesus' name.

Likewise, Corinthian scepticism concerning the place of the body in the afterlife is perfectly understandable in a Graeco-Roman setting. That Paul felt it necessary to explain at length, 'With what kind of body do they come?', is explicable precisely because his Gentile contemporaries had no notion of bodily resurrection.[19]

The quotation from Menander in 15:33, rather than being a clue as to the sources of Paul's own thought, as Martin himself points out, indicates Paul's sense of where the ideas he is countering come from:

> The abrupt interjection of the saying in Paul's argument may indicate that he believes the Corinthians' skepticism to be due to influences from other sources — in fact to persons who have only 'ignorance of God' — a description often used by Jews to refer to Gentiles ... All

---

[18] B. W. Winter, *After Paul Left Corinth: The Influence of Secular Ethics and Social Change* (Grand Rapids: Eerdmans, 2001).

[19] Ironically, in our day the possibility of 'the resurrection of the body', if not the person, via cloning with only the smallest amount of DNA is perfectly conceivable.

this suggests that Paul attributes the Corinthian doubts [about bodily resurrection] to Greek philosophy.[20]

It is thus by way of contrast to Paul that Graeco-Roman background proves to be most useful.

In discussing the 'background' to 1 Corinthians Bruce Winter makes the same distinction, between 'the cultural background of the Corinthian Christians and the theological background of Paul which he drew on when he framed his answers to the Corinthians' letter and the reports he heard of their conduct'.[21] The latter Winter takes to include 'the Old Testament, intertestamental Judaism, and early Christian traditions',[22] the areas we consider in the next two sections.

Biblical and Jewish Background

It is clear from no less than nine intertextual connections in 1 Cor 15, some of which are indispensable to his argument, that Paul is dependent on the Jewish Scriptures in his treatment of the theme of resurrection. These include: (1) the Adam/Christ typology in 15:21-22; (2) the allusion to Pss 110:1 and 8:6 in 1 Cor 15:25, 27; (3) the language of continual opposition to God's people in 15:30 which echoes Pss 44:22 and 119:109; (4) the quotation of Isa 22:13 in 15:32; (5) the scornful rebuke, ἄφρων, in 15:36 which echoes Ps 14:1 (LXX, ἄφρων — a Psalm Paul quotes from in Rom 3:11-12); (6) the allusions to Adam in 15:45-49 ('the first man', 'the man of dust', both twice); (7) the trumpet as a sign of the day of the Lord in 15:52 which recalls Isa 27:13, Joel 2:1 and Zeph 1:14-16 (cf. 2 Esdr 6:23); (8) the quotation from Isa 25:8 in 15:54; and (9) the quotation of Hos 13:14 in 15:55.

Unlike Graeco-Roman philosophy, Paul's Jewish inheritance, including both the Jewish Scriptures and their interpretation and elaboration in intertestamental Jewish literature, does affirm, albeit with variations in the details, a sturdy belief in the resurrection of the

---

[20] Martin, *The Corinthian Body*, 275.
[21] Winter, *After Paul Left Corinth*, xii.
[22] Winter, *After Paul Left Corinth*, xii.

body.[23] While explicit affirmation is reserved for certain Old Testament prophets, its foundations, as Richard Bauckham argues, are firmly laid in the Old Testament portrayal of God as Sovereign Creator, Righteous Judge and Divine Warrior.[24] In the inter-testamental period, these three motifs form the basis on which a belief in resurrection is founded (see the texts cited below). In this sense resurrection faith is not so much 'on the fringe of the Hebrew Bible'[25] as it is 'an intelligible development'.[26]

Whereas some Old Testament texts use resurrection language to refer to national restoration (e.g. Ezek 37:1-14), at least two texts declare a resurrection of the dead as a personal hope of life after death which is bodily in nature.[27] Isa 26:19 promises a resurrection ('your dead shall live') which is explicitly corporeal ('their corpses shall rise').[28] That this text envisages a literal, physical resurrection and not just a metaphorical national restoration from exile is clear from two observations: first, the broader context of chapter 26 has a universal focus and not simply a nationalistic one; and secondly, the referent of 'the dead' is in context 'the dead' of v. 14 who are righteous indi-

---

[23] Cf. R. J. Sider, "The Pauline Conception of the Resurrection Body in I Corinthians XV.35-54," *NTS* 21 (1974-75): 438: '[A]s a good first-century Pharisee, Paul could not conceive of the resurrection of the dead in purely immaterial terms.'

[24] Richard Bauckham, *The Fate of the Dead: Studies on the Jewish and Christian Apocalypses* (Leiden: Brill, 1998), 86: 'It was not from reflection on what human nature is that Jews came to hope for eternal life, but from reflection on who God is.'

[25] H. C. C. Cavallin, *Life after Death: Paul's Argument for the Resurrection of the Dead in 1 Corinthians 15* (Coniectanea Biblica 7; Lund: Almqvist & Wiksell, 1974), 23.

[26] Mark Stephens, "'This Mortal Body Shall Put on Immortality': Paul's View of Resurrection Bodies in Historical Context," 11.

[27] Other texts, such as Job 14:14, Pss 16:10; 49:15; 73:24, also seem to imply belief in life after death, although their exegesis is more controversial.

[28] The awakening from 'the dust' also implies a recreation of the whole person since the Old Testament describes death as a lying down or descending in the dust (e.g. Job 7:21; 17:16; Pss 22:15; 90:3; cf. Gen 3:19).

viduals who are no longer living. Isa 26:19 proclaims the sovereignty of Yahweh over all powers including death.

A second text, Dan 12:1-3, is just as explicit about bodily resurrection: 'Many of those who sleep in the dust of the earth shall awake, some to everlasting life, and some to shame and everlasting contempt' (12:2). If the passage in Isaiah predicated resurrection on the sovereignty of the Creator, the passage in Daniel sees it as a demonstration of the righteousness of God the Judge who will act to vindicate the faithful and condemn the unrighteous.

Whereas the Old Testament supplies only a few explicit reflections on the afterlife, many non-canonical Jewish intertestamental writings have resurrection as central to their beliefs.[29] A full survey is beyond the scope of this essay. Instead, aware of the diversity of opinion, we shall concentrate on a representative range of texts drawn from apocalyptic, testamentary and historical literature which teach about resurrection and may be of interest to Paul's own conception.

Four apocalyptic texts deserve mention:[30]

> *1 En.* 51:1: 'In those days Sheol will return all the deposits which she had received and hell will give back all that which it owes.'

> *1 En.* 62:14-16: 'The Lord of the Spirits will abide over them; they shall eat and rest and rise with that Son of Man forever and ever. The righteous and elect ones shall rise from the earth and shall cease being of downcast face. They shall wear garments of glory. These garments of yours shall become the garments of life from the Lord of the Spirits. Neither shall your garments wear out, nor your glory come to an end before the Lord of the Spirits.'[31]

---

[29] Richard Bauckham, *The Fate of the Dead*, 82, cites Ben Sira as the last Jewish writer (second century BC) categorically to deny the possibility of an individual afterlife.

[30] Translations are from J. H. Charlesworth, ed., *The Old Testament Pseudepigrapha, Vol. 1: Apocalyptic Literature and Testaments* (New York: Darton, Longman & Todd, 1983).

[31] Both the *1 En.* texts are found in the Similitudes of Enoch, which most scholars regard as Jewish in origin and written around the turn of the era.

4 Ezra 7:32-33a: 'The earth shall give up those who are asleep in it, and the dust those who rest there in silence; and the chambers shall give up the souls that have been committed to them. The Most High shall be revealed on the seat of judgement.'

2 Bar. 50:2, 4: '[T]he earth will surely give back the dead at that time; it receives them now in order to keep them, not changing anything in their form. ... And it will be that when they have recognised each other, those who know each other at this moment, then my judgement will be strong, and those things which have been spoken of before will come.'[32]

With regard to the role of the body, the first, third and fourth texts describe resurrection in terms of the place where the dead are kept (variously as Sheol, hell, the earth, dust and the chambers) 'giving back' the deceased. Richard Bauckham is right to see in such language, which is common in Jewish and Christian apocalyptic, 'an assertion of God's sovereignty over the realm of the dead',[33] a theme clearly present in 1 Cor 15:15, 27, 57. That *bodily* resurrection is in view is clear from this motif in that the 'giving back' implies a full restoration of the person to bodily life. This is confirmed in the second text where those who rise eat, rest and are clothed.[34]

However, *2 Bar.* is the most explicit in reflecting on the notion of resurrection bodies. In fact the author in 49:2 poses almost the same question as Paul, which is the focus of this essay, framed in a prayer: 'In what shape will those live who live in your day?' His answer in 50:1-5, like Paul's, takes for granted that the body will be involved. But unlike Paul, *2 Bar.* asserts that the body will be unchanged ('not changing anything in their form'), apparently asserting a greater de-

---

[32] Both *4 Ezra* and *2 Bar.* postdate Paul but remain of interest in tracing how Jewish conceptions of resurrection developed.

[33] Bauckham, *The Fate of the Dead*, 278.

[34] The reference to their faces may also be evidence, but it could be taken purely figuratively as referring to the transformation of their mood from sadness to joy.

gree of continuity than found in 1 Cor 15 ('we shall all be changed' [15:51]; 'you do not sow the body that is to be' [15:37a]).

A prominent example of testamentary literature which reflects on the afterlife is the *Testaments of the Twelve Patriarchs*.[35] Not infrequently the heroes of the faith including the patriarchs themselves are cited in connection with resurrection language (e.g. *T. Sim.* 6:7; *T. Jud.* 25:1-2; *T. Zeb.* 10:2). Some of these texts imply a more general resurrection, in that a patriarch may be described as assuming leadership over their tribe (e.g. *T. Zeb.* 10:2; *T. Ben.* 10:7). This assumption is made explicit in at least two texts. *T. Jud.* 25:4-6 affirms the resurrection of those who have died in sorrow, poverty or on account of the Lord; *T. Ben.* 10:6-10 mentions a resurrection in which 'all are changed', with some to expect glory and others dishonour. Tantalisingly no further explanation is offered. As Perkins notes, the main function of resurrection in the *Testaments of the Twelve Patriarchs* is to articulate the hope of a renewed and restored Israel.[36] That resurrection is bodily seems to be assumed without need for comment.

In terms of historical literature, 2 Macc unmistakably views resurrection as including the body.[37] Several of the brothers who choose to be martyred rather than violate Jewish food laws express fervently their hope of resurrection. In particular, the third and fourth brothers clearly speak of a bodily resurrection (7:10-13), with the former expecting the return of his tongue and hands which are being offered to the executioner. Likewise, Razis, one of the faithful elders of Jerusalem, hopes to receive back the very entrails which have been

---

[35] The problem of Christian interpolation is not relevant to the texts cited in connection with the theme of resurrection.

[36] P. Perkins, *Resurrection: New Testament Witness and Contemporary Reflection* (London: Chapman, 1984), 43-44.

[37] For the argument that Tobit, a moralistic historical novel, affirms a resurrection hope, see Peter G. Bolt, "What Were the Pharisees Reading? An Enquiry into the Literary Background of Mark 12:18-23," *TynB* 45 (1994): 379-94.

torn out of him (14:46). This admittedly crudely physical view of resurrection is qualified by clear affirmations of the eternal character of resurrection life (e.g. 7:9: 'The king of the universe will raise us up [ἀναστήσει] to an everlasting renewal of life [αἰώνιον ἀναβίωσιν ζωῆς] because we have died for our laws');[38] presumably some kind of transformation of bodily existence was assumed if not explicated by these texts.

Whereas the historian Josephus' own views on post-mortem existence in *Against Apion* do not explicitly assign the body a role (phrases like a 'renewed existence' and a 'better life' are ambiguous), in the *Jewish War* he does speak of 'the revolution of the ages' in terms of a new habitation of a chaste body (*B.J.* 3.374). More informative is his description of the beliefs of the Pharisees in both *Jewish War* and *Antiquities* where the idea is of a soul passing from one body to another. If 2 Maccabees stressed continuity, Josephus, perhaps as a concession to his Hellenistic readers, puts the accent on discontinuity, albeit without denying the involvement of a body in one way or another.

It is of course not that Paul always agrees with his Jewish forebears and contemporaries. On some issues, like election and the inclusion of the Gentiles, he swims against the tide.[39] And of course Jews did not always agree with each other. For our purposes Philo on Gen 1–2 is instructive. Whereas for Paul the earthly man is Adam and the heavenly man is Christ, for Philo both of these can be found in Genesis (albeit allegorically).[40] Nonetheless, if the key word for Graeco-Roman background is *contrast*, *similarity* sums up the essence of biblical and Jewish background with reference to Paul. As

---

[38] See Stephens, "'This Mortal Body Shall Put on Immortality,'" 31.

[39] In Rom 9–11 where he treats these issues he quotes the Old Testament over thirty times, presumably to make his disagreement plain.

[40] See Philo, *Legum allegoriae* 1.31-32. The earthly man represented the carnal person devoted to things that will pass away, the heavenly man the ideal spiritual state with the mind set on heavenly things.

this survey has shown, Paul's discussion of bodily resurrection fits comfortably into a Jewish milieu.

Jesus Tradition

'With what kind of body do they come?' Paul's answer in 1 Cor 15 is that the resurrection body will be an imperishable, powerful, glorious and spiritual body, brought about by the power and grace of God, fit for life in the age to come, which involves not only a mortal transformation but a moral one.

Against a Graeco-Roman background this answer (and indeed the question itself) would have struck naked incredulity. On the other hand, even if the broad lines of Paul's answer are in keeping with a Jewish background, as we have seen, it does not find consistent or detailed precedent there. As 1 Cor 15:45-49 make clear, Paul's conception of the resurrection body of believers ultimately owes its origin to the resurrected Christ, 'the life-giving spirit' (15:45), 'the man of heaven' to whose 'image' believers will conform (15:49). Paul makes the same connection elsewhere: at the parousia 'the Lord Jesus Christ ... will change our lowly body to be *like his* (σύμμορφον τῷ σώματι τῆς δόξης αὐτοῦ) glorious body' (Phil 3:20-21); for 'we shall certainly be united with him in a resurrection *like his*' (Rom 6:5b; cf. 6:8b). Christ, the eschatological Adam, is the founder of a new and better humanity.[41]

It is thus no coincidence that the words Paul uses to describe believers' resurrection are roughly the same as when he speaks of the resurrection of Christ.[42] This is true of all of the main terms, including: ἀνίστημι ('raise up'), ἐγείρω ('raise'), ἀνάστασις ('resurrection') and ζάω ('to live'). Only the related compounds ἐξεγείρω ('raise up') and ἐξανάστασις ('resurrection'), which occur

---

[41] As I. H. Marshall, *Jesus the Saviour: Studies in New Testament Theology* (London: SPCK, 1990), 173, points out, 1 Cor 15:21-22, 45-49 show that Paul regards the heavenly Lord Jesus as still being a human being.
[42] For a detailed chart see M. E. Dahl, *The Resurrection of the Body* (London: SCM, 1962).

once in 1 Cor 6:14 and Phil 3:11 respectively, with reference to the resurrection of believers, are not used of Christ's resurrection. The use of the συν- prefix in συζήσομεν ('we will live with [him]'; Rom 6:8; 2 Tim 2:11), συνδοξασθῶμεν ('we may be glorified with [him]'; Rom 8:17), συνεγείρω ('raise up together'; Col 2:12; 3:1), and συνεζωοποίησεν ('he made alive together with [him]'; Col 2:13; Eph 2:5) make the link between the two explicit at the lexical level.

In the light of this, Paul's view of the resurrection body as encompassing both continuity with and transformation of the present body, what Murray Harris calls 'identity with difference',[43] may well find its best precedent in the accounts of the resurrection appearances of the Jesus in the New Testament Gospels. Here Jesus is recognisable to his followers, but clearly has a different mode of existence, to which adjectives like imperishable, powerful, glorious and spiritual are appropriate.

Three things Paul says about the resurrection body in 1 Cor 15 in particular can be seen plausibly to derive from the prototypical resurrection of Jesus, specifically what he teaches concerning the latter in Rom 1, 4 and 6. First, according to v. 43 the believer ἐγείρεται ἐν δυνάμει, 'is raised in power'. Likewise, Rom 1:4 asserts that Jesus Christ is declared to be or designated the Son of God ἐν δυνάμει by his resurrection from the dead.

Secondly, Paul's treatment of the resurrection in 1 Cor 15 stresses the crucial role of the sovereign grace of God as the only sure ground of Christian hope, an appropriate climax to the epistle as a whole.[44] This theme is introduced with reference to Paul's own conversion and calling in 15:8-11 (where χάρις is repeated three times) and in 15:38 it is the ultimate explanation for how the dead are raised (cf. 15:35a):

---

[43] M. J. Harris, *Raised Immortal: Resurrection and Immortality in the New Testament* (London: Marshall, Morgan & Scott, 1983), 126.

[44] See in particular the comments of Barth, Luther and Calvin, carried forward in Anthony C. Thiselton, *The First Epistle to the Corinthians* (NIGTC; Grand Rapids: Eerdmans, 2000), 1169-71.

ὁ δὲ θεὸς δίδωσιν αὐτῷ σῶμα καθὼς ἠθέλησεν, 'but *God gives* it a body, *just as he wishes*' (which is not unlike the affirmation in 2 Cor 5:1, 'we have a building *from God* [ἐκ θεοῦ]'). The notion of resurrection as a free gift is expressed in Rom 4 (with ultimate reference to the resurrection of Jesus), where Abraham is said to have believed in God 'who gives life to the dead' (4:17; cf. 4:25b). The need for the grace of God is nowhere more evident than in the case of resurrection where the recipients self-evidently can contribute nothing whatsoever.

Thirdly, the 'spiritual (πνευματικός) body' of which Paul speaks (1 Cor 15:44) is not a concession to Hellenistic thought, referring to the non-physical nature of the resurrection body, but to a new mode of existence, life directed and empowered by the Spirit, suitable to the age to come, a body untainted by sin and death in every sense. In Rom 6 the 'resurrection like his' which believers await (6:5) is not only one that guarantees mortal transformation but also moral transformation, a 'walk in newness of life' (6:4), an existence that begins in the present.

Conclusion

What then of the general questions which opened this essay? Where does Paul sit vis-à-vis the various backgrounds commonly adduced in the study of his letters? Given the uniqueness of the resurrection of Jesus, it would be wise not to generalise too hastily. Nonetheless, while in no way decisive on its own, this short study adds another piece to the puzzle of determining the relative status of Paul's various 'backgrounds'. As far as his conception of resurrection bodies is concerned, Paul's teaching is framed in sharp relief by Graeco-Roman contrasting views, sketched in outline from biblical and Jewish sources but given its distinctive hues from the palette of the risen Christ. To switch metaphors, if this case study is typical, in Paul's letters he swims against the tide of Graeco-Roman teaching, and with the flow of the Old Testament and its Jewish interpreters, but rides the wave created by the coming of Jesus.

The Summing Up of All Things

(Ephesians 1:10)

Peter T. O'Brien

Introduction

The precise meaning of the expression, ἀνακεφαλαιώσασθαι τὰ πάντα ἐν τῷ Χριστῷ in Eph 1:10,[1] which has been described as 'an unusual and arresting term to use for the action of God in Christ',[2] has been unclear to Christian interpreters from earliest times and has led to many different renderings.

A brief survey of the better known English versions reveals considerable diversity. The AV reads 'that he might gather together in one all things in Christ'; the RV of 1881, 'to sum up all things in Christ'; the RSV (cf. ESV), 'to unite all things in him'; the NEB, 'that the universe might be brought into a unity in Christ' (cf. TEV); and the NRSV, 'to gather up all things in him'.[3] Following a somewhat different tradition the JB reads 'that he would bring everything together under Christ, the head', and this is similar to the NIV's 'to bring all things together under one head, even Christ'.[4] Both of these

---

[1] This essay is dedicated with gratitude and much affection to Dr Bruce Winter, friend and colleague for many years.

[2] M. Kitchen, "The ἀνακεφαλαίωσις of All Things in Christ: Theology and Purpose in the Epistle to the Ephesians" (unpublished Ph.D. thesis, Manchester, 1988), 69.

[3] Note Louw and Nida, § 63.8, 'to bring everything together in terms of some unifying principle or person', so 'to bring everything together in Christ'; BDAG, 65, 'to bring everything together in Christ'.

[4] Interestingly, the TNIV (2002) renders the expression as 'to bring unity to all things in heaven and on earth under Christ', thus dropping the word 'head' (from the NIV) but rendering ἐν τῷ Χριστῷ as 'under Christ'. Note the discussion below.

renderings place 'at least equal, if not more, emphasis on Christ's headship than on the unification of creation'.[5]

Not surprisingly, patristic writers offered a range of interpretations as they sought to grapple with the meaning of the expression in a letter which focuses on unity and cosmic reconciliation.[6] Some thought that the verb ἀνακεφαλαιόω connoted repetition or recapitulation because of the prefix ἀνα- ('again'). The general lines of Irenaeus' interpretation are well known.[7] For him the key thought was the recapitulation of the incarnate Word of God.[8] Christ is the new man in whom humanity, indeed the whole universe, is incorporated and being renewed. Origen, who claimed that the verb ἀνακεφαλαιόω was derived from the noun κεφάλαιον ('principal part', 'sum', 'total'), then linked it with κεφαλή. He understood God's saving acts in the Old Testament as pointing to Christ in a preparatory way, and they were 'recapitulated' in him.[9] Chrysostom recognized the customary rhetorical meaning of ἀνακεφαλαιόω ('a brief summary of what has been said at great length'), but asserted that in Eph 1:10 to sum up or

---

[5] J. McHugh, "A Reconsideration of Ephesians 1.10b in the Light of Irenaeus," in *Paul and Paulinism: Essays in Honour of C. K. Barrett* (ed. M. D. Hooker and S. G. Wilson; London: SPCK, 1982), 302-09, esp. 302.

[6] Note the references in G. W. H. Lampe, ed., *A Patristic Greek Lexicon* (Oxford: Clarendon, 1961), 106, under both ἀνακεφαλαιόω and ἀνακεφαλαίωσις.

[7] Note J. Lawson, *The Biblical Theology of Saint Irenaeus* (London: Epworth, 1948), 140-54; R. Schnackenburg, *The Epistle to the Ephesians* (Edinburgh: T & T Clark, 1991), 315-18; also the chapter by B. de Margerie, *An Introduction to the History of Exegesis: Vol. 1, The Greek Fathers* (Petersham, Mass.: St. Bede's Publications, 1993), 51-77. For a twentieth-century attempt to interpret Eph 1:10 along similar lines to that of Irenaeus, see McHugh, "Ephesians 1.10b," 302-09.

[8] Irenaeus cites Eph 1:10 on several occasions when writing of the recapitulation (e.g. *Adversus haereses* 1.10.1; 3.16.6; 4.6.2). According to the *Thesaurus Linguae Graecae* (on which see below), he uses ἀνακεφαλαιόω ten times and the cognate noun on three occasions.

[9] J. A. F. Gregg, "The Commentary of Origen upon the Epistle to the Ephesians," *JTS* 3 (1901-02): 241. Origen employs the verb ἀνακεφαλαιόω twelve times, and the noun ἀνακεφαλαίωσις on five occasions.

recapitulate signifies 'to join together'.[10] God's providential ordering over a long period of time has been recapitulated once for all in the Son. Chrysostom adds: 'There is also another meaning: In Christ's incarnation God has given a single head to all creation, both angels and humans.'[11]

Before interacting with some modern interpretations we shall examine the material now available in the canon of the *Thesaurus Linguae Graecae*.[12] However, even if we are able to provide an appropriate rendering of this enigmatic Greek expression in the immediate context of Eph 1:10, it still does not explain the underlying thought of the apostle or its significance within the wider context of the letter. We shall return to these two issues in due course.

Harvesting the Results of the Thesaurus Linguae Graecae (TLG)
Until fairly recently only a few attestations of the verb ἀνα-κεφαλαιόω and its cognate noun were accessible.[13] The rich evidence that is now available in the canon of the *TLG* is of special importance in helping us determine the semantic range and uses of ἀνακεφαλαιόω that are contemporaneous with and subsequent to Paul.[14] J. B. Maclean has surveyed this material and contends that this

---

[10]   John Chrysostom, *In epistulam ad Ephesios* 62.16.13. Cf. M. J. Edwards, ed., *Ancient Christian Commentary on Scripture: New Testament, VIII: Galatians, Ephesians, Philippians* (Downers Grove: InterVarsity, 1999), 116. Chrysostom uses the word group thirty-six times.
[11]   Edwards, *Ancient Christian Commentary*, 116.
[12]   The *TLG* is a collection of texts written in Greek from Homer (eighth century BC) to the Fall of Byzantium (AD 1453), and disseminated in CD-ROM format.
[13]   Three are listed in LSJ, which restricts itself to the original meaning of the root in rhetoric, to 'sum up the argument'; it mentions Rom 13:9 but omits Eph 1:10 (as does the *Supplement*); see McHugh, "Ephesians 1.10b," 302. H. Schlier, "κεφαλή, ἀνακεφαλαιόομαι," *TDNT* 3:681-82, provides several instances from Christian sources that postdate Ephesians.
[14]   In a recent search of the *TLG* (CD-ROM E) I found more than 300 instances of the ἀνακεφαλα- word group in material from the fourth century BC to the fourth century AD.

verb has a single meaning when it appears in rhetorical manuals and three distinct, though related, meanings in commentaries on philosophical, medical and religious texts.[15] As the point of departure for our own examination we shall summarize her findings:

(1) In the rhetorical manuals, the meaning of ἀνακεφαλαιόω as 'to conclude an argument by briefly recounting the proofs' is well known to modern scholarship. Aristotle divided rhetorical compositions into four sections, the last of which was to 'sum up' (ἀνακεφαλαιόω) the oration, and remind the audience of what had been said.[16]

(2) Likewise in the commentaries on Plato and Aristotle, the verb was employed to summarize a discussion in the earlier text. So in Aristotle's *Metaphysics*, his restatement of definitions of substance, genus and essence is picked up by Alexander of Aphrodisias with his use of ἀνακεφαλαιόω.[17] Similarly, Hippolytus employed the verb in this way when he stated that John summarized the prophetic message in John 1:1-3.[18]

(3) Also in the philosophical commentaries from the second century AD onwards ἀνακεφαλαιόω could refer to 'a previous author's conclusion of a discussion'. Maclean cites the example of Alexander of Aphrodisias who comments on the final lines of Aristotle's *On the Senses*: 'When he had demonstrated these things, he briefly summarized (ἀνακεφαλαιοῦται) his statements in the book.' Aristotle did not repeat the main points, but simply restated the topics he had cov-

---

[15] J. B. Maclean, "Ephesians and the Problem of Colossians: Interpretation of Texts and Traditions in Ephesians 1:1-2:10" (unpublished Ph.D. thesis, Harvard, 1995), 52-58.

[16] ἀνακεφαλαιώσασθαι πρὸς ἀνάμνησιν ('to stimulate the memory'), Aristotle, *Fragmenta varia* 3.22.133.8, cited by Maclean, "Ephesians," 53, n. 27. See also Dionysius of Halicarnassus, *Ant. Rom.* 1.90.2.6. Cf. BDAG, 65.

[17] For example, Alexander, *In Aristotelis metaphysica commentaria* 516.30, comments: 'He [Aristotle] sums up (ἀνακεφαλαιοῦται) the things said in the previous book and the book before that — not all of them ... but the most important things.'

[18] Hippolytus, *Contra haeresin Noeti* 12.3.1.

ered and brought the section to an end.[19] It has been suggested that this meaning clarifies the Theodotion (and the Quinta) translation of Ps 71:20 (MT 72:20), which reads ἀνακεφαλαιώθησαν προσευχαὶ Δαυίδ and should be rendered 'the prayers of David are finished'.[20]

(4) The final use of ἀνακεφαλαιόω, which is both early and widely attested, is to introduce a summary quotation from a text that is being explained. This usage is found in a medical commentary of Apollonius of Citium (first century BC), as well as in Christian writers who 'introduce quotations of biblical texts valued for their concise summarization of key ideas'.[21] In Rom 13:9 Paul introduces a quotation of Lev 19:8 with the words, 'If there is any other commandment, it is summed up (ἀνακεφαλαιοῦται) in this saying ...' Other examples of this use, according to Maclean, appear in Origen and Eusebius.[22]

Maclean concludes that none of the first three uses of ἀνακεφαλαιόω, each of which is literal, makes sense of Eph 1:10. The object of the verb, that is, τὰ πάντα, does not refer to 'the things previously mentioned' (i.e. in Eph 1:3-9), which would be necessary if ἀνακεφαλαιόω was being employed in a rhetorical and literal sense of 'to sum up' (1) and (2), or 'to bring a section to an end' (3). In its context τὰ πάντα is amplified as 'things in heaven and things on earth', which is quite different. Accordingly, Maclean thinks, only the

---

[19] Aristotle, *Sens.* 49B.1-3; Alexander, *In librum de sensu commentarium* 173.11.

[20] An alternative rendering is that the prayers of David have been 'gathered together'; cf. H. W. Hoehner, *Ephesians: An Exegetical Commentary* (Grand Rapids: Baker, 2002), 219.

[21] Apollonius, *In Hippocratis de articulis commentarius* 32.35. Maclean, "Ephesians," 56. Cf. Theophilus the apologist who uses ἀνακεφαλαιοῦται to introduce Gen 2:4-5 as a summary of the creation story (*Ad Autolycum* 2.19.4).

[22] See Origen, *De oratione* 9.3.2, where he conflates Jer 7:22-23 and Zech 7:10 as a summary of the law. Eusebius, *Praep. ev.* 7.11.3.4, quotes Gen 2:4 with the following words: 'but the scripture summarizing (ἀνακεφαλαιούμενος) the whole story, says ...'

last use of ἀνακεφαλαιόω (4) fits the context. The verb introduces a summary quotation from a text being explained, namely Col 1:16. In Eph 1:10 τὰ πάντα is amplified as 'things in heaven and things on earth', and this is believed to be a conscious allusion to Colossians, especially the formula in the hymn of 1:15-20. Further, this coherent meaning for Eph 1:10 is based upon the contemporary semantic range of ἀνακεφαλαιόω and the basic relationship between Ephesians and Colossians. Moreover, a great strength of this interpretation, according to Maclean, is that 'there is no need to assume a *metaphorical meaning* for ἀνακεφαλαιόομαι that would designate a specific eschatological action of God parallel to the other verbs often supplied', such as 'create', or 'reconcile'.[23]

But Maclean's arguments that ἀνακεφαλαιόω introduces a summary quotation from the Colossian hymn are unconvincing. It neither provides a coherent meaning within the movement of vv. 3-14, nor catches the right nuance of ἐν αὐτῷ. Instead, it gratuitously assumes that τὰ πάντα is a conscious allusion to the Colossian hymn and presupposes a possible but unproven relationship between Ephesians and Colossians. The net result is that none of the four contemporary literary or rhetorical uses of ἀνακεφαλαιόω precisely fits Eph 1:10.

We have seen from the *TLG* evidence that ἀνακεφαλαιόω in the rhetorical works is used to sum up or recapitulate an argument, a 'summing up' which signifies a 'drawing together of the main points'. Is it possible, then, that this verb in Eph 1 signifies to 'sum up' or 'bring things to a focal point or climax' — but now in a non-literary or non-rhetorical sense — to designate a specific eschatological action of God in Christ? The only other example of this verb in the New Testament, namely Paul's use of the word in Rom 13:9, suggests this is possible. Here the apostle employs ἀνακεφαλαιόω of love as the comprehensive command that brings the other commands together

---

[23] Maclean, "Ephesians," 59 (emphasis added). She asserts that 'there is no contemporary evidence for metaphorical uses of this term except from later exegetes of Ephesians, whose results provide no consensus' (n. 53).

under the one focal point.[24] When the same verb is then applied to 'Christ's eschatological relationship to a multitude of entities (including personal beings) scattered throughout the cosmos, it is inviting to understand God's "summing up" of these entities in Christ as his act of bringing all things together in … Christ,'[25] an idea that is akin to the reconciliation of all things in Col 1:20, even if there is a different eschatological emphasis. The notion of unity may not be part of the semantic range of the term, but it certainly seems to be an implication that Paul himself draws from the word in its sentence (Eph 1:9, 10), and which becomes an important integrating theme throughout the rest of Ephesians, as we shall endeavour to show in due course.

The bringing of all things together in Christ has often been thought of as involving a recapitulation. But it is doubtful whether the prefix ἀνα- in ἀνακεφαλαιόω should be given the sense of 'again'. A summary to some extent always entails some repetition. In the rhetorical works where this verb brings an argument to a conclusion through a summation of the main points, the whole argument is not repeated. Moreover, prepositions in compounds in Hellenistic Greek do not always carry their full weight, but often indicate simply an in-

---

[24] B. Byrne, *Romans* (SP; Collegeville: Liturgical, 1996), 396, rightly observes that ἀνακεφαλαιόω was used of the summary of the main points made by a speaker at the end of an oration, and states in relation to its use here: 'The sense is therefore that of drawing all things together under a single statement which can stand for all.' Note also C. E. B. Cranfield, *The Epistle to the Romans 9-16* (ICC; Edinburgh: T & T Clark, 1979), 677; E. Käsemann, *Commentary on Romans* (Grand Rapids: Eerdmans, 1980), 360; J. D. G. Dunn, *Romans 9-16* (WBC; Dallas: Word, 1988), 778; T. R. Schreiner, *Romans* (BECNT; Grand Rapids: Baker, 1998), 692; and M. Turner, "Mission and Meaning in Terms of 'Unity' in Ephesians," in *Mission and Meaning: Essays Presented to Peter Cotterell* (ed. A. Billington, T. Lane and M. Turner; Carlisle: Paternoster, 1995), 138-66, esp. 139. This differs from Maclean, "Ephesians," 56, who regards the verb as introducing the summary quotation of Lev 19:18, that is being explained, i.e. category (4) above.

[25] Turner, "Mission and Meaning," 139, following Lincoln, *Ephesians*, 33.

tensification of the thought of the root.[26] If it is appropriate to speak
of a 'recapitulation' at all, it is better to regard it as an *implication* of
God's bringing all things together into unity in Christ (which is spelled out later in Ephesians), rather than part of the word's semantic
range.

A similar point could be made in relation to the rendering of
ἀνακεφαλαιόω as to 'bring [all things] together under one head'
(NIV; cf. JB). This follows an exegetical tradition that takes the verb
as deriving from the noun κεφαλή.[27] Moreover, since Christ's role in
relation to the cosmos is spoken of in terms of headship later in
Ephesians (κεφαλή, 1:22), it is claimed that this notion confirms the
rendering of ἀνακεφαλαιόω as to 'bring [all things] under one head'.
So H. Schlier alleged that the meaning of the latter involves the sub-
jection of the cosmos to Christ as its head, while M. Barth understood
ἀνακεφαλαιόω to mean to 'be comprehended under one head'.[28] But
this procedure has rightly been criticized.[29] It is certainly appropriate
to place the thought of 1:10 within the context of the letter as a whole,
and this will involve linking it with passages that point to Christ's
relation to the cosmos (such as 1:22). But the meaning of 1:10, and
especially the verb ἀνακεφαλαιόω, ought to be determined first
within the immediate context, before turning to the rest of Ephesians.
Accordingly, it is preferable to understand ἀνακεφαλαιόω here as
describing the divine intention to sum up all things in Christ as the
focal point. When later it is asserted (1:22) that God has 'appointed

---

[26] E. Best, *A Critical and Exegetical Commentary on Ephesians* (ICC;
Edinburgh: T & T Clark, 1998), 140.

[27] The increasing consensus among modern scholars is that ἀνακεφαλαιόω
derives from κεφάλαιον ('main point, summary'), rather than κεφαλή
('head'), so that the basic meaning of the verb is 'to bring something to a
κεφάλαιον', or 'sum up'.

[28] H. Schlier, "κεφαλή, ἀνακεφαλαιόομαι," *TDNT* 3:681-82; M. Barth,
Ephesians 1-3 (AB; Garden City: Doubleday, 1974), 89-92.

[29] Note A. T. Lincoln, *Ephesians* (WBC; Dallas: Word, 1990), 33, and
especially J. Barr, *The Semantics of Biblical Language* (Oxford: OUP,
1961), 237-38.

him to be head (κεφαλή) over everything for the church', then this event, which occurs at the point of Christ's exaltation, is to be understood as a specific step taken by God in the onward movement of achieving his grand purpose of summing up all things in Christ.

ἀνακεφαλαιόω in Its Context of Ephesians 1

In elucidating the meaning of Paul's enigmatic phrase within its immediate context we notice several important syntactical and exegetical features. First, the bringing together of all things in Christ is the content of the mystery which has been disclosed to believers in accordance with God's purposes. The infinitival clause of v. 10, ἀνακεφαλαιώσασθαι τὰ πάντα ἐν τῷ Χριστῷ, stands in apposition to and is explanatory of τὸ μυστήριον τοῦ θελήματος αὐτοῦ ('the mystery of his will', v. 9).[30]

Secondly, within the long sentence of vv. 3-14 the God and Father of our Lord Jesus Christ is praised for blessing Christians with every spiritual blessing in the heavenly places in Christ. This opening paragraph which celebrates the accomplishment of God's gracious purposes in Christ provides a sweep from eternity to eternity, and the climactic note is struck with the mention of the mystery and its content (vv. 9, 10). Syntactically and structurally, the explication of the mystery in terms of the 'bringing all things together' is the 'high point' of the eulogy.[31] The immediately following words (vv. 11-14) stress that the magnificent blessings already described are for both Jewish and Gentile believers.

Thirdly, as throughout the rest of the eulogy the divine purpose is said to be accomplished 'in Christ', and this point is emphatically reiterated in the concluding words of v. 10, 'in him'. Although this ex-

---

[30] So most commentators.

[31] C. C. Caragounis, *The Ephesian Mysterion: Meaning and Content* (Lund: Gleerup, 1977), 143; T. Moritz, "'Summing Up All Things': Religious Pluralism and Universalism in Ephesians," in *One God, One Lord* (ed. B. W. Winter and A. D. Clarke; Cambridge/Grand Rapids: Tyndale House/Baker, 1991), 96.

pression might be understood as instrumental, suggesting that the Messiah is the means (or instrument) through whom God sums up the universe, it is better to take the phrase as referring to him as the sphere, in line with earlier instances of this phrase within the paragraph (vv. 3-7, 9). Christ is the one *in whom* God chooses to bring all things together in unity, thereby restoring harmony to the universe.[32]

Fourthly, the 'all things' which are to be summed up as a whole are amplified by the following parallel statement, 'things in heaven and things on earth'. This expression is not simply a rhetorical flourish but points to two important strands running throughout the epistle which signify two separate spheres. Ephesians has distinctive things to say about 'the heavenlies' (1:3, 10, 20; 2:6; 3:10; 6:12; cf. 3:15; 4:10; 6:9), as well as about 'the things on earth' (1:10; 3:15; 4:9; 6:3). God's intention of summing up everything in Christ has to do with each of these two spheres and what is represented by them. At the same time there is an inseparable connection between them, so that we may speak of both heaven and earth being summed up as a totality in him. As Paul proceeds to explain this throughout the letter, he concentrates on two representatives of these spheres, namely the *powers* representing 'the things in heaven', and the *church* (particularly Jews and Gentiles in the body of Christ) standing for 'the things on earth'.[33] The two obstacles which need to be dealt with before the divine purposes of summing up everything in Christ can be fulfilled are: the rebellion of the powers, and the alienation of the Jews from the Gentiles (as well as the estrangement of both from God, 2:11-22). Much of the rest of Ephesians is given over to explaining, in relation to these two spheres, the steps taken to achieve this goal.

---

[32] Lincoln, *Ephesians*, 34.

[33] This point has been argued at length by Caragounis, *Mysterion*, 96; 144-46; see also P. T. O'Brien, *The Letter to the Ephesians* (PNTC; Grand Rapids/Leicester: Eerdmans/Apollos, 1999), 112-13.

Finally, as to the timing of this summing up, although the content of God's plan *has been* revealed (he has made known[34] the 'mystery of his will'), its implementation is yet to be completed.[35] The apocalyptic expression 'when the times will have reached their fulfilment' looks forward to the consummation of God's purposes, while the infinitive 'to bring all things together' points to the goal to be achieved.

Making Sense of Ephesians 1:10 in the Letter As a Whole
The rest of Ephesians is consistent with this overall thrust of all things being brought together in Christ as the focal point. Moreover, significant steps have already been taken to achieve this goal, as we have noted. Through Christ's death on the cross not only has the revelation of the mystery's content been graciously given (1:7-9), but also Gentiles who were without God or hope have now been reconciled and incorporated along with Jews into the 'one new humanity' (εἰς ἕνα καινὸν ἄνθρωπον), the body of Christ (2:14-18). The divine intention, now revealed in the 'mystery' (3:3-6), was to make the Gentiles '*co-heirs, co-body members* ... of a new people of God, and *co-sharers* of the promise of the new creation in Christ' (3:6).[36]

God has raised Christ on high to a position of unparalleled honour and universal authority. He has placed all things under his feet so that the whole hierarchy of principalities and authorities, including death, is subject to the risen and exalted Lord. God has appointed him to be head over everything for the church (1:21-22). Gentiles and Jews alike have been brought into life-giving union with Christ and participate in his resurrection and exaltation in the heavenly places (cf.

---

[34] The aorist participle γνωρίσας ('made known') following the principal verb ἐπερίσσευσεν ('he lavished') describes coincident action: 'he lavished his grace on us in all wisdom and insight in that he made known to us the mystery of his will'. For further details, see O'Brien, *Ephesians*, 108-15.
[35] An architect's plan for a building which is submitted well in advance of the actual construction of the building may be a helpful analogy.
[36] Turner, "Mission and Meaning," 145.

2:5-6 with 1:20-21; cf. 4:8). Their destiny is now bound up with his destiny.

With the reconciliation of Jews and Gentiles in the body of Christ, a significant advance has been made towards the consummation of the divine purposes: 'the manifold wisdom of God has been made known to the rulers and authorities in the heavenly realms *through the church*' (3:9-10). The very existence of God's new people is a reminder that the authority of the powers has been decisively broken, and that their final defeat is imminent.

Eph 1-3 with its broad sweep of God's saving purposes provides the theological basis for the long paraenesis of chs 4-6 which are fundamentally an exhortation to unity. These chapters clarify the kind of unity[37] which Paul sees as being implied by God's intention to sum up all things in Christ. The opening admonition (4:1-6) is to a life which expresses the new creation harmony that God has inaugurated. The 'unity of the Spirit', which believers are urged to maintain (4:3), is the unity in Christ which God has inaugurated through the events described in 2:11-22, particularly his Son's death, by which Jew and Gentile believers together have access to God 'in one Spirit' (2:18).

Other aspects of this unity follow. Christ's victory gifts, given to various members of his people, are meant to contribute to the unity and maturity of the whole body (4:7-16). 4:17-5:2 describe first what it means to live according to the new humanity in contrast to the old (vv. 17-24), and culminate in an admonition to be imitators of God (5:1-2). Significantly, Paul's exhortations are directed against those sins, such as anger and falsehood (4:25-26), which cause dissension and alienation within the body, and therefore work against its *unity*.

Wise, godly living involves being filled by the Spirit (5:18), the results of which are evident in Christian behaviour (5:18-21), especially within the household (5:22-6:9). Here Paul deals with re-

---

[37] On the issue of unity in Ephesians see A. G. Patzia, *Ephesians, Colossians, Philemon* (Peabody: Hendrickson, 1990), 133-39, in addition to Turner, "Mission and Meaning," 138-66.

lationships between husbands and wives (5:22-33), focusing on the
ideal of Christian marriage and its relationship to the union of Christ
and his church. Marriage between Christians serves as an example of
the kind of unity the apostle has in mind between the 'head' (both the
husband and Christ) and his 'body' (the wife and the church). Such a
marriage bears living testimony to the meaning of 'the two becoming
one', and reproduces in miniature the beauty shared between the
Bridegroom and the Bride. Within the wider context of Ephesians, the
union between Christian husband and wife, which is part of the unity
between Christ and the church, is a pledge of God's overarching
purpose of summing up all things in Christ.

Paul's concluding appeal of 6:10-20 catches up many of the theological and ethical concerns of the letter, as he describes in cosmic
terms believers' responsibilities while they live in the world. Using
the sustained imagery of a spiritual battle, he depicts the Christian life
as a struggle against evil supernatural forces. These foes which are
arrayed against God and his people have already been defeated by
Christ (1:20-23). Nevertheless, they continue to exist and are im-
placably opposed to God and his purposes. But the ultimate outcome
is certain: God will fulfil his plan of uniting all things together in
Christ.

Some Conclusions

The verb ἀνακεφαλαιόω, which was used from the fourth century BC
to the fourth century AD of a literary or rhetorical summation, has
now been creatively employed by the apostle Paul in a non-rhetorical
sense to describe the magnificent goal of God's gracious purposes for
the whole of creation, namely, his 'bringing together or summing up'
all things in Christ, with the implication of his unifying them all in his
Son (1:10).

This divine intention to sum up all things in Christ is the content
of the mystery that has been disclosed to believers (1:9-10). Paul's
explication of this mystery is the high point of his opening paragraph
(1:3-14), which celebrates the accomplishment of God's gracious

purposes in Christ from eternity to eternity, and where he praises the God and Father of our Lord Jesus Christ for having blessed Christians with every spiritual blessing in the heavenly places in Christ (1:3). He is the one in whom God has chosen to bring all things together, thereby restoring harmony to the universe. The 'all things' that are to be summed up consist of two spheres, 'the things in heaven' and 'the things on earth'; there is an inseparable connection between them, so that we may speak of both heaven and earth, together with their representatives (the *powers* and the *church* comprising Jews and Gentiles in the body of Christ), being summed up as a totality in him. Much of the rest of Ephesians is given over to explaining, in relation to these spheres, the steps already taken to accomplish God's grand purpose that will be completed on the final day ('when the times will have reached their fulfilment', v. 10).

The statement of Eph 1:9-10, which proclaims that God has made known to us the mystery of his will, the content of which is that it is his intention to 'sum up all things in Christ', is the key text of the letter. It unlocks the epistle's glorious treasures, links with many of its major themes and enables us to gain an integrated picture of Ephesians as a whole, the central message of which is cosmic reconciliation and unity in Christ.

A Saviour for the Cities of Crete:

The Roman Background to the Epistle to Titus

David W. J. Gill

Paul's commission to Titus in Crete was that he 'might put what remained into order, and appoint elders in every town (κατὰ πόλιν) as I directed you' (Titus 1:5, ESV). The issue is what would these πόλεις on Crete have been like in the mid-first century AD.[1] Πόλις is rarely used in the New Testament epistles and would appear to be here identifying the urban, political units of the Roman province of Crete and Cyrenaica, which is how the term is used in the Greek world.[2]

The establishment of churches throughout the island is mirrored by events in the adjacent provinces of Achaea (Corinth), Macedonia (Philippi, Thessalonica), and Asia (Ephesus) where the major cities became the focus for evangelism.[3] At the time of writing to Titus Paul expected to winter at Nicopolis (Epirus) on the Adriatic (Titus 3:12) which pointed him westwards to Italy and perhaps beyond to the western Mediterranean.

Strabo and the Topography of Crete
A contemporary view of Crete is provided by the geographer Strabo,[4] which although written from the perspective of the Augustan period

---

[1] Paul's winter at Nicopolis (Titus 3:12) is perhaps best dated to AD 65-66.
[2] See A. H. M. Jones, *The Greek City from Alexander to Justinian* (Oxford: Clarendon, 1940).
[3] For an overview of events in Achaea, Macedonia and Asia see D. W. J. Gill and C. Gempf, eds., *The Book of Acts in Its Graeco-Roman Setting* (The Book of Acts in Its First-Century Setting 2; Grand Rapids: Eerdmans, 1994).
[4] Strabo, *Geographia* 10 (Jones, LCL).

drew on earlier sources. The mountainous nature of Crete made land communication difficult, and there is little evidence for a Roman road system.[5] However, the quaestor Q. Paconius Agrippinus is recorded as responsible for repairing roads and *androbamones* in the region of Hieropytna in the south of the island during the reign of Claudius.[6]

Recent field surveys have begun to expand knowledge of Crete in the Roman period, especially the Lassithi plateau which lies to the south of modern Malia,[7] though other results include material from the Ayiofarango Valley in the south of the island.[8]

The Roman Administration of Crete
Rome had intervened on Crete because of the problem of pirates.[9] The campaign was led by Quintus Caecilius Metellus who took three legions to the island in 69 BC. Campaigns led to the fall of Eleutherna,

---

[5]   J. D. S. Pendlebury, *The Archaeology of Crete: An Introduction* (London: Methuen, 1939), 365, suggested that the paved roads often attributed to late periods might in fact be Roman in origin. See also Oliver Rackham and Jennifer Moody, *The Making of the Cretan Landscape* (Manchester: Manchester University Press, 1996), 155-56.

[6]   I. F. Sanders, *Roman Crete: An Archaeological Survey and Gazeteer of Late Hellenistic, Roman and Early Byzantine Crete* (Warminster: Aris & Phillips, 1982), 7. *IC* III.iii.25-29.

[7]   L. V. Watrous, *Lasithi: A History of Settlement on a Highland Plain in Crete* (*Hesperia* suppl. 18; Princeton: American School of Classical Studies at Athens, 1982).

[8]   D. Blackman and K. Branigan, "An Archaeological Survey of the Lower Catchment of the Ayiofarango Valley," *Annual of the British School at Athens* 72 (1977): 13-84, esp. 72-76 (Hellenistic and Roman periods). See also D. Blackman and K. Branigan, "An Archaeological Survey on the South Coast of Crete, between the Ayiofarango and Chrisostomos," *Annual of the British School at Athens* 70 (1975): 17-36. See also the Sphakia survey: http://sphakia.classics.ox.ac.uk.

[9]   See Sanders, *Roman Crete*, 3-4. See also Sara Paton, "Hellenistic and Roman Crete," in *Cretan Quests: British Explorers, Excavators and Historians* (ed. Davina Huxley; London: British School at Athens, 2000), 174-81; S. E. Alcock, *Archaeologies of the Greek Past: Landscapes, Monument, and Memories* (Cambridge: CUP, 2002), 99-131 ('Cretan Inventions').

and Metellus established Gortyn as the capital of the island. Crete seems to have been linked with the administration of governor, and one of the first known governors, Cn. Tremellius Scrofa (50 BC), was proconsul of Crete and Cyrenaica.[10]

After the assassination of Julius Caesar and the formation of the Triumvirate, Crete was one of the provinces assigned to Mark Antony. He in turn seems to have given Cleopatra control of Itanos in the east of the island in 37-36 BC.[11] Following Actium, and the eventual defeat and death of Cleopatra and Antony, Crete was restored to Roman administration and following Augustus' reforms of 27 BC, Crete and Cyrenaica became a single province again under the control of the Senate. Under Tiberius the island was used for those exiled from Rome.[12] Alongside the Roman administration was the Koinon of the island, bringing together the different cities, organising quinquennial games and issuing coinage.[13] Such an institution helped to maintain a Greek identity on the island.

The Cities of Crete

The πόλεις of Crete were considered to number one hundred. A literate audience would know the lines from Homer:

> Idoemeneus the spear-famed was leader of the Kretans, Those who held Knosos and Gortyna of the great walls, Lyktos and Miletos and silver-shining Lykastos, and Phaistos and Rhytion, all towns well

---

[10] Sanders, *Roman Crete*, 176. See also Cicero, *Atticum* 6.1.13, dated to February 50 BC. See D. R. Shackleton Bailey, ed., *Cicero's Letters to Atticus* III (Cambridge: CUP, 1968), 246.

[11] Sanders, *Roman Crete*, 5. For the grant to Cleopatra: Dio Cassius, *Historia Romana* 49.32.4-5. For Itanos: S. Spyridakis, *Ptolemaic Itanos and Hellenistic Crete* (Berkeley: University of California Press, 1970). See also T. Kalpaxis, A. Schnapp and D. Viviers, "Itanos (Crète orientale)," *BCH* 119 (1995): 711-36.

[12] The exile of Cassius Severus: Tacitus, *Ann.* 4.21.

[13] Sanders, *Roman Crete*, 8.

established, and others who dwelt beside them in Krete of the hundred cities.[14]

This Homeric description of the island continued into the Roman period as it is repeated in the epitaph of a gladiator from Gortyn.[15]

	Issuing coins	Evidence of κόσμοι
Aptera		●
Arcades		●
Axos	● Tiberius; Claudius	●
Chersonisos		● ?
Cydonia	● Augustus; Tiberius; Claudius; Nero	
Eleutherna	● Tiberius	●
Gortyna	● Augustus; Tiberius; Caligula	●
Hierapytna	● Tiberius; Caligula	●
Itanos		●
Kisamos		●
Knossos	● Augustus; Tiberius; Caligula; Claudius; Nero	●
Lappa	● Augustus; Tiberius	●
Lato	● Caligula	●
Lyttos	● Caligula	●
Olus		●
Polyrrhenia	● Tiberius; Caligula	●
Priansos		●

Table 1. Roman cities on Crete[16]

During the Hellenistic period some 40 πόλεις are known to have been viable political units.[17] This number seems to have been roughly halved by the Roman period given the evidence from cities which issued their own coinage or had their own magistrates (κόσμοι).[18] By

---

[14] 'Catalogue of the Ships', Homer, *Il.* 2.645-49. See also Sanders, *Roman Crete*, 11; Alcock, *Archaeologies of the Greek Past*, 103; P. Perlman, "One Hundred-citied Crete and the 'Cretan Politeia'," *CP* 87 (1992): 193-205.

[15] *IC* III.373, line 10: Ἑκατονταπολῖται.

[16] Based on Sanders, *Roman Crete*, fig. 2, and p. 13, fig. 132.

[17] Sanders, *Roman Crete*, 11.

[18] Sanders, *Roman Crete*, 12. A useful, though dated, summary of sites (with references to archaeological work) on Crete can be found in D. Leekley and R. Noyes, *Archaeological Excavations in the Greek Islands*

the second century AD three Cretan cities were included as members of the Panhellenion with its focus on Athens.[19]

Among the main πόλεις of the island in the early Roman period were Gortyn, Eleutherna, Knossos, Hierapytna and Kydonia.

Gortyn

The administrative capital of the province of Crete and Cyrene was Gortyn which lies on the north side of the Mesara plain.[20] The site lying to the west of Ayii Deka, was first excavated in the 1880s by F. Halbherr, and subsequently by the Italian Archaeological Mission. The city was established in the Geometric period, and by the beginning of the classical period it codified its law in the celebrated 'Gortyn Code'. During the Hellenistic period Gortyn was linked to the Ptolemies, and its possible neutrality during the campaigns of Metellus in 69-67 BC allowed it to become the leading city of the island. Roman veterans may have been settled at Gortyn and were recruited from the island by Pompey during the Civil War.[21] During the fighting between Mark Antony (and Cleopatra) and Octavian, it took the side of the latter. This earned the city favour as its great rival Knossos had taken the side of the losers.[22] The city benefited from a

---

(Park Ridge: Noyes Press, 1975). An annual survey of work on Crete can be found in *Archaeological Reports.*

[19] Lyttos, Gortyn and Hierapytna. See A. J. S. Spawforth and S. Walker, "The World of the Panhellenion I: Athens and Eleusis," *JRS* 75 (1985): 80-82, 85.

[20] Antonino Di Vita, "Gortyn," in *The Aerial Atlas of Ancient Crete* (ed. J. Wilson Myers, E. Emlen Myers and Gerald Cadogan; Berkeley/Los Angeles: University of California Press, 1992), 96-103. For the monograph series see A. Di Vita, ed., *Gortina* (Rome: Monografie della Scuola Archeologica di Atene e delle Missioni Italiane in Oriente, 1988-). See also the review articles: George W. M. Harrison, review of *Gortina I*, in *Journal of Roman Archaeology* 3 (1990): 502-05; Jane Frances and George W. M. Harrison, "Gortyn: First City of Roman Crete," *American Journal of Archaeology* 107 (2003): 487-92.

[21] Caesar, *BC* 3.4.1. See also the tombstone (in Greek) of the centurion Q. Munatidius Maximus: *IC* IV.220. See also Sanders, *Roman Crete*, 5.

[22] In the province of Achaea, Athens found itself supporting the losing side.

range of public buildings, and at its greatest extent probably covered some 400 ha.[23]

Eleutherna

The city of Eleutherna is located in north central Crete.[24] It was excavated by members of the British School at Athens in 1928, and since the 1960s by the Greek Archaeological Service and more recently the University of Crete.[25] Some of the inscriptions come from the Julio-Claudian period.[26]

Knossos

The settlement of Knossos is perhaps best known for its Bronze Age 'palace'. However the site continued to be occupied in the Roman period, and was the site of a Roman colony, *Colonia Iulia Nobilis Cnossus*, probably established by Augustus.[27] Latin seems to have been the standard language in use on both coins and in its inscriptions. The Hellenistic and Roman city lay to the north of the

---

[23] It is reported that the Roman city and its necropolis covered some 430 ha: James Whitley, "Archaeology in Greece 2002-2003," *Archaeological Reports* 49 (2003): 81.

[24] Petros Themelis, "Eleutherna," in *Aerial Atlas of Ancient Crete* (ed. Myers et al.), 91-95. For a summary of the British excavations: A. M. Woodward, "Archaeology in Greece, 1928-29," *Journal of Hellenic Studies* 49 (1929): 224-26. For summary: Sanders, *Roman Crete*, 162-63. For earlier periods see, e.g., N. Stampolidis, "Eleutherna on Crete: An Interim Report on the Geometric-Archaic Cemetery," *Annual of the British School at Athens* 85 (1990): 375-403; A. Nakassis, "The Bridges of Ancient Eleutherna," *Annual of the British School at Athens* 95 (2000): 353-65.

[25] For the most recent work see the summary report in James Whitley, "Archaeology in Greece 2002-2003," *Archaeological Reports* 49 (2003): 86-87.

[26] *IC* II.xi.27-29.

[27] L. H. Sackett, ed., *Knossos: From Greek City to Roman Colony: Excavations at the Unexplored Mansion* (London: British School at Athens, 1992); S. Paton, "Roman Knossos and the Colonia Julia Nobilis Cnossus," in *Knossos: A Labyrinth of History: Papers in Honour of Sinclair Hood* (ed. D. Evely, H. Hughes-Brock and N. Momigliano; Oxford: Oxbow, 1994), 141-53. For a discussion of possible dates: Sanders, *Roman Crete*, 14.

Bronze Age remains.[28] There is evidence from the Shrine of Glaukos that cult activity was discontinued when the city was captured.[29]

An inscription alludes to *ludi* in the colony, which would indicate the presence of an amphitheatre where such spectacles could be mounted.[30] Excavations in the region of the so-called 'Unexplored Mansion' have also suggested that there was rebuilding of the city in the mid to late first century AD, possibly due to earthquake damage.[31] First-century tombs have been located in the region of Marathianou Lakkos.[32]

Hierapytna

This coastal city (at the modern port of Ierapetra) in eastern Crete has yet to be explored in detail.[33] The site is strategic as it dominates the southern end of the narrow isthmus of Ierapetra. There is a possible portrait of Augustus, and other sculptures of the first century AD.

---

[28] Sanders, *Roman Crete*, 152-53.
[29] P. J. Callaghan, "KRS 1976: Excavations at a Shrine of Glaukos, Knossos," *Annual of the British School at Athens* 73 (1978): 28.
[30] *IC* I.viii.51.
[31] Sanders, *Roman Crete*, 152-53, with n. 7. See L. H. Sackett, "The Unexplored Mansion at Knossos: A Preliminary Report on the Excavations from 1967 to 1972: Part II: Post-Minoan Occupation above the Unexplored Mansion," *Archaeological Reports* 19 (1972-73): 62-71; John W. Hayes, "The Villa Dionysos Excavations, Knossos: The Pottery," *Annual of the British School at Athens* 78 (1983): 97-169; Sackett, ed., *Knossos*.
[32] K. A. Wardle, "Two Notes from Knossos," *Annual of the British School in Athens* 67 (1972): 271-84.
[33] For a plan: Sanders, *Roman Crete*, 139, fig. 49. For an overview of some of the finds: Nikos P. Papadakis, *The Exiled Archaeological Treasures of Ierapetra* (Ierapetra: The Prefectural Council of Lassithi and the Morfotiki Stegi Ierapetras, 1997). For the most recent report: James Whitley, "Archaeology in Greece 2002-2003," *Archaeological Reports* 49 (2003): 84. For a new architectural inscription: M. W. Baldwin Bowsky, "Eight Inscriptions from Roman Crete," *ZPE* 108 (1995): 263-80, no. 1.

Kydonia

Kydonia is largely hidden under the modern Chania, though remains of the Roman city have been discovered.[34]

The Cult of Asklepios at Lebena

A wide range of cults were active on the island during the Roman period. In the colony at Knossos there was a cult of the deified Claudius,[35] and a member of the local elite had served as the *flamen* of the divine Vespasian,[36] and at Gortyn there may have been a cult of Roma and Augustus.[37] One of the most popular Olympian deities was Zeus.[38] The second most popular cult was that of Asklepios; this is found in at least 18 locations across the island.[39]

'Saviour' in Titus and on Crete

The term 'Saviour' is a frequent one in the epistle to Titus. Paul's preaching had been entrusted to him by 'God our Saviour' (ὃ ἐπιστεύθην ἐγὼ κατ' ἐπιταγὴν τοῦ σωτῆρος ἡμῶν θεοῦ, Titus 1:3). The opening greeting is in the name of 'God the Father and Christ Jesus our Saviour' (χάρις καὶ εἰρήνη ἀπὸ θεοῦ πατρὸς καὶ Χριστοῦ Ἰησοῦ τοῦ σωτῆρος ἡμῶν, Titus 1:4). The conduct of slaves should be such that 'in everything they may adorn the doctrine of God our Saviour' (ἵνα τὴν διδασκαλίαν τὴν τοῦ σωτῆρος ἡμῶν θεοῦ

---

[34] Sanders, *Roman Crete*, 169-70. For the most recent work see James Whitley, "Archaeology in Greece 2002-2003," *Archaeological Reports* 49 (2003): 86. For epigraphy: Baldwin Bowsky, "Eight Inscriptions from Roman Crete," esp. nos 3 and 6.

[35] *IC* I.viii.49.

[36] *IC* I.viii. 54. See Sanders, *Roman Crete*, 38.

[37] *IC* IV.270. This is based on a very fragmentary inscription: ...] et Aug[...

[38] Sanders, *Roman Crete*, 36.

[39] These include the Cult of Asklepios and Hygeia at Lissos belonging to the first century BC, to the first century AD and almost certainly later: Myers et al., *Aerial Atlas of Ancient Crete*, 168-71. For what appears to be a Hadrianic dedication from Lisos: Baldwin Bowsky, "Eight Inscriptions from Roman Crete," no. 2 (dedication by P. Aelius Leonas).

κοσμῶσιν ἐν πᾶσιν, Titus 2:10). There is a looking forward to 'the appearing of the glory of our great God and Saviour Jesus Christ' (ἐπιφάνειαν τῆς δόξης τοῦ μεγάλου θεοῦ καὶ σωτῆρος ἡμῶν Ἰησοῦ Χριστοῦ, Titus 2:13). Paul's conversion was through the appearance of 'the goodness and lovingkindness of God our Saviour' (ὅτε δὲ ἡ χρηστότης καὶ ἡ φιλανθρωπία ἐπεφάνη τοῦ σωτῆρος ἡμῶν θεοῦ, Titus 3:4). Finally, the outpouring of the Holy Spirit was 'through Jesus Christ our Saviour' (διὰ Ἰησοῦ Χριστοῦ τοῦ σωτῆρος ἡμῶν, Titus 3:6). Although there are parallels with the other pastoral epistles (e.g. 1 Tim 1:1, 2 Tim 1:10), the use of 'Saviour' in Titus is striking.

If Titus was based in Gortyn such language could have been given new meaning. On the south coast of Crete, immediately to the south of Gortyn, but separated by the Asterousia mountain range, was the sanctuary of Asklepios at Lebena.[40] The sanctuary seems to have been established in the fourth century BC from Epidauros,[41] in contrast to the other important strand of the cult with its focus at Pergamon. The cult remained important through the Hellenistic and Roman periods as is attested by a series of inscriptions recovered from the site.[42] The use of the sanctuary in the first century AD is supported by a dedication in Latin by Q. Fulvius Tuscus, a Roman quaestor.[43] The cult site is also reported to have had strong links with North Africa, in particular Cyrenaica, as 'large numbers of Libyans too make the crossing to it, for it looks over to the Libyan sea close to Phaestus'.[44]

---

[40] Despina Haczi-Vallianou, *Lebena: The Ancient City and the Shrine of Asclepius* (Athens: Ministry of Culture Archaeological Receipts Fund, 1989); Chiara Tarditi, "Lebena-Asklepieion," in Myers et al., *Aerial Atlas of Ancient Crete*, 160-63.

[41] For the epithet, *IC* I.xvii.7-8: Asklepios ἐξ Ἐπιδαύρω ἐς Λεβηναίος (no. 7), ἐν Ἐπιδαύρω (no. 8).

[42] For the inscriptions: *IC* I.xvii.1-60. See also M. Guarducci, "I miracoli di Asclepio a Lebena," *Historia* 8 (1934): 410-38.

[43] *IC* I.xviii.54. See also Sanders, *Roman Crete*, 178.

[44] Philostratus, *Vita Apollonii* 4.34. See Graham Anderson, *Philostratus: Biography and Belles Lettres in the Third Century A.D.* (London: Croom Helm, 1986), 200-02.

Although the site has been partially excavated by the Italian Archaeological School as well as by the (Greek) Archaeological Society, the site was explored by the British topographer Captain Thomas A. B. Spratt RN, following up earlier investigations by Belli in the late sixteenth century. Among the inscriptions removed by Spratt and presented to the University of Cambridge was a stone base originally carrying a pair of dedications, perhaps dedicated in the second century AD.[45]

Δοιούς σοι Διόδω-
ρος ἐθήκατο, Σῶτερ,
Ὀνείρους
ἀντὶ διπλῶν ὅσσων
φωτὸς ἐπαυράμενος

Diodoros dedicated to you, Saviour, two dreams,
in return for twofold eyes, light being restored.

Facsimile of the inscription from the sanctuary
of Asklepios at Lebena.

---

[45] *IC* I.xvii.24. The base is now in the Fitzwilliam Museum (GR.2.1854). For Spratt's donations to Cambridge, see Churchill Babington, "Inscriptiones Sprattianae," *Journal of Sacred and Classical Philology* 2 (1855): 98-109. The inscription is noted in D. W. J. Gill, "Behind the Classical Façade: Local Religions of the Roman Empire," in A. D. Clarke and B. W. Winter, eds., *One God, One Lord in a World of Religious Pluralism* (Cambridge: Tyndale House, 1991), 78. I am grateful to Dr Kevin Butcher for first discussing this inscription with me.

The 'dreams' themselves have not survived though there are two pairs of marks on the top of the block which suggest that they appeared to be anthropomorphic.[46] The use of Σῶτερ is a reference to Asklepios. Its use on its own is in contrast with the epistle to Titus where the word is qualified with Θεός or Χριστός. The epithet is also found attached to Zeus in a Greek dedication from Knossos made by one Plotios from Corinth.[47]

Conclusion

Although the members of the church on Crete in the time of Titus may have been drawn from the Greek and Roman communities of the island, there is a hint of converts from among the Jewish community. There is mention of 'the circumcision party' (1:10), those who 'devote themselves to Jewish myths' (1:14). Cretans were among those gathered in Jerusalem at Pentecost (Acts 2:11), though the reference to them is noticeably separated from Jews from Cyrenaica who are rather linked with Egypt (Acts 2:10). In the time of Augustus the Jewish community were hoodwinked into giving money to a charlatan from Sidon.[48]

The careful way that Paul makes an unambiguous reference to the 'saving' nature of Jesus Christ would mean that those coming from a Gentile background would not be confused by the language commonly used by pagan cults on Crete during the Roman period. This would be especially important as the gospel penetrated beyond the provincial capital of Gortyn, and the Roman colony of Knossos, to the long-established Greek cities of the island.

---

[46] There are in fact two sets of three holes for mounting the dedications. Two pairs of holes seem to be for feet.
[47] *IC* I.viii.17.
[48] Josephus, *A.J.* 17.327: 'he landed in Crete [and] won the confidence of all the Jews with whom he came into contact. And being well supplied with money as a result of their gifts, he sailed across to Melos' (LCL).

A Place for Hebrews?

Contexts for a First-Century Sermon

Peter Walker

> I have a lively, or rather deadly, recollection of a certain series of dis-
> courses on the Hebrews, which made a deep impression on my mind
> of a most undesirable kind. I wished frequently that the Hebrews had
> kept the Epistle to themselves, for it sadly bored a poor Gentile lad.[1]

So spoke the great nineteenth-century preacher, Charles Spurgeon.
Before his conversion, the Epistle to the Hebrews had not been his
favourite book. Many today, both in the academy and the church,
would probably agree. By contrast this essay considers ways in which
the letter has reason to claim a central place both in academic circles
and in the church.

The reasons for Hebrews' comparative unpopularity in the church
are not hard to find. Congregations may find its Jewish worldview
(focusing, for example, on temple sacrifices, Melchizedek and the
Levitical priesthood) quite alienating, its vision of God too awesome
(e.g. 10:31) and its warnings against apostasy (6:4-6; 10:26-31) un-
comfortable.

Meanwhile in scholarly circles, Hebrews has hardly been a centre
of recent debate. There is no 'New Perspective' on Hebrews, and no
opportunity for comparing it with another work by the same author.
Eucharistic debates (about the 'once for all' nature of Jesus' sacrifice)[2] no longer seem to concern us, and Hebrews' portrait of the

---

[1]   C. H. Spurgeon, *The Early Years, 1834-1859* (Edinburgh: Banner of
Truth, 1962), 48.
[2]   See, e.g., B. F. Westcott, *The Epistle to the Hebrews* (London:
MacMillan, 1914), 346-49, 455-63.

'historical Jesus' (though it speaks more frequently than Paul about Jesus' human life) is not readily admitted as real evidence.[3]

A key reason, however, for this comparative neglect is the acknowledged uncertainty about Hebrews' precise setting. Most English-speaking scholars may now lean towards a date before AD 70,[4] but there is no *consensus* about its authorship or audience.[5] Scholars and preachers alike are thus prevented from outlining the original situation with any confidence, and congregations cannot establish a rapport with the original author who, being anonymous, remains somewhat aloof. Paradoxically, preachers may avoid Hebrews as *too* historical (bound up with an ancient, now irrelevant, situation), whilst scholars avoid it as not historical enough (not giving sufficient opportunity for historical reconstruction).

A second reason for neglect is that this uncertainty extends to issues of real substance. The author speaks with passion and urgency, but it is unclear exactly what problem he is seeking to address. In

---

[3] 'Historical Jesus' studies inevitably focus almost exclusively on the Synoptic Gospels to the exclusion of John, Paul and Hebrews; on the dangers of this, see, e.g., N. T. Wright, *The New Testament and the People of God* (London: SPCK, 1992), ch. 13.

[4] Those favouring a date prior to AD 70 include commentators such as F. F. Bruce, P. Ellingworth, G. H. Guthrie, D. A. Hagner, P. E. Hughes, W. L. Lane, H. Montefiore, A. Strobel, as well as B. Lindars, *The Theology of the Letter to the Hebrews* (Cambridge: CUP, 1991), 10-21, and D. A. DeSilva, *Perseverance in Gratitude* (Grand Rapids: Eerdmans, 2000), 20. For a later date, see, e.g., M. E. Isaacs, *Sacred Space: An Approach to the Theology of the Epistle to the Hebrews* (Sheffield: JSOT, 1992), 44, 67; J. D. G. Dunn, *The Partings of the Ways* (London: SCM, 1991), 87.

[5] Even those who favour the most popular solution (of an audience located in Rome) are aware that this is still an enlightened piece of guesswork: W. L. Lane, *Hebrews* (2 vols.; WBC; Dallas: Word, 1991), 1:lviii, speaks of the 'considerable risk' of basing exegesis on this supposition that can 'never be proven'; cf., e.g., D. A. Hagner, *Hebrews* (NIBC; Peabody: Hendrickson, 1990), 7. Lane is critiqued for building too much on this mere 'hypothesis' by DeSilva, *Perseverance in Gratitude*, 1, 21; cf. too C. R. Koester, *Hebrews* (New York: Doubleday, 2001), 52.

what follows we will look at how this uncertainty about both the setting and substance of Hebrews may affect our reading of the text.

The Unique Sermon

There is some irony in Hebrews' being neglected — in particular, by preachers. For Hebrews is itself the nearest we get to an example of first-century biblical preaching. Almost certainly this 'word of exhortation' (13:22) functioned as a sermon treatise: its first recipients would have heard it, not just as a letter, but as a sermon from an absentee friend.[6] If so, it is without parallel in the New Testament. The speeches in Acts are no more than short summaries; here alone do we have an extended sermon (which could be delivered orally in about 45 minutes). Moreover, in our day when there is some new discussion of the value of 'expository' preaching,[7] we note that Hebrews, with its frequent discussion of Old Testament passages, is itself 'expository'.[8]

Key homiletical insights can be drawn from this ancient sermon. For example: the way the preacher, though starting in a grand style, nevertheless establishes rapport with his audience (building on concepts they share);[9] his pastoral sensitivity to their possible feelings, with his constant oscillation between encouragement and challenge;[10] his strong appeals at two key places which motivate the audience to keep on listening (5:11–6:6; 10:26-31); his occasional 'plateaux' when he summarises his argument before climbing the next peak (e.g.

---

6   See, e.g., Hagner, *Hebrews*, 12; Lane, *Hebrews*, lxx-lxxxv.

7   See, e.g., S. Greidanus, *The Modern Preacher and the Ancient Text* (Grand Rapids: Eerdmans, 1988); P. Adam, *Speaking God's Words* (Leicester: IVP, 1996); H. W. Robinson, *Expository Preaching* (2nd ed.; Leicester: IVP, 2001); C. Green and D. Jackman, eds., *When God's Voice Is Heard* (2nd ed.; Leicester: IVP, 2003).

8   See R. T. France, "The Writer of Hebrews As a Biblical Expositor," *TynB* 47 (1996): 245-76.

9   See B. Lindars, "The Rhetorical Structure of Hebrews," *NTS* 35 (1989): 390: the author 'starts with propositions that are not in dispute'.

10   Passages of exhortation and encouragement begin at 1:1; 2:5; 4:14; 6:9; 10:32; 12:22; 13:1 and 13:15; these are interspersed with passages of provocative challenge, beginning at 2:1; 3:1; 5:11; 10:25; 12:1, 25 and 13:9.

4:14-16; 10:19-25); the sense of cumulative dynamism which takes the listeners forward on their journey or 'race' (12:1) towards the climax focused on the heavenly Jerusalem (12:22) and the vision of God as a 'consuming fire' (12:29); his gentle, more pastoral manner in the final chapter (when nevertheless he exposes perhaps the key presenting problem);[11] and the way he raises this issue in the presence of Jesus ('the same yesterday, today and forever', 13:8), leaving his final appeal to come, as it were, not from him but rather from the Lord Jesus himself.

Those with a concern for biblical preaching would thus do well to heed, not avoid, this first-century sermon.

The Presenting Problem

So can we uncover more precisely the nature of the author's concerns? Clearly he had several positive truths which he wished to convey — not least the humanity and deity of the Lord Jesus Christ (chs 1–2), and the 'once-for-all' nature of his sacrificial death for sins in his role as great High Priest (2:17; 5:5; 7:24–8:2; 9:11–10:22, etc). Yet what was the problem that occasioned this creative exposition? What precisely was he preaching or teaching *against*?

At a general level we can note the following list: a crippling fear of death (2:15) or hardship (12:4); spiritual laziness (6:12) or bitterness (12:15); lack of perseverance or confidence (3:14; 4:14-16; 10:19-22, 35-36; 13:6); active faithlessness and hardened hearts that refuse to listen to God (3:12; 4:2, 11; 12:25); wandering 'astray' (5:2); immaturity (5:14); apostasy (6:4-6; 10:26-31); failing to keep meeting together (10:25); immorality (12:16; 13:4); disobeying church leadership (13:17). But is there a unifying principle underlying this expansive list of warnings? Unlike some New Testament letters (e.g. 1 Peter) Hebrews is not an unspecific letter sent to a variety of churches, where the author deals in generalizations because he does not know the local situation in detail. Instead it reads as a focused

---

[11] See below n. 25.

letter, written by someone who apparently knew his audience well, and who was seeking to dissuade them from a specific action — an action which they imminently intended, but which he perceived as potentially disastrous.

A Relapse into Judaism?

Most commentators suggest that the action intended by the audience was a lapse (of some kind) into non-Christian Judaism.[12] On this reading the later designation πρὸς Ἑβραίους ('to the Hebrews') accurately reflects the sense that the letter's audience were *Jewish-Christians*; as such their temptation to apostasy almost certainly would entail a return to their Jewish roots without Jesus — an abandonment of their faith in Jesus as Israel's Messiah.

This interpretation makes sense. What is less clear is the precise cause of this temptation: the author's concerns (listed above) might initially suggest anything from mere weariness and disillusionment through to positive love of their former Jewish practice; or from bowing to social pressure from their fellow Jews through to fear of Roman persecution. If, for example, the audience were 'second generation' Christians in Nero's Rome,[13] then we can readily imagine how a good many of these factors were playing some part in their temptation. However, the fact that the author fears his hearers will commit apostasy, *whilst believing that they themselves do not see it in those terms*, strongly suggests that one of these options is incorrect: they were not driven by a positive re-attraction to Judaism. In other

---

[12] See, e.g., W. Manson, *The Epistle to the Hebrews* (London: Hodder & Stoughton, 1951); Lane, *Hebrews*, 545; Hagner, *Hebrews*, 243-45; R. C. Stedman, *Hebrews* (Downers Grove: IVP, 1992); also F. V. Filson, *Yesterday: A Study of Hebrews in the Light of Chapter 13* (London: SCM, 1967), 61-66. This is now critiqued by DeSilva, *Perseverance in Gratitude*, who argues that the audience may have included a good proportion of gentiles and that the implied critique of Judaism serves only the positive purpose of emphasising the value of what they have in Jesus; cf. Koester, *Hebrews*, 72.

[13] On possible settings, see below on 'Finding Its Ancient Place'.

words, they were not consciously intending theological apostasy. Instead they were contemplating an action without having thought through its implications; their intended action was not the result of a conscious theological decision against Christ. This is important. Hebrews becomes for us a model of a sermon concerned to reveal the unintended consequences of a congregation's unclear thinking.

But if Hebrews is indeed written to prevent a lapse back into Judaism, there are some further major questions. For, in order to achieve his goal, the author must necessarily cast some aspersions on that to which he desires them not to return. Consequently the readers of Hebrews are intended by the author to hear a critique of Judaism, their 'parent body'.

The Author's Conscious but Careful Response

In practice this critique is not hard to hear. The law is imperfect and powerless (7:19) and 'only a shadow of the good things that are coming' (10:1-4); the old covenant is flawed and becoming 'obsolete' (8:7, 13). The Jerusalem Temple is also a 'shadow' and not the 'true tabernacle' (8:5; cf. 9:11, 24); it depends on 'external regulations', which were always intended as temporary 'until the time of the new order' (9:10), and it has now been eclipsed by the unique sacrifice of Christ (9:14, 26; 10:10). Unlike other high priests, Jesus can 'take away sins' (10:11-14), thereby offering a 'better hope' and a 'better covenant' founded on 'better promises' (7:19, 22; 8:6). Compared with great Moses (the faithful 'servant' *within* God's house), Jesus is the 'son' *over* God's house (3:1-6). Jesus thus offers something 'better' than anything found in Judaism alone.

None of this, of course, is written in a rude or dismissive spirit towards what had gone before. It was the author's own treasured heritage. There is no anti-Semitism here. This is an intramural debate, with one Jew telling other Jews where the truth of their faith now lies.[14] Yet there is a clear *and fully intended* statement that Judaism without Jesus is not a Christian option. If the author thought it was, the whole purpose of his sermon would be futile.

Indeed, he seems to imply that Judaism without Jesus is, strictly, no longer even a truly Jewish option. For on several occasions he hints that faith in Jesus brings to pass a 'fulfilled Judaism' such that believing Christians are effectively the embodiment of authentic Judaism. For example, Old Testament believers would have recognised the salvation now accomplished in Christ: the 'prophets' would have welcomed the 'Son' (1:1-2; 3:6); the heroes of faith looked forward to something better and only become perfect 'together with us' (11:1-40); Moses himself experienced 'disgrace for the sake of Christ' (11:26). Above all, God's great promise to Abraham finds its fulfilment in Jesus (6:13-20). As believers in Jesus they have moved forward into the fullness of what God intended; the past can therefore be treasured, but only so long as it remains just that — the *past*. They must not return to it. To lose Jesus would be to lose the heart of their Judaism and its divinely intended goal.

These are powerful claims, which we now can only read in the wake of centuries of debate between church and synagogue. We are well aware that many will dispute Hebrews' claims for Jesus and question the author's presentation of Judaism — not least as it has developed since the Temple's destruction.[15] Yet the key point is this:

---

[14] See W. Klassen, "To the Hebrews or against the Hebrews?," in *Anti-Judaism in Early Christianity: Vol. 2: Separation and Polemic* (ed. S. G. Wilson; Waterloo: Wilfrid Laurier University, 1986), 1-16. Scholars are rightly wary of allowing the New Testament to be read as *racially* anti-Semitic. Yet sometimes this is taken further to imply that the authors were not in any way opposed *theologically* to Judaism without Jesus and that they are not 'anti-Judaism' even in this sense. For a helpful overview of this problem in the New Testament, see C. A. Evans and D. A. Hagner, eds., *Anti-Semitism and Early Christianity* (Minneapolis: Fortress, 1993).

[15] A Temple-less Judaism would of course escape some of Hebrews' critique, but no doubt the author would have seen the Temple's destruction

here is a biblical warrant for a Jew to speak about Jesus as Messiah in a way that is critical of Judaism.

Here, of course, we need to tread with the utmost care. It is with good reason that anything that smacks of anti-Judaism is viewed with suspicion — 'anti-Semitism' has found too much ground in the church. Christian preachers in particular have sometimes used the pulpit to say awful things: caricaturing Judaism as a religion of works, or portraying Jesus as somehow opposed to the essence of Judaism. The work of Tom Wright in recent years helps us instead to see a thoroughly Jewish Jesus who argued with his fellow Jews not about religion but about eschatology, and who was crucified because of the claims he was making for himself.[16] The key issues that divide Christian and Jew are therefore not about religion as such but rather primarily about Christology and eschatology — the questions of who exactly Jesus was, and whether he was the divinely intended fulfilment of Israel's previous history. The author of Hebrews encourages his hearers to hold fast to the truths of Christ's unique person and work, and to see Jesus as truly that intended fulfilment. The preacher and scholar, who would honour the epistle, can do no other.

For our argument, the important point is this: Hebrews is fully conscious of this negative aspect of its message and intends its hearers to note it.[17] The whole force of the author's appeal is lost if they fail to pick up this implication. If they merely warm to his positive portrayal of Jesus without seeing that they must view their

---

in AD 70 precisely as the vindication of his position on the essential fulfilment of Judaism as now realised in Jesus.

[16] N. T. Wright, *Jesus and the Victory of God*, esp. chs 11-13.

[17] See, e.g., Dunn, *Partings of the Ways*, 91. In discussing this delicate issue, Lane, *Hebrews*, cxxv-cxxxv, is aware of the danger of anti-Judaic polemic. In this context he therefore suggests that a return to the synagogue was not one of the author's concerns. Yet this sits uneasily with his argument elsewhere that the audience might lapse back into Jewish traditions (see above, n. 12).

Judaism without Jesus as incomplete and therefore wrong in key areas, then his argument is unsuccessful. He is not asking them to abandon every aspect of their Jewish heritage, but he is giving them grounds for critiquing their ancestral faith and for distancing themselves from it in certain symbolic ways.

The Author's Sensitivity: The Temple

This conscious critique of Judaism is sometimes missed or denied by commentators. This may stem from an understandable desire to clear Hebrews of being 'anti-Jewish', but it also emanates from a failure to note the delicate pastoral context in which the author was writing. This context is well portrayed by Lindars:

> The author is dealing with an extremely urgent practical situation that demands his utmost skill in the art of persuasion, if disaster is to be averted ... They are heading for apostasy, and the purpose of the whole letter is to draw them back from the brink before it is too late. He has a delicate task to perform, because the efforts of the leaders have not been successful, and he has been approached as a last resort.[18]

If so, not only must he do everything he can to establish rapport with his audience and build up his argument from shared presuppositions; *he must also understate his applications.* If he had opened his sermon with the bald statement that they should have nothing further to do with the synagogue, he would have lost his audience immediately. He had to tread with incredible care. The critique had to be set within a positive context (concerning Jesus) and some of the practical implications must be left for the audience to draw out for themselves.[19] Those in the know would pick up the understated implications, though those of us reading it centuries later may miss them.

---

[18]   Lindars, "Rhetorical Structure," 384, 390.
[19]   This then adequately explains the otherwise puzzling fact that the contrast with Judaism comes only in the exegetical passages, not explicitly in the sections of exhortation and application.

This issue comes to the fore when we try to discern the author's attitude towards the Jerusalem Temple. Some commentators suggest our author had little interest in what was going on 'on the ground' in Jerusalem: his discussion of the Temple, we are told, is purely theoretical — hence his continual reference to the wilderness 'tabernacle', not to the physical sanctuary in contemporary Jerusalem.[20] Yet this is precisely to miss the point of Hebrews' careful strategy. To be sure, it does not present a frontal attack on the Jerusalem Temple, but the Temple is within his sights throughout. The author's mention of the 'tabernacle' might be inspired by his portrait of Israel in the wilderness (chs 3–4) and occasioned by the key verse in Exodus (25:40) that Moses was to construct it as a copy of the 'heavenly tabernacle' (Heb 8:5), yet the result is not intended to be merely theoretical. In fact the focus on the origins of the tabernacle enables him effectively to undercut the Temple system at its very *fons et origo* — a tactic far more weighty than (for example) expressing some mere practical grievance against the current Temple administrators.[21] Hebrews' analysis goes right to the root, seeing the Temple as God-ordained in its time but now eclipsed through the coming of Jesus. It is a bombshell — but one dropped with exceeding caution. To quote Motyer: 'The Temple does *not* appear in Hebrews precisely so that the profound message of the letter *about the Temple*

---

[20] See, e.g., Filson, *Yesterday*, 48; R. McL. Wilson, *Hebrews* (NCBC; Basingstoke: Marshall, Morgan & Scott, 1987), 140; P. Ellingworth, *The Epistle to the Hebrews* (EC; London: Epworth, 1991), viii; cf. also his 1993 work of the same title, 710.

[21] See, e.g., Dunn, *Partings of the Ways*, 87; Hagner, *Hebrews*, 3-4. This tactic is similar to that used by Stephen according to Acts 7:44-53. For possible parallels between Hebrews and Stephen, see L. D. Hurst, *The Epistle to the Hebrews: Its Background of Thought* (Cambridge: CUP, 1990) and Lane, *Hebrews*, cxlvi-cl.

may actually be heard in its scriptural depth, and not be rejected out of hand'.[22]

The Widening Critique

Once one is attuned to the author's careful strategy, one begins to notice some further implied critiques of Judaism. What, for example, if their interest in the Temple was part of a whole bundle of ideas (both religious and political) which also involved maintaining an affinity to the city of Jerusalem and to the land of Israel?

There is enough in Hebrews to suggest that these also were aspects of Judaism which the author wanted to be re-evaluated in the light of Jesus. First, there are several references to the land. chs. 3 and 4 imply that the land's true significance has to do with the divine promise of 'rest' — a 'rest' not fully achieved under Joshua but available now for 'the people of God' (4:8-9). This is then developed in ch. 11, when the patriarchs' desire for the 'land of promise' (11:9) is described as a 'longing for a better country — a heavenly one', the 'city' prepared for them by God (11:16). The writer is suggesting that his audience, like the patriarchs, should not focus on the physical land of Israel, but rather on the future 'Sabbath rest' which God has prepared for them.

We see the same, secondly, concerning their mother city, Jerusalem. As the sermon moves towards its climax, the theme of Jerusalem comes naturally to the fore as an enticing goal. The writer lures them on a pilgrimage, but the goal of this spiritual 'race' of faith turns out to be not the physical Jerusalem but rather the 'heavenly Jerusalem, the city of the living God' (12:22). In the final chapter he then hints at what this might mean for their attitude to the physical city of Jerusalem: 'here we do not have an enduring city, but we are looking for the city that is to come' (13:14). In other words, as be-

---

[22] S. Motyer, "The Temple in Hebrews: Is It There?," in *Heaven on Earth: The Temple in Biblical Theology* (ed. T. D. Alexander and S. J. Gathercole; Carlisle: Paternoster, forthcoming, 2004), italics original.

lievers in Jesus (who himself suffered 'outside' Jerusalem's gate: 13:12), they were not to pin their hopes (religious or political) on Jerusalem, which itself might not 'endure' forever. Jerusalem had lost its 'redemptive significance'.[23] The certain goal, the true object of faith and pilgrimage, was the heavenly city. This point was all the more striking because this is the only time when the author candidly admits that being a follower of Jesus involves an aspect of loss: believers in Jesus truly have 'rest', a 'High Priest', an 'altar', a 'hope', a 'kingdom' but 'the only thing which we do *not* have is an earthly territorial city'.[24]

So Hebrews has a critique not just of the Temple, but also of the two other geographical entities that were significant within first-century Judaism — the land and the city. Modern readers may miss this, precisely because the author has deliberately avoided open po-lemic. Yet his understated approach does not mean the matters were unimportant. Rather they were so important that he had to win his audience with great care.[25] So we are acting in accord with the author's intention when we detect this critique and draw out its im-plications for ourselves.

Finding Hebrews a Modern Place

A further reason why readers may miss these implications is that they are often not in the same position as the first audience, either chrono-logically or by religious background. Yet there is still a location where a significant number of people are much closer to the situation of the first audience, namely Jerusalem and the modern land of Israel.

---

[23] V. C. Pfitzner, *Hebrews* (ANTC; Nashville: Abingdon, 1997), 200.

[24] C. J. H. Wright, "A Christian Approach to Old Testament Prophecy concerning Israel," in *Jerusalem Past and Present in the Purposes of God* (ed. P. W. L. Walker; Carlisle: Paternoster, 1994), 18-19 (italics original).

[25] It is for this reason that the climax of his argument is given so carefully and pastorally in his summary of his argument in 13:9-14: see Lindars, "Rhetorical Structure," 388, 404; cf. my *Jesus and the Holy City* (Grand Rapids: Eerdmans, 1996), 223-26.

A 'Messianic' Reading

The *Jewish New Testament*, an English translation designed for believers in Israel, translates the title 'to the Hebrews' as 'to the Messianic Jews'.[26] With the increasing number of Jews in the last 20 years who have professed faith in Jesus (or Yeshua) as Messiah, there is now for the first time since the first century a group within the Church who identify themselves as 'Jewish Christians' or (as they prefer) 'Messianic believers'. Hebrews at last has whole congregations that can identify closely with the original congregation.

Ironically however, the message of Hebrews is not (in my experience) given much space amongst such believers.[27] They value Hebrews because it confirms the Jewishness of the New Testament; they also treasure its positive affirmation that Jesus is the authentic fulfilment of their ancestral Jewish faith. Less popular are any implications that true loyalty to Jesus might involve giving up certain aspects of that Jewish heritage. Suddenly it becomes quite urgent to know what exactly Hebrews was speaking out against.

For example, was it against *every* attendance at the synagogue or just a failure to meet as believers in Jesus (10:25)? Was it against *all* forms of Jewish national life, or only those that denied the significance of Jesus' person and work? At what point, according to Hebrews, would they be fatally compromised? These are urgent questions for modern Jewish believers who dislike the 'gentilization' of the Church and want to affirm their Jewish heritage. Their understanding of Hebrews will affect their choices next Saturday (Shabbat),

---

[26] See D. Stern, *The Jewish New Testament* (Jerusalem: New Testament Publications, 1992).

[27] This perception is based on various experiences within modern Israel, especially a series of annual consultations (1996-2000) bringing together Palestinian and Jewish believers: some of the papers were published in *The Bible and the Land: Israeli, Palestinian and Western Perspectives* (ed. M. Wood, L. Loden and P. W. L. Walker; Bethlehem: Musalaha, 2000); cf. also P. S. Johnston and P. W. L. Walker, eds., *The Land of Promise* (Leicester: Apollos, 2000).

as well as their whole approach to the state of Israel in its political and national aspirations. Put bluntly, what does it mean to 'follow Jesus outside the gate, bearing the disgrace he bore' (13:13)?

It is now that we sense the poignancy of Hebrews. This, the most Jewish document in the New Testament, is simultaneously the most thorough treatment of the insufficiency of Judaism without Jesus. Thus, the more that Messianic believers note its Jewishness and feel its relevance, the more they are exposed to its critique of Judaism and feel its challenge.

From conversations with them, the following themes in Hebrews prove less attractive to Messianic believers today: the application of the 'shadow to reality' motif; the sharp divide between the 'new' covenant and the 'old' one that is now 'obsolete' (8:13); and, of course, the implied critique (noted above) of Jewish attachment to Jerusalem and the Land. In other words, when assessing the negative implications of Hebrews, the tendency is to regard that negative critique as focused exclusively on the issue of the Temple. Yes, the Jerusalem Temple has clearly had its day,[28] but the coming of Jesus did *not* effect much else — certainly not the spiritual primacy of Jerusalem, the eternal significance of the 'promised land', or the continuing priority which is given in God's purposes to ethnic Israel and God's particular call to the descendants of Abraham. Thus the sharp contrasts which Hebrews paints between the old and □s, between the shadow and the reality, between the old order and the time of the 'new order' (9:10), are allowed to speak about the Temple, but not about anything else. Messianic believers wish to forge a new

---

[28] There is here a significant contrast between most messianic believers and Christian Zionists (often gentile sympathizers); many of the latter look for the building of a new third Temple. See, e.g., R. Price, *Jerusalem in Prophecy* (Eugene: Harvest House Publishers, 1998). The Messianic community tends to accept the message of Hebrews that because of Jesus there is no further need of such a temple. For a good overview of 'fundamentalist' attitudes to the Temple Mount, see G. Gorenberg, *The End of Days* (New York: Simon & Schuster, 2000).

paradigm for biblical theology — characterised more by continuity than by discontinuity. 'Fulfilment' is allowed, but rarely (except with the Temple) is one encouraged to speak of 'replacement'.

An Alternative Response

There are however some other believers, living nearby, who see things quite differently, namely the Palestinian Christian community.[29] For these believers there are equally urgent questions: does the land, which they think of as their 'home', really belong to Israel by divine right? Does God really want Jerusalem to be the 'eternal capital' of the Jewish nation? Does not the coming of their Saviour, Jesus Christ, open up God's purpose to the whole world and mark a shift in the divine economy relating to such things as Jerusalem and the Land?

So they too find Hebrews a source of great encouragement, for here is a Jewish believer telling his fellow Jews that God's purposes have moved forwards and they must not return to older ways of thinking: some parts of their Jewish understanding must be left behind because of their commitment to Jesus. Not everything that is Jewish is automatically right. If we are to fix our eyes on Jesus (12:2), they argue, we cannot be fixated with possession of Jerusalem and the Land. Followers of Jesus must have a distinctive approach to these issues, in contrast to both Judaism and (now) Islam. So Palestinian Christians must occasionally run the risk of reproach by following Jesus 'outside the city gate' (being distinctive from the Muslim majority amongst their fellow Palestinians), but so too Jewish Christians must run the risk of being distinctive from their fellow Israelis — especially in their attitude towards Jerusalem and the land.

In this way contemporary expositors can claim that Hebrews is indeed of particular relevance in the contemporary Church: in fact, its

---

[29] Estimates in recent articles in *Mishkhan* (a Jerusalem journal for Messianic believers) suggest that, despite emigrations, there are still c. 100,000 Palestinian Christians throughout the land, compared with c. 5,000 Messianic believers.

teaching has relevance for one of the most urgent political situations in the modern world. Could the tiny New Testament help unlock the current deadlock in Israel/Palestine? Could this political crisis, itself caused in no small part by certain readings of the biblical text, paradoxically only be resolved by a deeper appreciation of that text? Could it be that what the world needs is that elusive and even maligned discipline — biblical theology?

Finding Its Ancient Place

This modern discussion (highlighting the particular relevance of Hebrews for those living in the land of Jesus) then sends us back with a new interest to the historical question of Hebrews' original setting. Is this a document that emanated *from* Jerusalem or, conversely, one sent to Jerusalem?

There is no scholarly consensus on the provenance of the epistle. An intriguing case has been made that the audience lived in Corinth.[30] Some scholars have been willing to suggest Jerusalem[31] or Palestine more generally.[32] The majority of recent studies, however, if they posit a likely location at all, now converge on Rome.[33]

Moreover, most scholars argue, not least because of its 'Alexandrian' flavour, that Hebrews owes its roots to Diaspora Judaism. This is probably right concerning the location of the author, but this does not fully foreclose the issue of the *audience's* location. A location for the audience in Jerusalem (or Palestine) is worth reconsideration on at least two accounts. First, where else would one find a

---

[30] See H. Montefiore, *A Commentary on the Epistle to the Hebrews* (BNTC; New York: Harper, 1964), 11-30.

[31] See G. Buchanan, *To the Hebrews* (AB; New York: Doubleday, 1972) and those listed in C. Spicq, *L'Epître aux Hébreux* (2 vols.; Paris: Gabalda, 1952-53), 1:239, n. 1.

[32] This was the view of older commentators such as Delitzsch, Westcott, Ramsay, Turner and Spicq; it has been revived as a possibility by Isaacs, *Sacred Space*, 22-45.

[33] Lane, *Hebrews*, lviii; Hagner, *Hebrews*, 7; but see, e.g., DeSilva, *Perseverance in Gratitude*, 22.

whole community of Jewish Christians, separating themselves from other believers on matters relating to the Temple? Secondly, as seen above, the author's interest in Jerusalem and its Temple is not simply theoretical.[34] The great caution and sensitivity the writer displayed would make eminent sense if his audience was near Jerusalem; the issue of the Temple (for example) would then be a local and 'live' issue, positively requiring him to write with the utmost care.

However, we simply cannot be certain, and, on balance, it may be wise to accept the position of Lindars: 'the best that can be said is that nothing forbids the view that Hebrews is addressed to comparatively well-educated Jewish Christians somewhere in the Mediterranean Diaspora.[35]

Even so, the question still arises: even if Hebrews were not actually sent directly to believers in Jerusalem, how would this letter have been viewed once it came into the hands of those who *did* live there? Would its radical view of the Temple's redundancy have found a welcome response? Or is its view that of one so remote from the Temple that it could only have caused grief for those who were right in the thick of the problem?

Reconstructing the beliefs of the believers in Jerusalem in the tumultuous years prior to the siege and fall of the city (AD 67-70) is notoriously difficult.[36] The task of James, the Lord's brother, was particularly difficult — caught between the nationalism of his fellow Jews on the one side and the expansion of the Jesus movement into

---

[34] See above n. 22. For a recent defence of a Jerusalem audience, see R. C. Gleason, "The Old Testament Background of the Warning in Hebrews 6:4-8," *BibSac* 155 (1998): 62-91.

[35] Lindars, *Theology of the Letter to the Hebrews*, 19.

[36] For overviews, see F. F. Bruce, "The Church of Jerusalem in the Acts of the Apostles," *BJRL* (1985): 641-61; J. J. Scott, "Parties in the Church of Jerusalem As Seen in the Book of Acts," *JETS* 18 (1975): 217-27; and R. J. Bauckham, "James and the Jerusalem Church," in *The Book of Acts in Its Palestinian Setting* (ed. R. J. Bauckham; The Book of Acts in Its First Century Setting; Carlisle: Paternoster, 1995), 415-80.

gentile lands on the other. He was martyred in AD 62, but there may
have been other 'moderates' who continued to try to be loyal to the
Temple, pursuing a policy of identifying with the ancestral faith for as
long as possible.[37] If so, the argument of Hebrews (which saw a renewed commitment to the Temple sacrifices as a denial of Jesus)
might well have been too much to endorse straightforwardly. The
author of Hebrews might see their policy as compromise; they, on the
other hand, might see it as a matter of plain survival. For their part,
believers resident in Jerusalem might concur with Hebrews that the
coming of Jesus had now placed a huge question mark over
Jerusalem's Temple, but so long as it still stood, it was not for the
followers of Jesus to abandon it.

So Hebrews can be seen as a document which, whilst pertinent to
Jerusalem, was not the kind of thing that could easily have emanated
from Jerusalem or been sent *to* it in its time of looming crisis. Instead
it would prove to be a prophetic piece, almost certainly written by
someone fully aware of the crisis brewing in Palestine, but offered to
believers in the Diaspora as a warning not to hanker after the survival
of the Temple: their faith was to be anchored elsewhere (cf. 6:19). It
was a summons to leave the Temple to its fate. This sentiment was, of
course, fully in keeping with Jesus' solemn warning that his disciples
should 'flee to the mountains' (Mark 13:14), but it was one which
those in Jerusalem might only be able to heed when all other avenues
of hope had departed. Quite possibly, by the time the text of Hebrews
found its way to Palestine, its central argument had been fully vin-
dicated in history, and the Temple had already been destroyed.

Conclusion
Significantly, it was Hebrews (and not the views of those caught up in
Jerusalem's crisis), which became the definitive New Testament

---

[37] This pragmatic policy may well have been pursued in full awareness of
the Synoptic tradition warning of the Temple's imminent destruction (Mark
13:2; Luke 19:43; Matt 23:38): its end was nigh.

voice on this subject. It was able, with a combination of prophetic distance and yet close pastoral concern, to formulate a theology that would stand the test of time. We will never know exactly how much of the author's thesis was original to him. Yet he has clearly pondered the challenges that were implicit within Jesus' ministry. Although it is often thought that Jesus never explicitly compared himself to the High Priest,[38] the author argues that this is who he truly was — the eternal High Priest who eclipsed those, like Caiaphas, who had held this office in his own day. More openly, Jesus had spoken of his death in sacrificial terms and posed a significant challenge to the Temple. Hebrews ponders all this, picturing Jesus in the garden of Gethsemane below the Temple's walls (5:7-9) and his being led 'outside the city gate' (13:13) to offer his life in a sacrifice which would eventually nullify the *raison d'être* of that Temple on the opposite hill. With lucidity the author draws out the implications of what had only previously been hinted: the eclipse of Jerusalem and its Temple by the full radiance of God's eternal Son.

No doubt he did so with mixed feelings, for the things eclipsed by Jesus were precious to his heart too. But he had his eyes fixed firmly on Jesus and asks his hearers to consider all these things as empty compared with the greatness of Jesus. If this message, which draws people away from territorial attachment, were applied to the contemporary Middle East, it could yet be a force for peace.

---

[38] In recent years, however, C. Fletcher-Louis has developed some significant arguments for this comparison to the High Priest in Jesus' ministry: see his *All the Glory of Adam* (Leiden: Brill, 2002).

James As a Sermon on the Trials of Abraham

David Instone-Brewer

James appears to be a collection of short treatises concerning a handful of themes,[1] though there have been several attempts to find a single overarching structure. Some, like Davids,[2] construct careful schemes where individual themes run in parallel occasionally interacting with each other, while others, like Moo,[3] content themselves with identifying repeated themes. Those who have been most successful at identifying an overall structure are probably Wall, who finds three neat points ('Quick to Hear' 1:22–2:26, 'Slow to Speak' 3:1-18, 'Slow to Anger' 4:1–5:6)[4] or Cabaniss, who thinks that James addressed different strata in the church (bishops 1:2-27, deacons 2:1-26, teachers 3:1-18, widows 4:1-10, penitents 4:11–5:12, and the faithful

---

[1] Luther accused James of 'throwing things together ... chaotically' ("Preface to the New Testament," 1522, *Luther's Works* 33:397). This view is also reflected in Martin Dibelius' commentary, *James: A Commentary on the Epistle of James* (Hermeneia; Philadelphia: Fortress, 1976), 4-11, which regards James as a series of loosely connected paraenetic passages, though he regards this lack of structure as one of the characteristics of paraenetic discourse.

[2] Peter H. Davids, *The Epistle of James: A Commentary on the Greek Text* (NIGTC; Exeter: Paternoster, 1982), 25-30.

[3] Douglas J. Moo, *The Letter of James: An Introduction and Commentary* (TNTC; Grand Rapids/Leicester: Eerdmans/IVP, 1985), 43-46. E. Fry also traces a number of different themes which he plots on a graph to uncover a complex (and improbable) pattern; see "The Testing of Faith: A Study of the Structure of the Book of James," *Bible Translator* 29 (1978): 427-35.

[4] Robert W. Wall, "The Intertextuality of Scripture: The Example of Rahab (James 2:25)," in *The Bible at Qumran: Text, Shape and Interpretation* (ed. Peter W. Flint; Studies in the Dead Sea Scrolls and Related Literature; Grand Rapids: Eerdmans, 2000), 217-36.

5:13-20).[5] Forbes suggested that the epistle was written in two halves to be read out loud in two sessions because themes are repeated[6] while Gertner linked various themes to Ps 12 by means of midrashic techniques.[7] Johnson, who has a useful analysis of these and other attempts at finding a structure, concludes that the best one can hope to find is 'an important organizing (and selecting) principle' which 'undergirds the inclusion and shaping of James' material',[8] and this principle is the opposition of friendship with the world and friendship with God.[9]

This paper will propose that James is structured as a sermon based on the Trials of Abraham. This theme and structure would have been easily identified by a first-century Jewish audience without any special skills or knowledge, except that which would have been picked up at Sabbath school and regular listening to sermons.

This paper will not come to any conclusion about the authorship of the epistle, and will simply refer to the author as 'James'. Neither will it deal with the much-debated relationship with the epistles of Paul, other than some limited comparisons. The main purpose of this paper is to discover the subtext of the epistle which would have been in the minds of an average Hellenistic Jewish audience in the first century.

---

[5]   A. Cabaniss, "A Note on Jacob's Homily," *EvQ* 47 (1975): 219-22.
[6]   P. B. R. Forbes, "The Structure of the Epistle of James," *EvQ* 44 (1972): 147-53.
[7]   M. Gertner, "Midrashim in the New Testament," *JSS* 7 (1962): 267-92. Luke T. Johnson also thinks that it may be based on a single passage (Lev 19); see his "Friendship with the World/Friendship with God: A Study of Discipleship in James," in *Discipleship in the New Testament* (ed. F. F. Segovia; Philadelphia: Fortress, 1985), 166-83.
[8]   Luke Timothy Johnson, *The Letter of James: A New Translation with Introduction and Commentary* (AB; New York: Doubleday, 1995), 11-15; quotation from p. 14.
[9]   Johnson, "Friendship with the World."

Abraham's Faith and Works in Jubilees

Abraham was, for both Paul and James, the perfect illustration of faith and works. For James, Abraham showed that works were not only a demonstration of faith but they could even be regarded as a proof, because Abraham's faith in Gen 15:6 was traditionally seen as verified by ten Trials, the last of which was the sacrifice of Isaac in Gen 22.[10] Bauckham lists a multitude of Jewish texts which link Gen 22 to Abraham's faith,[11] though for James the most significant of these texts is *Jubilees* because it not only emphasises the concept of faith, but also contains several details to which James alludes throughout his epistle.

Jubilees originated in the second century BC probably in Palestine and was particularly popular among Jews of the first and second centuries AD – as evidenced by the fragments from 15 separate copies spread over five caves at Qumran (in the original Hebrew), and its translation into Greek (though only a very few fragments survive). It remained popular and was translated into Latin, Ethiopic (which is the only version in which the whole text has survived) and possibly Syriac. It is cited in the *Damascus Document* (*CD* 16:2-5) and it may be a source for the *Genesis Apocryphon*.[12]

Jubilees consists largely of a retelling of the stories of Genesis and Exodus by an angel to Moses during his forty days on Mount Sinai. This retelling summarises some events, expands others and inserts a few events which are not found in the Torah. In some places *Jubilees*

---

[10] Richard Longenecker found themes from the Trials of Abraham in several New Testament epistles; see his "'Faith of Abraham' Theme in Paul, James and Hebrews: A Study in the Circumstantial Nature of New Testament Teaching," *JETS* 20 (1977): 203-12.

[11] Richard Bauckham, *James: Wisdom of James, Disciple of Jesus the Sage* (New Testament Readings; London: Routledge, 1999), 122-23.

[12] According to J. A. Fitzmyer, *The Genesis Apocryphon of Qumran Cave 1: A Commentary* (Biblica et Orientalia 18A; Rome: Pontifical Biblical Institute, 1966), 14. However, *Jubilees* and the *Genesis Apocryphon* may also have used similar common sources.

is content simply to paraphrase Genesis, such as its first reference to Abraham's faith:

> He believed the Lord and it was counted for him as righteousness. (*Jub.* 14:6-7 // Gen 15:6)[13]

The concept of Abraham's faith is very important to the author of *Jubilees* because he inserts another reference to it which is not found in Genesis:

> Abram rejoiced and he told all of these things to Sarai, his wife. And he believed that he would have seed. (*Jub.* 14:21-22 — inserted between the account of Gen 15 and 16)[14]

A very large insertion of non-biblical material in *Jubilees* occurs just before the Trial concerning Isaac, and this too concentrates on Abraham's faith:

> Words came in heaven concerning Abraham that he was faithful in everything which was told him and he loved the Lord and was faithful in all affliction. And Prince Mastema [the lord of evil spirits; cf. *Jub.* 10:7-8] came and he said before God, 'Behold, Abraham loves Isaac, his son. And he is more pleased with him than everything. Tell him to offer him (as) a burnt offering upon the altar. And you will see whether he will do this thing. And you will know whether he is faithful in everything in which you test him.'

> And the Lord was aware that Abraham was faithful in all of his afflictions because he tested him with his land, and with famine. And he tested him with the wealth of kings. And he tested him again with his wife, when she was taken (from him), and with circumcision. And he tested him with Ishmael and with Hagar, his maidservant, when he

---

[13] This and other quotations from *Jubilees* come from O. S. Wintermute's translation of the Ethiopic text in J. H. Charlesworth, ed., *The Old Testament Pseudepigrapha* (New York: Doubleday, 1985), 2:35-142. They have been checked against the translations of R. H. Charles, *The Apocrypha and Pseudepigrapha of the Old Testament in English, with Introductions and Critical and Explanatory Notes to the Several Books* (Oxford: Clarendon, 1913). Differences are noted when they are significant.

[14] It is interesting to see that Paul also regarded belief in Sarah's pregnancy as a key aspect of Abraham's faith (Rom 4:17-20).

> sent them away. And in everything in which he tested him, he was found faithful. And his soul was not impatient. And he was not slow to act because he was faithful and a lover of the Lord. (*Jub.* 17:15-18)

The tenth Trial of Abraham's faith came when Sarah died, which *Jubilees* regards as a Trial of Abraham's 'patience' or 'self-control':[15]

> And Abraham went to weep for her and bury her. And we were testing him whether he would exercise self-control. And he was not impatient with the words of his mouth and he was found self-controlled in this also and he was not filled with anxiety because with the self-control of his spirit he spoke with the sons of Heth. (Gen 23:3)

> This is the tenth trial with which Abraham was tried. He was found faithful, controlled of spirit. (*Jub.* 19:3-4, 8-9)

Abraham, as a result of these tests, was a model of good works. At the end of his life *Jubilees* adds a touching funeral scene, which includes the tribute that

> Abraham was perfect in all of his works with the Lord, and was pleasing through righteousness all the days of his life. (*Jub.* 23:10)[16]

These portions of *Jubilees* have not survived among the Qumran fragments in the original Hebrew, so the nearest we have is the Ethiopic translation of a Greek translation. The exact wording is therefore lost, but the emphasis on 'faith' in *Jubilees* is clear. The material which is additional to Genesis is very interesting in that it contains both a reference to faith as mental assent ('he believed that he would have seed'), and to faith as verified by works (testing whether he would 'do this command' as well as the conclusion that he was 'perfect in all his works'). All this is ideal for James who wants to show that Abraham's faith in Gen 15:6 was merely the start of his life of faith which was evidenced through his works.

---

[15] Charles' translation has 'patience' whenever Wintermute translates 'self-control'.

[16] The translation 'works' comes from Charles. Wintermute translates 'works as actions'.

When James linked Gen 15 with Gen 22 he was merely following the traditional link which is found throughout Jewish literature.[17] In contrast, Paul was being innovative when he pointed out the chronological distance between Abraham being declared 'righteous' (in Gen 15:6) and the first 'work' of circumcision (in Gen 17:10-14). Paul did not deny the value of works, but he brought faith to the fore and said that works *follow* faith (Rom 4:9-12). Paul denied that 'works of the law' had any role in salvation (Rom 4:2-3), though we will see that James also denied this. For James and his audience it was self-evident that believers had faith which was evidenced by works, but James felt that many had neglected the latter, so he used the story of Abraham's Trial concerning Isaac to remind them.

But this was not the only Trial of Abraham which he referred to in this epistle. James only referred to Abraham directly at 2:21-24, which concerns the sacrifice of Isaac, but he spoke about the 'works of Abraham' (i.e. more than one 'work') by which 'his faith was made complete' (2:22) — implying that he was also thinking about other incidents in Abraham's life where an action demonstrated his faith. We will see that James alluded at several points to incidents that are recorded in *Jubilees*.

A Sermon on the Trials of Abraham
Parallels between James and the Trials of Abraham in *Jubilees* provide the clue that this epistle was a sermon based on these traditions. As well as those mentioned above, there are other minor parallels,[18] and when these are all considered together they indicate that James and his audience had something *like Jubilees* in mind.[19]

---

[17] Bauckham, *James*, 123.
[18] Various parallels are discussed later in this paper, such as Firstfruits (*Jub.* 6:21-22; 16:13-14; 22:1; cf. Jas 1:18), monotheism (*Jub.* 12:1-8, 12-14, 19-21; cf. Jas 2:19), and dangers of wealth (*Jub.* 13:28-29; 17:17; cf. Jas 5:5).
[19] The version of *Jubilees* surviving in Ethiopic and in Qumran fragments was not the only version in the first century, as seen by the citation from 'The book of divisions of periods according to their Jubilees' in *CD* 16:4-5.

James could assume that his audience was familiar with the collection of stories about the Trials of Abraham because these were widely known. They are alluded to in many types of Jewish literature including Philo,[20] Josephus,[21] other Hellenistic works,[22] the New Testament[23] and Rabbinic traditions.[24] The only full account of these stories dating from New Testament times is found in *Jubilees*,[25] though they may have occurred in other literature which has not survived. The large number of allusions to them suggests that these stories were so well known that it was unnecessary to retell them in most circumstances because the majority of his audience would be very familiar with them.

Most Jews would have known these stories from regular Sabbath preaching, rather than from literature. They did not need to be reminded of them, any more than a modern Christian congregation needs to be told the parable of the Good Samaritan. What *would* make

---

[20] *Somn.* 1.194-95.

[21] *A.J.* 1.223, 233.

[22] Jdt 8:26-27; Sir 44:19-20; 1 Macc 2:52.

[23] Heb 11:17.

[24] Pseudo-Philo, who knew about these stories (Pseudo-Philo, *L.A.B.* 40.2, 5) records stories which were better known in Rabbinic Judaism than Hellenistic Judaism — for example, the only lengthy extra-biblical expansion concerning Abraham in *L.A.B.* is the story of surviving the furnace (*L.A.B.* 6.11-18), which is alluded to very frequently in Rabbinic texts but not in Hellenistic literature. There is a second-century reference to the 'Ten Trials of Abraham' in *m. Ab.* 5.3 and several references in later centuries (e.g. *b. San.* 89b; *Ex. R.* 30.16; *Num. R.* 14.11; 15.12).

[25] Pseudo-Philo includes only the extra-biblical story of Abraham and the furnace (*L.A.B.* 6). Josephus concentrates on political details and adds almost nothing to the biblical text (*A.J.* 1.154-238). Philo allegorises at great length in *De migratione Abrahami*, in *De Abrahamo*, and in various places within *Legum allegoriae* and other works, but he is not very interested in stories about his life. The *Testament of Abraham* and *Apocalypse of Abraham* describe Abraham as a famous person who finds out about death and eternity, and therefore cover very little of his life. Rabbinic literature preserves stories in *Gen. R.* 39-62 and *Pirqe de Rabbi Eliezer* 26-32, but these are both late compilations which have little overlap with *Jubilees*.

a congregation take note is any variation in a well-known story; so if a preacher said that 'a tax collector and a Roman passed by' instead of 'a priest and a Levite', the congregation would correctly wonder about the reason for this change. By this method a preacher can give his own emphasis while using a familiar story and we will see that James used this method on a couple of occasions in this epistle.

The epistle opens by saying that the subject is 'trials' (1:2-4) and some of his audience might have identified the well-known theme of the 'Trials of Abraham' simply from this reference. Their hunch would be confirmed when James turned immediately to the subject of 'wisdom' (1:5), for which Abraham was famous,[26] and then to 'doubt' (1:6-8), which was the subject of Abraham's tenth Trial.[27] By the time that James says 'God tempts no one', all of his audience would recognise the allusion to the story of Satan testing Abraham with regard to Isaac — i.e. Mastema, the lord of the evil spirits (*Jub.* 10:7-8) who stood accusing Abraham before God's throne (17:15-16). There was no need to tell this story of this trial, because a Jewish audience was familiar with this homiletic expansion of Gen 22, which they had heard in countless sermons. We are fortunate to have a full account of the story in *Jubilees*, because on other occasions the story is simply alluded to rather than narrated.[28] This story was probably popular because it helped to avoid the suggestion that God would demand hu-

---

[26] Philo is very interested in Abraham's wisdom (e.g. *Leg.* 3.244; *Cher.* 10, 18, 31, 106; *Sacr.* 122; *Post.* 27, etc.). He calls him 'wise Abraham' on more than 40 occasions.

[27] In *Jub.* 19:3-4, the angel said that when Sarah died 'we tried him to see if his spirit were patient in this and was not disturbed.' Philo is also interested in Abraham's unchanging faith and lack of doubt (e.g. *Migr.* 44; *Abr.* 270; *Leg.* 3.228; *Her.* 90 based on Gen 15:6; *Migr.* 132 based on Gen 18:23; *Cher.* 19; *QG.* 3.58; cf. Jas 1:6-8).

[28] This story was not only well known in Jewish Hellenistic circles, from which *Jubilees* came, but also Aramaic-speaking Judaism — see, e.g., a late third-century tradition in *b. San.* 89b where 'Satan' tests Abraham and first-century *L.A.B.* 32.1 where Abraham is told to make the sacrifice because 'all the angels were jealous of him'.

man sacrifice, by saying that the temptation came from Satan and not from God.

When James alluded to this story, he introduced a variation which would have made a Jewish audience take note. Instead of referring to a temptation from Satan, James said that temptation comes when someone 'is lured and enticed by his own desire'. James did not reject the concept of a personal devil (cf. Jas 4:6), and he could not have meant that Abraham was incited by his own desire to sacrifice Isaac, so he could not be attempting to change the story. If he was not changing the story, then he was changing the *application* which the audience would draw from it, by making a startling change in emphasis. But what was his new application?

Without having yet answered this question, James turned the story round. He has already likened believers to Abraham when he was tested, and now he likens believers to Isaac, the product of a promise. God 'gave us birth through the word of truth' (1:18) which is like the promise made to Abraham by the 'Father of heavenly lights' (1:17) — a promise that he would have a son whose descendants would be as numerous as the stars (Gen 22:17; *Jub.* 18:15). James called Isaac 'a kind of firstfruits' (1:18) of all those promised children, so that believers are firstfruits 'of all he created' (1:18).

The Festival of Firstfruits is very important in *Jubilees*, especially in the stories of Abraham who is almost regarded as the patron of this particular festival.[29] Firstfruits were very important to Diaspora Jews (to whom this letter is addressed) because these were the only personal offerings which they could send to Jerusalem each year even if they could not attend themselves. Representatives of each town brought a collection of the Firstfruits of their community, often forming a procession led by a sacrificial ox decorated with a crown of

---

[29] Abraham is described as sacrificing firstfruits on several occasions; sometimes the description is in detail (*Jub.* 6:21-22; 16:13-14; 22:1).

leaves between its horns.[30] James may be alluding to this popular image when he says that, believers wear a 'crown of life' (1:12).

James then introduced one of the major themes in this epistle — controlling the tongue. This theme is found both in Abraham's Trial concerning Isaac and in his tenth Trial concerning Sarah's death – two trials which are closely linked in *Jubilees*.[31] When Sarah died, Abraham had to control what he said and speak graciously to the sons of Heth who were employing all the cunning stratagems of oriental haggling to get the best price for her grave. In *Jubilees* the angel tells Moses that

> ... we were testing him whether he would exercise self-control. And he was not impatient with the words of his mouth. (*Jub.* 19:3)

This is similar to the Trial concerning Isaac which was a test to show that 'his soul was not impatient. And he was not slow to act' (*Jub.* 17:18). This description appears to be contradictory unless the 'not impatient' refers to speaking, which is what the Trial concerning Sarah suggests, so we should read 'not impatient [to speak] and not slow to act'. He was 'not slow to act' because as soon as God called, he answered, and when he was told what to do, 'he arose while it was still dark' to obey God without saying or asking anything more (Gen 22:3; *Jub.* 18:3). He was 'quick to listen, slow to speak, and slow to become angry' (Jas 1:19), even when asked to sacrifice his son, and he did not 'merely listen to the word' but immediately went to 'do what it says' (Jas 1:22).

After exploring these issues, the epistle leaves the story of Gen 22 and moves on to criticising the favouritism which was shown to

---

[30] *m. Bik.* 3.2-3. This tradition is likely to originate before AD 70 because it is told from the point of view of priests, rather than the scholars or rabbis who later compiled the Mishnah who are unlikely to have recorded it like this unless they had received it in this form.

[31] The two stories are next to each other in *Jubilees* and they are both concerned with the theme of 'patience' — *Jub.* 17:18, 'his soul was not impatient' and *Jub.* 19:3, 'he was not impatient with the words of his mouth'.

wealthy visitors and the comparative rejection of the poor (Jas 2:1-13). There are no definite allusions to stories of Abraham in this section, though there is a thematic link with the story of Abraham's hospitality to three strangers who turned out to be angels in disguise (Gen 18). Unfortunately this incident is missing from most of the early sources,[32] so we do not now know how the story was preached in first-century Judaism and it is therefore possible that there are allusions to the story in this section which we cannot recognise. We do know one way in which it was preached because Philo used it to emphasise Abraham's hospitality[33] and it was used in Heb 13:2 to teach hospitality to strangers, which presumably meant 'poor strangers' because no one needed encouragement to give hospitality to rich strangers.

This story made Abraham into an exemplar of hospitality in later Judaism,[34] and these two early sources make it likely this was the way that the story was often preached in the first century. This means that James' audience would have recognised his section on welcoming the poor as an application of the story of Abraham's hospitality in Gen 18. Once this link is made, then James' conclusion that 'mercy triumphs over judgement' (Jas 2:13) becomes an allusion to the conclusion of Abraham's prayer for Sodom (which arises from his talk with the angels): 'Shall not the Judge of all the earth do right?' (Gen

---

[32] It is passed over without details in *Jubilees*, passed over completely in Pseudo-Philo and this section is missing from the fragments of the *Genesis Apocryphon* in the Dead Sea Scrolls. Josephus records only the details found in Genesis, though he adds that they were 'angels', that Abraham offered them 'entertainment', and that the angels 'made a show of eating' (*A.J.* 1.196-97). Philo also emphasises that they only 'seemed to drink ... and eat' because they were 'incorporeal' (Philo, *Abr.* 118).

[33] Philo elaborated on the hospitality which Abraham demonstrated even though he thought they were merely three human strangers (*Abr.* 107-09).

[34] As Louis Ginzberg, *The Legends of the Jews* (Philadelphia: Jewish Publication Society of America, 1913-67), notes re Gen 18:1; cf. Roy-Bowen Ward, "Works of Abraham: James 2:14-26," *HTR* 61 (1968): 283-90, esp. 286-87.

18:25). James said to those who discriminated against the poor that 'you have become judges with evil thoughts' (Jas 2:4), as an appeal to them that they should judge like God does.

James then turns to the matter of faith and works, which is at the centre of the story of Abraham's Trials, and especially his Trial concerning Isaac (Jas 2:14-26), as outlined above. To emphasise that this combination of faith and works did not only apply to Abraham, James adds the example of Rahab 'who was considered righteous for what she did' (Jas 2:25). Wall[35] has pointed out that the language which James used of Rahab has clearer linguistic links with the story of Abraham's hospitality than with the story of Rahab — like a good host she 'lodged them' (ὑποδέχομαι) then 'sent them' on their journey (ἐκβάλλω); and her guests are even called 'angels' or 'messengers' (ἄγγελοι). This helps to confirm that James was also alluding to Abraham's hospitality in 2:1-13.

Exhortations Arising from the Theme

All the themes which are derived from the Trials of Abraham in the first half of James' sermon are applied in personal and direct ways in the second half, unlike the first half which is almost all in the third person. In ch. 1 he talked about 'one who doubts' (1:6), 'one who is rich' (1:10), 'one who is tempted' (1:13), 'one who listens to the word but does not do what it says' (1:22), etc. In ch. 2 he talked *to* them, but only hypothetically: 'if a man comes in to your synagogue' (2:1), 'if you really keep the royal law' (2:8); and then he goes back to the third person, 'if a man claims to have faith but has no deeds' (2:14). In the second half everything becomes very personal: 'we who teach' (3:1), 'we all stumble' (3:2), 'with the tongue we praise ... or we curse' (3:9), 'who is wise and understanding among you?' (3:13), 'what causes fights and quarrels among you?' (4:1). The epistle ends with personal criticisms and calls to repentance: 'you adulterous

---

[35] Robert W. Wall, "The Intertextuality of Scripture," in *The Bible at Qumran* (ed. Flint), 217-36. See also Ward, "Works of Abraham."

people' (4:4), 'submit yourselves to God' (4:7), 'do not slander one another' (4:11), 'you rich, weep and wail' (5:1), 'be patient till the Lord's coming' (5:7).

The exhortatory second half of the sermon is based largely on the themes which were derived in the first half from stories of the Trials of Abraham: self-control of the tongue (3:1-12; cf. 1:19-21); wisdom and humility (3:13–4:10; cf. 1:5-12); slander, favouritism and wealth (4:11–5:6; cf. 2:1-7). Consequently there are few references to Abraham in the second half, except when new sub-themes are introduced — quarrels at 4:1-7 and warnings about riches at 5:1-6.

Quarrels, says James, are evidence that they are spiritually 'adulterous', because they practise 'friendship with the world' (4:4) and they should 'submit to God' instead. Abraham was widely known as the 'friend of God' which would be seen as the antithesis of 'friendship with the world'.[36] Jas 4:5 apparently contains a citation, though it is impossible to identify, because it does not match anything in the Old Testament or any extra-biblical texts which have survived.[37] However, the theme of jealousy is clear in this citation, and the subject of God's jealousy due to spiritual adultery is a common theme in the Old Testament prophets, who likened idolatry to adultery and the exile of Israel to a divorce by a jealous husband.[38]

The theme of spiritual adultery would therefore remind a first-century Jewish audience about the first Trial of Abraham which concerned his rejection of idols. This extra-biblical story, which is very

---

[36] Although it is in Scripture (Isa 41:8; 2 Chr 20:7), it is also specifically associated with Abraham's Trial concerning Isaac in *Jubilees* and Philo (*Jub.* 17:16, 18; 19:9; 30:19-20; Philo, *Abr.* 271).

[37] Perhaps this is a reference to a Greek version of Mal 2:15 which is equally difficult to translate from the Hebrew which has survived, but which speaks about a spirit dwelling inside, in the context of marriage breakup. See the analysis of this text in G. P. Hugenberger, *Marriage As a Covenant: A Study of Biblical Law and Ethics Governing Marriage, Developed from the Perspective of Malachi* (SVT 52; Leiden: Brill, 1994), 124-32.

[38] E.g. Jer 3; Ezek 16 and 23.

important in Jewish literature, is recorded at length in *Jubilees* which includes a long poetic appeal to Terah, on the lines of an Isaianic complaint about the vanity of idols (*Jub.* 12:2-5), as well as the story of burning the idols of Ur (*Jub.* 12:12-14). In this story, Abraham discovers monotheism (*Jub.* 12:16-21), which James may be alluding to when he says that even demons believe that 'God is one'.

James' conclusion in 4:7 that one should 'submit to God; resist the devil and he will flee' is similar to the story of Abraham's circumcision. This story is missing from all the extant texts of *Jubilees*, but part of it is found in the *Damascus Document* where it appears to cite a passage from *Jubilees* which is not found in any surviving version. It says that the following was found in 'The book of the divisions of the periods according to their Jubilees and their weeks':

> And on the day on which the man has pledged himself to return to the law of Moses, the angel Mastema [the lord of evil angels] will turn aside from following him, should he keep his word. This is why Abraham circumcised himself on the day of his knowledge. (*CD* 16:4-5)[39]

This suggests that at least some versions of *Jubilees* contained the story of Abraham's circumcision and that his obedience to this precept was regarded as the key to his protection from Satan (Mastema). James' version at 4:7 is clearly different, because he has replaced submission to the Law of Moses with submission to God. This is probably a deliberate variation by which he would capture his audience's attention, like he did at 1:13-14 where he replaced Satan with human desires. As on that occasion, James does not state his reasons for doing so at this point in the sermon.

---

[39] Translation from Florentino García Martínez, *The Dead Sea Scrolls Translated: The Qumran Texts in English* (Leiden: Brill, 1994). It is not clear where the citation from the book of *Jubilees* starts or ends, but it almost certainly included the reference to 'Mastema' which is the name for the lord of evil spirits in *Jubilees* (it occurs only here in *CD*, but 12 times in *Jubilees*).

The second new sub-theme, the warning about riches at 5:1-6, has a tenuous link to Abraham's Trial of Riches of Kings (*Jub.* 17:17). Perhaps James felt that it was not necessary at this stage in the sermon to flag his allusions more clearly, because his audience would be looking out for them. *Jubilees* does not clearly state what the 'Trial of Riches of Kings' was, but it is most likely a reference to the offer by the King of Sodom to keep the war booty in return for the people (*Jub.* 13:28-29 // Gen 14:21-24). This explains James' otherwise extreme words, 'you fatted yourselves in a day of slaughter' (Jas 5:5).

The End and the Aim of the Sermon
The sermon ends at 5:11, with a final reminder that the Lord's coming is near (5:7-9) and with a return to the opening theme of Abraham's patience in his Trials (5:11; cf. 1:2-3). He links this theme with the story of Job, which was clearly the model for the story in *Jubilees* about the debate in heaven concerning the sacrifice of Isaac (*Jub.* 17:15-18). The final words of the sermon are 'The Lord is full of compassion and mercy' so that, like a model sermon of early Judaism, it ends with a word of consolation.[40]

This ending may be telling us that the 'text' of the sermon was the story of Job. The 'text' of a sermon in early Judaism was typically only referred to at the end and sometimes at the beginning, while the main body of a sermon was based on a series of incidents which could be verbally or thematically linked to this text.[41] If this reference to Job

---

[40] In early Judaism, a sermon should end with a word of consolation. Joseph Heinemann found this as far back as 2 Macc 8:23; see his *Prayer in the Talmud: Forms and Patterns* (Berlin/New York: de Gruyter, 1977), 228.
[41] This was the typical structure of a sermon of the 'Proem' form, which is found frequently in aggadic Rabbinic literature; see the introduction by Isaiah Sonne in *The Bible As Read and Preached in the Old Synagogue* (ed. Jacob Mann; Vol. 1, New York: KTAV, 1971; Vol. 2, Cincinnati: Hebrew Union College, 1966). Unfortunately the Rabbinic collections containing these sermons were compiled relatively late, and individual sermons are almost impossible to date. However, this sermon form can be identified in

is the revelation of the 'text', we can see the rationale behind the choice of the main themes which he picked out of the Trials of Abraham — they were all themes which are also found in Job: gaining wisdom through trials, the transience of riches, listening rather than speaking and the danger of the tongue.[42]

The last few verses (5:12-20) are some final exhortations and advice which were added when the sermon became an epistle. This is similar to the final exhortations which are found in other New Testament epistles.[43] Although the sermon is over, the themes of Abraham and Job are carried over into this codicil. The teaching on swearing was probably prompted by the Lord saying 'I swear by myself ...' immediately after the Trial concerning Isaac,[44] and although Elijah is named as someone who prayed with faith, it was Abraham and not Elijah who prayed for the healing of an illness caused by sin.[45] Job also contains both the themes of swearing[46] and healing through prayer.[47]

---

the New Testament; see John Westerdale Bowker, "Speeches in Acts: A Study in Proem and *yelammedenu* Form," *NTS* 14 (1967): 96-111, esp. 100.

[42] Job 1:22: 'Job did not sin by charging God with wrongdoing.'

[43] Cf. Rom 16:17-20; 1 Cor 16:22; 2 Cor 13:11; 1 Thess 5:12-22; 1 Tim 6:17-20; Titus 3:14.

[44] Gen 22:16; *Jub.* 18:15.

[45] Gen 20:17-18. The whole incident with Abimelech and Sarah is missing from *Jubilees* as well as the similar incident of Abimelech and Isaac's wife (Gen 26:6-11), because the author of *Jubilees* does not want to record anything negative about Abraham. However, the previous similar incident concerning Pharaoh and Sarah in Gen 12:10-20 *is* recorded briefly (*Jub.* 13:13-15) as a test concerning 'when his wife was taken' (*Jub.* 17:17). Other Hellenistic retellings of Abraham's Trials do mention Abraham's healing powers with regard to this story, such as a mid-third-century tradition in *Gen. R.* 39.11 and, more importantly, the fragmentary account in the *Genesis Apocryphon* 19–20 which says that Abraham 'laid hands' on Pharaoh's head to heal him, which made an evil spirit stop attacking him (20.20, 29). In the *Testament of Abraham* (first or second century AD) Abraham prays for a soul whose good works and sins are balanced equally (*Testament of Abraham* A.12), and his 'righteous prayers' result in the soul's salvation (*T. Abr.* A.14 esp. v. 8).

The aim of the sermon should not be sought so much in the text or the other sources which he has used (which may have been determined by a lectionary or by tradition) but by the ways in which James has *departed* from his sources — themes which were not present in the sources or themes which he has ignored, and variations which he has introduced to the traditional stories. His use of these traditional stories does not mean that he believes in their historicity or puts them on a par with Scripture, but he is able to use them as illustrations in a sermon in much the same way as a modern preacher might refer to the life of a saint. The variations which he introduces are not intended to be corrections, but a different emphasis or a different application which stands out simply *because* it is different.

We noted two departures where he varied from the familiar stories: first, he replaced temptation by Satan with temptation by internal desires (1:13-14) and, secondly, he talked about submission to God instead of submission to the Law (4:7). The first variation would have stood out very obviously to his audience because the story of Satan's request to test God's saint was so well known both in the Trials of Abraham and at the beginning of Job. The second variation may have been less obvious because the tradition it is based on is a less familiar theme — the circumcision of Abraham is recorded in only one surviving source. James does not spell out the reason for either variation, so presumably the messages he wants to derive from them must be found elsewhere in his sermon.

The second variation involves a de-emphasis of submission to the Law, which concurs with another way in which James departs from his sources — he never speaks about keeping the ceremonial law, whereas *Jubilees* considers it to be very important. *Jubilees* tries to show that Abraham obeyed all of that law which was later called the

---

[46] Job 2:9: 'curse God and die'.

[47] In Job 42:9-10 Job was healed after praying for his friends, like Sarah's barrenness was healed after Abraham interceded concerning the barrenness of the Egyptians caused by their taking Sarah (Gen 20:17–21:2).

Law of Moses. Abraham paid tithes of everything 'to his priests' (*Jub.* 13:25-27), offered his Firstfruits of crops and herds on the correct date (15:1-2; 22:4),[48] circumcised his household (15:11-14, 23-34 — an expansive enlargement of the biblical text), kept the Festival of Booths by building a Booth of branches and making all the correct offerings (16:20-31; 22:1-4), and on his deathbed he gave detailed prescriptions about how to make sacrifices in accordance with Lev 3:7-11 which he found written 'in the books of my forefathers, and in the words of Enoch and in the words of Noah' (*Jub.* 21:6-10). None of this emphasis is found in James.

James repeatedly reminds his audience about the value of 'works', but the works described and called for by James are all moral good works, in stark contrast to *Jubilees* which is mainly concerned with what Paul calls 'works of the Law'. This makes James' ethical teaching stand out vividly against the background of the sources with which he and his audience were familiar. This is the same contrast which we find in Paul, who commented negatively about 'works of the Law' but who commented three times as often about the positive value of 'works' (i.e. morally good works).[49]

The message implied by the first variation, which de-emphasised Satan, is probably related to this. As pointed out above, James was not trying to change the story, but was presenting a different application of the story. Presumably he was warning his audience against applying the story of Abraham's Trial in the wrong way — i.e. by concluding that temptations generally come from the devil. This type of misapplication provides people with an excuse for evil,

---

[48] Unlike Rabbinic Judaism which allowed Firstfruits to be presented any time between the feasts of Weeks and Booths (*m. Bik.* 1.3, 10), *Jubilees* is concerned that they should only be presented on the last day of Weeks.

[49] Johnson points out that although Paul refers negatively to 'works of the Law', 17 of the 50 references to 'works' in the Pauline corpus are actually positive references to good works of charity or moral works — see details at Johnson, *James*, 60. Sometimes even 'work(s) of the law' can refer to ethical good works (e.g. Rom 2:15).

by saying that 'the devil made me do it'. James' reply to them is that 'each one is tempted ... by his own evil desire'. He wanted to emphasise that they should make a conscious effort to avoid evil works in the same way that they should strive to do good works.

In conclusion, James' message is a call to a moral lifestyle — they should do good works and they should not do evil deeds. He illustrated this by the Trials of Abraham in order to emphasise that their faith was on trial, and the evidence presented in this trial is based on their works. This conclusion is confirmed if we collect the direct personal statements and imperatives which are found in the epistle: 'do not show favouritism' (2:1), 'you have insulted the poor' (2:6), 'speak and act as those who are going to be judged by the law of freedom' (2:12), 'you adulterous people' (4:4), 'wash your hands, you sinners, and purify your hearts you double-minded' (4:8), 'do not slander' (4:11), 'you boast and brag' (4:16), 'you rich, weep and wail' (5:1), 'be patient ... until the Lord's coming' (5:7-8).

James' overall teaching is therefore that believers are tested in this lifetime like Abraham and Job were. Like them, it is not their works which are on trial, but their faith as evidenced by their works.

'You Have No Need That Anyone Should Teach You' (1 John 2:27):

An Old Testament Allusion That Determines the Interpretation

D. A. Carson

In an unguarded moment some years ago, in a book treating the use of the Old Testament in the New, I wrote, 'The most striking feature relevant to our subject in these [Johannine] epistles is the absence not only of OT quotations but even of many unambiguous allusions to the OT.'[1] At one time, I think, Judith Lieu would have agreed; even the one Old Testament name, the reference to Cain (1 John 3:12), she had written, more likely springs from Christian catechesis than from independent use of the Old Testament.[2] Subsequently, however, she argued that my published judgement is 'wrong'[3] because 'the Cain narrative may be already in mind in 3:7 and even continue to the end of the chapter; behind 2:11 lies Isa 6:10; other passages too may go back to OT passages and their exegesis, while … many of the images have Old Testament roots.'[4] Still more recently, she has developed her argument regarding the Cain narrative lurking behind much of 1 John 3,

---

[1]   D. A. Carson, "John and the Johannine Epistles," in *It Is Written: Scripture Citing Scripture* (Fs. Barnabas Lindars; ed. D. A. Carson and H. G. M. Williamson; Cambridge: CUP, 1988), 256.
[2]   Judith M. Lieu, *The Second and Third Epistles of John: History and Background* (Edinburgh: T & T Clark, 1986), 181-82, 188-89.
[3]   Judith M. Lieu, *The Theology of the Johannine Epistles* (Cambridge: CUP, 1991), 87, n. 99 (though she misquotes it).
[4]   Lieu, *Theology of the Johannine Epistles*, 87.

and in addition has traced Old Testament roots behind 1:9–2:2 and behind 2:11.[5]

Old Testament Roots

Formally, I suppose, my quotation is correct: there is no explicit Old Testament quotation in the Johannine Epistles, and, on a tight definition of 'allusions' and a generous reading of 'many', there are not 'many unambiguous allusions' either. Nevertheless, my statement is misleading in two respects. The first is that the Old Testament is John's Bible: it is the matrix out of which his understanding of Christ and the gospel grew, the seedbed for many of his categories. As Lieu puts it, many of the images have Old Testament roots, even if in some cases they have been mediated through the gospel: light and darkness, son of God, Christ, ἱλασμός, and certain covenantal notions. Even the insistence that valid knowledge of God is accompanied by principled obedience sounds very much like an Old Testament theme. On the other hand, these developments in Old Testament categories mostly build upon broad themes and recurrent usage, rather than upon discrete and identifiable texts. Still, my statement could have been more nuanced.

Old Testament Theme

The second misleading element in my quotation is that in addition to the passages in which Lieu detects Old Testament rootage, there is one particular Old Testament text that goes a long way to explaining an important theme in 1 John.

To get at it, we must come to a decision on the extent to which covenantal notions play an important part in this epistle. Almost a century ago, Kennedy argued that, despite the fact that 1 John does not explicitly use the word 'covenant', covenantal patterns of thought

---

[5]   Judith M. Lieu, "What Was from the Beginning: Scripture and Tradition in the Johannine Epistles," *NTS* 39 (1993): 458-77.

are never far away.[6] The covenant idea in the Old Testament is bound
up with the 'religious community', i.e. with the relation of the people
to the God whose call and care constitute them. So John says that
'what we have seen and heard' we 'announce also to you', and the
purpose of this proclamation is that the 'you' may have 'fellowship'
with 'us', and 'our fellowship' is with the Father and his Son. If then
we make certain claims to have fellowship with God while walking in
the darkness, we lie, we are not practising the truth (1 John 1:3-4, 6-
7). Indeed, the sharp antithesis between the faithful community and
those who belong to the world reflects this consciousness of a 'society
constituted by fellowship with God in Christ', and this 'calls up the
Covenant-conception of the ideal of the Hebrew community'.[7]
Kennedy also argues that, just as under the Mosaic covenant the
problem of sin was dealt with by the sacrifice prescribed for the Day
of Atonement, so John deals with the problem of sin in the community by referring to the sacrifice of Christ (1:9; 2:1-2): Jesus is the
ἱλασμός, a word used more than once to render כִּפֻּרִים (kippurim,
'atonement', e.g. Lev 25:9; Num 5:8), 'which belongs to the very
heart of the covenant-ceremonial'.[8] Obedience is bound up with the
covenant (Exod 24:7); here we are sure that we know God if we obey
his commands (1 John 2:3). On God's part, divine fidelity is what
establishes the faith of the people; so in 1 John 1:9, God is 'faithful
and just', or the terms of the new covenant could not be counted on.
Kennedy also argues that while the closest New Testament parallel to
the 'sin unto death' in 1 John 5:14-15 is Heb 10:26-29 (which is
awash with covenant categories), the Old Testament passage behind
both of them is Num 15:22-30, which specifies at what point a person
may be cut off from the covenant community.

---

[6]   H. A. A. Kennedy, "The Covenant-conception in the First Epistle of
John," *ExpT* 28 (1916): 23-26.
[7]   Kennedy, "Covenant-conception," 24.
[8]   Kennedy, "Covenant-conception," 25.

Old Testament Categories

In 1949, without referring to Kennedy, Boismard published an important article arguing that the knowledge of God in 1 John derives its categories from Old Testament promises of the new covenant, especially the characteristics of the knowledge of God under the new covenant (especially Jer 31 and Ezek 36).[9] His arguments are in the main convincing, and need not be repeated. In 1978, Malatesta published his doctoral dissertation, tying the categories εἶναι ἐν and μένειν ἐν, so important to 1 John, to 'interiority and covenant'.[10] One need not agree with every jot and tittle in these works (dissertations commonly go over the top) to perceive their importance, and many of their arguments have been taken up in recent commentaries. Nevertheless, it is vital to recall that the promise of the new covenant in Jer 31 and Ezek 36 specifies that it will come to pass in the last days. It is not only a covenant of eternal life, but it is an internalized covenant: God will write his law on the hearts of his people, or (in Ezekiel) pour out his Spirit upon them, with the result that they will obey him. It was a covenant for the whole people of God (young, old, men, women — all flesh), and dealt radically with the problem of sin. It is difficult not to overhear echoes of such themes in 1 John.

Indeed, the arguments in support of the importance of covenantal categories in 1 John can be strengthened if we are right in seeing the same author behind both the Fourth Gospel and 1 John. Pryor has shown that many of the Gospel's themes are covenant categories: the use of ἴδιοι in 1:11 with reference to Israel and in 13:1 with reference to Jesus' followers, the true vine language (John 15), the portrayal of

---

[9]   M.-E. Boismard, "La connaissance de Dieu dans l'Alliance Nouvelle d'après la première épître de S. Jean," *RevBib* 56 (1949): 365-91. A more popular version appeared elsewhere: see his "'Je ferai avec vous une alliance nouvelle' (introduction à la première épître de saint Jean)," *LumVie* 8 (1953): 94-109.

[10] Edward Malatesta, *Interiority and Covenant: A Study of εἶναι ἐν and μένειν ἐν in the First Letter of Saint John* (Analecta Biblica 69; Rome: Biblical Institute Press, 1978).

Jesus as the Mosaic prophet, some of the 'sending' terminology (cf. Num 16:8), the shepherd and flock categories, the links between Jesus' glory dwelling among us (viz. the messianic community) and the Old Testament covenantal antecedents (1:14-18; cf. Exod 32–34), and much more.[11] Why Smith, following Bultmann, says that in the Fourth Gospel 'the concept of God's covenant with his people Israel, his election of them, plays no explicit role (cf. Romans 9–11)',[12] I am uncertain. True, John does not use the word 'covenant', but then again neither does he use the word 'church', yet most commentators find not a little to say on ecclesiastical matters. There is no explicit mention of the election of Israel, yet there is a systematic theological interchange between Jesus and his opponents as to what it means to be a son of Abraham (John 8) — and in any case the plentiful election terminology in John is now focused on the messianic community.[13] In my commentary on John, I strongly sided with those who see Ezek 36:25-27 behind John 3:3, 5, and tied some of the Holy Spirit passages to other new covenant passages (e.g. Joel 2).[14]

None of this authorizes us to read material of the Fourth Gospel into 1 John. Yet given the strong reasons for thinking that there is a common author, or (if you prefer) at very least a more or less unified tradition, and that the two books were written perhaps a decade or so apart, there is little reason to think that some fundamental shift has taken place in the move from one to the other. 1 John is saturated with the categories deployed in the Fourth Gospel; and those categories are

---

[11] John W. Pryor, *John: Evangelist of the Covenant People* (London: Darton, Longman and Todd, 1992).

[12] D. Moody Smith, *The Theology of the Gospel of John* (Cambridge: CUP, 1995), 67; Rudolf Bultmann, *Theology of the New Testament* (2 vols.; London: SCM, 1952-55), 2:7-8.

[13] Cf. D. A. Carson, *Divine Sovereignty and Human Responsibility: Biblical Themes in Tension* (London: Marshall, Morgan and Scott, 1981), 181-92.

[14] D. A. Carson, *The Gospel according to John* (Grand Rapids: Eerdmans, 1991), 191-96, *passim*.

saturated with the imagery and language, and sometimes the quotations, of the Old Testament Scriptures. In 1 John the Old Testament is not so much a source that is quoted as the very matrix of reflection of a Christian who for many years has thought hard about the relation of Christian truth to antecedent revelation.

Old Testament Allusion

In this light, one element in particular from Jer 31 casts considerable light on 1 John 2:20, 27. John's readers are told that they all know (οἴδατε πάντες, 2:20), and need no one to teach them (οὐ χρείαν ἔχετε ἵνα τις διδάσκῃ ὑμᾶς, 2:27). Many have noted the parallel with Jer 33:34 (LXX 38:34): οὐ μὴ διδάξωσιν ... ἕκαστος τὸν ἀδελφὸν αὐτοῦ λέγων Γνῶθι τὸν κύριον, ὅτι πάντες εἰδήσουσιν με ... Assuming the reading πάντες in 1 John 2:20, it is hard not to detect a link with Jeremiah's promise that under the new covenant *all* Israel will know the Lord, from the least to the greatest. The parallel has been picked up by commentators as diverse as Westcott and Brown.[15]

Yet despite this rather obvious connection with an Old Testament passage, it appears that one important element of the Jeremiah text is regularly overlooked. It might be simplest to quote Brown at length:

> Nevertheless, in his opposition to false teaching the author goes to the extreme of denying the need of any teacher. Other NT works inculcate the need for authoritative teachers (I Tim 4:11: 'Command and teach these things'), and indeed 'prophets and teachers' were a regular feature in many churches (I Cor 12:23; Eph 4:11; Acts 13:1) ... Since it is the anointing of the Christian that dispenses with the need for a teacher, the author is most likely basing himself on the promise of Jesus that the Paraclete would teach all things and guide the Johannine Christians along the way of all truth (John 14:26; 16:13) ...

---

[15] B. F. Westcott, *The Epistles of St John: The Greek Text with Notes* (Grand Rapids: Eerdmans, 1966 [1892]), 79; Raymond E. Brown, *The Epistles of John* (AB; London: Geoffrey Chapman, 1983), 349.

Despite the author's clear statement against the need for human teachers, some scholars persist in referring to the 'we' of 1 John 1:1-5 and 4:6 as if a group of apostolic teachers were involved. I have argued that more likely the Johannine School (including the author) thought of themselves as 'witnesses,' a title that would offer no rivalry to an anointing by the Spirit. ... I have suggested that the lack of organized teaching authority in the author's branch of the Johannine Community was what made the propaganda of the secessionists such a threat, and that eventually some churches in that Community had to develop local authority with the power to teach. Even if I am correct in judging that the author's vision of a Christianity without human teachers ultimately failed, subsequent Christianity, which had a fully developed magisterium of human teachers, still accepted into its canonical Scripture his dictum, 'You have no need for anyone to teach you.' Already Augustine, a teaching bishop himself, wrestled with this problem (*In Epist.* 3.13; SC 75, 210): 'There is here, my brothers, a great mystery on which to meditate: the sound of my voice strikes your ears, but the real Teacher is within. Do not think that one learns anything from another human being. We can draw your attention by the sound of our voice; but if within there is not the One who instructs, the noise of our words is in vain. ... The internal Master who teaches is Christ the teacher; his inspiration teaches. Where his inspiration and anointing are not found, the external words are in vain.' ... Among the many commentators who have opted for an interior teaching by the Spirit corresponding to an exterior teaching are Belser, Bonsirven, Chaine, de Ambroggi. A particular variant is expounded by Paulinus of Nola (*Epistolae* 23.26; CSEL 29, 193) who died *ca.* 431. He points out that since the Spirit dwells in each faithful Christian, the faithful as a whole have a guide to the truth. This has resulted in the thesis that the universal and constant belief of the Christian community guarantees Christian truth. Still another interpretation is that the anointing of a Christian by the Spirit guarantees the private exegesis of the Scripture. Obviously these interpretations go beyond what the author had in mind, but all of them reflect a continuation of the line of thought he represented. In the long run, his position has meant that the Church has to live with a tension between authoritative teachers and the Spirit enlightening individual Christians, both of which are attested in the NT.[16]

All sides recognize, of course, that elsewhere the author provides other firm advice as to how to remain faithful. It appears that the secessionists thought of themselves as progressives (2 John 7, 9). Against this John urges that true believers must maintain what was taught from the beginning (e.g. 1 John 2:7), and that the 'anointing' that they have received (most plausibly referring to the Spirit) teaches them about all things (1 John 2:27). If that were all our author said, there would be no puzzle. But for him to ban all teachers, when transparently what he is doing is teaching himself, seems, on first reading, to be more than a little strange. If that is what he is doing (as Brown, for instance, thinks, as witnessed in the extensive quotation, above), it is difficult to avoid charging the author with rather serious (however unconscious) inconsistency.[17] It is as if he were saying, 'Ban all teachers, look to yourself and the work of the Holy Spirit within you — provided you agree with my teaching.'[18] Add in all the usual caveats — that any teaching has to be 'tested' for its truth (4:1-5; 2 John 9-10),[19] that the 'truth' in question may be primarily the kind of basic Christological truth that establishes who is 'in' or 'out' and

---

[16] Brown, *Epistles*, 374-76. Cf. similarly Georg Strecker, *The Johannine Letters* (Hermeneia; Minneapolis: Fortress, 1996), 76-77; and many others.

[17] Cf. Hans-Josef Klauck, *Der erste Johannesbrief* (EKK; Zürich/Neukirchen-Vluyn: Benziger/Neukirchener, 1991), 168-70.

[18] Cf. Stephen S. Smalley, *1, 2, 3 John* (WBC; Waco: Word, 1984), 125: 'So complete is the spiritual instruction which the true believer has received, John concludes, that the need for temporal teaching is removed. However, as many commentators point out, this absolute declaration about the dispensability of earthly teachers appears in the course of a document which is heavily didactic!'

[19] On which see especially R. Schnackenburg, *The Johannine Epistles: Introduction and Commentary* (London: Burns & Oates, 1992), 149-50 — though, strangely, Schnackenburg does not think that the 'anyone to teach you' clause could have the heretics in view. See also Pierre Bonnard, *Les épîtres johanniques* (CNT; Genève: Labor et Fides, 1983), 62.

nothing more basic, that the opponents may well be Gnostics who think they 'know' everything and that John is determined to take them down a peg or two — and the fact remains that this way of wording things is still somewhat puzzling. John does not simply say that his readers do not need any new teaching, or that they should not listen to any false teaching, but that they do not need anyone to teach them.

One of the most denunciatory assessments to arise from this clause comes from Rensberger:

> By identifying the opponents with the expected antichrist, the author has transferred the concept of a leader of evil *outside* Christianity to the realm of *internal* Christian dissension. This is a step with potentially dangerous consequences, the first of many such identifications in Christian history. It opens the way for Christians who disagree with other Christians to demonize them altogether, as indeed the author will do in chapter 3.
>
> At the end of this section, the author puts forward a powerfully antiauthoritarian, nearly anarchic concept of the church and of Christian doctrine, by declaring that the only teaching needed is that which comes directly from the Spirit.[20]

What Rensberger prefers is an ongoing tension between the work of the Spirit and the authority of tradition.[21]

But all of this indignation may be entirely misplaced if we observe a little more closely the context of the Old Testament passages to which (most scholars agree) John is making reference. In particular, Jeremiah's promise of a new covenant (Jer 31:31-34) is preceded by

---

[20]   David Rensberger, *1 John, 2 John, 3 John* (ANTC; Nashville: Abingdon, 1997), 83.

[21]   Rensberger's argument begs several issues that are not germane to my argument in this paper, but which should not go unnoticed. In particular, he assumes that because the secessionists emerged from the church (1 John 2:19) that they are still Christians. The conflict, then, becomes the equivalent of denominational squabbling wrongly labelled something more substantive. That is certainly not the author's view, of course, and Rensberger can adopt this view only by saying that John's theological arguments as to what constitutes a Christian do not stand up.

the comment, 'In those days people will no longer say, "The fathers have eaten sour grapes, and the children's teeth are set on edge." Instead, everyone will die for his own sin; whoever eats sour grapes — his own teeth will be set on edge' (Jer 31:29-30). The proverb is clearly the same as that in Ezek 18:2, though the application in the two contexts is somewhat different. There is a trend in recent commentaries on Jeremiah to argue, correctly, that this proverb is not meant to justify a mere individualizing of religion. Instead, it is commonly argued, the blessings associated with the new covenant will be so sweeping in their extent ('they will all know me', 31:34) that the experience of judgment will fade into the past.[22] Doubtless this is true as far as it goes, but it does not deal adequately with the *structural* change that the wording implies. True, Yahweh will bring about an amazing transformation, caused by his writing his law on the hearts of all the people (31:33). But notice the antithesis in the new covenant promises that mirrors the antithesis in the rejection of the old proverb: the new covenant will *not* be like the old covenant, in exactly the same way that the people will *not* say what they used to say in the words of the old proverb. In both instances, the change is the same. Under the new covenant, *all* will be transformed (which suggests not only that there is an increased intensity of religious faithfulness, but an increased sweep of those affected); and under the expectation that the proverb will no longer apply, *all* face judgment without facing the judgment inherited from the 'fathers'.

The point is that the old covenant was tribal and representative. Prophets, priests, kings and a few others received special endowment of the Spirit, and functioned as intermediaries, charged, amongst other things, with telling the rest of the covenant community, 'Know the Lord.' In such a tribal and representative system, when the leaders

---

[22] See, among others, William McKane, *A Critical and Exegetical Commentary on Jeremiah* (2 vols.; ICC; Edinburgh: T & T Clark, 1986-96), 815-17, 820-27; Gerald L. Keown, Pamela J. Scalise and Thomas G. Smothers, *Jeremiah 26-52* (WBC; Dallas: Word, 1995), 134-35.

(the 'fathers') went astray, judgment fell on all — an experience not rare in the history of Israel, as even David managed to demonstrate. All of these intermediaries were in some ways Israel's teachers. But under the terms of the new covenant, they will no longer be needed, for all who are under that new covenant will know the Lord. In short, those who will no longer be needed, according to this context, are not simply teachers, but intermediary teachers.[23]

If this is the thrust of Jer 31, and if John understands it, then his allusion takes on new specificity. By telling his readers that 'you do not need anyone to teach you' (2:27; cf. John 6:45; 1 Thess 4:8-9; Heb 8:11), he is, by the allusion, actually saying, 'You do not need any mediating teacher to teach you', or, 'You do not need anyone to teach you in a mediating sort of way.' The context of Jer 31 makes it clear that what is in view is the *mediating* teacher. Under the old covenant, ideally teaching was mediated to the people through specially endowed prophets, priests, kings; there would be no need for such mediation under the new covenant, for all who are under this covenant would know the Lord. Thus if any group claims, as some Gnostics were wont to do, a special insight that only they and those who joined them enjoyed, part of John's response is in terms of Johannine theology that itself claims to fulfil Old Testament promises regarding the dawning and nature of the new covenant, a new covenant that would guarantee the gift of the Spirit and consequent illumination to all within its embrace, forever relegating to the sidelines those who claim the authority of specially endowed mediating teachers.

---

[23] Occasionally commentaries pick up on this distinction, but most do not make much of it. See, for instance, J. A. Thompson, *The Book of Jeremiah* (NICOT; Grand Rapids: Eerdmans, 1980), 581: 'The extent of the transformation *in those days* would be that intermediaries like Moses, priests, prophets, teachers, would no longer be needed to instruct people and say "Know Yahweh," because all of them shall *know* (*yāḍaʻ*) him, young and old, from the least to the greatest.'

Although it would take another essay to demonstrate the point, all this is happily in line with Johannine theology. It is often noted, for instance, that in the Fourth Gospel Jesus becomes the new temple, the new Passover, the new lamb; he takes over the rites of the Feast of Tabernacles and provides the rest of the Sabbath. The old covenant was tribal and representative; the new covenant extends to the world, and abolishes the representative structures that were constitutive of the Mosaic legislation. That, at any rate, is how John reads Jer 31 and Ezek 36 — and he is not the only New Testament writer to read Old Testament promises that way. This is also why John keeps reiterating that all true Christians must simply hold on to the gospel that has been there from the beginning. To follow the teaching of the secessionists would be to follow something esoteric, something for an inside group that claims a mediating teaching role.

This in turn suggests that some of the categories that many schol-ars have used to wrestle with 1 John 2:27 — the claims of the Spirit versus the authority of tradition, the universality of the 'anointing' but the need for teachers provided that what they teach is appropriately tested — though important in their own right, rather miss the mark here. The Protognostics appear to have been claiming that they have a special insight, a special γνῶσις, that only they, on the inside track, could impart. But that would elevate them to the role of mediating teacher, to the position of those who do more than expound the truth that is in the domain of the entire church and accessible to the entire church: they claim to teach from the vantage point of superiors, the elite of the elect, the mediators. And that class of teacher, the sixth-century prophets foresaw, would forever be abolished.

Rome, Provincial Cities and the Seven Churches of Revelation 2–3

Bruce W. Longenecker

Although scholars frequently refer to the first-century world as the 'Graeco-Roman' world, pockets of that world were noticeably more Roman than Greek. Bruce Winter (among others) has claimed this to be the case both for Corinth in Achaea and for Galatia in central Asia Minor.[1] The same was also true for the territories between those two areas, western Asia Minor, the region in which the seven churches addressed in Rev 2–3 were located. The Roman character of the main cities of this area is particularly evident in their aspirations and their manner of governance. In western Asia Minor the Greek ideals of the independent 'city-state' as the basis for governance and civic dealings had long since been supplanted by a new style of governance. In the cities of first-century western Asia Minor, civic governance was marked out by one overriding feature: allegiance to Rome — the single great city that interconnected and governed the whole of the world that mattered (at least in the eyes of those whose world was centred in the Mediterranean basin). In this important regard, many of the cities in the provinces of Asia Minor had been thoroughly Romanized.[2]

A key ingredient in this Romanization of the empire's provinces was the cultivation among the provincial elite of the expectation that

---

[1] With regard to Corinth, see, for instance, B. W. Winter, "The Achaean Federal Imperial Cult II: The Corinthian Church," *TynB* 46 (1995): 177-78 and works cited there. With regard to Galatia, see B. W. Winter, *Seek the Welfare of the City: Christians As Benefactors and Citizens* (Grand Rapids: Eerdmans, 1994), 123-43.

[2] Cf. T. Mommsen, *The Provinces of the Roman Empire: The European Provinces* (Chicago: University of Chicago Press, 1968).

they, and consequently their city, would benefit through association with Rome.[3] The provincial elite became, in effect, the unpaid bureaucracy of the Roman empire, as they sought to implement socioeconomic structures within their local contexts that enhanced their cities' prospects for advancement within the empire. In this way, through the efforts of the urban elite, the provincial cities became 'both the major cultural conveyor and the construct of Roman imperialism'.[4]

Included within these dynamics was the thriving cult of the Roman emperor, who was proclaimed by the local promoters of the imperial cult as an incarnate deity and to whom sacrifices were to be offered. Belligerent aversion to the imperial cult could bring upon an objector the charge of 'atheism' — i.e. the refusal to worship the traditional gods of Rome and the emperor. To be guilty of 'atheism' of this kind was to draw the harsh condemnation of peers and/or overlords, and frequently ended in exile or, in extreme cases, death (e.g. the case of Antipas in Rev 2:13).[5] Consequently, it was well within the interests of the provincial elite to promote the worship of the emperor as an intrinsic part of their attempts at self- and civic-advancement.

Much of this is testified to within the Johannine apocalypse, with its maze of symbolic imagery and allusive language. The author of Revelation sought to unmask the vagaries and perversities of imperial Rome and the cult of the emperor, demonstrating them to be an affront against the sovereign reign of Israel's God. Whereas God is sovereign, eternal and the only true authority, those acclamations had

---

[3]   Cf. W. S. Hanson, "Forces of Change and Methods of Control," in *Dialogues in Roman Imperialism: Power, Discourse and Discrepant Experience in the Roman Empire* (ed. D. J. Mattingly; Ann Arbor: Journal of Roman Archaeology, 1997), 67-80.

[4]   C. R. Whittaker, "Imperialism and Culture: The Roman Initiative," in *Dialogues in Roman Imperialism* (ed. Mattingly), 145.

[5]   For a 'historical fiction' depicting Antipas' last year of life, see my *The Lost Letters of Pergamum: A Story from the New Testament World* (Grand Rapids: Baker Academic, 2003).

been usurped by Rome, proclaimed to be the sovereign, immutable and eternal city, with the Roman emperor paraded as an incarnate god, thereby shoring up Rome's legitimacy as favoured by the gods.

So, for instance, Rev 13 depicts the power, authority and might of the Dragon (Rev 12) as incarnating the reign of the Beast from the sea, the Dragon being identified as the Evil One and the Beast as the world-wide system of Roman rule, dominance and religion. As a variety of interpreters have suggested,[6] the First Beast of Rev 13:1-10 appears to be a veiled depiction of the military-political dimension of the Roman system (e.g. 'Who is like the Beast, and who can fight against it?', 13:4); the Second Beast of Rev 13:11-15 is a veiled depiction of the religio-political dimension of the Roman empire (i.e. the localised imperial cult that promoted the worship of the emperor; cf. 13:12, 15); and Rev 13:16-17 depicts Rome's economic-political aspect — a depiction which becomes magnified in the extensive depiction of the Harlot[7] and her downfall in Rev 17–18.

What Revelation further illustrates is the enormous attractiveness of the Roman system, which even John the seer seems to recognise ('When I saw her [the harlot] I marvelled', 17:6).[8] Rev 17–18 depicts the inhabitants of the earth falling over themselves to participate in the vast luxuries propagated by the Satanic system (e.g. 17:2; 18:3, 9, 19, 22-23), these extensive luxuries and resources being outlined in 18:12-17. Most of the seven cities of Asia Minor mentioned in Rev 2-3 were deeply entrenched in the Roman system, acting as

---

[6] See, e.g., R. J. Bauckham, "The Lion, The Lamb and the Dragon" and "The Economic Critique of Rome in Revelation 18," in his *The Climax of Prophecy* (Edinburgh: T & T Clark, 1993), 174-98, 338-83.

[7] Rev 17:18 identifies her as 'the great city which has dominion over the kings of the earth', while Rev 17:9 identifies the Harlot's seven heads as 'seven mountains', just as Rome was known to be built upon seven hills.

[8] That John is favourably impressed with the awe-inspiring grandeur of the Satanic system seems implied by what appears to be a rebuke in 17:7, 'Why do you wonder at this?' Moreover, the reference to the 'wilderness' in 17:3 might suggest that the vision of the Harlot is a temptation along the lines of Jesus' temptation by Satan in the wilderness.

administrative, commercial and/or religious centres of Roman culture. Revelation depicts the nations growing 'rich from the power of her luxury' (18:3), a depiction that marked out nearly all of the seven cities mentioned in Rev 2–3. Some Christians in those cities seem to have advocated working within the Roman socio-economic system (e.g. 2:6, 14, 15, 20), but the Johannine seer likens such involvement with the Roman system to intercourse with the great Harlot, urging Christians instead to 'Come out of her, my people, so that you do not take part in her sins, and so that you do not share in her plagues' (18:4).

The mythological depiction of these social realities within the narrative of the Johannine apocalypse corresponds precisely to indicators of the same phenomena from literary, epigraphical and numismatic remains from ancient Asia Minor. In their quest to appropriate as much honour as possible within the Roman system, the cities of western Asia Minor were no different from the rest of the Romanized cities of the empire. Their wellbeing depended on seeking out and vying for imperial favours.[9]

Take, for instance, the cities of Pergamum and Ephesus, two of the seven cities mentioned in Rev 2–3. Throughout the first century, the two cities had been in a nose-to-nose race to emerge as the leading city of western Asia Minor (a race that many other cities had sought to win as well). Early in the race Pergamum had established a good footing to take that accolade by means of a series of alliances with Rome.[10] An easy point of comparison involves the imperial temples of the two cities.[11] The officials of Pergamum had been quick off the

---

[9]   Cf. B. Levick, *Roman Colonies in Southern Asia Minor* (Oxford: Clarendon, 1967), 104-05.

[10]   See E. Gruen, *Studies in Greek Culture and Roman Policy* (Leiden: Brill, 1990), 11-21, where Pergamum's importance in the establishment of the Magna Mater cult in Rome is discussed as one example of this.

[11]   Other comparisons would involve their respective Asklepia, libraries, coinage, building projects, civic games and gladiatorial contests. On the latter T. Wiedemann, *Emperors and Gladiators* (London: Routledge, 1992),

mark to establish favourable relations with Rome under Augustus' rule during the last third of the first century BC. Having defeated Antony and Cleopatra's forces (31 BC), Augustus (i.e. Octavian) returned triumphantly to Rome in 29 BC, the undisputed master of the Roman empire, becoming installed as the first emperor of Rome two years later (27 BC–AD 14). Pergamum was the first city of Asia to honour Augustus in his undisputed role, erecting in 29 BC a temple dedicated to him and to Rome. Around this time Pergamum also instituted athletic games, again dedicating them to Augustus and Rome. Nine years later (20 BC), a statue of Augustus was erected in the Pergamene Sanctuary of Athena to reinforce the city's honourable stature in the eyes of Rome.[12] Pergamum's currency as a leading Romanised city of western Asia Minor had been so well cultivated that in AD 77 Pliny the Elder could describe Pergamum as 'by far the most distinguished city in Asia'.[13]

But the prospects for Ephesus were increasingly promising. In the second half of the first century, Ephesus assembled a series of notable accolades in its own favour. During the time of Domitian's reign as emperor (AD 81-96), the Ephesians erected a magnificent complex with baths and gymnasiums in honour of Domitian, and established Olympian games at which he was honoured as the high god Jupiter,

---

43 (cf. 144-45), writes: 'In Roman colonies …, *munera* [gladiatorial contest days] could serve as a symbol that the population (whatever their ethnic origin) was genuinely Roman and superior to the Hellenistic communities in the rest of the province.' Even sexual relationships entered the fray of influence; the emperor Domitian's homosexual attachment to the Pergamene Earinus was a likely factor in bolstering the Asklepios cult in Pergamum, with the emperor himself contributing funds to its renovation. See M. P. Bonz, "Beneath the Gaze of the Gods: The Pergamon Evidence for a Developing Theology of Empire," in *Pergamon, Citadel of the Gods: Archaeological Record, Literary Description, and Religious Development* (ed. H. Koester; Harrisburg: Trinity Press International, 1998), 255.

[12] For discussion of these and other points, see D. N. Schowalter, "The Zeus Philios and Trajan Temple: A Context for Imperial Honours," in *Pergamon, Citadel of the Gods* (ed. Koester), 236-39.

[13] Pliny, *Nat.* 5.30.

known to the Greeks as Zeus Olympios.[14] Around this time the
Ephesians minted a coin in which the head of Domitian appeared on
one side and the image of Olympian Zeus/Jupiter on the other. This
coinage, then, affirmed both (1) the connection between the high god
and the emperor, and (2) the relationship between Rome and Ephesus,
since the high god is depicted as holding a likeness of the Ephesian
god Artemis in his hand.[15] It is little surprise, then, that during his
reign as emperor (AD 81-96) Domitian financed the improvements in
the Ephesian temple of Artemis,[16] or that in AD 89 he granted to
Ephesus the right to establish an imperial temple to service the bur-
geoning emperor cult in its region. The residents of Ephesus took
great pride in this distinctive privilege, and publicised their city far
and wide as 'neokoros' — i.e. warden of an imperial temple.[17]

But the Pergamenes responded in kind. Since their city had
established an imperial temple over a century earlier, they noted that
Pergamum was not simply 'neokoros', but was 'protos neokoros' (i.e.
first warden of an imperial temple). Processes were set in motion in
Pergamum that came to fruition later under Trajan's rule (AD 98-117),
with Pergamum establishing yet another imperial temple, the Temple
of Zeus Philios and Trajan. With this, it had outstripped Ephesus in
the number of imperial temples of which it could boast, and it adver-
tised itself now as 'protos kai dis neokoros' (i.e. first and twice war-

---

[14] See S. J. Friesen, Twice Neokoros: Ephesus, Asia and the Cult of the
Flavian Imperial Family (Leiden: Brill, 1993), 117-19.
[15] See Friesen, Twice Neokoros, 119.
[16] See D. Knibbe, R. Meric and R. Merkelbach, "Der Grundbesitz der
ephesischen Artemis im Kaystrostal," ZPE 33 (1979): 139-42.
[17] See Friesen, Twice Neokoros. Ephesian enchantment with Rome was
deeply rooted. One Ephesian inscription dating from 85 BC reads as follows:
'the people [of Ephesus] preserves its old goodwill towards the Romans, the
saviours of all, and readily agrees to their ordinances in all things. And
because from the beginning our people has maintained goodwill towards the
Romans ... it has resolved to undertake the war against the Mithridates for
the Roman empire and for common freedom'; see SIG³ 685:14-15.

den of an imperial temple).[18] But the Pergamene privilege of being distinctively 'twice *neokoros*' did not last long, with Ephesus building a second imperial temple during the reign of Hadrian (AD 117-38). In his time, Hadrian built up both cities, upgrading Pergamum from the status of city to that of metropolis, but likewise declaring Ephesus to be 'the first and greatest metropolis of Asia'. Hadrian's estimate was probably the predominant view, since Ephesus had emerged from the contest as the dominant metropolis, a status that it would continue to hold for centuries to come, with Pergamum and Smyrna falling below it in the pecking order of leading Roman cities in the region.[19]

This rough outline of one dimension of the inter-city relations between Pergamum and Ephesus is enough to demonstrate the keen attentiveness of the leading citizens of Asia Minor to matters of civic prestige in the first centuries of the common era. The same could be demonstrated for other dimensions of this single relationship, as well as for almost all other cities in their region. But the point should be clear from even this brief sketch, which amplifies W. M. Ramsay's observation that throughout this region 'there was keen competition for the title "first of the province" (or "the district"). Every city which could pretend to the first place in respect of any qualification called itself "first", and roused the jealousy of other cities which counted themselves equally good.'[20] And being 'first' usually involved being thoroughly committed to the ways of Rome.[21]

---

[18] See Schowalter, "The Zeus Philios and Trajan Temple," 233-49.
[19] See L. M. White, "Counting the Costs of Nobility: The Social Economy of Roman Pergamon," in *Pergamon, Citadel of the Gods* (ed. Koester), 339; S. Mitchell, *Anatolia: Land, Men and Gods in Asia Minor* (Oxford: Clarendon, 1993), 1:203-06.
[20] W. M. Ramsay, *The Letters to the Seven Churches* (2nd ed.; Peabody: Hendrickson, 1994), 99-100. On p. 99 he speaks of 'the jealousies and rivalries of these great cities' as being 'a quaint feature of their history in the Roman period'.
[21] So again Ramsay, *Letters to the Seven Churches*, 84, '[T]here was nothing else to hold the province together in a unity except the enthusiastic loyalty which all felt to the Roman imperial government.'

One other feature, however, does require mention: that is, inter-city alliances. Coinage from the ancient world commonly testifies to the existence of inter-city *homonoia*, a union of 'harmony' or alliance. In these widespread coins,[22] the representatives of the two cities (usually their distinctive gods) are depicted side by side. It is not wholly clear what circumstances mitigated *homonoia* associations. *Homonoia* associations may have been undertaken simply in the spirit of the much publicised *Pax Romana* (i.e. the peace brought about by Rome), with inter-city concord itself testifying to the cities' credentials as full participants in the project of the Roman empire.[23] On occasion, *homonoia* associations signalled the end of an inter-city controversy regarding the ranking of regional cities, and might even have been entered into under order of Rome.[24] In most cases, however, *homonoia* associations were probably established simply for the mutual benefit of each partner, with the associated cities profiting from the strengths of each other's distinctive reputations[25] and with the minted *homonoia* coinage publicising their profitable association.

One example will illustrate the kind of inter-city *homonoia* relationships that were typical of the cities throughout the empire, including the seven of Revelation. When Pergamum had established its second imperial temple under Trajan (mentioned above), two cities minted *homonoia* coinage to promote their reputations. One of these was Thyatira (cf. Rev 2:18-29) which took the occasion to bask in the

---

[22] P. R. Franke, *Kleinasien zur Römerzeit: griechisches Leben im Spiegel der Münzen* (Munich: Beck, 1968), 24, identifies seventy-eight *homonoia* cities minting coins in 110 combinations of relationship.

[23] So K. Wengst, *Pax Romana and the Peace of Jesus Christ* (London: SCM, 1987), 22.

[24] So Franke, *Kleinasien zur Römerzeit*, 24. Cf. John Paul Lotz, "The *homonoia* Coins of Asia Minor and Ephesians 1:21," *TynB* 50 (1999): 173-88.

[25] In antiquity, as in much of the world today, similar purposes are sometimes served through marriages arranged between the family members of leading figures of neighbouring cities.

reflected glory of Pergamum by minting *homonoia* coins to commemorate an alliance with Pergamum. The other city to mint coins in the wake of the establishment of its second imperial temple was Pergamum itself, which reaffirmed or issued a new alliance with Ephesus and paraded that alliance in a *homonoia* coinage.[26]

Within this context of civic prestige, competition and alliances, the epistolary character of the Johannine apocalypse takes on special significance. The inhabitants of the seven cities of Revelation, in particular the elite who controlled the mechanisms of civic life, were characterised by a profound concern to enhance the honour of the cities in which they lived, engaging them in an intensely competitive programme in relation to their neighbouring cities. They defined honour and shame in terms defined by Roman society, headed by the emperor. Their sights were set on outdoing neighbouring cities in advocating the ways of Rome, elevating their city's profile and enhancing the prospects of their urban elite. They judged themselves in terms of their success in acquiring honour in the eyes of Rome and kept a finely calculated 'league table' to assess their position against other cities.[27]

Against this backdrop, if readers of this essay would simply reread Rev 1–3, the next few paragraphs will prove to be virtually superfluous. One of the things that they will find there is a complete reorientation of the inter-city registry. The churches of those cities are not to fall into the conventional patterns of behaviour thought by the civic

---

[26] See U. Kampmann, "*Homonoia* Politics in Asia Minor: The Example of Pergamon," in *Pergamon, Citadel of the Gods* (ed. Koester), 373-93, esp. 377; helpful studies in *homonoia* relationships include U. Kampmann, *Die Homonoia-Verbindungen der Stadt Pergamon* (Saarbrücken: SDV, 1996) and D. Kienast, "Zu den Homonoia-Vereinbarungen in der römischen Kaiserzeit," *ZPE* 109 (1964): 267-81.

[27] This aspect of civic life in Asia Minor is underemphasised in C. J. Hemer, *The Letters to the Seven Churches of Asia in Their Local Setting* (Sheffield: Sheffield Academic Press, 1986), where the focus is more 'intra-city' than 'inter-city'. The same might be true for Ramsay, *Letters to the Seven Churches*, except for the material quoted at n. 20 above.

majority to be natural and sensible. As a text that unmasks the pretensions of its world, the Johannine apocalypse illustrates how honour
and shame fall upon the churches of the seven cities in a manner that
runs contrary to indigenously determined patterns. The recon-
figuration of cultural honour codes is ultimately derived from 'the revelation of Jesus Christ' (1:1). The Christological basis for this recon-
figured system of honour is projected onto the screen of the heavens
(e.g. 1:12-16) and rooted in the very core of unfalsified reality (e.g.
Rev 4–5). It involves an empire — not the empire of Rome but of
God who has made his people to be 'an empire' (βασιλείαν, 1:6; cf.
1:9; 5:10) with Jesus Christ himself as 'the ruler of the
kings/emperors [βασιλέων] of the earth' (1:5). It is an empire in
which transpire works of love, faithfulness (τὴν πίστιν), service and
endurance (2:19; cf. 2:2; 3:10). It is an empire that knows no
compromise in this regard (as in 2:4-6, 14-16, 20-23; 3:1-3, 15-19).
The faithful lives of Christians are testaments that the empire of
Rome (which paraded itself as eternal, sovereign and immutable) had
not usurped the eternal, sovereign and immutable empire of God. In
this, there is a Christological precedent; just as Jesus Christ himself
was 'the witness' *par excellence* because he was 'the faithful one' *par
excellence* (ὁ πιστός, 1:5),[28] so too the churches in these Romanised
cities are called upon to replicate 'the faith of Jesus' (τὴν πίστιν
Ἰησοῦ, 14:12) in ever-new configurations of fidelity to God's empire
throughout Roman Asia Minor.

'Let the one who has an ear hear what the Spirit is saying to the
churches'; so conclude the words of the risen Lord to each of the
seven churches (2:7, 11, 17, 29; 3:6, 13, 22). The plural 'churches' is
certainly significant. In the centuries since the writing of the
Johannine apocalypse, this phrase has frequently been understood to
highlight the importance of the various messages for the benefit of
later ecclesiastical generations. In the original context of the text,

---

[28] My reading of ὁ μάρτυς ὁ πιστός assumes that these are both
substantives separable by a comma.

however, circulated as it was amongst at least the seven churches of Asia Minor (and presumably more), this repeated phrase would have served the particular function of drawing the churches together in a common relationship of accountability before their exalted Lord. What the Spirit was saying to the seven churches collectively is that they should be seeking to outdo each other not in gaining esteem in relation to the empire of Rome, which was certain to fall before the sovereign power of the only true God.[29] Instead they should outdo each other in finding honour before the sovereign Lord of the universe, whose kingdom will have no end. Instead of calculating, comparing and appraising each other's merits and entitlements within the empire of Rome, they were to attend to their corporate responsibilities within the empire of God.

We have seen, then, that an extraordinary and fiercely competitive pro-Roman sentiment had overrun the first-century provincial cities of Asia Minor. For the benefit of the churches in seven of those cities, the Johannine seer depicts the risen Christ as inspecting his churches according to categories of honour and shame that diverged radically from those that animated the idolatrous empire of the day. No doubt the seer would have thought that his message would also be relevant to Christians living long after the fall of the Roman empire who may have become complacent with systems of honour and shame that run contrary to the empire of God.[30]

---

[29] So, for instance, Rev 16:10 speaks of the empire (βασιλεία) of the Beast (Rome) being plunged into darkness.

[30] I am indebted to the Alexander von Humboldt Stiftung for providing the funding for a research period during which this article was written.

Revelation 12:

An Apocalyptic 'Church History'?

Paul Barnett

This paper[1] focuses on Rev 12 and seeks to inquire whether it is rooted in past 'Christian' history.[2] Most commentators see this chapter as informed by the 'combat myth',[3] whether explicitly or implicitly. Few scholars consulted made any connections with Herod or the Slaughter of the Innocents.[4]

This chapter commences a long and important sequence extending to 14:20. Unlike earlier sequences it lacks specific numbering, though a similar format of six sections followed by a (two-part) interlude ahead of a seventh section can be discerned.

---

[1]   I am delighted to share with others in acknowledging the academic contributions of my friend and fellow Australian, Dr Bruce Winter. His leadership in promoting major publishing enterprises (in particular the Acts series) together with his own very important research-based works have enriched the quest for the life-setting of the New Testament.
[2]   For a review of interpretations of Rev 12 see P. Prigent, *Apocalypse 12: Histoire de l'exégèse* (Tübingen: Mohr, 1959).
[3]   A major discussion of the 'combat myth' idea (from Old Testament, ancient near eastern, Egyptian, Greek sources) is A. Yarbro Collins, *The Combat Myth in the Book of Revelation* (Missoula: Scholars, 1976). For a sustained review of various possible mythological influences on Rev 12 see D. Aune, *Revelation* (WBC; Nashville: Nelson, 1998), 660-74. R. Bauckham, *The Climax of Prophecy: Studies on the Book of Revelation* (Edinburgh: T & T Clark, 1993), 185-98, acknowledges mythical symbols underlying Rev 12–13 but sees Old Testament texts, chiefly Gen 3, as the inspiration for John's vision.
[4]   One exception is H. Alford, *The Greek Testament*, IV (Cambridge: Deighton, 1886), ad loc.

The Two Beasts (Revelation 13) and Ephesus

Preterist interpreters see in this sequence (Rev 13) the likely centre-piece of the Apocalypse as a whole. The Dragon, cast down from heaven and frustrated by his attempts to destroy the woman, 'gives his power and authority' (δύναμις ... ἐξουσία) to the Beast from the Sea (13:1-10). In turn, the Beast from the Earth (13:11-18) exercises the authority of the first beast in its presence and 'makes' everyone worship the first beast.

These are thinly veiled references to invincible Roman power exercised locally in provinces, specifically the Province of Asia in the city of Ephesus.

The compulsion to worship 'the first beast' fits well with the general ethos of Roman Asia where the ruler cult had its historic genesis.[5] As early as 195 BC, half a century before the Kingdom of Pergamum became the Province of Asia (129 BC), the city of Smyrna had established temples and rituals to 'the goddess Roma'. Accelerated by the Pax Romana following Augustus' victory at Actium in 31 BC there was a veritable explosion of cult centres in Asia.[6] In 9 BC the cities of Asia decreed that their calendar must have as their New Year's Day the birthday of 'their saviour and god', Augustus (23 September).[7] The people of Myra hailed Augustus as 'the god Augustus Caesar, son of a god, ruler of land and sea, benefactor and saviour of the whole world.'[8]

The Julio-Claudians are well known for resisting deification during their lifetimes. This changed under Domitian, in whose latter years most believe Revelation to have been written. According to Dio Cassius, Domitian 'insisted on being considered a god and was ex-

---

[5] See generally S. R. F. Price, *Rituals of Power* (Cambridge: CUP, 1984); P. W. Barnett, "Revelation in Its Roman Setting," *RTR* 50 (1991): 59-68.

[6] See the map in Price, *Rituals of Power*, xxv.

[7] *Orientis Graeci Inscriptiones Selectae* (1903-05), 458, cited in N. Lewis and M. Reinhold, *Roman Civilization* II, 64-65.

[8] *IGR* 3.719, cited in Lewis and Reinhold, *Roman Civilization* II, 64, n. 191.

ceedingly proud to be called "master and god'" (*dominus et deus*).[9] Suetonius states that "'Lord God" became his regular title, both in writing and conversation.'[10] The court poet Statius referred to his master as 'offspring and sire of mighty deities ... whose godhead I heard from afar.'[11]

Domitian probably affected the people of Asia in particular, due to their long fascination with the ruler cult. Following the advent of Domitian the cities of Asia competed for the privilege of erecting a temple to the emperor. Ephesus was granted this honour, with the much-sought title νεωκόρος, 'temple sweeper'.

A vast temple was erected in the best and most central site in the city near the state agora. Outside the temple was a huge statue of Domitian, eight metres high (if standing). The well-preserved head is on view in the local museum (Selçuk).

Rev 13 can be regarded as the Seer's interpretation of this fairly recent development in Ephesus with its tragic consequences for Christian believers 'made to worship' this beast by local officials and priests.[12] Jews received immunity on account of the *Fiscus Judaicus* but there was no such protection for the Christians. Recent developments in Ephesus served only to make a difficult situation worse. Ephesus was already the cult centre for Artemis and, as Millar has shown,[13] the Romans had easily merged the worship of Roma and Princeps with such local deities.

In light of these long term and more recent developments the situation of Christians in Ephesus was serious indeed and most likely

---

[9] Dio Cassius, *Historia Romana* 67.5.7.
[10] Suetonius, *Dom.* 13.
[11] Statius, *Silv.* 1.1.66.
[12] See B. F. Harris, "Domitian, the Emperor Cult and Revelation," *Prudentia* 11 (1979): 15-25.
[13] Fergus Millar, "The Imperial Cult and the Persecutions," in *Le culte des souverains dans l'Empire Romain* (ed. E. Bickerman and Willem den Boer; Vandœuvres-Genève: Fondation Hardt, 1973), 145 ff.

represents the historical catalyst for John's exile on Patmos and the writing of the Apocalypse.

Persecution Reflected in Revelation 12

In Rev 12–13 an evil triadic hierarchy is revealed, the Dragon/the Devil and Satan, the Beast from the Sea and the Beast from the Earth. The Dragon delegates his power and authority to the Beast from the Sea who delegates it to the Beast from the Earth. The Dragon, the supernatural Source of the evil, has a single-minded intent to win the war against the Male-Son (υἱὸν ἄρσεν) caught up to heaven to rule the nations. That war spills out from heaven, casting the Dragon to earth where his surrogates continue 'to wage war against the saints, to conquer them' (13:7; cf. 12:17).

This is expressed in what sounds like a forensic setting: 'the accuser (ὁ κατήγωρ) of our brothers ... accuses (ὁ κατηγορῶν) them day and night before our God' (12:10). We note that the vocabulary is used elsewhere in judicial contexts (e.g. Acts 23:30, 35; cf. *TDNT* 3:636-37).

It is likely that in these words we see a similar setting to the trials of Christians described by Pliny to Trajan a few years later in neighbouring Bithynia.

> I have asked them in person if they are Christians, and if they admit it, I repeat the question a second and a third time, with a warning of the punishment awaiting them. If they persist I order them to be led away for execution ...

> I considered that I should dismiss any who denied that they were or ever had been Christians when they repeated after me a formula of invocation to the gods and made offerings of wine and incense to your statue ... and furthermore had reviled the name of Christ ...[14]

Pliny's circumstances in Bithynia are sufficiently close in time and place to those of Asia in the nineties for the governor's description to cast some light on the ordeal of Ephesian believers. After all, Pliny is

---

[14]   Pliny, *Ep.* 10.96.

not likely to have instituted his proceedings without some kind of local and regional precedent. That Trajan was unaware of the details presents no obstacle to this; Bithynia and Asia were unusual in their high concentrations of Christians.

The ordeal being endured by Christians appears to have included 'accusation' at the official level as well as economic sanctions ('... no one could buy or sell ...') at the grass roots (Rev 13:16-17; cf. 2:9; 6:5-6).

Accordingly it is reasonable to view Rev 12–13 as John's apocalyptic commentary on the grievous circumstances he and his fellow brothers and sisters were suffering in the nineties under the Principate of Domitian.

What, then, of Rev 12:1-6, with which the sequence begins?

Revelation 12: An Apocalyptic Church History
It is worth considering whether this passage is a kind of church history, set out allegorically, in apocalyptic terms. The various elements in the passage appear to represent people and events from the past century.

The opening section (12:1-6) sets the scene for the 'war in heaven' (12:7) that, due to the Dragon's defeat there by the ascended Male-Son, is now waged on earth against the saints (13:7).

To begin (12:1) we meet 'a woman clothed with the sun, with the moon under her feet, and on her head a crown of twelve stars.' The 'twelve stars' help identify her as Israel in terms of twelve patriarchs or tribes. This is confirmed by Joseph's offensive dream that the sun and the moon and the *eleven* stars were bowing down to him (Gen 37:11). Furthermore, in the *T. Naph.* 5:3-8 the twelve patriarchs on the Mount of Olives saw that the sun and moon were standing still, ready to be seized. The twelve run to lay hold of sun and moon and Levi grasped the sun and Judah the moon, and both were lifted up with them.

Clearly, then, 12:1 is to be understood from the biblical and apocalyptic traditions as a reference to Israel. Yet why is a *woman* clothed with sun, moon and stars when these have previously been connected with men?

The symbol of a woman is only now introduced in the Apocalypse. The Seer sets various elements in pairs of opposites[15] that Deissmann had suggestively referred to as 'polemical parallelism'.[16] The 'pairing' or 'parallelism' sets the 'bride, wife of the Lamb' (21:2, 9; 22:17) against the 'great harlot seated on many waters' (17:1). The former is the community wedded to the Lion-Lamb and the consort of the latter is the 'kings of the earth' with whom the 'great Harlot' fornicates (17:2). She is Rome, the Beast from the Sea, now portrayed under an equally sinister image.

Who, then, is the 'woman … with child' (ἐν γαστρὶ ἔχουσα) in 12:1-2? Since her clothing with sun, moon and stars identifies her in 'patriarchal' terms, I conclude that she is faithful Israel, embodied in Mary, the mother-to-be of Jesus, the Messiah.[17] Mary and Joseph, along with folk like Anna and Simeon belong to a devout remnant of the Chosen People, whose fidelity was in contrast with Herod whose evils had corrupted Jewish society from the top to the bottom. Among those 'poor' and holy ones at the 'bottom' came the Messiah, born by an otherwise undistinguished young Jewess. Strikingly, she is called 'a great sign in heaven' (σημεῖον μέγα … ἐν τῷ οὐρανῷ).

The 'Male-Son' she 'brought forth' was born on earth; he was later 'caught up' to God and his throne. The great red Dragon who menaced the woman at the time of her delivery is, by allegorical inter-

---

[15] P. W. Barnett, "Polemical Parallelism: Some Further Reflections on the Apocalypse," *JSNT* 35 (1989): 111-20.

[16] A. Deissmann, *Light from the Ancient East* (New York/London: Hodder & Stoughton, 1910), 346.

[17] True, there are evocative 'mother' images from the Old Testament (Isa 54:1; 66:7-9; Mic 5:3) and Qumran (1QH 3:7-12), though the sun, moon and twelve stars of Rev 12:1 are rather specific. M. E. Boring, *Revelation* (Interpretation; Louisville: John Knox, 1989): 'The woman is not Mary, nor Israel, nor the church but less and more than all of them' (152) is unconvincing.

pretation, the human Herod. His murder of the boys of Bethlehem is known outside the biblical tradition in Macrobius,[18] as well as inside that tradition in the Gospel according to Matthew (2:1-18). The Seer, John, will know that tradition.

This narrative jumps from the birth to the ascension of the messianic Male-Son. The Messiah does not teach or heal, nor is he crucified or raised from the dead in this account, but is 'caught up' immediately to God. Here the Seer invokes the two-person language of Ps 2, Yahweh and his Anointed King. The Anointed King is the Male-Son, whom Yahweh calls, 'My Son' (cf. 11:15). He is 'to rule (ποιμαίνειν) all the nations with an iron rod.' A parallel two-person format (the 'Lord and Christ' who is exalted at 'God's right hand') is heard from the lips of Peter on the Day of Pentecost (based not on Ps 2, but on Ps 110).

In consequence of the exaltation of the Male-Son as ruler of the nations, the armies of Michael war against the Dragon who is 'cast down' (ἐβλήθη — aorist passive, i.e. by God) to the earth. This, says our text, coincides with the era of the Dragon's deception of the whole world (whom the Male-Son is to rule) and his war (persecution) against the saints. Historically, this began in Jerusalem at the hands of the Jewish hierarchs reaching an early climax with the depredations of Saul of Tarsus but not ending with his conversion (1 Thess 2:14-15).

---

[18] Macrobius, *Saturnalia* 2.4 (tr. P. V. Davis; New York: Columbia University Press, 1969). The Macrobius information is problematic, however, due to its lateness and the uncertain path it may have followed to find its way into this text. So R. T. France, "Herod and the Children of Bethlehem," *NovT* 21 (1979): 117-19, who urges that Macrobius' evidence merely points to an awareness of Christian tradition in 'educated circles' c. AD 400. On the other hand, the 'educated circles' associated with Macrobius were culturally distant from the church and likely unaware of Christian belief at this point. Hence a tradition stream parallel with Matthew's tradition is conceivable.

In particular, the Dragon pursued the woman who had borne the Male-Son (12:13). Who is this woman? With dazzling merging of imagery John appears to be saying that the mother of the Male-Son is now the church of the Messiah, that is, his bride (anticipating the later 'bride' references). That is, she gave birth to the Messiah and she has now become the Messiah's people, specifically *Jewish* Christians. Despite the Dragon's determination to destroy her she finds refuge and nourishment in the wilderness. Is this reference broad and vague? Arguably it refers to the escape of the Jerusalem church from their fellow Jews in *c.* AD 67 to Pella in the Decapolis, on the east bank of the Jordan, referred to by Eusebius[19] and Epiphanius, both depending on Hegesippus.

Frustrated, the Dragon 'went off to make war on the rest of her offspring' (12:17). These are described as 'those who keep the commandments of God and bear testimony to Jesus.' Their locale is not described, but it may be inferred from the narrative as it continues into ch. 13. After the Dragon stands on the sand of the sea he then re-emerges from the water as the 'beast rising out of the sea.' The Dragon in Palestine pursuing the Jewish church has surfaced, submarine-like, in Asia as the Beast from the Sea and his delegate, the Beast from the Earth waging war now on gentile believers.

Rev 13:1 is particularly vivid. We easily imagine the Roman trireme rounding the bend of the Cayster sweeping up the harbour to the wharf at the waterfront of Harbour Street of Ephesus, with the Roman Proconsul at the prow with all sinister pomp and circumstance and with many Ephesians watching. He has come to make war on the Christians.

And so the grim story unfolds in ch. 13, the centrepiece of the Apocalypse.

---

[19]   Eusebius, *Hist. eccl.* 3.5.3.

Conclusion

Much of the Apocalypse is John's inspired commentary on contemporary events and pastoral encouragement in the face of those
events, in particular the persecutions of ch. 13. In our view, ch. 12,
which begins that section, begins with its historical antecedent from
Israel/Mary's safe delivery of the Male-Son, through his rapture to the
throne of God as ruler of the nations, to the persecutions of Jewish
believers ending in the persecution of gentile believers in Ephesus in
Roman Asia.

Some years earlier Luke wrote his magisterial two-volume history
covering a similar historical sweep, though in more recognisably
'historical' terms. If the foregoing argument is correct, however, it
means that Luke was not the only historian of early Christianity.
Notwithstanding its different literary category as 'apocalyptic', Rev
12–13, is at the same time 'historical' or at least, informed by history.
Nonetheless, many years would pass before other historians, that is,
Hegesippus (now lost) and Eusebius, would take up pens to write
their own (very different) versions of the 'history of the church.'

Jewish apocalyptic writers narrate history, for example, the
anonymous author of the *Assumption of Moses* (ch. 6). He encom-
passes a span of several hundred years from the Hasmonaean Priest-
Kings through the Herodian dynasts until the Roman siege of
Jerusalem. In common with the Seer of Revelation he employs coded
references to people and events from the past. There are differences.
The *Assumption of Moses* is an entirely retrospective account of a
span of history that purports to be prophetic of the future. In Rev 12–
14, however, the Seer narrates earlier events relating to the birth of
and rapture of the man-child as still being played out in the present
afflictions of the 'woman' suffered at the hand of the 'dragon' and his
two beast-like accomplices. Here is a form of history, past and present, through the apocalyptist's eyes. This is history-in-the-making, in
apocalyptic dress.

Index of Ancient Sources

Index of Modern Authors